Teacher Education Reform
as Political Theater

Teacher Education Reform as Political Theater

RUSSIAN POLICY DRAMAS

Elena Aydarova

Cover art: Valeriy Yaroslavtsev, *Concert*, 2008. Oil on canvas, 150 × 100cm. Reprinted with permission of the artist.

Published by State University of New York Press, Albany

© 2019 State University of New York

All rights reserved

No part of this book may be used or reproduced in any manner whatsoever without written permission. No part of this book may be stored in a retrieval system or transmitted in any form or by any means including electronic, electrostatic, magnetic tape, mechanical, photocopying, recording, or otherwise without the prior permission in writing of the publisher.

For information, contact State University of New York Press, Albany, NY
www.sunypress.edu

Library of Congress Cataloging-in-Publication Data

Names: Aydarova, Elena, 1982– author.
Title: Teacher education reform as political theater : Russian policy dramas / Elena Aydarova.
Description: Albany : State University of New York Press, Albany, [2019] | Includes bibliographical references and index.
Identifiers: LCCN 2018052655 | ISBN 9781438476155 (hardcover) |
    ISBN 9781438476148 (pbk.) | ISBN 9781438476162 (ebook) Subjects: LCSH:
            Teachers—Training of—Russia (Federation) | Education and
state—Russia (Federation) | Educational change—Russia (Federation)
Classification: LCC LB1725.R8 A93 2019 | DDC 371.102—dc23
LC record available at https://lccn.loc.gov/2018052655

10 9 8 7 6 5 4 3 2 1

To Bevin and Zoya

Contents

List of Illustrations ... ix

Acknowledgments ... xi

Introduction ... xiii

Part I
Historical Context: Sowing the Seeds of Discontent / 1

Part II
Directing Social Change: Russian Policy Dramas / 35

1. Actors ... 37

2. Masks and Guises ... 61

3. Dress Rehearsals and Missing Directors ... 89

4. Light and Shadows ... 121

5. Props, Scripts, and Playwrights ... 155

6. Money Matters ... 183

Epilogue ... 215

Appendix A. Summary of the Policy 235

Appendix B. Theoretical Foundations 239

Appendix C. Methodology and Data Analysis 249

Notes 259

References 267

Index 289

Illustrations

Figures

1. Types of institutions most commonly involved in teacher preparation in Russia 1917 to the present — 13
2. Public service announcement in downtown Moscow, June 2011 — 33
3. Reformers' networks — 48
4. Diagram from the policy text — 83
5. Diagram from the original study — 83
6. Representations of pedagogical university applicants' performance on the Unified State Exam in reformers' presentations — 123
7. Percentages of "effective" institutions among pedagogical universities based on MOE criteria — 127
8. Portrait of a graduate — 135
9. December 1, 2013—A day of protests against educational reforms across Russian cities — 186

Tables

1. Policy words and their English and Russian counterparts — 79
2. Comparison between pedagogical and medical universities in the number of students with a Unified State Exam average score higher than 70 — 124

3. Teachers' labor functions according to the new professional standards 139
4. Comparison of the McKinsey report suggestions for improving teacher quality and the Concept of Teacher Education Modernization measures 171
5. Summary of grants awarded to project participants in 2014 195

Acknowledgments

Acknowledgments are like family albums. Allow me to share my family album with you.

First and foremost, I am endlessly grateful to every faculty member, student, administrator, policymaker, and educational researcher I met through my wanderings across the Russian Federation and the world. I can't name many of you, but you should know that without your tender care at times of confusion, rejection, suspicion, and doubt, I would never have come this far. If my project has not lived up to your expectations, please, forgive me.

No words can express my gratitude to many mentors who offered guidance during my work on this book. First, I am thankful to Lynn Paine, Michael Sedlak, Avner Segall, Alaina Lemon, and Chantal Tetreault for advice and generous readings of the earlier versions of this work. I owe an enormous intellectual debt to Suzanne Wilson, who first suggested that I look at teacher education reform as a form of theater. Without the support of David Post and David Berliner, this book would not have seen the light of the day. I am grateful to those who guided me through the earlier stages of this research project—Kyle Greenwalt, Peter Youngs, Aaron Bodle, and Todd Drummond. I thank many others for powerful conversations that pushed my thinking—Kathy Anderson-Levitt, Cynthia Dillard, Lesley Bartlett, Radhika Gorur, Iveta Silova, David Phillips, Francine Menashy, Kristine Phillips, Amy Stambach, Francine Vavrus, Nancy Kendall, Johnny Saldaña, Meg Gardinier, Eugene Matusov, Ana Marjanovic-Shane, and Tatyana Tsyrlina-Spady. Much helpful support came from mentoring opportunities created by the New Scholars Committee at the Comparative and International Education Society and the Council of Anthropology and Education of the American Anthropological Association.

I am thankful to Sheila Marquardt and Joshua Olmsted for opening their home to me when I needed to get away and write. I also owe huge thanks to Ricky Greenwell and Patrick Carriere at Minnesota State University for the crash course on theater they provided to a weary scholar in search of a better-fitting theoretical framework.

I would never have been able to go through all the research trips, analysis, and writing without the support of my spouse, Bevin Roue. Thank you for holding down the fort when I was roaming the earth and for taking so many burdens on yourself when I needed it most. I am also grateful to my family in Russia and Ukraine, who collected policy documents, forwarded newspaper articles, and debated politics with me throughout my research. Without my family's help, this project would never have come to fruition.

This project was made possible through a Fulbright Hays Doctoral Dissertation Research Abroad Fellowship and generous funding from Michigan State University's College of Education.

Some of the work for this book took place at the University of Illinois Summer Slavic Lab. I am thankful for the helpful guidance of librarians at the University of Illinois at Urbana-Champaign, particularly Joe Lenkart, who many times helped me fish out obscure but tremendously valuable Russian sources across many different libraries and hidden nooks of the internet.

Special words of gratitude go to my editor at State University of New York Press, Rebecca Colesworthy, for her support and guidance. I am also thankful to the anonymous reviewers of the manuscript, who provided generous and helpful suggestions for revision.

I take full responsibility for any errors that this text may contain.

Introduction

On a sunny day in May of 2012, I made my way to one of the top teacher preparation institutions in Russia—Ognensk State Pedagogical University.[1] Located in a historic downtown area, OSPU occupied a block of ornate buildings inherited from Russia's imperial past. I was there for an education conference that brought together teacher educators, principals, teachers, and educational researchers from around the country. Marble statues, oil paintings, and red carpets adorning the interior of the main administration building where the conference took place impressed visitors with the institution's status as one of the oldest pedagogical universities in the country. Balloons hanging along the hallways created a festive atmosphere; professionally designed posters and banners informed participants about the main developments in Russian education. As I walked to the opening plenary, I watched men and women shaking hands, embracing, kissing each other on both cheeks, and laughing about how much they had changed since they last saw one another.

With velvet seats facing a stage draped in dark pleated curtains, the large plenary auditorium resembled a theater. Half of the seats were reserved for esteemed visitors: university rectors, school principals, members of the Scientific Council, and others. In the balconies above the auditorium sat students who appeared to be in awe of what they saw in front of them. Large TV screens displayed announcements, graduation pictures, and images of books published by OSPU's professors. Music from old Soviet school films played in the background. Forty-five minutes after the scheduled start, someone stood up, motioning others to follow suit in order to greet the governor.

The governor's speech was short. He noted that it was important to carry out the tasks set by the country's leaders. Even though education was a conservative field, it had to be reformed to initiate change in other sectors of the economy and society. With that, the governor called for implementation of Our New School, a policy issued in 2010, stating that it served as "the starting point for the modernization of the nation's education." The governor also congratulated the university on its two-hundred-year anniversary and praised it for supplying high-quality teachers for the city's schools, saying that half of the city's sixty thousand teachers were graduates of the university.

The irony of the governor's speech was that Our New School argued for a complete elimination of pedagogical universities—a point that concerned many in the educational community. In the plenaries and sessions that followed, organizers and speakers from OSPU emphasized the need for participants to consider the points laid out in the conference resolution. The four-page document distributed among the participants highlighted both the achievements of Russian pedagogical education and the challenges it was facing. Its conclusion stated:

> Concerned with the emerging practice of transforming pedagogical universities into general higher education institutions, the assembly participants underscore the necessity of preserving and strengthening the national tradition of preparing teachers in pedagogical universities. (Resolution 2012, 3)[2]

The despair veiled by the bureaucratese of the resolution became most tangible during the closing plenary when one of the conference organizers pleaded with the audience: "Colleagues, I just want to remind you. We have to sign this resolution as soon as possible and direct it to the powers above. If we don't do it, if we don't act soon, there might be no pedagogical education left in Russia in several years' time." When I heard those words, I froze in my seat. I became familiar with the attacks on university-based teacher education in the United States, United Kingdom, and other international contexts when I embarked on my multi-sited ethnography of Russian educational reforms. Hearing this story of attacks echoed in a country with a distinct educational history, far removed from the troubles of American or British politics and seemingly untouched by the rise of corporate control of education, was, to put it mildly, unsettling. The festive atmosphere of the conference, I came to realize, had a dark underside. Among other things, it was pedagogical universities' desperate attempt to survive in the onslaught of globally circulated neoliberal reforms. To tackle these challenges, the organizers tried to mobilize participants to create networks, working groups, and partnerships to counteract the changes that were coming from "above."

When I returned to Russia in August 2013, I learned that one such change from "above" was the Concept of Support for the Development of Teacher Education[3]—also called the Concept of Teacher Education Modernization (referred to as the Concept throughout this text and summarized in appendix A). According to its creators, the Concept sought to improve the quality of teacher education. This improvement was to be accomplished by creating multiple paths into the teaching profession, increasing practical preparation in teacher education programs, making preparation competency based, and introducing a certification exam for those who wanted to teach. Even though many of these measures resembled proposals promoted by reformers in other countries (Darling-Hammond and Lieberman 2012; Furlong, Cochran-Smith, and Brennan 2009; Trippestad, Swennen, and Werler 2017), there were no references to international experiences in the official text. It only stated that the introduction of new standards for K–12 schooling and new teachers' professional standards in Russia necessitated teacher education reforms. As I came to realize later, working in tandem, the new standards and the Concept significantly changed the purposes of schooling, deprofessionalized teaching, and radically redesigned teacher education. These changes came to naturalize social inequality and depoliticize education. This reorientation of an educational system is noteworthy because of Russia's socialist past as well as its prior commitments to educational equity (Zajda 2003) and to a professionalized teaching force (Counts 1961) that was trained predominantly in pedagogical universities or stand-alone teacher education institutions.

In order to understand these changes, I focused on the Concept and followed the work of reformers who orchestrated its development and implementation. During my ethnographic fieldwork, I encountered discrepancies between reformers' public and private justifications for this reform; mimicry, masking, double-talk around this policy across various sites; as well as creative forms of coercion deployed to induce educators to accept reform ideology. Throughout my research, I often encountered participants who described what was happening in Russian education through the metaphor of theater. Thus, this book draws on the construct of political theater to reveal and disrupt the dramas unfolding in the world of educational policymaking in Russia and across the globe.

Drawing on several years of ethnographic research in Russia, I argue that teacher education reforms work as political theater that uses ideas of higher quality to disguise the sociocultural change pursued by reformers and mystifies policy processes so that the audience would accept this change.

Throughout the book, I analyze the dramas that unfolded in Russia as an observer who seeks to understand how reformers deploy dramaturgical techniques to introduce globally circulated policy scripts for educational reforms into national and subnational spaces despite opposition from educators and the public. The globally interconnected processes and transnational flows of ideologies I describe have a bearing not only for the future of Russia but also for other countries around the world. In what follows, I discuss global transformations in education and what the Russian context can offer for extending our understanding of these processes. I then discuss the conceptual framework of political theater used in this book and anthropology of policy as the methodological approach of this study. In the final section, I provide an overview of the book.

Teacher Education Reforms in the Global Neoliberal Context

In many ways, this book is about a small group of Russian reformers who pursued educational modernization under the influence of the global neoliberal imaginary (Rizvi and Lingard 2010). In conceptualizing neoliberalism, I draw on Wacquant (2012), who approaches it as a political project that reengineers the state to serve markets and to produce new subjectivities through disciplinary policies. The prevalence of market thinking means that education around the world is framed in terms of its significance for economic competitiveness and efficiency rather than social cohesiveness, cultural continuity, or democratic equality (Rizvi and Lingard 2010). Reformers identify accountability, efficiency, and cost-benefit analyses as key priority areas. The production of new subjectivities (Davies and Bansel 2007), on the other hand, reflects a turn toward a conservative modernization (Apple 2006), which creates flexible, responsibilized subjects (Ong 2006), consumers (Ward 2012), or workers who imagine themselves as "bundles of skills" (Urciuoli 2010, 162).

In the changing relationships between the state and the private sector, teachers are increasingly positioned as strategic resources for achieving national economic competitiveness on the global stage (Maguire 2002, 2010) and as managers of human capital (Ellis and McNicholl 2015; Smyth 2006). These transformations lead to the construction of a "global teacher" with "the emphasis . . . on compliance with competencies rather than thinking critically about practice; focusing on teaching rather than learning; doing rather than thinking; skills rather than values" (Maguire 2010, 61).

The repositioning of teachers in national or global agendas has immediate implications for teacher education (Maguire 2010). Approaching teacher education as "a public policy problem," policymakers try to identify "which of its broad parameters . . . can be controlled . . . to enhance teacher quality and thus have a positive impact on desired school outcomes" (Cochran-Smith 2005, 4). This framing of teacher education as a policy problem occurs both in the United States and around the world, often with references to globalization, economic competition, and rapid change (Darling-Hammond and Lieberman 2012; Earley, Imig, and Michelli 2011; Furlong, Cochran-Smith, and Brennan 2009; Paine, Blömeke, and Aydarova 2016; Trippestad, Swennen, and Werler 2017; Zeichner 2010). Yet the pursuit of teacher quality is wrought with contradictions. Some policy actors advocate for complete elimination of university-based preparation (Hanushek and Rivkin 2004) or opening routes into teaching to those who were trained for other jobs (Gladwell 2009; Hess 2002). Others argue that teacher education programs should be held responsible for their graduates' job placement (DeStefano 2013) and for academic achievement of their graduates' students through value-added measures (Hanushek and Rivkin 2010). Less radical but much more common proposals include increasing teachers' practical preparation through partnerships with schools (Beauchamp et al. 2016; Ellis and McNicholl 2015; Zeichner 2017), making teacher education more outcome-oriented and competency-based (Darling-Hammond 2010; Darling-Hammond and Lieberman 2012; Sälzer and Prenzel 2018), and using tests to determine who can gain entry into the profession (Darling-Hammond 2010; Kobakhidze 2013). In the struggle over which parameters will improve teacher quality, private sector actors and alternative providers exercise greater power both over the direction of new policies and over actual preparation of teachers (Chudgar 2013; Kumashiro 2010; Zeichner and Peña-Sandoval 2015; Zeichner and Conklin 2016). Crisscrossing the globe, most of these measures appeared in one way or the other in the proposals of Russian reformers.

The fields of comparative and international education as well as global policy offer three perspectives on how and why globally circulated policies made their way to Russia. On the one hand, world culture theorists argue that shared beliefs about the role of education in nation building drive governments around the world to adopt similar educational approaches (Baker and LeTendre 2005; Boli 2005; Boli, Ramirez, and Meyer 1985). Policymakers choose Western models as more efficient or rational solutions to the problems at hand. In a similar vein, world society theory suggests that global circulation of myths about individuals and nation-states explains the growing homogenization of education worldwide (Ramirez 2012). Noting increased similarities in how government officials prioritize educational quality and equity, theorists working in this paradigm argue that loose coupling explains variation in how these policies manifest themselves on the ground. These macro-level approaches, however, have recently come under significant scrutiny. Critics contend that world culture theory assumes homogeneity where there might be none, overlooks conflict and coercion that accompany educational standardization, and ignores participants' lived experiences in different corners of the world (Anderson-Levitt 2003, 2012; Carney, Rappleye, and Silova 2012; Caruso 2008; Griffiths and Arnove 2015; Rappleye 2015; Silova and Brehm 2015; Takayama 2015).

Theories of educational borrowing and lending, also known as educational transfer (Rappleye 2012) or policy recontextualization (Verger, Novelli, and Altinyelken 2012), provide an alternative explanation. Steiner-Khamsi (2004, 2010) argues that in cases of apparent similarities between different policies, it is only discourses that end up being borrowed. Governments often use references to global models or international "best practices" to justify and legitimize contentious policies at home, evoking "external authority for implementing reforms that otherwise would have been resisted" (Steiner-Khamsi 2004, 203). Referencing other countries helps policymakers build coalitions among otherwise dissenting groups and build momentum for large-scale systemic changes (Rappleye 2012; Takayama 2008, 2010). But with Russia's long-standing struggle between those who look to the West for modernization designs and those who vehemently oppose the introduction of foreign ideas, referencing external forms only intensifies conflicts around controversial reforms. While transformations in Russian education can perhaps be seen as "silent borrowing" of international forms (Waldow 2009), this explains neither how the process of engaging with global forms unfolds in such a politically charged context nor what the ultimate goal in engaging these policies might be.

Most recently, scholars attending to the global circulation of educational policies shifted the focus of their explorations from governments to governance (S. Ball and Junemann 2012; Rizvi and Lingard 2010), highlighting "the different forms of individual and institutional agency that play a role in constructing a nascent global policy" (Mundy, Green, Lingard, and Verger 2016, 8). These studies examine how international organizations, such as the Organisation for Economic Co-operation and Development (Morgan and Shahjahan 2014; Sellar and Lingard 2013), the World Bank (Mundy and Verger 2015; Zapp 2017), UNESCO (Edwards, Okitsu, da Costa, and Kitamura 2017), and WTO (Robertson, Bonal and Dale 2002; Sidhu 2007; Verger 2009) engage in normative and epistemic governance. They do so by circulating knowledge and policy prescriptions through monitoring reports (Read 2019), technical assistance (Klees, Samoff, and Stromquist 2012), and sponsored projects (Rappleye and Un 2018). In other words, international organizations "exert influence through their governance instruments, which range from norm setting, opinion formation, financial means, coordinative activities to consulting services" (Bieber 2010, 106; see also Martens, Nagel, Windzio, and Weymann 2010).

International assessments, such as the Programme for International Student Assessment (PISA) administered by the OECD, constitute an important mechanism in global governance (Sellar and Lingard 2013, 2014), because the benchmarking they produce influences national decisions to adopt global policy scripts (Meyer and Benavot 2013). Other assessments such as TALIS[4] and policy evaluation procedures such as SABER[5] work to streamline policies targeting teachers, thus placing them in the center of global neoliberal governance (Robertson 2012, 2013, 2016). Corporate actors are another force to reckon with, as they seek to shape policies that would either facilitate the expansion of educational markets or produce a workforce they can employ (S. Ball 2007; Menashy 2016; Spring 2015a, 2015b; Steiner-Khamsi 2018).

Building on the observations of global governance scholarship, this book explores how multiple positions that Russian reformers occupied in international organizations' epistemic communities, global policy networks, as well as national policymaking circles provided them with resources to conceptualize and enact a controversial reform of teacher education. Reformers deployed these resources as much to accomplish global agendas of creating a knowledge economy as to introduce a conservative modernization that would purportedly restore Russia's greatness on the global stage. To untangle the complexities of reformers' engagement with global policies and national scripts, this book departs from rationalist macro-level examination of nation-states predominant in the study of global policies. Instead, it focuses on the micro-politics of policy actors' activities in order to analyze the discrepancies, mismatches, and ruptures between the public appearances of teacher education reform and reformers' backstage discussions of its conceptualization, implementation, and consequences. Political constructions of global education policies in the Russian context make this study relevant to audiences in other countries, which I will discuss next.

Research Context: Educational Change in Russia

While global transformations in teacher education and in educational policymaking have received some attention, particularly in the Anglo-Saxon world, perspectives from postsocialist contexts have been uncommon (for exceptions see D. Johnson 2010; Niyozov, 2008; Steiner-Khamsi and Stolpe 2006; Webster, Silova, Moyer, and McAllister 2011). A lack of attention to developments in Russian education can partly be explained by the assumptions of its uniqueness, difference, and divergence from the West (Alexander 2000). Yet sometimes this emphasis treads on the verge of exoticizing, Orientalizing, and Othering Russia in ways that are reminiscent of the Cold War era (Aydarova, Millei, Piattoeva, and Silova 2016; Chatterjee 2015). Even though there was a historical moment of Russia's limited participation in transnational educational flows (Schriewer and Martinez 2004), Russia's involvement with international influences and global policies was strong before the formation of the Soviet Union and since its collapse in 1991 (Alexander 2009; Gounko 2008; Gounko and Smale 2007; Timoshenko 2011). Exchanges between Russia and different parts of the world continued even during the Soviet era: Dewey influenced the early Soviet school (Mchitarjan 2000); Vygotsky and Bakhtin had a significant impact on educational philosophies in the West (Wertsch 1998).

Despite cultural differences, the ongoing policy dialogues between Russia and the West created many commonalities. The fact that school vouchers were tested in Russia before they were introduced in the United States (M. Johnson 1997) demonstrates that old assumptions about other nations' present being advanced nations' past no longer hold in the era of networked globalization. Vying to restore its position of power on the global stage, Russia also actively engages in the efforts to outdo and outperform the Western world even in the Western world's creations, such as neoliberalism and market mechanisms across the social sector (Hemment 2009; Matza 2010). For this reason, research in postsocialist contexts such as Russia can extend our understandings of how global neoliberal policies traverse the globe.

Despite prior attempts at decentralization, Russia continues to run a relatively centralized system of education headed by the Ministry of Education (MOE). The ministry is in charge of issuing directives that regulate the functioning of the educational system, which include standards for general education (K–12), professional preparation, and the teaching profession. A World Bank study of Russian education (Nikolaev and Chugunov 2012) stated that in the last ten to fifteen years there were several programs of modernization targeting different levels of education. Ongoing modernization efforts allow globally circulated ideas to cut through Russia's centralized educational system with incredible speed, making visible the processes that could take much longer to trace in more decentralized systems.

According to the OECD's *Education at a Glance* (2016), Russia has one of the highest levels of higher education attainment among OECD countries. Based on the national statistics from 2015 (*Indikatory Obrazovaniia* 2017), at 54.4 percent, education had the highest proportion of employees with higher education degrees compared to 33 percent in the economy overall. By 2015, 82.7 percent of Russian teachers had higher education degrees and 77.5 percent were graduates of pedagogical universities. Only 16.2 percent of teachers held secondary vocational degrees. The proportion of teachers with secondary vocational degrees depends on the level of schooling. In early childhood education, 50.7 percent of teachers had higher education and 47.7 percent had secondary vocational education. Among teachers for grades 1 through 4, 74.3 percent had higher education degrees and 24.7 percent had secondary vocational education. For grades 5 to 9, the proportion of teachers with higher education degrees hovers around 90 percent. The preponderance of teachers with higher education degrees, particularly from pedagogical universities, raises an important question about reforms that seek to eliminate or radically transform higher education institutions dedicated to teacher education—how and why do the institutions that prepare most of the country's teachers become the target of such drastic reforms?

Of great significance for this book are the blurred lines between reality and fiction that characterize much of Russian politics and life. Peter Pomerantsev in *Nothing Is True and Everything Is Possible* explores the life of Russian politics and society where nothing is what it seems. The surreal nature of interactions between politicians, oligarchs, opposition, and society implode the traditional notions of linearity and rationality. In this situation, realistic accounts so common in policy research run the danger of misrepresenting people's lives and state-level decision-making processes (Pisano 2014). But these blurred lines no longer characterize lives in the postsocialist world only. The rise of the audit culture (S. Ball 2003; Shore and Wright 1999; Strathern 2000), neoliberal governmentality (Ferguson and Gupta 2002), and corporate involvement in policymaking (S. Ball 2007, 2012) facilitates the spread of these surreal arrangements around the globe (Amann 2003; Aydarova, Millei, Piattoeva, and Silova 2016; Brandist 2014, 2016). The Russian case, in this situation, is helpful for understanding the processes that surface around the globe with growing regularity, particularly if viewed through the lens of political theater, which I describe next.

Political Theater as a Conceptual Framework

There are two distinct approaches to political theater. One uses theater as a conceptual lens for exploring the blurry lines between truth and fiction in social lives, politics, and policies (Edelman 1988; Goffman 1974; Scott 1990; Turner 1975). The other focuses on the liberating potential of theater that draws the audience's attention to the injustices and inequalities around them (Boal 1979; Conquergood and Johnson 2013; Kushner 1997; Willett 1964). This book straddles the divide between these approaches by examining the theatricality of policymaking and the dramas of educational reforms in order to suggest potential emancipatory paths out of the deadlock of global neoliberal transformations in education.

By attending to the blurry lines between reality and fiction, the first approach echoes the notion of political spectacle (Edelman 1988). Policymaking viewed from this lens "resemble[s] theater, complete with directors, stages, casts of actors, narrative plots, and (most importantly) a curtain that separates the action onstage (what the audience has access to) from the backstage, where 'real allocation of values' takes place" (Smith et al. 2004, 11). The power of political spectacle is particularly striking in the differences between what actors perform onstage and how they interpret that performance backstage. Different actors perform for different audiences: reformers arguing for the necessity of school accountability to improve educational quality (Smith et al. 2004), students in an urban setting performing the role of destitute but deserving children for school funders (Brown 2015), or principals evoking global competitiveness to justify high-stakes testing (Koyama 2013).

According to Edelman (1988), policy problems are constructed in ways that allow political elites to advance their agendas. The reformers' goal then is to convince the audience of their definition of the problem and get them to accept the reform proposal as the only way to address that problem (Anderson 2005; Granger 2008; Smyth 2006). For example, in the United States reformers such as Ron Unz argued that Spanish-speaking children show low academic achievement because of bilingual education and the only way to address this problem was through English only policies (Wright 2005). These arguments were touted as based on the best scientific evidence even though they ran counter to well-documented research findings (Hakuta 2011). Wright (2005) argued that "the use of symbolic language, the use of plots and story lines, the creation of leaders (heroes) and enemies, [and] the evoking of symbols of rationality" evident in the introduction and implementation of English only policies in Arizona revealed the political spectacle of these reforms. Adamson, Forestier, Morris, and Han (2017) observed a similar trend in Britain where reformers constructed a crisis around low PISA scores, presenting members of the educational establishment as villains responsible for the educational failure and themselves as heroes able to fix it.

Spectacle and theater as analytical frames reveal how some ideas are disguised, other ideas are modified, and still others remain completely invisible to the audience. Central in this analysis is the role of shadows that obscure the involvement of actors that are not ordinarily imagined as participants in educational policies in democratic societies. Largely invisible to the general public remains the presence of philanthropic foundations using grant funding to advance their agendas (Tompkins-Stange 2016), corporations venturing into the educational sector to increase their market value (Gunter, Hall, and Apple 2017), and private companies profiting from schools' failure to meet adequate yearly progress under the No Child Left Behind Act (Koyama 2010). It is not only the presence of other actors that is obscured in the political spectacle. Arguments about educational quality, choice, and opportunity similarly disguise the growing disparities among privileged and underprivileged groups. By extension, this disguise normalizes and naturalizes social inequality (Koyama and Bartlett 2011), placing the responsibility for low achievement on individual students, their communities, or their schools rather than structural inequalities (Koyama and Cofield 2013).

Modernization dramas common around the world seek to destroy political possibilities of addressing these structural inequalities and attempt to create economic utopias most conducive to corporate and oligarchic prosperity. The processes of introducing educational reforms that retrench inequality, introduce conservative values, and reengineer societies unfold in ways that create an illusion of democratic participation (Smith et al. 2004). These reforms appear to be open to debate, but reformers and policymakers adopt a monologic position and rarely take opposition to them seriously. Consider, for example, the opt-out movement in the United States. Even though families in different communities around the country began to raise serious objections to the testing their children are subjected to, their resistance is coopted into the political spectacle as yet another oppositional force that hero-reformers have to combat (Szolowicz 2017). Diverse voices that question, challenge, or critique the direction of change chosen by political elites are often silenced or drowned out as irrelevant, uninformed, misguided, and detrimental for the nation's future (Smith et al. 2004).

What can be done in such a challenging political moment is the prerogative of the second approach to political theater. Brecht (Willett 1964) and Boal (1979) argued that Greek tragedies are staged in ways that coerce the audience to empathize with the characters onstage and experience catharsis at the end of the performance. This way tragedies mold the audience into accepting the status quo. Modernization dramas and reformers' justifications for neoliberal policies similarly seek to mold the audience into accepting their version of reality and into maintaining the status quo that upholds injustice and inequality. Brecht argued that alienation from the act onstage is necessary to distance the audience from the fiction of the play to propel them to action (Willett 1964). Seen from this perspective, a book that tells the story of neoliberal reforms in another country could serve as a potential catalyst to stop taking neoliberalization and marketization of education in one's own context for granted. Building on Brecht's observations, Boal (1979) developed the Theater of the Oppressed "to change the people—'spectators,' passive beings in the theatrical phenomenon—into subjects, into actors, transformers of the dramatic action" (122). I draw on the framework of political theater in the hope of not only critiquing but also imagining possibilities for praxis.

The focus on political theater as an art form also allows me to bring together politics, ethics, and aesthetics into my policy analysis. Bakhtin (1990, 1993) writes of authors' aesthetic responsibility that any product that an artist creates bears his or her signature that testifies to its authorship. In networked states, where responsibility for policies is increasingly dissolved, a lack of policymakers' accountability and responsibility for changes is paralyzing to those who become the target of reforms. In presenting my analysis through the lens of theater, I explore how the process of diffusing responsibility is accomplished. By focusing on individual actors involved in reforms, I also seek to make visible the roles played by actual people behind seemingly impersonal modernization reforms. While my analysis will not lead to specific individuals being held accountable for their roles (I use pseudonyms throughout the text), it nevertheless affords opportunities to reexamine how policy analysis can be carried out in ways that will keep playwrights, directors, and actors of reform aesthetically, ethically, and politically responsible for their productions.

Finally, the framework of political theater puts the ethnographer who enters spaces of struggle and contestation in a unique position like that of the fool, the joker, or the clown in Bakhtin's (1981) account of the "theatrical trappings of the public square" (159). These figures question and challenge authority. As outsiders, they create opportunities to scrutinize the duplicity, banality, and hypocrisy of those who currently hold power (Aydarova "Jokers"). In an ethnographic context, an outsider, such as myself, can perform the role of a fool who observes and analyzes events, and who may be particularly well poised to do so if insiders are under the threat of repercussion for speaking out.

Building on these two approaches, I conceptualize political theater as a multifaceted process, in which reformers stage performances that create an imaginary world dedicated to the orchestration of conservative social change through modernization reforms. To demystify policymaking processes and reformers' performances, I use dramaturgical components and techniques, including masks (chapter 2), event sequence in theatrical productions (chapter 3), selective focus accomplished through the use of light and shadows (chapter 4), props and scripts (chapter 5), and actor training (chapter 6) as tools for policy analysis. In offering this analysis, I also explore possibilities of alternative constructions and integrate multiple participants' perspectives on the issues entangled in or obscured by the political theater of teacher education reforms. Connecting a diversity of perspectives on the performances onstage allows me to disrupt the monologic unitary construction of problems and solutions that reformers advocate and offer insights into alternative paths of change. I share Boal's hope that readers of this book would consider active positions available to them to respond to the policy dramas they are observing. A more detailed explanation of this work's theoretical foundations is provided in appendix B.

Anthropology of Policy as the Methodological Approach

It is common for global education policy studies to trace processes from policy formation to policy implementation. In addition to constructing policy processes in a linear fashion, there is a common tendency to ascribe authorship for the changes to the visible actors—international organizations, national governments, ministries of education, or expert communities (see Martens et al. 2010; Verger, Novelli, and Altinyelken 2012). Occasionally, the presence of other actors is recognized (see S. Ball 2007, 2012; Menashy

2016; Spring 2015a, 2015b; Gunter, Hall, and Apple 2017; Hursh 2016; Kovacs 2011; Tompkins-Stange 2016), but their activities are often approached in a rational manner. The guiding assumption for analyzing those actors' words and works is that they do what they say they do. Finally, studies in global governance tend to deal with final products—reports or policies that have been proposed or implemented, leaving the processes of arriving at those products largely unattended. While this approach is helpful for shedding light on possible movements in the field, it remains insufficient for capturing the inner workings of power and for attending to how some voices drown out others in national and subnational debates on global policies. To address these gaps, I turn to the methodological approaches of anthropology of policy to make visible the inconsistencies in policy actors' performances, to disrupt certainties about policy formation processes, and to reconsider ethical and aesthetic responsibilities in policymaking in the age of spectacle.

Anthropology of policy departs from a linear construction of policy formation and policy implementation. Associated closely with the interpretive policy analysis (Yanow 2000), it instead attends to the messy, contested, and contingent nature of policies that work as instruments of governing and power (Shore, Wright, and Però 2011; Sutton and Levinson 2001). Moving away from the realist rational frame, anthropology of policy expands the notion of how policies can be studied as "contested narratives which define the problems of the present in such a way as to either condemn or condone the past, and project only one viable pathway to its resolution" (Shore, Wright, and Però 2011, 13). For an ethnographer to study a contested narrative means that she must give credence to multiple voices in policy debates and attend to the fragmentations within the policy (Shore and Wright 1997). Apart from a distinct conceptual focus, anthropology of policy reconsiders ethnography's "geographic coherence" (Hamann and Rosen 2011, 466) and expands an anthropologist's use of evidence. Site ethnography in policy research may not always be accessible, but rich insights into unfolding processes can be gained through the use of published and unpublished reports, newspaper accounts, memos, and public interviews. In drawing on this approach, I similarly incorporate different types of evidence into my account.

Research Sites and Data Sources

My research journey in Russia began in 2011. I did not go there to study the dismantling of teacher education. I went with questions about educational reforms imbued with global neoliberal discourses, the budding effects of which I began to observe in government reports and policy briefs. I started with an ethnographic study of changes at Dobrolyubov State Pedagogical University in Siberia in 2011. Constant talk of the Bologna Process and modernization policies made me wonder how the story of reforms would unfold over time. I thought I knew the answer. I imagined that with strong academic traditions, resistance against globally circulated reforms would prevail. When I returned in 2012, I added fieldwork at Ognensk State Pedagogical University—located centrally both geographically and politically—planning to observe how that resistance would unfold. That summer, a colleague put me in contact with a collaborator who quite fortuitously was connected to the reformers' networks. Because of my interest in educational reforms, she recommended that I connect with the folks from Lyutvino Economics University (LEU) as they were now running much of the show. She put me in touch with a couple of people working there who I managed to interview at that time. Those interviews had a strong global and neoliberal flavor, with references to problem constructions and analyses of educational trends reminiscent of US and UK reform discourses.

When I returned to Russia in 2013, I decided to incorporate all three sites into a critical multi-sited ethnography: Ognensk and Dobrolyubov State Pedagogical Universities to capture the variation in how pedagogical universities were dealing with reforms and LEU to understand how these reforms came to acquire so much of the global flavor. Research at the pedagogical universities could help me "study through" the policies (Wedel et al. 2005), whereas LEU would offer an opportunity to "study up" (Nader 1972).

I spent several months conducting ethnographic research at foreign languages and pedagogy departments at Ognensk and Dobrolyubov State Pedagogical Universities. Life at pedagogical universities generally rotated around classes, breaks between classes in the offices shared by as many as fifteen or twenty faculty, and occasional faculty meetings. I spent most of my time "hanging out" in shared faculty offices, in classrooms, and in the hallways where students waited for their classes. I participated in university conferences, department events, and conducted classroom observations. When students were on their teaching practicums, I traveled to the schools where they were placed and spent time observing their teaching and their interactions with K–12 teachers and students. In my observations, I focused on how teaching and learning proceeded in teacher education, paying particular attention to how different participants made sense of reforms associated with educational modernization.

I conducted focus groups with students and interviewed faculty, administrators, and educational researchers to learn about their perspectives on and experiences with educational modernization. OSPU was actively engaged in contesting teacher education modernization, so the university leadership put together a working group that was preparing an alternative policy proposal. I interviewed members of the working group and included the publications and presentations of this group's members in my analysis. Many of my participants knew about the developments in teacher education modernization and repeatedly gave me two or three names of reformers who worked for the LEU as the people I should definitely interview for my project. These people subsequently became key characters in this text. Due to Dobrolyubov's remote location, there was less awareness of the specifics of modernization policies when I was collecting data. There was, however, a general sense among faculty members of being overwhelmed with the onslaught of reforms and constantly changing expectations (Aydarova "Fiction-Making").

I first traveled to Lyutvino to attend a conference organized by LEU and to meet with the secretary of the working group that developed the Concept. I followed some of the developments around the policy through webinars, media interviews, and public announcements remotely. When I returned to Lyutvino in January of 2014, I was assigned a desk in an office shared with the working group secretary. I do not know if I was placed there so that I could learn what I needed or so she could keep an eye on me. Both are equally possible.

Life at LEU did not have a familiar flow. Because the Education Department did not serve any undergraduate classes and most of their master's programs did not have a residential requirement, it did not have a regular rhythm of classes, with students' voices filling the hallways during breaks. Faculty shared offices, but they had only two or three people in each. Most of what was happening occurred behind closed doors in offices or in conference rooms. There were no communal spaces where people congregated, so I had to find new ways to "hang out." I attended weekly seminars open to the public and separate seminars for the employees and affiliates of the Education Department. I still observed different classes and gained valuable insights since there was a significant variation in ideological orientations within LEU, with the least visible faculty being most opposed to reforms.

Early on, I learned about an official working group of twenty-two people that the Ministry of Education allegedly created to draft the Concept.

The working group secretary promised to ask the members of that group for an interview on my behalf. After waiting for two weeks, I learned that only two people agreed to do an interview with me. After another two weeks, I learned that my request for an interview never went out to the group as a whole and was only discussed in the reformers' inner circle. This experience was indicative of the challenges I had to navigate at other sites where my presence was carefully managed to contain what I could learn. To work my way through these challenges at LEU, I started with the two interviews I was offered but used every imaginable opportunity to ask others for an interview or for a conversation. I approached folks during seminars at LEU, during educational and noneducational conferences, and even during an educational Olympiad—a competition organized to identify the best among teacher education students. During each interview, I also asked my interviewees for recommendations about who I should interview next. Through this reputational sampling (Farquharson 2005), useful for studying policy elites and for tracing their networks, I was able to conduct close to forty interviews, incorporating the perspectives of those who belonged to the reformers' networks and those who worked outside of them.

During my time in Lyutvino, my interviews were spread throughout the city. Those interviews took me to university buildings constructed during imperial times, to the offices in the buildings where famous Soviet chocolates used to be made, to research institutes speckled around different neighborhoods, to recently built high-rises of presidential academies. Every time I had an interview, I would get lost. I eventually accepted this as an inalienable part of a multi-sited ethnography of policy in a large metropolitan area. In the apartment I rented in the outskirts of Lyutvino, I created detailed observation narratives from the jottings I took during the day, wrote interview summaries, and meticulously mapped out reformers' networks, trying to figure out who knew whom, for how long, and through what channels. In the summer of 2014, I came back to Lyutvino to collect more interviews and observations and to conduct archival research for the historical background of these reforms.

From the time of fieldwork to the follow-up trips in November and December 2015, I followed reform developments online and through personal contacts. I went back for a conference in Lyutvino in November 2015 to learn that my assumptions about resistance were too simplistic. Despite the foreignness of reform ideas, representatives of pedagogical universities continued to struggle with what they meant for their practice but appeared to embrace change. I also conducted follow-up interviews with faculty and administrators in Dobrolyubov and reformers in Lyutvino, trying to understand how this change was accomplished.

On my last night in Lyutvino in December 2015, a colleague took me for a drive around the city. The landmarks I saw during my fieldwork, the large and small streets where I got lost, all of a sudden came together. I realized how interconnected everything was in the city: international organizations' offices stood close to embassies and consulates, research institutes circled academies, and LEU buildings were not far from ministry offices. It also dawned on me then that I no longer got lost on my excursions to conduct final interviews. That final drive through Lyutvino streets—unusually rainy for December—made that strange city finally familiar. My study was brought full circle.

Overall, I was able to conduct eighty interviews with reformers, teacher education faculty, pedagogical university administrators, as well as educational researchers, in addition to fifteen focus groups with teacher education students. Following the methodological approach of anthropology of policy, I incorporated into my analysis policy texts, background reports, academic publications, media reports, video recordings of reformers' presentations, and archival materials (more on methodology in appendix C).

The Researcher as Intern

In different contexts, I was called Olena, Helen, or Elena and was often asked where I was from. "I was born in Russia but grew up in Ukraine," became my standard, polished response. "I am working on a research project focusing on teacher education modernization in Russia," I would add right away. As someone with a native Russian-language proficiency, I often got a more intimate side of the story. Some people occasionally commented that I sounded like an American. The more time I spent in the field, the less frequent those comments became. Those I interacted with for my research often asked if I graduated from a pedagogical university. I did not. I graduated from a state (also known as classical) university, which made my degree more legitimate in reformers' eyes but put a distance between me and my participants from the teacher education community.

At some point, I had to ask myself what was it that got me into researching teacher education. What possessed me to choose that path after degrees in philology and linguistics? One of the reformers nudged me, "I also was young once and cared deeply about politics." He was right. I had cared about politics since high school. This interest was deepened by the influence of the years spent teaching at teacher training colleges in China and the United Arab Emirates. The educational modernization reforms that those countries were introducing cut straight to the heart of communities where I was working, raising difficult questions concerning values, priorities, and beliefs. Because of these experiences, I came to Russia trying to understand what happens to teachers, teaching, and teacher education in the context of those reforms.

I grew up in poverty and attended school in Odessa, Ukraine, in the nineties when the rapid introduction of a market economy destroyed industries and decimated livelihoods. In reading about alternative routes into teacher education in the United States and the United Kingdom, such as Teach For America, I wrote on the margins about my memories of being taught by people who were never trained to be teachers. A math teacher in the seventh grade came to work at my school because she lost her job as an engineer at a factory. She would silently write solutions to algebraic equations on the board to punish the class for their misbehavior. Those who did not care continued misbehaving. Those who did care copied those equations from the board trying in utter desperation to understand what they actually meant. At the end of the year, everyone failed the math exam. The next year, the math teacher was gone and the class was turned over to the strictest but also the strongest mathematician of the school. It took her fifteen seconds to get the class quiet. She caught the class up on the lost grade and moved us significantly ahead. Whatever was taught that year became my ticket to graduate school in the United States: there were no GRE prep schools in Ukraine at that time and I could only rely on the math I learned in school to pass that exam. This was not an isolated experience. I had other unpleasant encounters with teachers who walked into teaching after losing employment elsewhere. These experiences as well as my own professional path in teacher education made me rather skeptical of reformers' proposals when I first encountered them.

At all three sites, I was officially or unofficially labeled an intern—or *stazher*. This helped justify taking notes in a notebook during classes and asking what seemed like naive questions. During fieldwork, particularly in Lyutvino, I was acutely aware of my age and gender. Most of the people I interacted with for my research were older, and most were men. Being a young woman created certain barriers: my interactions with the reformers occurred mostly within the formal settings of workplaces, conferences, or academic events. That clearly shaped the stories that were shared with me. It is likely that a man would have had greater freedom in accessing reformers in more informal contexts, but alas, you do what you can with the body you are given. However, there were moments when forms of protectorate and paternal benevolence were extended to me—in helping arrange interviews with other people in the network or in getting access to relevant materials. This was tremendously helpful. The use of the first name and patronymic for most of the participants in this text, however, is a clear sign of the position from which I as a researcher saw these performances—as a younger woman, generally of a lower socioeconomic status, and certainly in a position with no power, in a distant semi-professional relationship with the participants. Only with students and some faculty at pedagogical universities I was able to develop warm and caring friendships.

My association with an American university provided some prestige in the reformers' networks but was not universally welcome in other contexts. Older academics labeled me "a spy"[6] or chided me for a lack of patriotism for leaving my country and for betraying my Motherland. That often hurt, particularly because returning to do this research in Russia was about giving back to the Motherland—the Motherland that actually did not care much either for me or for them, for that matter. Eavan Boland's poem in *A Woman Without a Country* expressed it best, "What troubled me was not whether she included her country in her short life. But whether that country included her."

Overview

This text consists of an introduction, a historical overview, an ethnography, and an epilogue. I have labeled the historical overview part 1 and the ethnography part 2 because they use different analytical approaches and genres. Part 1 uses historical evidence to report on the transformations in Russian teacher education that took place in the past and is written in a more traditional style. Part 2, on the other hand, subjects various sources to scrutiny to uncover hidden agendas, origins, or implications and is written in the style of a narrative ethnography (Stoller 2007; Narayan 2012). The stylistic and methodological differences between the two parts stem from the exigencies of the context—fiction-making that takes place in the present is more accessible to critical analysis than what took place in a more or less distant past.

In part 1, I explore the historical and sociopolitical context of teacher education reforms in Russia to situate the events and perceptions that emerge in part 2. Based on analysis of archival materials, historical documents, and interview accounts, I show how teacher preparation in Russia, throughout its development, had a complex relationship with the state and society: it stood on the crossroads of competing priorities that placed contradictory demands on its performance. On the one hand, the state invested in expansive and demanding teacher preparation, so that teachers could participate in transforming society to build a new future. The state simultaneously used affirmative action policies in teacher education to right the wrongs of low-quality education provided to historically underserved communities. With the growing prestige of higher education, students increasingly used teacher education as an opportunity for social mobility. The affirmative action policies provided opportunities for members of underserved groups to rise up the social ladder, moving away from their communities and from teaching in schools. Ministry officials and educational reformers saw this as a betrayal of the pedagogical university's mission. This conflict undermined the status of pedagogical universities and allowed authorities to view those institutions as failures in subsequent decades, eventually justifying their closures or mergers with other institutions of higher education.

Part 2, titled "Directing Social Change: Russian Policy Dramas," is an ethnographic account of the most recent reform activities I witnessed and examines the theatricality of educational policy by attending to different dramaturgical elements present in Russian teacher education reforms. In writing this account I chose to use the style of narrative ethnography because stories are a way for us to partake in our shared humanity (Stoller 2007), to gaze into the Other's eyes and see that the Other is us and we are the Other (Agar 1996). To keep a consistent narrative flow, quotations in part 2 are integrated with the main text rather than set off as block quotes. I wanted to avoid creating a jagged text that keeps shrinking and extending, depending on whose voice it represents. I share extended quotes from my data—from texts and from participants—inviting the reader to pursue their own interpretations of the events that unfolded and policies that were implemented. This is my way of saying that in the world of blurred boundaries between fiction and reality, you do not need another author telling you what to think. That is the power in art and theater—to awaken the senses through a provocative encounter and to sharpen conceptual tools for greater engagement instead of maintaining the status quo with ready-made explanations (Rancière 2011, 2016).

I use pseudonyms for most places and people mentioned in this text. I do it knowing that readers familiar with the Russian context would identify the main characters of this drama without much effort. The use of pseudonyms may appear counter to my own intentions—of putting faces on policies, of arguing for responsibility and accountability, of making visible processes in an attempt to demystify some of the behind-the-curtain banter or struggles. What's worse, I am doing it despite the wishes of my participants, who for the most part wanted me to use their real names.

I chose not to use real names for two reasons. First, the changing Russian political landscape can guarantee security and safety neither to my participants, nor to myself. I do not shun the responsibility to write dangerously (Dandicat 2010) and enter dangerous spaces (Madison 2009), but I feel that revealing these stories and disrupting these narratives is already close enough to the razor's edge for everyone involved. Second, in writing this text, my goal was not to create an analysis in the genre of *j'accuse*. My goal was to make visible the processes that are likely to take place in other contexts of the world, to trouble the linearity and objectivity of global policy analysis, as well as to think of alternative readings that can be reinserted into policy-related performances. Thus, I encourage my readers to resist connecting characters and places in this drama with specific places and people because that would detract from the main point of what I write about—teacher education reform as political theater. Given the global contexts in which dramas of education reforms unfold, they could be performed similarly in other places, with slightly different characters.

Part 2 consists of six chapters that demonstrate how policy dramas mystify processes of change, depersonalize decisions, and obscure reformers' ultimate goal of creating social change through educational reforms. In chapter 1, I describe the main actors most actively involved in Russian teacher education modernization. Affiliated with an economic university, these actors drew on twenty years of experience with educational reforms in Russia to reshape the teaching profession so that Russia would "catch up with the rest of the world" and become competitive in the global economy. I show how the various connections and associations in their networks provided them with resources for occupying positions of power in Russian educational policymaking. Of particular importance are the elements of reformers' biographies that link them to transnational policy networks and ground their proposals in neoliberal ideologies.

In chapter 2, I analyze the text of the Concept of Teacher Education Modernization and explore how masks of the name, intentions, origins, uncertainty, and evidence were used to disguise the policy's attempt to drastically transform Russian teacher education. Even though the name of the text suggested that the policy would support and develop teacher education, reformers acknowledged that the real intention of the policy was to decrease the state's expenditures on teacher preparation and create alternative routes into teaching. The key ideology driving reform efforts is the notion that those who are not prepared to teach are better at teaching because "they bring a wealth of professional experience into their classrooms." Despite the visible presence of international influences, however, the text of the Concept masked the origin of these ideas by deploying new words to describe proposed changes.

Chapter 3 examines the development of teacher education modernization policy text as a production sequence that includes both auditions and a series of dress rehearsals. The chronological narratives presented by reformers suggested that the Concept emerged out of multiple discussions that solicited input from the teacher education community. I show, however, that the main aspects of reform were prepared before by the Ministry of Education created a working group to design this policy. This means that meetings with teacher educators served to create an illusion of democratic participation and worked only as dress rehearsals for the official release of the policy. Furthermore, I demonstrate how reformers consistently identified the president and the Ministry of Education as directors of reform efforts, even as they themselves continued directing the drama of Russian teacher education and used the president as the mouthpiece for their proposals. Discrepancies in the chronologies reveal ways in which actor and director roles were reshuffled to obscure who directed reform processes, leaving no one accountable for the reforms' outcomes.

Chapter 4 uses the metaphor of selective focus to examine how reformers drew the audience's attention toward "low-quality" teacher education institutions and away from the ideologies that drove reform efforts. The crisis of "low-quality" teacher education was instigated through the use of such tropes as "only the weakest students go to pedagogical universities" and "most pedagogical universities are ineffective." Yet these tropes were based on fictionalized data, arbitrary measures, and unsubstantiated claims. The light focused on that crisis obscured ways in which teacher education was positioned as an instrument of conservative social change and education was being redesigned to serve the interests of the corporate sector. In their writing and public engagements, reformers argued that teacher education has to prepare teachers who would regulate students' behaviors and participate in students' socialization, instead of transmitting knowledge or engaging students in knowledge production. Through a set of policies that accompanied teacher education modernization, reformers reoriented the system of Russian education toward the production of compliant workers, consumers, and spectators.

In chapter 5, I examine the Concept's global connections. I explore how international assessments and references to global transformations were used as props to support reformers' production concept. Similar to politicians and reformers in other contexts, reformers used references to international assessments to justify the implementation of the policies they devised. They dismissed the results that showed the performance of Russian students in a positive light and instead focused on the failures revealed by PISA. Taking a cue from Michael Barber's report *How the World's Best-Performing School Systems Come Out on Top*, reformers selectively used international assessment results to instigate crisis narratives that necessitated drastic reforms. The comparative analysis of the Concept and Barber's report shows uncanny similarities, demonstrating how that report served as a foundational script for the Concept and its implementation.

Chapter 6 captures how, despite significant pushback, critique, and opposition from educators and the public, teacher education modernization became implemented. Highlighting the role of sponsors and donors in reform implementation, this chapter analyzes how participants' acquiescence was purchased through competitive grant funding. It also explores how teacher educators were trained as actors to perform acquiescence to new ideologies in front of MOE officials to ensure continued funding of the reform.

I conclude with an epilogue rather than a conclusion to underscore the unending nature of political theater and struggles associated with it. In the epilogue, I examine how the political, aesthetic, and ethical dimensions used in the world of theater can be helpful in subjecting policymakers' performances to critique. Drawing on Bakhtin's (1993) discussion of ethical imperatives, I discuss how role reshuffling obscures authorship of reforms and leaves no one answerable for the changes introduced. I also show that aesthetic principles that guide the construction of powerful art are useful for reexamining the relationships between policymakers and the populations they attempt to govern through their policies. Instead of attempting to control these populations, policymakers could give them greater freedom to innovate, develop, and undergo the open-ended process of becoming; instead of creating grotesque portrayals that exaggerate the population's features, policymakers could see individuals in their wholeness. Finally, I problematize political theater as a form of coercion that minimizes opportunities for critical engagement and dialogue over the proposed measures.

To counteract the insidious effect of teacher education reform as political theater, I suggest that teacher educators around the world reappropriate reforms as theater of liberation. To do that, I suggest they build networks of collectivity and transnational collaborations, seek out opportunities for dialogic engagement with a variety of stakeholders, and root their effort in the historical struggles over schooling and the teaching profession.

Part I

Historical Context

Sowing the Seeds of Discontent

Russia had seen so many worlds flick through in such blistering progression—from communism to perestroika to shock therapy to penury to oligarchy to mafia state to mega-rich—that its new heroes were left with the sense that life is just one glittering masquerade, where every role and any position or belief is mutable.

—Peter Pomerantsev, *Nothing Is True and Everything Is Possible*

Throughout its development, teacher preparation in Russia had a complex relationship with the state and with the society: it stood on the crossroads of competing priorities that placed contradictory demands on its performance. In this chapter, I present a synopsis of how pedagogical universities as standalone institutions dedicated to teacher education evolved in the Russian context. My goal, however, is not to present a comprehensive account of this evolvement as this has been done by others (see Long and Long 1999). Rather, I foreground some of the issues that gained particular significance in the current context of its reforms and provide descriptions of key features of the system to situate the drama that unfolded in the last couple of years.

I break up my narrative by several different decades but do not follow a strict chronological timeline. Instead, I trace how the change introduced at one point in time mutated through subsequent decades to produce the kind of results that subsequently made the work of pedagogical universities particularly challenging. In presenting my analysis, I abstain from demonizing the Soviet state, as is customary in the accounts of that period. Instead, I focus on the evidence that is available to me—primary sources from the Russian archives, a variety of secondary sources in Russian and English, as well as interview data. In doing so, however, I am aware that the line between reality and fiction was blurry in the Soviet Union as much as it currently is in modern Russia. Multiple sources of evidence might state the same lies. While others abandoned any attempts to contextualize their projects in official historical documents for this reason and turned instead to personal accounts only (see Matza 2010), I bring various sources together to allow them to corroborate or challenge the storyline presented.

On the Eve of the Revolution: Education and Teacher Preparation in Imperial Russia

The Russian Empire did not have compulsory education. A variety of schools existed: some were run by local authorities, some by the ministry, some by churches. Schools that provided access to higher education—such as gymnasiums or lyceums—were not equally accessible to children from different social classes. In fact, the *Cook's Circular* of 1887 stated that "gymnasiums and progymnasiums are freed from receiving the children of coachmen, servants, cooks, laundresses, small tradesmen, and the like" (as quoted in Long and Long 1999, 5). Many could not rely on formal schools to provide basic instruction and had to learn from any individual available to teach them. Literacy rates varied significantly between urban centers and rural areas: they rarely rose above 47 percent among the adult population in Saint Petersburg and Moscow and dropped to about 14 percent in Siberian regions (Bogdanov 1964). Literacy rates among males were often twice as high as literacy rates among females.

Teachers who taught in Russian schools varied in the extent of their preparation as well. For basic schools that offered elementary education, most teachers were prepared in pedagogical gymnasiums that were equivalent to high schools. Other teachers came from universities, teacher institutes, and teacher seminaries. While universities offered a range of educational specializations, those who graduated from them received no training in pedagogy or teaching methods. Teacher seminaries and teacher institutes focused exclusively on teacher preparation and offered courses in pedagogy. They, however, were not considered higher education institutions and did not give their graduates the right to enter universities upon graduation. Teacher institutes were nicknamed "plebeian universities" because they were more accessible to those who came from lower middle classes (Panachin 1979).

Teacher seminaries were the most prevalent teacher preparation institutions in Imperial Russia (Panachin 1979). These were schools that opened in Russia in the second half of the nineteenth century to prepare teachers who would know both the subjects they would be teaching and pedagogy. By 1917, there were 183 teacher seminaries with about 120–150 students in each (Prokof'yev et al. 1967). Their goal was to train politically trustworthy teachers who identified with teaching as a profession rather than a temporary position. Grigor'yev in his *Historical Essay on the Russian School* describes the principles that were foundational to teachers' seminaries:

> The education of the seminary's students is created according to their future mission. They must be confirmed in the holy truths of faith, receive clear knowledge in it, and with that, the main effort should be directed toward arousing in their hearts warm feelings of faithful love to God and the Holy Savior and passionate faithfulness to the Lord Emperor. Respect for law and civil order, love for their labor and a desire of their soul

to pour into the hearts of children under their care a feeling of faith and virtuousness should be made a part of all the students' thinking. (Grigor'yev 1900, 447)

This description reflects the central role of religion in teacher preparation—the first subject on the list of courses offered in teacher seminaries was "The Divine Law." The Bible teaching was fused with instilling in students faithfulness to the tsar as well as "respect for law and civil order." Seeing the growing unrest among the Russian population, imperial ministers hoped to use teachers to prevent a larger uprising. This heavy emphasis on divine law limited teachers' knowledge of natural sciences and other disciplines: students spent four times more on Bible classes than on the study of all the natural sciences combined (Panachin 1979).

Teacher institutes were similar to teacher seminaries but were not quite as numerous—by 1914 there were about forty-four teacher institutes spread around the Russian Empire. Unlike teacher seminaries that enrolled men and women, institutes admitted only men. Students in both teacher institutes and teacher seminaries received their education at the expense of the state but then were required to work at a school for no less than six years. Together with the provision of preparation for teachers, more forward-looking statesmen supported the establishment of teaching as a profession with the help of teachers' professional meetings and publications. Even though those were on the rise at the turn of the century, the tsar's desire for a tighter rein on his subjects resulted in an abrupt end of support for these endeavors (Long and Long 1999).

To become a teacher in imperial Russia, however, one was not required to have professional training. Instead, it was possible to take an exam to receive a permission to work at a school. Those exams took place in universities. Those who had university education could take an abridged version of an exam; those who did not have a higher education degree had to take a full exam. Usually an exam consisted of a written and an oral portion and two demonstrations of a lesson. Most exams checked candidates' knowledge of the subjects they would be teaching, but some later started adding questions about pedagogy. Panachin (1979) notes that often exams were used not to determine those who were best fit for teaching but rather those who were "politically trustworthy"—candidates were required to submit paperwork proving that they were not involved in any political activities or had any conflicts with authorities. By the end of the nineteenth century, about 20 percent of elementary school teachers took an exam to receive permission to work at a school. Permissions for teaching varied depending on the candidates' educational background. Those who lacked higher levels of education received permission to be private tutors or "home teachers." During Soviet times and subsequently post-Soviet times, exams were for the most part eliminated as an entry into the profession. Based on the Central Committee's Decree No. 19 from 1936, one could receive a title of teacher after some form of pedagogical education and working at a school for a year, if one did not have prior work experience at an educational institution. In 1939, a follow-up decree canceled the one-year requirement and stated that one could be awarded the title of teacher based on a diploma from a pedagogical institute, a teachers institute, or a pedagogical college (Karpova and Severtseva 1957, 162). This practice remained in effect until the current wave of teacher education reforms.

The low levels of education across vast swaths of the population did not escape the attention of those who fought to overthrow the tsar. In a 1913 speech to be delivered by a Bolshevist member of the parliament, Lenin (1957) wrote about the dismal state of affairs in Russian education. Quoting the data published in an *Annual Russian Handbook*, he emphasized that less than fifty people out of a thousand had access to education, when the proportion of school-aged children constituted about one-fifth of the total population. Of great concern to Lenin were deplorable conditions of living that many teachers, particularly in rural areas, were subjected to, together with the miserly pay they were receiving for their work. "There is not a single other savage country where masses of people would have been robbed of education, light, and knowledge left in Europe, except for Russia" (Lenin 1957, 145). Throughout the rest of the speech, constant comparisons were drawn between the "civilized" and "developed" countries of the West, where illiteracy was all but eradicated and where education was generously financed by governments, and "backward" Russia, where none of this was happening. America occupied a prominent place among these examples. Lenin noted how even though the United States did not have as high an educational achievement as some of the European states, it had four times the number of students than Russia did and was spending 426 million dollars on education. "Of course, we receive objections . . . that Russia is poor," he went on to say, but that poverty only manifested itself in the state's inability to provide education for its population. Russia was not poor when it came down to lavish expenses on the police, army, military interventions, and state bureaucrats.

The member of the parliament who was to deliver that speech did not get a chance to finish it—he was stopped when he began saying that this injustice would only end when the people would rise up and topple the government of that time. But the speech captured an important juxtaposition: Russia as "backward" and "savage" against the "developed" and "civilized" West. This juxtaposition demonstrated the reflexive gaze that came to dominate discursive shifts in Soviet educational politics throughout the twentieth century and reemerged in the 2010s among the reformers who became key participants in my research. If the Soviet state later came to use that reflexive gaze to emphasize Russia's accomplishments in education, then modern-day policymakers drew on the same language that Lenin used to justify radical reforms in order to overcome Russia's "backwardness." It also captured an important irony that continues to ring true nowadays: How is it that in a country with high oil and natural gas revenues, education remains so underfunded?

The Revolution and the 1920s: The Time of Experiments and a Pursuit of New Forms

With the Revolution of 1917, education was in the limelight. After all, socialism and communism as ideological systems rested on the assumption that for the working class to govern itself it needed to be highly educated or enlightened. Education became the cornerstone of social transformation and economic development. One of the first decisions made by the Soviet leaders was to introduce the so-called "Unified Labor School." Unlike its many predecessors, the Unified Labor School was supposed to be the same for children from all different social backgrounds. It was based on Dewey's principles of student-centered learning and activity-based approaches to education (Mchitarjan 2000). In labor schools, project work was used to bring together intellectual, physical, and moral development of new generations. In a six-week teacher preparation program in 1920, the purpose of the labor school was described as follows:

> The ideal of the modern labor school must ensue from the main purposes of the state, which is in the hands of the working class. Its task is the upbringing of proletariat children to be people developed in multiple dimensions (or well rounded, cultured),

> called to be conscious creators of the new society and new culture, natural participants in proletarian "dictatorship" as a regime that realizes truly human freedom and rights of a human personality [Rus. *lichnost'*] by destroying the class-based state. (*Obyasnitelnaya Zapiska k Obshchestvenno-Politicheskoy Chasti Programmy 6-nedelnyh Kursov 1920*, GARF, A2306, 10, 236)[1]

This vision for the labor school captures the school's responsibility for creating the New Man—"a man marked by selfless love of the motherland, unquestioned loyalty to the Party, devotion to the cause of proletarian internationalism, respect for public property, dedication to socially useful labor, and such traits of character as discipline, obedience, courage, and creativity" (Counts 1961, 13).[2] It also reveals several important aspects of the philosophical foundations of Soviet education. The school sought to create "multiple-dimension people," which in Russian carries a strong intellectual overtone (Dimov 1981). Even though critics of the Soviet system often claim that education was expected to serve the needs of the economy and not the individual, this criticism is not completely fair. Reading was encouraged and heavily subsidized by the state not because it could increase workers' productivity but because it could support spiritual growth among Soviet citizens as one of those multiple dimensions.

Schools were meant to prepare students to be "conscious creators of the new society and new culture." This is an important principle that runs through much Marxist theorizing on education throughout the twentieth century in Russia and in other countries. It underscores the role of education in enhancing the subjects' ability to shape the world around them—a principle that bears an important contrast with the current wave of reforms. Finally, this preparation was deemed necessary to create citizens ready for self-governing. Disputes among the political elite about the extent to which the working class would be able to govern itself eventually led to the creation of a system in which opportunities for self-governing were diminished and protests were violently stamped out. But the vision for schools and for education remained relatively consistent throughout the Soviet era. Some modern-day observers speculate that well-educated citizenry contributed more to the downfall of the Soviet state than its weak economy.

While the model of the school was chosen early on, the relationship between the state and the teacher took longer to define. Not all teachers supported the revolution and some staged protests against the Bolshevik uprising, albeit Soviet-era scholars called those "paid protests" (Kotomkina

2002). To create a dialogue with teachers, multiple conferences and congresses were organized. For example, an All-Russian Congress on Teacher Preparation took place in August 1919 (GARF, A2306, 10, 19). Its resolution called for a major overhaul of teacher preparation inherited from the Russian Empire to get rid of the past, so that new institutions could be built. More importantly, the debates revealed how uncertain the relationship between teachers and the new Soviet power was. Some among those in attendance argued that "a destruction of teachers' work was under way" and that representatives of the Soviet state should treat teachers with more respect. Stories were shared about teachers who refused to take orders from the commissars appointed in their areas. Their insubordination was met with violence, which the conference chair admitted were cases when the Soviet power may have gone "a little overboard." In conclusion, however, the organizers of the congress agreed that it was not necessary for all teachers to be devout followers of socialism. As the chairperson explained, "The Soviet power embodied by its representatives, such as Lunacharskiy and Pokrovskiy, does not demand that a teacher be a communist, but it does demand that a teacher be an honest worker, but of course, there should be some contact with the Soviet power."

This sentiment soon disappeared from debates on teachers' roles. In a meeting dedicated to the reform of pedagogical establishments held in 1920, speakers stressed the importance of bringing up generations of teachers that were good communists and socialists. During that meeting, attendees "unanimously accepted a resolution that the socialist labor school can only be built when there are enough socialist teachers. That is why the preparation of socialist teachers is the main task in a practical implementation of the idea of the labor school" (GARF, A2306, 10, 236).

The "preparation of socialist teachers," however, did not have ready-made forms and had to go through multiple transformations before it reached a semblance of the system that worked through most of the twentieth century. First, institutions that prepared teachers before the Revolution were transformed into Institutes of the People's Education—higher education institutions with three- to four-year-long courses of study. Two years later, those were eliminated. Pedagogical institutes and pedagogical colleges were created in their place. Later some of the pedagogical institutes were turned into departments of pedagogy of state universities. Even though higher education institutions proliferated, they were not supplying enough teachers. A variety of teacher preparation courses were opened. Some of those lasted a year, some two. The country's leadership called teacher education programs to recruit as many people as they could, but they could often get only a fraction of students to enroll—teachers' work was not popular and was perceived to be too strenuous (Kotomkina 2002). Multiple institutional forms that were being created had to address problems with teacher shortages and overcome barriers of high turnover among newly trained teachers.

Proliferation of institutional forms was also accompanied by diversity in curricula plans and teaching approaches (Panachin 1975). Many institutions ran programs that consisted of a large number of disparate and disconnected courses. The committee in charge of teacher preparation urged teacher educators to employ the principles of the labor school as a unifying principle in educating teachers. Shatskiy—one of the leading Soviet educators—proposed pedagogical courses where students "through the means of active independent work had to master the foundations of the labor school." That required physical labor in workshops that had to be accompanied by "conversations, seminars, reports, lectures, where the educational side of physical labor would be worked through" (GARF, A2306, 10, 23). Along with the experimental forms of pedagogy that this approach exemplified, a more traditional version that focused on philosophical underpinnings of educational processes was offered at pedagogical departments in universities. For example, Tambov University in 1918 offered courses in pedagogy that combined both the history of pedagogical ideas and teachings in general pedagogy (GARF, A2306, 18, 91). Popov (GARF, R9396, 16, 804) described pedagogy courses of that era as "applied philosophy." With multiple variations in curricular forms, most teacher preparation programs, however, did incorporate at least one course in political economy to prepare "socialist teachers" for the new school. Overall, these different approaches reveal that the 1920s were a decade of experiments and relative freedom in educational institutions.

Apart from giving shape to the system of teacher preparation, the general framework of higher education also had to be determined. Otto Schmidt—a famous Soviet mathematician—with the support of Narkompros (People's Committee on Enlightenment, which was in charge of education at that stage) argued for the creation of a two-pronged higher education system: "elite" preparation of scientists and higher education faculty and "mass" preparation of specialists for applied fields, such as teachers or engineers (GARF, A2306, 10, 311). The distinction between "elite" and "mass" education, in this case, did not rest on differences in social classes but rather on different functions that graduates would carry out. Schmidt's proposal rested on considerations for a delicate balance between theory and practice.

From his perspective, higher education in imperial Russia was so obsessed with its focus on theory that its science degraded into "dead scholasticism." For science to stay alive, it needed to be connected to practice. Graduates during the tsar's time, according to him, were also not prepared for their professional roles. But a heavy emphasis on practice alone without a vital connection with theory and science could cause "practice to become shallow and stop progressing."

According to Schmidt's proposal, elite preparation of scientists and a professoriate should proceed in departments of higher education institutions that focused on narrow disciplines. Those departments would occupy a higher position in the educational hierarchy than, for example, departments of pedagogy that were supposed to prepare "educated enough teachers on a mass scale for the Unified Labor School." This boundary between elite preparation of scientists and mass preparation for applied professions, such as teaching, served as the implicit framework for the organization of higher education throughout most of the Soviet era. This distinction sowed one of the paradoxes that has reemerged in the current wave of reforms as well. Modern-day reformers identify the mass nature of teacher preparation as one of its most problematic areas, one that diminishes its quality.

Amid the search for the appropriate institutional forms, there was also an attempt to define the relationship between the state and its people. The metaphor of a relationship between a teacher and his or her students was often evoked to capture that emergent relationship. Scott's (1998) analysis of Lenin's writing on the party's role in the development of socialism shows that the metaphor of a classroom teacher appears consistently: the party, like a teacher, has to bring up the working class. Lenin did not believe that the masses were able to identify a path of ideological clarity on their own and thought that the party could step in and provide that direction, just the way a teacher would with his or her students. Scott contrasts Lenin's position with that of Rosa Luxemburg and Alexandra Kollontai—feminist activists who were critical of Lenin's ideas. Continuing with the theme of party pedagogic activity, they argued that the party should be a teacher who learns from students rather than treating students in an authoritarian manner. Both Luxemburg and Kollontai believed that communism should not be assumed to have a predetermined form but rather should emerge organically out of the creative activity of the working class.

It is important that these political actors' writing drew on pedagogic metaphors that emerged out of their own experiences as teachers. This shows how political leaders often identified themselves with the teaching profession. This resulted in a symbolic conjoining between the emergent leadership's role in paving the way for its people toward progress and the teacher's role in leading students toward knowledge and enlightenment. By identifying the party with teachers, Soviet leaders in subsequent decades afforded teachers a position of trust and authority, treating them like heroes and celebrities (Counts 1961; Ewing 2004).

This position of trust and authority, however, was not earned, in Weberian terms, but rather bestowed on teachers by the country's political leadership. It was also zealously protected by the party. In 1955, for example, a communiqué regarding concerns about students' upbringing stated that it was unacceptable for parents to treat teachers with disrespect because "schools' and teacher's authority has to be protected" (Fursenko 2006, 116). In protecting teacher's authority, it is likely that the party was trying to protect its own authority. Ultimately, this zealous protection of teachers' position and status contributed significantly to strengthening the teaching profession throughout the twentieth century. This support most likely heralded the demise of the profession afterward as well: when the state collapsed in 1991, no external authority identified with teachers or defended their position in society.

Overall, the twenties was a decade of hardship. The country was destroyed by the Civil War and its economy was in tatters, which significantly undermined its ability to invest in education (Kiseleva 2002). Attempts to build new schools and train new teachers ran into a lack of basic resources to carry out this task (Long and Long 1999). Major shortages of teachers across all of Russia created enormous barriers to the eradication of illiteracy and to the expansion of school access among the population. The problem was not only that there were not enough trained teachers but also that their working conditions were so strenuous that few could last in their jobs. Teachers' salaries were lower than what they were before the Revolution. Their work conditions were so challenging that one of the regional educational ministers in 1919 asked for teachers' labor to be recognized as hard labor that should receive special protection because of "hygienically abnormal work conditions" (GARF, A2306, 10, 236).

Despite these challenges, the first decade of the Soviet state's existence represented a constant search for new forms, with the system of education in general and teacher preparation in particular experiencing much uncertainty and significant change. In this search, international experiences were studied and transferred to the Russian context—a practice that was soon abandoned (Schriewer and Martinez 2004) when the leadership chose a more distinct path of socialist development. By the end of the decade, a three-prong system of pedagogical education evolved: pedagogical institutes became stand-alone institutions that offered four-year higher education degrees, teachers institutes were two-year programs of incomplete higher education that prepared predominantly middle school teachers, and at the level of a technical school pedagogical colleges offered professional preparation to primary school teachers (fig. 1).

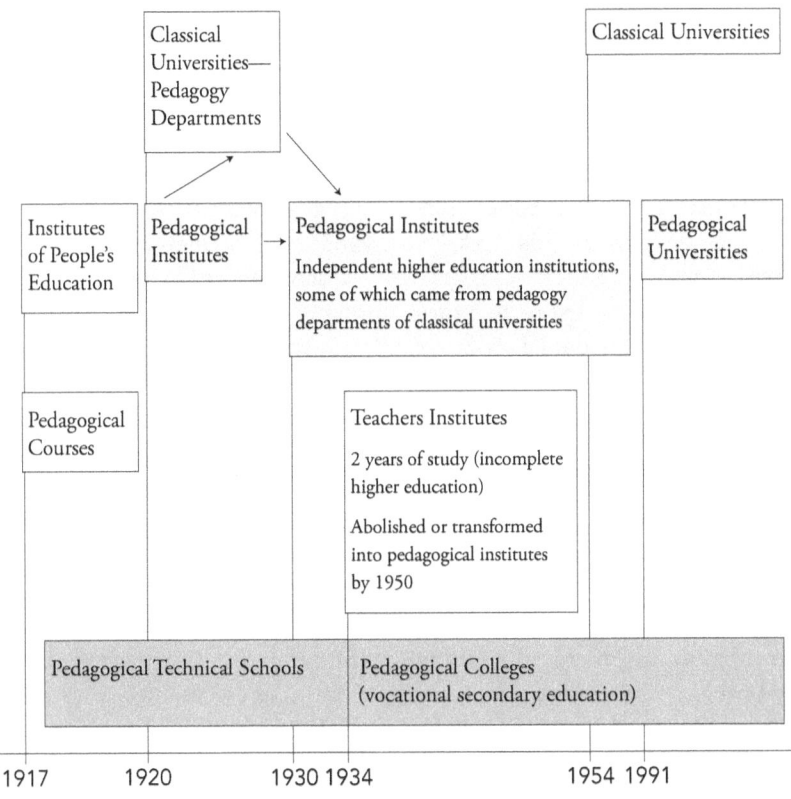

Figure 1. Types of institutions most commonly involved in teacher preparation in Russia 1917 to the present.

The 1930s: The Emergence of a Dichotomy between Classical Universities and Pedagogical Institutes

Across the educational system, the thirties saw both enormous strides in increasing access to education and the tightening of state control over institutions' activities, faculty's teaching approaches, and students' lives. Laws on compulsory education were introduced at the beginning of the decade. New schools were built throughout the country. Higher education institutions were expected to follow centrally issued decrees that determined many of the aspects of their lives: the length of semesters, dates when semesters would start, forms of teaching (lectures and seminars), and forms of assessment (oral exams)—all of which became rigidly prescribed by official decrees. The project method utilized in the 1920s was banned; instead, only lectures and seminars were allowed. Some of the "pedological" approaches developed in the twenties, such as standardized assessments, were described as perversions that did not belong in a socialist state. A more traditional turn in teaching was introduced, with less freedom for institutes to choose their own paths. Curricular plans, directions for curriculum implementation, guidelines for course content, university rule books, and budgets were streamlined through the central authorities in Moscow. Overall, the centralization of decision-making and funding as well as standardization of educational activities that occurred at this stage continued to be a defining feature of Russian education until post-Soviet reforms of the 1990s and 2000s, but even the decentralization introduced then was not long lasting.

One important development of this decade is the emergence of a dichotomy between classical universities and pedagogical institutes that continues to reverberate in the present day. From 1928 to 1930 many universities were closed; they reopened in 1931, but in new configurations: their pedagogical and medical departments became independent institutes. This model reflected Schmidt's proposal of separating education of the "elite" scientists from the preparation of "mass" specialists. Throughout the thirties, the number of pedagogical institutes throughout Russia grew rapidly: by 1947 there were about forty pedagogical institutes in comparison to about nine universities (Popov 1947; GARF, R9396, 16, 804). In many cases (but not all), the university begat the institute and both maintained a complex relationship with the changing demands of Soviet power.

The complex relationship between the university and the pedagogical institute is evident in the contrast between reports prepared by the two institutions in Gorky in 1947. Gorky State University was founded in 1918.

After the pedagogical and medical departments were removed, Gorky University reopened in 1931. It had four departments: physics and mathematics, chemistry, biology, and radiophysics. These departments reflected a specific scientific focus of the institution. Prominent scholars and famous researchers were working there; several of them were members of the Russian Academy of Sciences. Through decisions in Moscow, the university received most of the maps, museum pieces, and library books that constituted the collection of the pedagogical institute. It also received funding to build new buildings and dormitories. From 1945 to 1948, the university had a total of 818 students, with thirty-six students graduating in 1946 and sixty in 1947. The university had the right to award advanced degrees in math and sciences.

In contrast, the pedagogical institute underwent multiple transformations through the first two decades of its existence: from a teachers institute in 1915, to a pedagogical institute in 1917, to the Institute of the People's Education in 1918, to a department of the university in 1926, until it became independent in 1930. By 1947, it had departments of history, Russian language and literature, physics and mathematics, natural sciences, preschool education, geography, and physical education. Only one faculty member belonged to the Russian Academy of Sciences—the faculty member who was also a faculty member at Gorky State University. The institute had 1,606 students, and it graduated 251 students in 1946 and 369 in 1947. It had no right to award advanced degrees. The report did not indicate that the institute received any funding for research or for expanding its facilities.

Reports from these two institutions shed light on the stark contrast between universities and pedagogical institutes across the country. Universities had more resources than pedagogical institutes; subsequently, MOE officials criticized the latter for their lack of resources to enhance students' learning. Universities were relatively rare and more exclusive. They graduated on average thirty to seventy students a year compared to the three to four hundred that pedagogical institutes did. Universities' highly trained professoriate received significant support to conduct groundbreaking research, whereas pedagogical institutes had faculty who for the most part barely surpassed students in their educational attainment. These disparities were exacerbated by the difference in these institutions' ability to award advanced degrees. Very often faculty pursued advanced degrees as they were teaching in higher education institutions. Having access to advanced degrees in home institutions ensured a steady upgrading of the faculty's credentials. If faculty working for pedagogical institutes had no access to advanced degrees at their institutions or in their hometowns, they could rarely afford to travel elsewhere to get them. Finally, the contrast between the two is also striking in the universities' relatively steady identity and the pedagogical institutes' constant transformations in search of a suitable identity. While the universities clearly began to demonstrate a focus on more "elite" preparation, pedagogical institutes in the 1930s entered the path of becoming mass institutions hastily opened throughout the Russian Republic. These institutions' distinct identities created the appearance of an equilibrium in which classical universities and pedagogical institutes played different roles in the society.

But this equilibrium did not last long. In 1954, the Council of Ministers issued Decree No. 1863 demanding that universities stop preparing cadres that cannot be utilized in the national economy. Instead of preparing students with narrow specializations, universities were urged to produce more teachers and engineers. The Ministry of Higher Education was ordered to revise curriculum plans at universities to change the orientation of students' preparation, so that they would not be receiving "narrow profile" preparation but training that reflects "the needs of the national economy, culture, and enlightenment." Even though this decree was later revised and partially repealed, it refocused the mission of the university—not to provide elites for science but rather serve the specific needs of the economy in applied fields. This, in turn, placed classical universities and pedagogical institutes onto the same playing field. University graduates, with revised curriculum plans, would receive degrees that would qualify them to be teachers (by the 1970s, university graduates annually replenished about 15 percent of the teaching force in the Soviet Union [Panachin 1975]). This placed pedagogical institutes in a bit of an unfavorable comparison: better-resourced and more selective universities could now also provide the country with teachers. Why keep a distinct institution called a "pedagogical institute" then?

The question emerged soon after the Decree of 1954. The Council of Ministers started issuing decrees about combining if not entire institutions then at least some of their departments in order to "eliminate parallelism [or redundancy] in the preparation of cadres." For example, in 1956 there was an order to combine historical departments of Gorky State University and Gorky Pedagogical Institute (GARF, A2306, 73, 1444). The Ministry of Enlightenment that was in charge of pedagogical institutes responded that such a change would be unreasonable: the university had 136 students in their department, whereas the pedagogical institute had 676. But similar decrees were issued for institutions in other cities as well. In Kazan, the university had to take the History Department, but similarly to Gorky University, it had fewer students and therefore could not accommodate four or five times more students that were coming from the pedagogical institute. The Department of the Tartar Language, on the other hand, had to be moved to the pedagogical institute, but the faculty and the students from the university refused to hold their classes there and continued meeting at the university (GARF, A2306, 73, 1270). The conflict in Kazan, among other things, reflected how palpable the difference in status between the two institutions was: faculty and students from pedagogical institutes were willing to "move up," but the university faculty and students refused to "move down."

In response to these changes, in 1956 Arsen'yev—the director of the teacher preparation department at the Ministry of Enlightenment—wrote a report to the Central Committee of the Communist Party, explaining why pedagogical institutes should not be eliminated or merged with classical universities. In that report, Arsen'yev made two rhetorical moves. First, he emphasized that during imperial times, teachers who were prepared at universities had no pedagogical preparation. Second, he claimed:

> The creation of a scientifically based system of pedagogical education is an unquestionable accomplishment of the Soviet state. Only after the October Revolution in our country were pedagogical and teachers institutes created for the preparation of teachers and caretakers for different types of schools and establishments dedicated to the people's enlightenment. Soviet pedagogy, as a science of communist upbringing of the growing generations, serves as the foundation of pedagogical education in the USSR and is, like nowhere else in the world, connected very closely with other sciences (philosophy, psychology, anatomy, physiology, and so on). (GARF, A2306, 73, 1444)

So, why were pedagogical institutes important? According to Arsen'yev, those mattered because they represented the distinctness of the Soviet state. Pedagogy as science and pedagogical institutes as its keepers distinguished the Soviet Union from its past ("only after the October Revolution") and they set it apart from other countries in the world ("like nowhere else in the world"). The use of institutes to emphasize the distinctness of the Russian educational system became a common refrain throughout the Soviet era. For example, in a 1971 article published in the *International Review of Education*, Il'ina and Mishin stated, "Teacher training institutes are a completely new type of higher educational establishment founded in our country after the October Socialist Revolution. There are no educational institutions of this kind in other countries" (334). In Soviet attempts to develop an alternative form of modernity, these institutes became a sign of educational modernization. After the collapse of the Soviet Union, Russian educators dropped references to the connections between the Soviet state and pedagogical institutes but maintained the narrative of distinctness that these institutes represented.

This quote also reveals the aspect that became the eventual downfall of pedagogical institutes. Arsen'yev makes a point that "Soviet pedagogy" with its "focus on communist upbringing" serves as the foundation for Soviet pedagogical education. This later proved to be an unfortunate move. In Russia, "upbringing" (Rus. *vospitanie*; similar to the German concept of *Bildung*) was a constitutive part of educational processes that focused on the development of students' moral character and behavior both during imperial and Soviet times. But Soviet educators, for the most part, denied the continuity of traditions associated with upbringing, treating it as a distinctly Soviet approach. When the Soviet Union collapsed in 1991, the question of what "pedagogy" was a science of became more difficult to answer. For two subsequent decades, the notion of upbringing was largely abandoned and was brought back into the official policies only after 2010. During my fieldwork, however, I learned that reformers drew on the definition of "pedagogy as a science of communist upbringing" to discredit the system of pedagogical universities, claiming that after the collapse pedagogy became useless.

But the contrast between universities and pedagogical institutes that Arsen'yev laid out is quite instructive. He emphasized that university preparation was too narrow for well-qualified teachers: if a university student could specialize in medieval history, a pedagogical institute student had to know ancient history, medieval history, and modern history equally well. Pedagogical institutes also had stronger ties with schools where students had their practicums several times during their studies; university students were placed in labs or research institutes for their practical training. The final argument was very pragmatic: by midcentury the school system had grown so large and required so many teachers to continue growing that universities on their own could not meet those needs. Arsen'yev argued that each region had to have its own pedagogical institute (not each region had its own university) to guarantee a steady supply of teachers for the schools in the area. He won the argument for the time being and pedagogical institutes continued growing through the rest of the Soviet era, but with the collapse of the Soviet Union the same question had to be answered again—if universities could prepare teachers, why keep a distinct institution called "pedagogical university"? This time, however, there was no advocate to provide a cogent response about why the new state still needed those institutions.

The same question became particularly hard to answer because through the sixties and seventies Soviet authorities supported a convergence between university and pedagogical institute education. Curriculum plans for similar specializations in classical universities and in pedagogical institutes reveal that in terms of courses offered, the programs were quite comparable. One difference lay in a heavier dose of pedagogy and methods courses that students in pedagogical institutes received; another revealed different expectations in terms of performance. For example, foreign language departments at classical universities taught a number of courses in foreign languages; at the end of their program, students were expected to defend their capstone research project (diploma project) in the target language. Students in pedagogical institutes were taught most courses in their native language and were given the option of defending their research projects in Russian. With those differences, students who chose certain specializations in universities and pedagogical institutes received similar diplomas with a qualification of teacher, but university graduates appeared to be more qualified. Furthermore, having been placed on the same playing field, the two institutions were required to play by slightly different rules. I will return to this point later when I discuss the competing expectations placed on pedagogical institutes by the state and by society in the fifties.

The 1940s: The Aftermath of the War and the Trouble with Base Schools

World War II presented an enormous trial and created a new set of challenges for the educational system in Russia. But, unlike what is mentioned in other accounts (e.g., Long and Long 1999), the Soviet state quickly turned to teacher education even before the war was officially over. In February of 1945, three months before the end of the war, the Ministry of Enlightenment demanded that the department of pedagogical preparation report on the state of teacher preparation institutes around the country. Their state was dismal: faculty numbers remained relatively stable, but student numbers dropped precipitously because many young people went to fight; buildings were destroyed, pillaged, burned down, or repurposed as hospitals or recovery wards. The ministry demanded that repairs start as soon as possible and that local authorities find support for teacher education institutions to be ready for the new academic year. Institutes needed everything: construction materials, fuel, coal, cloth for blankets, pots, pans, bowls, spoons, and forks. According to the reports, the repurposed buildings were reluctantly, if ever, returned to the institutes; the resources necessary were either not provided or provided only as a fraction of what was needed.

The crisis moment of postwar restoration also served as a moment of introducing innovations into the system of teacher education. In December of 1946, amid the struggles of rebuilding the country after the war, the Council of Ministers issued Decree No. 2787 demanding that teacher education be improved, that teachers receive more practical training, and that each institute have a "base school" attached to it. Base schools, similar to laboratory schools in the United States, were supposed to serve two functions. First and foremost, their role was to allow students to practice teaching before they graduate. Second, they were supposed to be used by faculty from pedagogical institutes to conduct research relevant for improving classroom instruction and for developing pedagogical science. As Minister of Enlightenment Kairov later explained in one of his letters in 1955, base schools attached to pedagogical institutes had to "become such establishments that mass elementary and middle schools could look at them as models and learn from their positive experience how to teach and bring up students" (GARF, A2306, 73, 1119).

In theory, those were sound ideas. In practice, they did not often work. Institutes attached "base schools" to themselves, but the two institutions continued operating as separate entities. Even though some work was done in base schools, they could neither accommodate all students that needed practical training, nor were they always useful for faculty to conduct their research. This state of affairs eventually became known to the Ministry of Finances. There, this arrangement was regarded as an inefficient use of resources. Unlike other schools that were funded through local authorities, base schools received funding from the budget of the Republic just as pedagogical institutes did. In addition, pedagogical institutes were under the jurisdiction of the Republican Ministry of Enlightenment, but schools were first and foremost under the control of local authorities, which then reported to the ministry. Base schools, according to the Ministry of Finances, stopped being supervised by local authorities after they became attached to pedagogical institutes (Letter to the Council of Ministers, 1956; GARF, A2306, 73, 1440). The Ministry of Finances demanded that "base schools" should receive their funding from local authorities. The Ministry of Enlightenment responded that "base schools serve[d] the same function for pedagogical institutes as [teaching] clinics for medical institutes" and that they provided a platform for conducting pedagogical experiments that could not be carried out in a mass school (Letter to the Council of Ministers, 1956; GARF, A2306, 73, 1440). If base schools were moved under the funding of local authorities, close ties with pedagogical institutes would be lost and they would not be able to carry out these important functions.

An argument between the two ministries, with the involvement of the country's highest authorities, went on for several years. Eventually, the decision was made to move base schools under the funding of local authorities. While some institutes continued involvement in their schools after that stage, in most places the relationship between the institute and the school became either nominal or ceased to exist altogether. The new wave of reforms in the 2010s seeks to bring back the practice of base schools (though under a completely different name, see chapter 2), but without any recognition of previous (failed) attempts to yoke together institutions with different orientations, commitments, and funding structures.

Decades of the 1950s–1970s: The Rise of Competing Priorities

In the decades after the war, the Soviet state pursued three directions of school reforms: expanding access to education for the entire population, extending the length of schooling, and increasing the quality of educational provision. To meet these goals, it needed well-trained teachers, but the system continually experienced significant teacher shortages. For example, the average annual deficit of teachers was twenty-five thousand in 1961–1962; fifty thousand in 1962–1963, and forty-seven thousand in 1963–1964 (Panachin 1975, 120). To meet those needs, many teachers institutes that offered only two years of education were transformed into pedagogical institutes (others were closed and the practice of an incomplete higher education for teachers was quickly eliminated). The number of pedagogical institutes hovered around one hundred for two decades. In years when the demographic situation began to improve, pedagogical institutes were also allowed to increase the number of students they could admit to meet the state's plans for the number of graduates.

Even though fast enrollment expansion was a positive development, it created a number of problems due to a lack of facilities at pedagogical institutes to support that expansion. Many institutes remained dilapidated after the war; others had to be started in whatever buildings were available in the area. To address the shortages of the facilities, many institutes throughout the country ran classes in several shifts a day. For example, in 1953, Herzen State Pedagogical Institute worked in four shifts with classes being taught from eight in the morning until midnight. Classes were held in sheds, makeshift constructions, or even in hallways. Classroom buildings, if not closed because of the dangerous conditions they were in, could hold only a fraction of the students enrolled; dormitories could hold even less.

Throughout the next two decades, letters that institute administrators directed to the ministry reflected continual requests for building materials and financial resources to expand their campuses and enlarge their assets to accommodate the growing numbers of students. The repetitive nature of these requests along with direct complaints that they had not been met show that support for building projects in pedagogical institutes was slow in coming. While some institutes eventually received funding to expand, most did not. Some were also closed because ministry inspections showed that they did not have enough resources (such as classroom spaces) to continue operating. When in 2012 the Ministry of Education started its monitoring of effectiveness of higher education institutions, it designated many pedagogical universities as ineffective because of a lack of facilities.

But there was another dimension of the state's agenda to expand access to schooling that put pedagogical institutes at the crossroads of competing expectations. In the 1950s, party leaders began to express concerns for the conditions of rural schools and schools located away from the European part of Russia ("in the periphery," as those areas are still described, and how I will continue referring to them throughout). Students in those areas did not receive high-quality education because they did not have access to highly qualified teachers. As a result, students graduating from those schools were not competitive in entering institutions of higher learning. The periphery also needed to receive highly trained professionals for the expansion of industries and construction. To address the problem of dense concentration of professionals in the European part of Russia, the Central Committee issued a decree demanding that all graduates of institutions of higher learning be assigned to mandatory job placements based on the needs of the economy for a minimum of three years upon graduation (Council of Ministers Decree No. 660, May 18, 1956). This system of workforce distribution—*raspredeleniye*—applied to all fields and ensured that different geographic locations received the professionals they needed based on the centrally determined allocations.

This decree applied to pedagogical institutes just as much as it applied to any other institute or university. So, a graduate from Moscow could be sent to be a teacher in a small town in the Far East of Russia because that town experienced teacher shortages. The problem that emerged out of the job placement allocations in education was that students assigned to remote locations either did not show up (official numbers stated that on average only about 80 percent took their assigned posts [Miasnikov and Khromenkov 1981, 114]) or rarely stayed beyond the three required years. This created the problem of a revolving door in hard-to-staff areas, which was perceived as a waste of state resources because relocations and support for resettlement came from the state. This arrangement also failed to address the problem of low-quality education in rural and remote schools serving indigenous communities. In 1973, a decree titled "About the Measures of Improving the Work of Rural Schools" (TsK KPSS i Sovet Ministrov SSSR 1973) opened with the statement that twenty-two million children—or half of the country's students—were attending rural schools. The decree went on to say that rural children "continue to lag behind urban children in the quality of their knowledge."

To address the shortages of well-qualified teachers in rural and remote schools, a system of preferred admissions was introduced in pedagogical institutes. In general, to enter higher education institutions, applicants were required to go through a competitive process of taking challenging exams. Those exams weeded out academically weak candidates. Students from rural areas (or representatives of indigenous groups), as I mentioned before, were not prepared well enough to compete in the admission process. Therefore, through the system of preferred admissions (Rus. *vne konkursa*), students from rural areas were allowed to enter pedagogical institutes regardless of their performance on entrance exams.

Institutes were urged to graduate as many candidates from rural areas as possible, because rural schools needed more teachers. So, as early as 1961, the Ministry of Enlightenment reported to the Central Committee of the Communist Party that among first-year students in pedagogical institutes at least 50 percent came from rural areas (GARF, A2306, 73, 3204). By the end of the seventies, the Ministry of Enlightenment reported the number of students whose parents were "workers or farmers" rose to two-thirds of students enrolled in pedagogical institutes (Miasnikov and Khromenkov 1981,

97). Whether this change in the composition of the student body was real or fictional is hard to establish, but the intentionally created system of getting around entry requirements bred negative perceptions of these institutes in the years to come. According to some modern-day policymakers, pedagogical institutes became "academic ghettoes" (Interview No. 45; February 2014) predominantly because they were taking more students from rural areas who did not have to pass entry examinations to be admitted.

The problem with hard-to-staff schools, however, was not resolved. Students from rural areas did not always go back to their villages or hometowns. They tried to stay in the city where the quality of life was significantly better. Also, not all graduates were choosing to work in schools. Some reports stated that between 1947 and 1971, at least 20 percent of pedagogical institutes' graduates left teaching and joined other industries (Miasnikov and Khromenkov 1981, 115). The ministry issued multiple decrees urging the directors of pedagogical institutes to screen candidates better to make sure that students *do not* enter "just to study and receive higher education" (Ministry of Enlightenment Directive No. 36-5, June 1958). There were proposals to select students based on their motivation for teaching, but those did not become a widespread practice. Probably, it did not happen because in many institutes in the periphery by the end of the seventies, the number of those who applied only marginally exceeded the number of those they were required to admit by the plan.

This is how pedagogical institutes got caught in the streams of competing priorities. On the one hand, the state expected pedagogical institutes to provide teachers for all schools, including the ones that are located in rural and remote areas where living conditions were poor. On the other hand, students chose these institutes to pursue opportunities for a better life—either as teachers in urban areas or as specialists in other industries. As I will show later, reformers derided pedagogical universities for failing to prepare teachers and instead functioning as places that help villagers move to cities. They argued that social mobility became the institutes' most visible function, pushing preparation for teaching down the list of its priorities. The most troubling outcome of these competing demands was the growing stigma attached to these institutes because of their alleged lack of selectivity. The emergence of negative stereotypes of pedagogical institutes became reflected in folk sayings, such as "if you have no brains, go to a pedagogical institute" (Rus. *mozgov net, idi v ped*) or "if you have no road ahead of you, go become a pedagogue" (Rus. *net dorogi, idi v pedagogi*).

These sayings regularly peppered the speech of the modern-day reformers of Russian teacher education.

There was another way that the problems of rural schools influenced teacher preparation, and this influence revealed several important aspects of teacher education reforms in the Soviet era. While much in the life of educational institutions was determined by party decrees and Ministry of Enlightenment orders, some of the transformations occurred through the initiative of pedagogical institutes themselves. In 1955, faculty from Lenin's Moscow Pedagogical Institute wrote a letter in which they argued that in small rural schools, teachers who had only one major (which was typical for pedagogical institutes up to that point) could not get a full workload. To address teacher shortages, they continued, teachers should have broad preparation in at least two subjects. The Ministry of Enlightenment carried out an analysis of how many teachers could be supplied this way, how much their preparation would cost, and how a combination of two majors would benefit the economy. The debate about whether such broad preparation was financially feasible, whether such preparation would provide competent teachers, and how these teachers might be employed went on at the Ministry of Enlightenment and the Ministry of Higher Education for a year. Eventually, new curriculum plans were designed that allowed a five-year preparation of teachers with "a broad profile" (such as Russian language and literature and foreign languages, French and physics, math and biology, geography and chemistry, etc.) and a four-year preparation of teachers with "a narrow profile" (only Russian language and literature, only foreign languages, or only math, etc.).

Many pedagogical institutes adopted new curriculum plans, but this innovation was not equally popular with all actors. Students complained to the ministry that double majors significantly increased their workloads. For example, a student wrote a letter to the ministry arguing that preparation in Russian language and literature already carried a heavy load where students had to read about forty books a year. With the addition of foreign-language study on top of these expectations, students' workloads reached seventy hours a week. School administrators raised concerns about the quality of teachers' knowledge. They felt that teachers prepared with two majors did not know either subject well enough to teach. The reform was not long-lived, because from the mid-sixties to the beginning of the seventies, many institutes reverted back to mostly preparing teachers trained in one subject. What is important about this reform, however, is that it challenges the commonly held assumptions of exclusively top-down educational policymaking in the Soviet Union. This reform indicates that the field of policy formation and contestation was populated by a variety of actors, even in the highly centralized system of Soviet education.

It also reveals an important aspect of Soviet teacher preparation relevant for modern-day debates. While pedagogy and methods courses comprised a significant proportion of teacher education curriculum, teachers were first and foremost expected to be subject knowledge specialists. This reform failed because it went against this expectation. Modern-day reforms that are the subject of this book attempted to move away from the conception of the teacher as a subject specialist. But due to the long-standing tradition previously described, the educational community did not support this move.

During this period, subject knowledge became an integral part of an ambitious vision for teacher preparation. A curriculum guide in 1970s sets the following as the vision for the teacher as a graduate of a pedagogical institute:

> To the teacher belongs the deciding role of equipping learners with strong knowledge of science foundations, of developing a materialistic worldview and communist morality, as well as of preparing young people for life and for active participation in society. In our time, only the teacher who possesses a broad political and cultural horizon, has perfectly mastered the pedagogical craft, knows deeply the science of the taught discipline, and knows how to demonstrate its role in social and civil progress and in solving the tasks of communist development can work successfully in school, teach, and bring up young people. (*Uchebnye Plany Pedagogicheskih Institutov* 1970, 1)

The curriculum guide captures an expansive vision for a well-prepared teacher who is able to enact change not only in the classroom but also in society at large. This teacher's responsibility is to prepare students that can be active participants in social and political processes. To accomplish these purposes, this teacher has to have at least three elements in his or her preparation: "broad cultural and political horizon," "sound knowledge foundation," as well as "a mastery of pedagogical craft." While this document presented teaching as a craft, other documents emphasized its scientific base (pedagogy, psychology, and methods of teaching) as well as its creative nature. Numerous publications used in pedagogical institutes referred to teaching as an art (e.g., see Bondarenko 1974; Gritsevskiy and Gritsevskaya 1990).

Teachers were responsible for demonstrating the connections between what their students were learning in a particular discipline with transformations of the society and the world around them. Particularly with the decrees in the sixties and seventies that stressed the importance of connecting school knowledge with life outside schools, the teachers' responsibility was to teach the broad encyclopedic curriculum of the Soviet school and demonstrate how the knowledge of those disciplines can be applied in real life. The teacher, however, was not responsible solely for knowledge transmission but also for the upbringing of the students—the process of moral and spiritual development (as it pertains to a holistic understanding of a person, rather than any religion) that could provide students with resources to lead a meaningful life in the future. Curriculum plans used in pedagogical institutes provided the training that matched this vision. Ultimately, the party's involvement in creating a vision for the profession and the ministry-issued curriculum plans created a consensus around what constituted the knowledge necessary for teaching. This consensus was still palpable even after the collapse of the Soviet Union (Alexander 2000).

In sum, the decades of the fifties, sixties, and seventies were times of stabilization. Reforms were introduced, changes pursued and occasionally retracted, but those bore the semblance of tinkering with the system rather than dramatically transforming it. While many of the proposals for change allegedly came from the nation's leaders, such as Khrushchev with his decree on bringing school closer to life, some of the reform proposals did come from the institutes themselves. Many of the changes that the ministry proposed, along with the directions for transformations identified by the nation's leaders, were forwarded to pedagogical institutes for discussion and deliberation. For some of the reform proposals, feedback was solicited and incorporated into the final drafts of the changed policies, which points to a possibility that communication loops even in a highly centralized and allegedly authoritarian structure allowed for participants in the institutes to feel a part of the policymaking process. When faced with contradictory demands of providing rural schools with teachers and increasing the quality of pedagogical education, however, institutes willingly took up the challenge without raising objections to the transformations that greatly tarnished their reputation. Despite the competing expectations placed on them by the state and the society, they were urged to provide high-quality teachers and adhere to an expansive vision of the teacher's role in the society.

The 1980s: The Beginning of the End and the Era of Innovators in Education

The decade of the eighties brought with it many uncertainties about the future of the country. Pedagogical institutes were not subject to large-scale transformations at this time, but a school reform was introduced that extended the length of study to eleven years and added more vocational training (Long and Long 1999; Sutherland 1999). But these changes were seen as merely cosmetic by some educational activists. In an attempt to address the contradictions that emerged in Soviet schools, a grassroots movement of innovative educators sought to transform classroom instruction with new approaches. These innovations did not come from pedagogical institutes; they came from practicing teachers and from principals who were running experimental schools. Innovative educators—Shatalov, Lysenkova, Amonashvili, Ivanov, and Il'in—published accounts of their educational experiments in one of the leading educational newspapers. Together they authored the report "Pedagogy of Cooperation" (Uchitel'skaya Gazeta 2006) that urged educators to move away from teaching based on compulsion and intimidation toward a more supportive and creative approach. Those accounts stirred the imagination of teachers and teacher educators around the country. Participants in my study who worked in pedagogy departments described that time as a decade of excitement when multiple ideas bubbled around accompanied by a general sense of experimentation and a search for new forms (yet again).

The desire for change captured in the innovators' work caught on among those who wanted to see a radical transformation of the educational system. A temporary scholarly research collective called "School" (Rus. VNIK Shkola) under the leadership of Eduard Dneprov came together to draft a new Concept of Education (Dneprov 2006). Dneprov argued that the Soviet educational system was too authoritarian and too centralized: the ministry held all of the power in its hands and did not attend to the needs of those on the ground. In order to combat that, he suggested that the role of the state in education be reduced and educational structures be liberalized. This agenda became the foundation for the basic principles of the reform proposal that VNIK drafted: democratization, multiplicity of forms (variability and alternative approaches), national character of education, openness of education, regionalization of schools, humanization, humanitarization,[3] differentiation, developing an activity-based education, and lifelong learning.

The document caused significant upheaval and was resisted by the Russian Academy of Pedagogical Sciences. Even though the reform proposal was blocked, many of the principles laid out in the document became foundational in Russia's Law on Education in 1992. Dneprov's appointment as the minister of education and the move of VNIK Shkola's team into the ministry after the collapse of the Soviet Union facilitated the introduction of these principles into the new educational laws. Many among those who at that time came together under Dneprov's leadership to do away with the school of the Soviet past emerged as reformers of schooling and teacher education in the 2000s and 2010s. Some of those people became participants in my research.

The 1990s: Winds of Change Sweeping through the Country

In 1991, with the dissolution of the Soviet Union, the importance of education slid down the hierarchy of needs of a nation in survival mode. Aggressive market economy reforms left the country split between fabulously rich oligarchs and the rest of the population struggling to survive amid skyrocketing inflation and unemployment. The default of 1998 only further undermined the already weak economy. Funding for the educational sector fell precipitously—from 7 to 10 percent of GDP during the Soviet era to about 3 percent in the nineties. Salaries in the state sector were not paid for months and sometimes years. Strikes among teachers, miners, students, and doctors erupted with steady regularity. Mortality rates greatly increased; male life expectancy dropped by six years and female by three in that decade alone (Parsons 2014). Those were also disorienting times in terms of morality, values, aspirations, and social ties (Lemon 1998, 2009; Pesmen 2000; Ries 2002).

In the midst of these seismic changes, international organizations, such as the OECD, the World Bank, USAID, and others, became actively involved in many sectors of the Russian economy, including education. With support from international organizations, Eduard Dneprov and a group of like-minded reformers pursued a radical transformation of Russian education, introducing decentralization and market principles of educational provision. These autocratic reforms were met with significant resistance, which led to Dneprov's departure from the Ministry of Education (M. Johnson 1997).

His successors tried to reorient the educational system toward more centralized control. Despite the changes in ministers and in official priorities, many of the World Bank's recommendations for the restructuring of Russian education continued to be pursued: decentralization of decision making, a different approach to the contents of education, introduction of new state standards, diversification of the textbook market, changes in educational finance structures, introduction of quality assurance mechanisms and a system of national assessments, as well as a reorientation of professional preparation (Heyneman et al. 1995). Teacher education did not escape attention either. In their evaluation of Russian education policies, the World Bank team highlighted the problems in initial teacher training:

> While some pedagogical universities offer very good initial training and are actively revising their curricula to include needed new courses, such as education psychology, there is nonetheless a concern about the quality of many teacher training institutions. Often, pedagogical universities permit entry to those with a relatively low level of educational attainment (a system of positive discrimination) so as to address a problem of rural schools that have difficulty in attracting and retaining teachers. (Canning, Moock, and Heleniak 1999b, 7)

To address the problem of low-quality teacher preparation in Russia, the World Bank's reports recommended that teacher education become more "flexible and market-relevant" (Canning, Moock, and Heleniak 1999b, vii). The World Bank teams argued that this could be accomplished through the closure of pedagogical institutes, their merger with classical universities, or creation of regional base centers of teacher training (Heyneman et al. 1995; Canning, Moock, and Heleniak 1999a, 1999b). Many of the previously described initiatives were either implemented by the reformers who became the main characters of this book or became top priority items on their agendas.

Meanwhile teacher education pursued its own change. When in the nineties higher education institutions were given freedom to transform themselves, pedagogical institutes quickly embarked on a name change, dropping "institute" from their title and becoming universities (Khanzhiev 1994). Some dropped "pedagogical" from their title too, if they received permission to do so. By 2012, from a relatively stable system of about one hundred institutions, only seventy-four remained "pedagogical universities."

There was a change in schools: teachers were leaving their jobs because of low pay or significant delays in pay; high rates of unemployment among those who used to work at factories and plants created pools of those who had higher education degrees and were willing to work at a school for any pay. Thus, schools started hiring those who were not trained to be teachers. While there are no published accounts of those experiences, narratives shared in society at large (to which I am privy because of my own school experiences with nonpedagogues) generally state that those teachers rarely succeeded. Many did not last more than a year, and that one year was a loss for students. If nothing else, those years showed that to teach at a school and to do it well, just a higher education degree in any discipline was not enough.

Transformations in the New Millennium: Let Modernization Begin (Again)!

The 2000s introduced a distinct neoliberal bent in education (Gounko 2008; Timoshenko 2011). In 2001, the Ministry of Education issued the Concept of Educational Modernization, which initiated a change in how education was conceived and the role the state had to play in its provision (Aydarova 2014). Individuals became responsible for their education with a heavy emphasis on choice and flexibility that educational systems had to provide. The state's role was changed from a provider to an overseer of the educational sector. Additional groups, such as businesses, employers, and communities, were expected to play a greater role in setting educational priorities and agendas. This Concept set off a wave of modernization policies that targeted the education sector with efficiency formulas and accountability controls. OECD (2016) noted that Russia's educational expenditures have risen in the last decade from 2.7 percent in 2005 to 3.8 percent of its GDP but remained lower than the OECD average of 5.2 percent.

In 2003, Russia joined the Bologna Process, which only further instilled the value reorientation introduced by the Concept. The harmonization of higher education policies that swept across Europe reached Russia: the Program for Educational Development 2006–2010 identified restructuring of the higher education system to match the demands of the Bologna Process as one of its highest priorities. Thus, two-tiered degrees were introduced—bachelor's and master's—instead of the traditional five-year specialist degrees that all students received prior to this change. Academic hours were replaced by credits; curriculum plans were reduced significantly and set to match the European framework of competencies laid out in the project Tuning. Teacher education standards issued after the introduction of the Bologna Process were based on neoliberal principles (Aydarova 2014). This change was most apparent in the reduction of teachers' work from a public intellectual to a technocrat. At the same time, however, the new standards increased the number of practicum placements in undergraduate curriculums. Instead of a two-month student teaching experience in students' fifth year, the new standards required three placements with an increasing degree of student involvement in the work of schools. One placement was expected to happen over the summer, requiring students to work as summer camp counselors in order to develop skills of upbringing work.

After the turbulent nineties, many looked forward to reforms in education. Those inside the system hoped that reforms would bring back much-needed funding. Instead, under the guidance of international organizations, funding formulas were redefined to move away from normative needs-based funding toward per capita or project-based funding. For schools, per capita funding created a massive state of disarray—smaller schools were closed regardless of the quality of education they provided. In higher education, institutions started fighting for higher per-student allocations and for the ministry's permission to admit more students both as "budget" students (or those whose tuitions are completely subsidized by the state) and as "contract" tuition-paying students. Distinctions between different categories of students created tensions and conflicts within institutions because "budget" students became perceived as more capable and deserving of higher education than their fee-paying counterparts (Aydarova 2015b).

In 2009, high school graduates began to take the Unified State Exam to receive their high school diploma and to apply to higher education institutions. Prior to this exam, higher education institutions conducted their own admission exams. The Unified State Exam moved those responsibilities away from universities and gave students greater freedom to apply to multiple institutions. It was supposed to reduce corruption, but observers noted that corruption simply moved to schools. Multiple scandals with students cheating, purchasing test materials, or distributing answer keys through social networks before the day of the exam have shaken the country. Centralization of the exam under the jurisdiction of Federal Service on Supervision in Education and Science created multiple possibilities for corruption, which became more visible because of the national scale of the examination. Despite all the problematic aspects of this test, the Ministry of Education began to use applicants' scores on the Unified State Exam to evaluate the quality of educational institutions. Combined with several other measures (see chapter 4), this led to closures, mergers, and other punitive interventions.

Throughout the 2000s, the system of teacher recruitment maintained the Soviet legacy of relying on higher education diplomas as proof of one's qualification to teach at a school. What that meant was that pedagogical universities and many classical universities continued issuing degrees that qualified graduates to work as teachers in schools. Compulsory job placements were abandoned and graduates had to rely on informal networks of family and friends to find employment. Declining teacher salaries as well as teachers' low status in society, however, made teaching an unattractive career path (Aydarova 2016, 2017b). To address this problem, the government proclaimed 2010 the Year of the Teacher and introduced public announcements praising teacher's work (fig. 2). Those efforts, however, were rarely taken at face value as government support for teachers either through salaries or other benefits remained weak.

Figure 2. Public service announcement downtown Moscow, June 2011. Quotes from teachers on the billboard: "Dare to be wise" (*left*), "I give my heart away to children" (*center*), "There are no students who are not talented. There are those who are well behaved and not well behaved."

Concluding Thoughts

In this part, I have situated the relationships that emerged around pedagogical universities in the context of the Soviet modernization project where they were called to provide teachers for the expanding school system. Throughout the twentieth century, the identity of pedagogical universities was questioned when placed in contrast to classical universities. After pedagogical institutes were urged to admit students from rural areas without competition, their reputation was significantly undermined. When the Soviet Union collapsed and the foundation of "pedagogy as the science of communist upbringing" lost its purpose, these institutions were left with the difficult task of having to redefine themselves in the new millennium.

Ultimately, this complex relationship between the state and institutions that prepare teachers has one continual thread running through it: when a strong state needed those institutions and identified its role as metaphorically similar to teacher's role, they were able to maintain their distinct status. The collapse of the Soviet Union weakened their ability to defend themselves or find strong advocates to protect their identity.

Part II

Directing Social Change

Russian Policy Dramas

All that is solid melts into air.

—Karl Marx

1

Actors

On my first day at Lyutvino Economics University (LEU), Anton Mikhailovich and I had a chat about my research on teacher education modernization. According to those who carefully followed this reform, he played an important role in its development and was most readily recognized as the main reformer among five or six people involved in teacher education modernization. Knowing his role in the reforms intimidated me but also made me realize that I had to find a way to get along with him.

At the end of our conversation, he sized me up, "How can you be useful *to us*?"

I mumbled something incoherent in response.

"Oh, I know how we can use you. You will be our foreign expert."

I mumbled a semblance of an agreement.

It turned out that Anton Mikhailovich and two of his colleagues—Roman Valeryevich and Stepan Sergeyevich—were involved in a project helping Fevral'sk State Pedagogical University revamp itself into a school of social work and special education studies. The project had to be reviewed by experts and I could be one of them. The review involved more than simply reading a proposal. I had to evaluate the project, go with them to Fevral'sk, and present my review at a roundtable discussion of the project. For two weeks prior to the trip, Stepan Sergeyevich coached me on what to expect and how to approach this task.

"What am I doing here?" I kept wondering. "Am I expected to put an earnest effort into assessing this project? Am I qualified enough to evaluate this program's intentions for reinvention? Or is this just a performance and all I have to do is simply play along? What does this all mean for me as a researcher?" One thing I knew for sure—if I do it right, I might have an in; if I mess up, I can kiss the rest of my fieldwork good-bye. That in no way alleviated my anxieties. The night before I had to board the plane to Fevral'sk, I did not sleep.

It was a whirlwind trip. Board the plane on Thursday morning. Arrive in Fevral'sk Thursday evening. Spend all Friday at the roundtable event. Fly back to Lyutvino early Saturday morning. Enjoy minus-thirty-degree temperatures throughout.

Friday was long. There were presentations, questions, and discussions. There were important people from the regional Ministry of Education who had important things to say. There were faculty members who without much belief on their part presented aspects of the project trying to convince the local MOE officials that revamping could work. In the midst of presentations and conversations, someone asked a question about language: "We all seem to be saying words to each other but we don't fully understand what they mean." The president of the university leaned over to Anton Mikhailovich, "I do feel that there is a major fragmentation here. A fragmentation of understandings." Anton Mikhailovich's face melted into a large smile, "That's the kind of politics we now have."

In the second half of the day, the time came for me to present my review. I drew on what I knew best: research on professionalization and the relationship between higher education institutions and the labor market based on US examples. The group from LEU nodded in approval. The only part that Anton Mikhailovich spoke up against, almost immediately after I finished, was my comment about faculty's low pay and high workloads. "We are not even going to discuss that," he said in response.

At the end of the day, the president of the university took the floor and spoke for thirty minutes about all of the university's accomplishments far beyond anything that is done abroad (a prolonged look at me); Fevral'sk's remote geographic location slowing down change—"my grandma told me they did not know anything about the Revolution here until 1919"; and the impossibility of reform when funding is limited. During her tirade, Anton Mikhailovich folded his hands on his belly and dozed off. For him and his team, it was a long week of tough work trying to change people's minds about education and about how it could be done differently. His team encountered a major challenge: faculty only wanted to be told what to write in reports indicating that they had completed a project. This way they could move on with their lives, probably doing what they had always done before.

On Saturday, Anton Mikhailovich, his team, and I headed to the airport. He asked me what I thought of the event. I chose the most neutral response I could come up with, "It was interesting." We had a bit of time before take-off, so we all sat down at a table in the airport's café. Three men in their fifties and I—a woman in my mid-thirties. They all got tea. Someone got a cup for me, too. I could sense that the mood around the table was gloomy.

"How did you end up at LEU?" started Anton Mikhailovich.

I blinked. Is this a test? Is he checking whether I can be trusted? Have I done anything wrong? "Joseph Abramovich was at a conference and I . . ."

"And that's how you got here? Alright. You will be our intern [Rus. *stazher*] then. There is some dissatisfaction with our work."

Stepan Sergeyevich chimed in: "The leadership is dissatisfied. The faculty are all on fire. They figured out they could do things differently. But the president . . ."

"Well, you heard her speak. How could anyone have taken up so much time and say nothing of value?" added Roman Valeryevich.

Anton Mikhailovich took over, "See, you say it was interesting for you. Of course, it was your first time. But we have done so many of these projects. We want to see results. We pour ourselves into this. At least here we spent only a couple of days. We had universities that we worked with for months. We did so much and all of a sudden the president says, 'No. We are not going to change anything.' And there is no change."

"Well, do they have an explanation for it?" I wondered.

"They don't want to change."

"They are afraid of the new. They don't want to do anything with those who resist."

Anton Mikhailovich took a sip of tea and started again, "Generations have to change." Roman Valeryevich and Stepan Sergeyevich nodded their heads.

"The old generations have to physically disappear. Right now, university faculty are either over fifty or under thirty. There is no middle, no one of the most productive age. And it is the same at all universities. In the nineties no one wanted to go work at the institutes and universities. Those who had gotten jobs there before the nineties stayed and the rest left. They had to feed their families somehow. You see, we travel a lot. We went to Ozerskiy Pedagogical University. That is the only pedagogical university in that region. There are no other places to stick their children. A mum won't let her daughter go to Lyutvino. It is so far away. The girl would have to stay at the dorm. Someone will ruin her life."

"And if it is a boy, they will teach him to drink vodka."

"And there is the army as well."

"So, they send their children to pedagogical universities. They think, 'Let them study. They can get a different degree afterward.' And pedagogical universities? They are monopolists. They will always get students. Why change anything?"

"Pedagogical universities in large cities? Same thing. They will always get students. Why change anything?"

"And they will never care about the contents. They have some pedagogy classes, but all of it is just a formality. I was a student at a pedagogical university. I heard about Comenius, but I never read his works. I only read about him, some quotes from his works. But I don't know what he actually wrote. So we get this situation when the best teachers are those who never went to a pedagogical university. My friend here is a great example of that." Anton Mikhailovich turned his head to Stepan Sergeyevich.

"Yeah, I graduated from an engineering school. Afterward, I worked as a schoolteacher for twenty-one years."

Anton Mikhailovich listened for a minute or two, then interrupted and changed the subject slightly.

"Young people now say life was better during the Soviet Union times. Joseph Brodsky called the Soviet Union 'anthropological genocide.' You know what that means?"

Of course I knew what it meant, but the ethnographer in me got the upper hand. I asked him to explain.

"Anthropos—a man, genocide—destruction. Joseph Brodsky was a poet. A Nobel laureate."

This felt quite humiliating. I wanted to kill the ethnographer in me.

Anton Mikhailovich continued, "The Soviet Union was a proletarian country. When people applied to higher education institutions, workers and farmers received preferential treatment. They were more readily accepted and enrolled. I am from the intelligentsia. My father was a professor. Grandfather—a professor. And what could I do? But farmers were admitted without exams when they applied to institutes. So, they came to the cities and went to pedagogical institutes. Then they graduated, stayed in the city, and there appeared a chasm."

Not sure whether I was supposed to know what this chasm was about, I made a puzzled expression.

"So, they got their higher education degree, then what? Return to the village? So, she can marry a tractor driver there, but all that she would get out of it is physiological pleasure. Stay in the city? She can't fit in. Roman Valeryevich knows. He is also from the intelligentsia. They come from a village but they have nothing to talk about. A horrible situation. But all the smart and intelligent ones got destroyed. Soviet times were horrible times. We were so poor. We had absolutely nothing. When I was a principal, I arranged for my teachers to buy food from the cafeteria. They were so happy because if they had to wait until the end of the working day to go shopping, stores would be empty. They would have nothing to feed their families. The first time I went abroad, to Paris, I went to a store and I could not believe my eyes. All of this abundance in front of me. One of my colleagues was with me. She just started crying. A grown woman had tears running down her face. But I digress. Yes, pedagogical education. It never fulfilled its function."

"It was just an institution for social mobility and not teacher preparation."

"No, they had teacher preparation. It just wasn't their top priority," Anton Mikhailovich corrected his colleague.

"It just was on the third or fourth place."

"That's how it turns out that pedagogical education is the boggiest of all bogs," Anton Mikhailovich added slowly, looking away.

"And nothing changes."

"And no one goes to work in schools."

We could have continued, but the announcement for our flight came. I boarded separately, took my seat in a different section of the plane, and spent most of the time writing about this trip. This conversation was an important window into reformers' worlds. During the two weeks that I had spent at LEU prior to this trip, I started noticing how reformers perceived themselves as game-changers but struggled to see the game go on unchanged as if they did nothing; how they viewed pedagogical universities as low-ranking institutions that saw change as unnecessary; how they evaluated the Soviet past as a negative time of destruction; how they looked to the West as the place of abundance and order; and how they thought of those who came from less privileged backgrounds as intruders into their space who should never have attempted to move up the social ladder. Desire for change seemed to be their driving passion. They poured their energy into it and hated to see that energy wasted.

This was not simply about money, although a lot of it was channeled through their consulting. It did not seem to be simply about power, although they certainly enjoyed a great deal of it working on different projects. It was about eliminating the remnants of the Soviet past to build a different future—a future that would make Russia look more like the countries in the West. And teacher education became viewed as a barrier to this change. Bringing it down to open the way for change became the foundation for the modernization drama that unfolded.

Modernization Drama

"Modernization and innovative development are the only way that will allow Russia to become a competitive society in the world of the twenty-first century, guaranteeing a decent life to all of our citizens. Under the conditions of solving these strategic tasks, initiative-taking, the ability to think creatively and to find nonstandard solutions, the skill of choosing a professional path and of learning through life become the most important qualities of a person. All of these abilities [and skills] begin to develop in childhood" (Government of the Russian Federation 2010).[1]

This opening paragraph of Our New School—a policy that initiated a new wave of education reforms in 2010—captures many of the strands that comprise the current stage of Russian modernization. Russia had a long history of top-down modernizations imposed by its various rulers (Remington 2008). The new turn toward modernization yet again tries to erase the past and compress the present, so that the country could leap into the future. It does so not only with a reflexive gaze toward the West, but also with an eye toward an imagined "world of the twenty-first century." In that imagined world, Russia has to stake out a new position: it should emerge not as a subordinate global player, but as a leader; its economy should move away from its dependence on oil toward national sources of income that would protect its sovereignty and autonomy in global markets.

Ironically, the country's competitiveness depends on the individual—specific personal qualities instilled in the nation's children can allegedly guarantee Russia an edge in global markets. With this individual turn, modernization becomes a project of sociocultural change urging people to shed old values of waiting for the "paternalistic state" to provide for them and to adopt new values of individual responsibility for their success in the market economy. Since this value change has to be developed "from childhood," school becomes the site of change. According to Strategy 2020—a set of policy proposals targeting multiple dimensions of Russian economic and social development issued in 2013—the school's mission has to change: instead of ensuring cultural and historic continuity in society, it is now expected to help the nation respond to "the challenges of globalization" (Strategy 2020 2013). Our New School similarly reframes the purpose of schooling from learning from the past to preparing for the future, from mastering content to receiving socialization, from providing academic preparation to schools as "centers of leisure." New school standards introduced in 2012 follow this line of thinking and focus on students' personal qualities more than their academic preparation.

For the school to fulfill this new mission, it needs teachers fit for the task, but it runs into a problem: "The existing model of producing an excessive number of new teachers in specialized higher education institutions . . . does not guarantee teachers' professional competence that meets modern demands" (312). Even though Strategy 2020, fiercely opposed by multiple civic and social groups, was never signed into law, other policy proposals moved its agendas forward. New teachers' professional standards were signed into law in 2013 to reframe teachers' work from knowledge transmission to regulation of students' behavior. But that was not enough because teacher education had to change as well. Attacks on pedagogical universities captured in the preceding quote became the starting point for the Concept of Support for the Development of Teacher Education, also known as the Concept of Teacher Education Modernization. Yet another policy that was never signed into law because of contestations it engendered, the Concept initiated reforms that radically transformed the ideology of teacher preparation in Russia, making it more practice focused, school based, and competency oriented. The modernization narrative in Russia and around the world suggests that teachers trained this way would be better equipped to produce individuals who can respond to modern challenges.

Those who become the target of these changes do not always appreciate the modernization narrative performed by reformers and experts in their network in Russia and with some variation around the globe (Aydarova 2015a, 2017a). The conflicts and contestations this narrative engenders turn the whole project into a struggle over social change, the nation's past, and its possible futures. The rest of this book will delve into more detail of what modernization entails, how it becomes translated into specific reforms with the help of global scripts, and how it is presented to the public in ways that obscure those global connections. In this chapter, however, I present the setting of these policy changes and introduce the main actors involved in the modernization of Russian education.

The Setting: LEU and Other Institutions

LEU's campus was dispersed across several different locations in Lyutvino—a hub of political and economic life in Russia. In the early nineties, Yegor Gaidar—a Russian statesman who introduced market reforms in Russia—issued a decree to create a state university that would prepare a new generation of economists, managers, and administrators. That is how LEU came to be. Since its inception, it occupied a contradictory position. It was closely linked with Russia's key powerful actors. At the time of my fieldwork, the rector's wife was an insider in Putin's team (Ledeneva 2013); yet LEU also engaged in critiquing government policies. It was outward-looking—many of the practices, structures, and mechanisms that constituted the core of the university were allegedly borrowed from the West. Those associated with LEU were often called "Westernizers"—*zapadniki*—because the policies they proposed had a distinct foreign flavor, which often triggered immediate opposition. Yet, many of those who were familiar with LEU's practices noted that "it [was] neither of Russia, nor of the West."

This contradictory position, nevertheless, afforded opportunities for those affiliated with LEU to have a profound impact on Russian policymaking across economic and social spheres.[2] This impact manifested itself when LEU experts participated in drafting state policies and programs, such as Strategy 2020. Even if the policies and programs they proposed were not signed into law, ideas encapsulated in them became commonsense when they were disseminated through conferences and seminars organized by LEU. During the seminars open to the public, LEU experts and their invited speakers shared research findings on such topics as Russia's results on PISA, Russian higher education in the context of global change, teacher education modernization, privatization of Russian kindergartens, systemic reform of educational systems, and many others. Through these seminars and its many publications, LEU disseminated knowledge that supported their reform proposals. LEU did not prepare teachers and offered only two or three small master's programs for practicing teachers.

As an institution closely identified with the notion of modernization because of its political clout, LEU was connected to other institutions in Lyutvino that pursued a similar set of agendas. One such institution was Lyutvino Social Sciences University (LSSU). Similar to LEU, it was created in the nineties but as a private university that focused on preparing new managers and administrators based on the British model of higher education. While LSSU was smaller in size than LEU, its graduates occupied strategic positions in the government and in other sectors of the economy. Its role in shaping modernization agendas similarly played out during annual conferences and seminars that brought together various actors in the policymaking world. Similar to LEU, LSSU did not prepare teachers.

Another such institution was Skolkovo—an innovation hub created by President Medvedev's decree in 2010. Even though reformers call it "an unprecedented progressive structure," Skolkovo's name was mired in several corruption scandals in 2013.[3] Skolkovo's primary focus was on the development of sciences and technologies that could provide Russia a competitive edge in the global economy—telecommunications, space exploration, biomedical technologies, energy efficiency, information technologies, as well as nuclear science. Skolkovo was lauded as an emblem of modernization in Russia for its focus on these areas. But there were other activities that reflected similar agendas. The Skolkovo Foundation, together with the Ministry of Education and the Microsoft Corporation, conducted a competition entitled The School of the Future, which prioritized the creation of a school that significantly individualized learning.[4] The Moscow School of Management at Skolkovo organized several programs that trained various leaders and administrators to function according to the new ideologies of "the modern world." One such program was New Leaders of Higher Education, informally known as the 100 Rectors program, that prepared "rectors of the future" able "to understand modern trends and rely on international experience,"[5] so that they could reform their universities to better serve the needs of businesses and corporations.

LEU was also connected to Lyutvino Special Education University (LSEU). Similar to LEU, it was created in the nineties as a public university that focused on providing research- and practice-based preparation in psychology. The university prided itself on continuing research in sociocultural psychology and activity-based learning developed by Vygotsky, Leontyev, and Davydov. LSEU's influence in shaping teacher education policies first became evident when teacher education standards revised in 2009 abandoned their subject area focus. This change went against the wishes of the teacher education community, many of whom ascribed it to the LSEU rector's growing influence in educational politics. LSEU's role in reshaping Russian teacher education has grown exponentially since then.

While there were other institutions that played an important role in setting the modernization agendas or in trading expertise with LEU, these institutions were key in shaping educational policies and teacher education reforms.

Main Policy Actors

No matter how significant an institution can be in setting agendas for modernization, individual actors play an important role in putting together performances of educational policymaking. Akin to a theater actor, a policy actor "selects from memory and personal experience what he or she has seen, heard, felt, and experienced over a lifetime" (Barranger 2006, 201). Actors who put together policymaking performances draw on their personal biographies and professional experiences to conceptualize change. They also rely on their networks to access the resources for mobilizing change. In this section, I provide biographical sketches[6] of those who actively participated in Russian teacher education reforms initiated by the Concept of Support for the Development of Teacher Education. Officially, the Concept was developed by a working group of over twenty members. Unofficially, a core group of reformers identified as "the authors of the Concept" created the Concept and oversaw its implementation. In my description of this group, I highlight some of their key affiliations and show how their relational ties evolved over time (fig. 3 on pages 48 and 49).

Anton Mikhailovich

Anton Mikhailovich shared that he went to a pedagogical university because he was refused entry to a prestigious physics university. This happened because his mother was Jewish and his relatives were living abroad. "No, of course, it was interesting to me. I wanted to try out what it was like being a teacher," he added (Interview 48a, February 2014). This was a personal experience with injustice in which a pedagogical university was used by the Soviet government to punish those it considered dangerous. I sometimes wondered if this experience affected his reform commitments. Anton Mikhailovich prided himself on having firsthand experiences with teaching, even though he worked as a teacher only for a year and spent most of his time in schools as an assistant principal or a principal. In 2001 he moved on to the Lyutvino Social Sciences University and in 2011, he joined LEU where he had been working since.

Over his long career in education, he traveled abroad—France, the United States, England, the Netherlands—where he participated in professional development courses or conducted projects in education. He personally knew Michael Barber. With pride, he shared with me a story about Barber giving the group he was working with the same advice as

Anton Mikhailovich. Together with Joseph Abramovich, Anton Mikhailovich chaired the group Our New School for Strategy 2020. When I asked him whether debates about reforming teacher education started in the 2000s, he corrected me, "Much earlier than that. I gave my first presentation about it during a national teachers' assembly in December of 1988" (Interview 48b, March 2014). In 1989, when he conducted his first research project on pedagogical education, he met Vadim Alekseyevich.

Vadim Alekseyevich

I started my interview with Vadim Alekseyevich with the same wrong assumption that reforms of pedagogical education started in the 2000s. Similarly to Anton Mikhailovich, he corrected me, "Actually, that is not the case. Several of my colleagues, including Joseph Abramovich, and I started working on pedagogical education reform when we met Georgiy Shchedrovitsky. That was 1985" (Interview 55, February 2014). Under the influence of Shchedrovitsky's seminars and games (more on that later in this chapter), Vadim Alekseyevich, who at that time was a dean of the Department of Psychology and Pedagogy at Fevral'sk State University,[7] designed a new model of teacher preparation. In this model, students from other universities or from other majors could transfer to his department after the first two years of their studies and become trained as teachers of math or physics. This was a revolutionary move because the rest of the Soviet system relied predominantly on linear trajectories—students graduated with the same specializations that they chose when they first applied. The department also implemented new approaches to teaching: seminars, workshops, and games. In an article that Vadim Alekseyevich shared with me, he described the department.

"What is different about that department during that era? We used organizational activity games. We got students after they studied math and physics for two years. How could we get across to them this idea that they entered a different reality? That this is a different type of a department? Not based on the idea 'you have no brains, go to a pedagogical [university].' So, we started organizing games that were supposed to help students problematize their assumptions about pedagogy. Students were supposed to understand that the Department of Psychology and Pedagogy is not a reduced version of a math department or physics department, but it is a different reality" (Interview 55, February 2014).

When the Soviet Union collapsed, Eduard Dneprov—a reform-minded minister of education—invited Vadim Alekseyevich to work at the ministry.

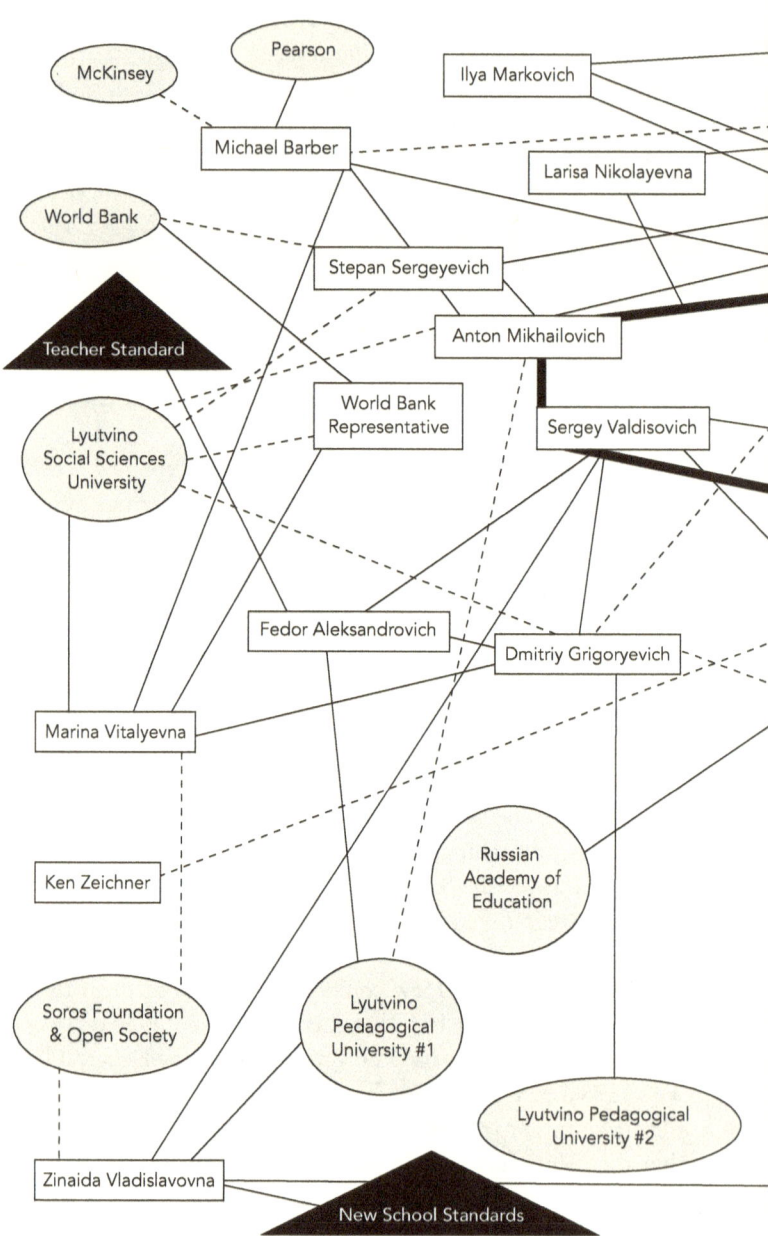

Figure 3. Reformers' networks.[8]

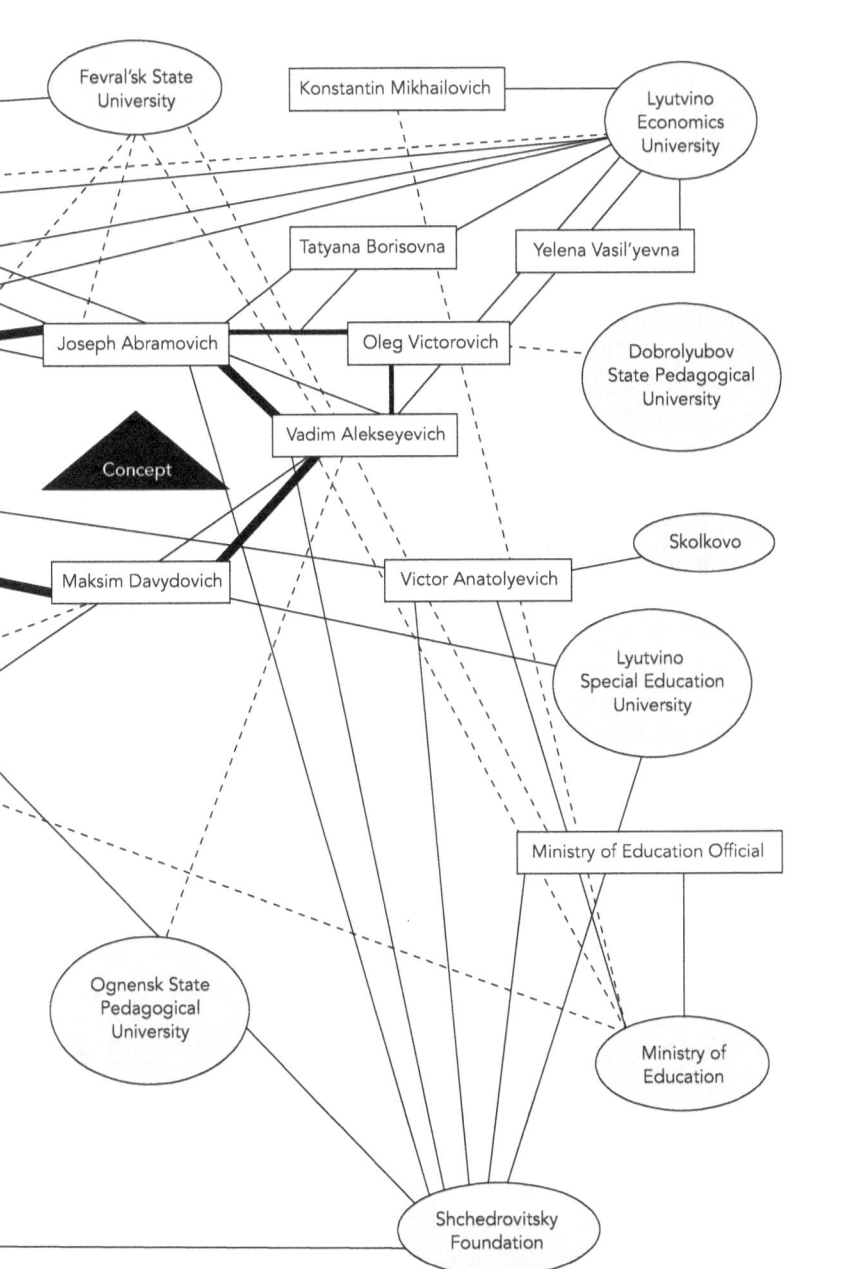

On joining, he realized that the "Fevral'sk model cannot be replicated in other contexts" (Interview 55, February 2014). Two reasons were key, according to him. The group who designed this new model of teacher education did not publish enough on the topic, leaving few records on how this approach can be replicated. To run this type of a program, it was also necessary to have methodologists trained in Shchedrovitsky's approaches. There were not enough of those people around to reform all of teacher education based on that model. Despite this observation, many of the elements of that model appeared in the Concept.

In the 1990s and 2000s, Vadim Alekseyevich facilitated the introduction of the Bologna Process in Russia. In 2000, he defended his doctoral dissertation on modernization of pedagogical education at Ognensk State Pedagogical University. Later, he became one of the working group members who put together the Program of Pedagogical Education Modernization in 2003. For the next several years, other projects "ate up all of his energy" as he worked at the Federal Service for Supervision in the Sphere of Science and Education on introducing the Unified State Exam.

In 2009, he joined LEU and became a member of the Russian Academy of Education. This prestigious association gave him a major advantage among the working group members. As Joseph Abramovich explained: "The Russian Academy of Education is the stronghold of conservative forces. Vadim Alekseyevich's presence there allowed them to think that they were also participating in this reform." His long-standing experiences in reforming teacher education are highly regarded by the expert community in Lyutvino. Together with Anton Mikhailovich and Joseph Abramovich, he was involved in developing blueprints for reforming Russian education for Strategy 2020.

Joseph Abramovich

When Vadim Alekseyevich created the Psychology-Pedagogy Department at Fevral'sk State University, Joseph Abramovich assisted him with the reforms. The department created a lab school and Joseph Abramovich became the principal of that school. At the same time that he taught at the school, he also taught at the Department of Psychology and Pedagogy at FSU. Even though not called such, lab schools appeared in the Concept despite the failure of their predecessor "base schools."

Similar to Vadim Alekseyevich, Joseph Abramovich acknowledged that Shchedrovitsky had a profound impact on his thinking. In 1999, he began working for the World Bank. When I asked him how working for the World Bank influenced him professionally, Joseph Abramovich explained that it allowed him to see that the narrow professional preparation that pedagogical universities provided was an "anachronism, an atavism" (Interview 47, February 2014). This statement reflected how he thought about teacher education. In a short exchange I had with him about the reform before I embarked on my research journey, Joseph Abramovich noted, "Anton Mikhailovich is trying to reform that which should have been destroyed a long time ago."

Joseph Abramovich joined LEU in 2009, where he soon became the head of the Education Department. Throughout most of his career, Joseph Abramovich advocated for allowing the market to increase the quality of education. After one of the LEU seminars devoted to the deregulation of kindergartens, Joseph Abramovich said to me with a smile, "See how much we are radical market advocates!" There was also a distinct way in which he regarded the West. During one of the LEU seminars, he noted, "I wonder how we could get the same educational achievements as they get in Europe but for a fraction of the cost." International experiences played an important role in how Joseph Abramovich approached problem-solving in Russian policymaking. He had been to the United States on an exchange program and regularly visited international conferences. He also knew Michael Barber for at least ten years prior to beginning work on the Concept. Together with Anton Mikhailovich, Joseph Abramovich chaired the group that developed education reform proposals for Strategy 2020. At the time of my fieldwork, Joseph Abramovich was spending a significant amount of time attending meetings at the Ministry of Education.

Maksim Davydovich

Unlike the other members of the core group, Maksim Davydovich was an administrator at Lyutvino Special Education University. In the nineties, he spent summers teaching classes in a teacher education program at one of the leading American universities where he first met Joseph Abramovich. He was well versed in Western scholarship on teacher education. In the nineties, he presented at the American Educational Research Association annual meeting. But then he got busy developing LSEU and most of his ties with the United States fell by the wayside. English words peppered his speech. Maksim Davydovich's name did not appear on the list of those who were associated with the Shchedrovitsky Foundation, but the university he worked for was an official partner of that organization.

Maksim Davydovich was an insider in the enterprise of preparing teachers. He was an ardent supporter of teacher professionalization and believed that teaching is one of the most important professions. Emphasizing the key role of education in building the future of societies, he noted, "Strugatsky's novel *Beetle in the Anthill* has a hierarchy of professions that I agree with. The job of a progressor who develops civilizations is primitive compared to the job of a pedagogue who develops a person" (Interview 78, December 2015).

His position inside the core group was probably more coincidental than anyone else's: the top administrator of his university—Alexander Dmitrievich—started out in the core group but got too busy with other projects. Maksim Davydovich took his place.

These four people—Anton Mikhailovich, Vadim Alekseyevich, Joseph Abramovich, and Maksim Davydovich—were most often referred to as "the active group," "the generators of ideas," or "the authors of the Concept" by those who belonged to the Lyutvino expert community. But there were others who appeared regularly in Concept discussions and presentations, the people I turn to next.

Sergey Valdisovich

Sergey Valdisovich volunteered for the Ministry of Education. He chose this route because to become a full-time ministry official would require him to give up his private business. He served as the ministry's coordinator of the working group that designed the Concept. Prior, Sergey Valdisovich had worked for private companies and various government agencies. He also chaired foundations that prepared new types of administrators and oversaw projects of training new leaders by Skolkovo and the Russian Academy of State Economy and Public Administration. "I have spent many years in education," he said defensively when I asked him about his professional path. "It was not in pedagogical education, but I understood its crucial role early on" (Interview 44, February 2014). Together with the other four members, he participated in weekly or biweekly meetings to discuss ideas, reform strategies, and reform plans. Sergey Valdisovich was actively involved in Shchedrovitsky's network and published a book on the use of organizational activity games. He described his experience with Shchedrovitsky's network as a transformative experience: "It is easy for me to state what game technology and methodology changed in my life—absolutely everything. I never went back to my prior specialization. My entire lifestyle changed dramatically. My sphere of interests, my way of reasoning, and my professional decisions—all of it carries an imprint [of these approaches] and that will last forever" (Interview 44, February 2014).

Oleg Victorovich

Oleg Victorovich graduated from a pedagogical university in Russia but then spent about twenty years working at several colleges of education in the West. He considered himself a part of the core group, but the other core group members saw him as an outsider who knew international practices well but did not know enough about Russia. They believed that it was important for me to talk to him but rarely mentioned him as influential in the decisions they made. The reason for that might be that he arrived to take a full-time job at LEU at about the same time that I came to do my fieldwork. Most of the work he did on the Concept was carried out long distance.

At the time of my fieldwork and beyond, Oleg Victorovich was developing a theory of deschooling society. His proposal was to pay children for the competencies they develop without requiring that they attend a formal institution of schooling. Even for LEU's faculty this theory appeared rather radical. When they raised questions and concerns after he presented his ideas at a seminar, he responded, "I am clearly more neoliberal than you all are."

Dmitriy Grigoryevich

Dmitriy Grigoryevich was a graduate of Fevral'sk State University. That is how he knew Vadim Alekseyevich and Joseph Abramovich. He spent many years in the Ministry of Education and was appointed rector of a pedagogical university in Lyutvino only in the summer of 2013, right before the Concept was first announced publicly. Dmitriy Grigoryevich received his master's degree from the Lyutvino Social Sciences University. Our New School, which he allegedly authored, bore the imprint of LSSU's influences as it argued for reforming teacher education based on the English model of multiple routes into the teaching profession. His proposal was to modernize teacher education by closing pedagogical universities or merging them with classical universities.

Fedor Aleksandrovich

Similar to Dmitriy Grigoryevich, Fedor Aleksandrovich was appointed rector of one of the Lyutvino pedagogical universities in the summer of

2013, right before the Concept was first announced publicly. Prior to that, Fedor Aleksandrovich was in charge of the institute that provided professional development for teachers. When I got a chance to interview him, we were interrupted by a phone call. After the phone call, he turned to me, "I intentionally wanted you to hear this conversation, so that you will know the challenges we are facing. Faculty members are calling to tell me that there are not enough chairs in the classrooms to allow all students to sit down. I am sharing this, so that you would understand the situation better" (Interview 54, February 2014). While this comment was intended to help me see the struggles of defunded pedagogical universities, I could not help but notice the twelve reclining leather chairs that flanked a large oak desk in his office. My eyes slid across the paintings on the walls and other expensive memorabilia proudly displayed on the shelves. Indeed, the funding challenges did not escape my attention.

Tatyana Borisovna

Tatyana Borisovna was a former school principal who worked at LEU at the time of my fieldwork. She came to Lyutvino from Fevral'sk. Tatyana Borisovna was the second working group secretary, responsible for collating different versions of the text, collecting various reports related to the Concept, and putting together the framework for the grant competition.

Larisa Nikolayevna

Larisa Nikolayevna was a former teacher educator who worked at LEU at the time of my fieldwork. She came to Lyutvino from a small city in the far east of Russia. Larisa Nikolayevna was the first working group secretary who was a part of the group since the beginning.

Stepan Sergeyevich

Stepan Sergeyevich started participating in this reform project in more of a support role, but gradually moved toward coordinating it on the LEU's side. He received his undergraduate degree from an engineering institute and worked at a factory until 1991. When the Soviet Union collapsed, he found a job as a teacher at a school and soon became principal. He received his master's from LSSU, worked there for several years, and then moved to LEU.

While most of the people described previously appeared on the official ministry list of the working group members, the new leaders of two key pedagogical universities—Dmitriy Grigoryevich and Fedor Aleksandrovich—did not. No one seemed to include them in the list of active creators of the Concept, except for themselves. Was it a coincidence that the ministry appointed new leaders for two key pedagogical universities several months before the Concept was presented to the public? Dmitriy Grigoryevich and Fedor Aleksandrovich did have a role to play and they did it faithfully. They were invited as discussants during public presentations of the Concept or as coparticipants in assistant ministers' interviews for newspapers or educational magazines. They were meant to represent pedagogical universities—the establishment that has been antagonistic toward modernization—but do so with enthusiastic support for the reform. A Russian journalist in a widely circulated 2011 article that critiqued Russian education reforms described this role as claqueurs in theater—those who are hired to demonstrate approval and applaud during a performance. Similar to others, they inserted English words here and there as they talked to me: "*full-time," "*part-time," "*subject matter preparation," "*tenure," "*cash."[9] During public meetings or group presentations, they congregated with the rest of the group with the mischievous look of coconspirators and accomplices.

There were many others who belonged to the reformers' network and whose names did or did not appear on the ministry's list of the working group that designed the Concept. Their ideas, however, were quite influential for the direction of the reform. One such person is Sir Michael Barber[10] and another is the late Georgiy Petrovich Shchedrovitsky.[11]

Michael Barber

Michael Barber worked as a teacher and briefly as a university professor before he joined Tony Blair's cabinet. There he was responsible for the implementation of policies in the social sphere, which included education. After overseeing several major reforms that targeted schools and the teaching profession in England, Barber joined McKinsey & Company—a global management consulting firm that offers services to businesses, governments, and nongovernmental organizations across a variety of sectors, including education. In 2007, Michael Barber coauthored a report that became very influential in educational policies around the world *How the World's*

Best-Performing School Systems Come Out on Top. He later became the chief education advisor to Pearson, which allowed him to be heavily involved in the world of global policymaking (Hogan, Sellar, and Lingard 2015). Since Barber was invited to Russia to teach several courses at a Russian university, he has maintained ties with his "Russian friends" by visiting the country to give talks, offer policy advice, or participate in their events. Several people in the reformers' network spoke about him as a personal connection whom they appreciated because of his charismatic personality.

Georgiy Petrovich Shchedrovitsky

Born at the end of the 1920s, Shchedrovitsky became a student at the Physics Department at Moscow State University after the war (Davydova 2005). He transferred to the Philosophy Department in his fourth year and started working as a school teacher teaching logic, psychology, and physics. During his time at the Philosophy Department, he became an ardent supporter of Vygotsky's work, which was banned in the USSR as subversive at that time (Shchedrovitsky 2001). It was also at this time that he developed friendships with Zinovyev, Mamardashvili, and Davydov. The first two became famous dissident philosophers during the sixties (Rus. *shestidesyatniki*); Davydov together with Elkonin later used Vygotsky's ideas as a foundation for the theory of developmental education (Rus. *razvivayushchee obuchenie*). This small group along with several others started the meetings of the Moscow Logic Circle, which after a split with Zinovyev became the Moscow Methodological Circle. The circle at first brought together "a small non-mainstream group of thinkers" (Tullar 1992, 17), many of whom later described their experiences as opportunities to enjoy intellectual freedom. In subsequent decades, the circle grew significantly and spread to other cities across Russia.

For several years, Shchedrovitsky was employed at the Academy of Pedagogical Sciences working on the *Soviet Dictionary of Pedagogy*; later he worked at a research institute dedicated to upbringing in preschools. He often switched jobs. In the sixties, Shchedrovitsky was expelled from the Communist Party. In the seventies, he ended up working at the Moscow Regional Institute of Physical Upbringing where he taught courses in pedagogy, methodology, and psychology. Transcripts of his lectures in pedagogy[12] reflect his critical appraisal of the Soviet pedagogy that "has not been fully developed as science" and outline ways in which pedagogy can be reframed for better use in developing society (more on that in chapter 4).

Shchedrovitsky's scholarly work—now accessible through the website of the Shchedrovitsky Foundation created in his honor—encompassed semiotics, hermeneutics, and psychology. One of his seminal pieces, "Technology of Thinking," was published in *Izvesitya*—one of the leading Soviet newspapers—in 1961. There, he argued that logic is necessary for "the technological modeling of thinking" (Shchedrovitsky 1961). Shchedrovitsky argued that a careful study of logic shows that school lessons in algebra and geometry, if reorganized and taught with different approaches, can be introduced as early as the first grade. In 1968, Shchedrovitsky's (1993) *Logic and Pedagogy*—a volume that explored some of these ideas further—was completed but not published because of his expulsion from the Communist Party.

Subsequently, Shchedrovitsky worked on developing a theory examining systems, thinking, and activity. It was based on one key principle: "Activity should not be regarded as an attribute of an individual but rather as an all-embracing system that 'captures' individuals and 'forces' them to behave in a certain way" (Grigorenko 2004, 201). In the seventies, Shchedrovitsky developed an approach called Organizational Activity Games (Rus. Organizatsionno-Deyatel'nostnye Igry). In the eighties, factories, plants, industries, and universities invited him to conduct the games to address issues that organizations were facing. Usually those were based on the topic at hand (such as "Higher Education" or "Architecture and Urban Development" [Tullar 1992]) and used to problematize existing approaches, reframe experience, and create alternatives through collective thinking. A colleague who had participated in those once or twice described his experience as being a part of a human computer. Through games like these, some of the reformers came in contact with Shchedrovitsky's ideas and joined his network in the eighties.

Before his death in 1994, Shchedrovitsky worked with several of his students in Tolyatti. Together they created a network of methodological laboratories for the design of modern education. Those who were involved in that work described the reasoning behind the network this way: "[We] discussed a new model of a human being: the model of free 'individual' [Rus. *individ-lichnost*] (that originated in the Renaissance era) must be replaced with an 'artificially technical' being or 'a thinking individual,' able to feel comfortable when surrounded by large 'organizational-technical systems' and global infrastructures. To grow such a new man, it was necessary to design new systems of preparation and education that would match the constantly changing situation of our life" (Zinchenko et al. 2003). According to the authors, Shchedrovitsky was involved in this project because he believed that this change was necessary "to restore Russia's greatness on the global stage." This project resulted in a major transformation of only two educational establishments: Tolyatti Academy of Management and Kiev Business College (LECOS). But when innovations in education evolved into an organized movement at the end of the eighties and the beginning of the nineties, Shchedrovitsky's son (who graduated from a pedagogical institute) became the president of the Association of Innovative Schools and Centers, which brought together many of the reformers. They "now occupy all the key positions [in education]" (Interview 50, February 2014).

Reformers' Networks

Reformers were positioned in an elaborate network of like-minded experts located in Lyutvino, across Russia, and across the world (fig. 3). The complexity and multiple dimensions of these relationships could be best understood through the lens of Wedel's (2011, 151) notion of flex nets—or a type of network that "draw[s] for membership on a limited circle of players who interact with each other in multiple roles, both inside and outside of government to achieve mutual and consistent goals over time." Reformers played different roles in government institutions, advisory boards, as well as international organizations' projects, which allowed them "to amass and coordinate both material and interpersonal resources" (Wedel 2009, 18) that facilitated policy mobility across global and national spaces (S. Ball 2016). It is through membership in these flex nets that these actors rose to power.

The emergence of reformers' networks was intricately connected with the international organizations' funding for different projects in Russian education. Zinaida Vladislavovna—a member of the Lyutvino expert community well connected to reformers—explained it the following way: "Soros started many things. The Open Society Institute. That's how we [the experts] met. We traveled to Europe together. Since 1988–1989, expert positions in the system of education began to develop. . . . In 1990–1991, grants appeared. The National Training Foundation [Rus. NFPK] appeared. Some of our people worked as experts for NFPK. I worked as an expert for the Soros Foundation in their educational program. There was a project of supporting innovative education in the regions [financed by the World Bank]. Dmitriy Grigoryevich was a part of that. . . . Through different programs in Russia that had some expert positions these people emerged. Now LEU gathered almost all of these people around them" (Interview 56, March 2014).

Similar to Zinaida Vladislavovna, other reformers and experts shared stories of receiving financial support from international organizations either in recognition of their accomplishments or with the goal of promoting specific reforms. For example, Anton Mikhailovich shared that he received "Soros' teacher" awards of $1,000 and $500 because a first-year student survey showed that he influenced a large number of students to enter university. Vadim Alekseyevich who worked for the Ministry of Education in the nineties, on the other hand, explained how he worked on MOE projects funded by the World Bank and the Soros Foundation to diversify the textbook market and to provide schools with access to the Internet.

Several of the reformers authored reports published in English by the World Bank; some of the reformers and experts in their networks wrote papers analyzing PISA data and evaluating Russian education based on the OECD's frameworks. This way they were not only the conduits of global neoliberal ideologies into the Russian space but also the voices of the "global-speak" (Steiner-Khamsi 2010) reaching out to international audiences. These multiplex entanglements made them part of international organizations' epistemic communities both as consumers and generators of knowledge aligned with global priorities (Lawn 2006; Sellar and Lingard 2013; Zapp 2017). In the context of the global rise of expertocracy supported by international organizations, these activities also made them the mediators through whom knowledge became policy (Grek 2013).

One of the distinguishing features of flex nets is actors' reliance on personal relationships that often go back twenty or thirty years (Wedel 2009). That is how many reformers explained how they became a part of the group working on the Concept. They shared a history of being affiliated with similar educational institutions or organizations, of working on educational innovation projects together, of collectively drafting various policy proposals, and of being singled out by international actors for training, grant support, or research. Of note here is the fact that most reformers were men, despite the fact that women constituted 82.2 percent of employees in the educational sector at large and 88.2 percent of school workers (*Indikatory Obrazovaniya* 2017). Even the distribution of roles in policy development captured gender inequality: men were the "authors of the Concept"; women, often despite their firsthand experience in teacher education, were only responsible for record-keeping or logistics. Gender homogeneity further strengthened personal relationship dimensions of reformers' work.

The links in the network varied in strength but were used to "coordinate power and influence from multiple vantage points" (Wedel 2009, 16), keeping the boundaries between different projects quite weak. For example, when I asked the leader of the working group on the teacher's professional standard for an interview, he responded, "I don't know if I can now. We are trying to get this pedagogical education reform pushed through." He was not officially affiliated with the teacher education modernization group but saw the ratification of that policy as a part of his personal mission. This incident also demonstrated ways in which members of reformers' flex nets shared conviction about the need for modernization, innovation, and competition as they worked together to achieve common objectives (Wedel 2009).

Flex net members are "frequent gatekeepers of inside access and 'knowledge' [which enables them] to brand information and control its applications" (Wedel 2009, 16). To support various projects under way, reformers and experts traded information, knowledge resources, and data to which only insiders were privy. When reformers needed statistical data on teacher oversupply, they turned to the member of their network who worked for a federal education monitoring agency. During my interview with that member, I asked whether educational data was available to the public and he responded, "Technically yes, but no one is going to give it to you. I had access to it because of my professional position and I was able to put these things together in a report. But no one is going to do anything like this for you" (Interview 52, February 2014). I was not an insider and therefore I did not receive any statistical data that I needed from him.

Finally, a distinguishing feature of flex nets is a theory their members share. Apart from subscribing to neoliberal ideologies of market and competition, many of the reformers followed Shchedrovitsky's teaching and were linked to the network of his followers, although there was a shroud of secrecy around those connections.[13] Shchedrovitsky's network was far-reaching and quite active: Skolkovo ran programs based on his teaching; Shchedrovitsky's disciples were advisors in several ministries, including the Ministry of Education; his followers did consulting for large state and private corporations. Shchedrovitsky's focus on engineering a social change aligned strongly with the reformers' sincere desire to change the world around them. This desire was overlaid with the reformers' neoliberal bent, which raised questions about the overall direction of educational reforms (chapter 4). In the next chapter, I will focus more closely on the interplay of ideas in the text of the teacher education modernization policy by analyzing which aspects of the proposal received overt attention and which ones were disguised in the public discussions of the policy.

2
Masks and Guises

When I first arrived in Lyutvino, Anton Mikhailovich told me that pedagogical education reform is connected to the project Institutional Transformations of Teacher Education. The next day, he told me about a couple of background reports that I should read. He was searching for documents on his computer and mumbled as he was typing the words for the search, "The Con-cept of Teach-er E-du-ca-tion Mo-der-ni-za-tion . . . OK. Here look. The Concept of Support for the Development of Teacher Education. Our project. There is a presentation and there is the Concept. But to tell you the truth we have already changed a lot in it. But it is not official yet. That is why . . . Everything that is official I give you . . . In other words, we don't know what it will come down to . . . [Rus. *Neizvestno chem eto vse konchitsya*]. Right now there is an ongoing struggle between researchers, politicians . . . You understand" (Field Notes, January 2014).

Either because of jetlag or because I was not sure which documents I needed, I did not fully comprehend what he was telling me. After that meeting, I kept searching for the Concept of Teacher Education Modernization because that was the document that Anton Mikhailovich presented in the fall and that seemed to be the policy that my participants in Ognensk talked about with concern. That seemed to be what I needed. But my attempts to find it online, however, were completely fruitless. The only thing that would come up in the search was the Program of Pedagogical Education Modernization from 2003.

When Tatyana Borisovna returned from an international conference, I got permission to sit at an unoccupied desk in her office. I asked her where I could find the document. Her response was simple, "It is on the

Ministry of Education's website. It should be quite easy to find." I continued searching in vain for another hour. Finally, I gave up and asked her if she could email it to me. When I got it, I realized my problem. I had been searching for the Concept of Teacher Education Modernization, but that was no longer the name of the policy. It was now called the Concept of Support for the Development of Teacher Education. That's what Anton Mikhailovich meant! I marveled at the transformations in the title of the policy. "Cheeky," I thought then. "If other people are like me and keep trying to find information on this policy based on the name it had in the fall, they won't have much luck."

But my struggles with the text did not end there. Even though I am literate in Russian and have read many Russian policy documents, I could not understand the nine pages of this policy no matter how hard I tried. I even asked Tatyana Borisovna for a print-out to see if I would do better if I had a hard copy. All I got out of this exercise was that the version she printed for me was a slightly different version from the one that was posted on the ministry website. Sadly, not much else. I reread the Concept before different interviews. During interviews I would ask what my participants would recommend I read—academic research, policy documents, legal statutes—and some would kindly say that I should read the text of the Concept. I would reassure them I was already doing that. Ironically, even those who belonged to the reformers' networks did not always seem to be well versed in the text either: some people celebrated measures that had by then been eliminated from the text or expressed regrets about elements missing from the text that were clearly still there.

But with each subsequent interview, with each new encounter, with each new turn in my research work, different parts of the text would come alive. Not because of how they were written, but because those who spoke them into existence connected for me the words on these pages with the worlds they hoped to see (Austin 1975). And that is how I began to understand what that policy might be about.

Looking back, I suspect that a part of the challenge was the structure of this text—it was unfamiliar and different from most policies I knew. Unlike other Russian educational modernization programs that tend to have a relatively linear structure, this text turned out to be more cyclical—with each subsequent part, one returned to the same proposed measures. The lack of movement forward stifled my progress through it because I kept getting lost in details and could not see that the details added through each cycle reinforced the set of solutions already offered.

I also wonder if it might have been the newness of the constructs that were setting the document into motion that hampered my understanding. There were no familiar references to the Bologna Process, or transnational policies, or international assessments. Instead, it was "universal bachelor's," "applied bachelor's," "practical training," "accompanying a young teacher," or "qualification tests." All those were new ideas that were expressed with familiar Russian words that had other meanings. This might have turned this text into an impenetrable forest of ideas with little tangible meaning attached to them.

But most importantly, through the interactions with the reformers around this text in different contexts, I came to realize that a much bigger reason for my apparent lack of ability to understand this policy was its masks. How the text was presented front-stage[1] to the public in its representation on the ministry's website (appendix A) was different from how it was presented backstage when only those close to the reformers' networks were present. The text communicated one message but left room for alternative readings—readings that, if made legally binding, could create the foundation for far-reaching change. In this chapter, I present an analysis that examines the policy's masks to show that what the text says does not match some of its underlying claims or intentions.[2] It is in the gap between what is stated publicly and what is known privately that the unsuspecting reader is caught.

The Mask of the Name

The first most visible mask of this text is the mask of the name. Both across time and across various contexts the policy appeared under different names, with each name suggesting something new about it. During the first stage of the group's work in the spring of 2013, the policy was discussed under the title Institutional Transformations in Teacher Education, which primarily targeted pedagogical universities as the objects of reform. In the documents from the fall of 2013, the Concept was referred to as the Concept of Teacher Education Modernization. During that discussion and afterward, reformers made a clear point that this policy was about improving pedagogical education across different institutions that offered this specialization and not just pedagogical universities. When the policy was released for public discussion, the text displayed on the ministry's website carried a different title—The Concept of Support for the Development of Teacher Education. That became the official name of the policy. The website devoted to the implementation of this policy, however, was called the Project of Teacher Education Modernization, which was also how reformers and experts referred to this policy. The focus on modernization, even though it disappeared from the official name of the policy, captured the continuity between the current waves of teacher education reforms, their earlier iterations, and other initiatives aimed at transforming Russian education (more on that in chapters 3 and 4).

Multiple names used for the policy during the period of its inception, public discussions, and implementation raise questions about how the title for the policy was chosen to elicit a particular response from the audience. Joseph Abramovich explained how the audience's perceptions of the title were important for the reformers: "In our first draft, the concept was called something like the Concept of a Radical Reform. And when the minister saw this, he said, 'Guys, do you want to get executed[3] [Rus. *zastrelili*] before they even read this text?' And we called it the Concept of Support for the Development of Teacher Education, so it is not reform, it is *support. And that is very important. Second, we emphasized that we don't want to close pedagogical universities or merge them with classical universities. We want to help them develop themselves" (Interview 47, February 2014).

Even though Joseph Abramovich described how calculated the move toward the policy's official name was, media articles about the Concept called it "a radical reform of pedagogical education." These discrepancies in the policy's titles are important to consider in light of what those titles conveyed to the audience and what they made invisible.

Modernization

Throughout the 2000s, multiple policies throughout Russia's economic and social spheres came under the banner of "modernization." The ubiquitous presence of this word not accompanied by any palpable change received much attention in the media. The famous Russian comedian Mikhail Zadornov devoted several of his performances to rants against modernization, coining a motto: "They modernized us, modernized us, but have not modernized us out." I encountered similar sentiments toward this word at teacher education institutions. During a focus group with second-year students from Ognensk State Pedagogical University, I asked them what they thought about educational modernization reforms. One of the girls looked at me and said, "People are afraid of this word now. They keep modernizing everything and it all just keeps getting worse" (Focus Group 2, November 2013).

But fear was not the only reaction I encountered. Some people became quite angry when I asked them about modernization. "They have made me sick with their modernization!" an elderly student affairs dean puffed at me during our interview. "They should just leave us alone and let us work! No, they have to get to us and try to modernize us!" (Interview 13, November 2013). This anger appeared reasonable when the ministry tried to modernize pedagogical universities by closing them down. There were also some who claimed that no matter what those in power did with their modernizations, faculty would just continue teaching and doing research the way they always did. This attitude reflected a distancing move that delineated the areas of personal influence that were protected from "modernization" to preserve the practices that have been developed over time. Neither fear, nor anger, nor distance bode well for effective transformations. It is likely that either reformers or ministry officials wanted to avoid evoking those sentiments when they presented the policy for public discussion.

The Promise of Support

If we return to the text of the Concept and examine the changed title from the position of these responses, then a different picture emerges. Let's pause for a second and imagine how someone expressing the aforementioned positions might read the title Concept of Support for the Development of Teacher Education. "Modernization" does not appear in the title. But the word "support" does. In Russian, "support" (Rus. *podderzhka*) conveys the notion of catching something and not letting it fall; providing help and assistance; expressing agreement, approval, and defense of someone; not letting something die, stop, or end (Ozhegov 2014). There is a promise in that word. That promise is further extended in the emphasis on "development." "Development" assumes that the existing organism or institutional structure will be given room to grow, become better or stronger, and have a future. "Support for development" promises preservation with some modifications.

But when one works through the text—that describes teacher education as delivered by ineffective institutions that admit "not the best students," use "outdated materials," lack quality assurance mechanisms, and fail to cultivate connections between schools and universities—one realizes that there are no warrants for the preservation of pedagogical education as it currently stands. The dismal state of affairs portrayed leaves no room for support or development; it paves the way for the elimination of the existing system to build something completely different (more on that in chapter 4).

Role of the Policy: Scale and Use of State Resources

The official title of the policy obscured the fact that one of this policy's purposes was to change "the scale of teacher preparation." Even though the text did not overtly state that fewer people should be allowed to become teachers, in interviews reformers identified large numbers of teacher education students as one of the problems in Russian pedagogical education. They claimed teacher preparation's "mass" scale undermined its quality.

The comparison between LEU's draft of the policy and the version displayed by the Ministry of Education sheds light on how the problem of scale was constructed. In describing the conditions of pedagogical education in Russia, LEU first provided the information about "ineffective" universities and then statistics about the number of students who enter and graduate from these universities. The ministry's text flipped this order: first the number of students, then the high number of "ineffective" institutions. LEU listed the total number of students in pedagogical education as well as the numbers for those who received state subsidy, whereas the ministry only provided statistics for students who entered pedagogical universities with state subsidies. The flipped order and the focus on state subsidies, following the paragraph on the closure of pedagogical universities, created a strong sense of a crisis and wasted resources. In fact, this is how the ministry and the reformers constructed the problem behind the scenes.

For example, Oleg Victorovich, drawing on his experiences abroad and on the analysis of international experiences in teacher education reform, described the role of the policy in the following way: "We had to understand which ideas would work in Russia and which ones would not because Russia has a unique mechanism of financing higher education. In Russia, you either get everything or nothing. You either get a one hundred percent discount as a student when you get a budget spot or you get nothing at all. This skews the process. And then in Russia there is no direct connection between which university you graduated from and what job you are going to get. Meaning, people go to universities to get some kind of higher education. There are many pedagogical universities and they have many budget spots. So, naturally, people apply to these universities even if they don't want to be teachers, these universities are easier to enter, admission scores are lower. Naturally, that plugs up the system [Rus. *zasoryayet sistemu*; lit., "fills the system with trash"]. Students who never wanted to be teachers enter these universities and then their job placement statistics are very sad. I don't remember exactly, maybe ten percent, less than twenty percent. And because the government pays for it, then as the minister's assistant said, the federal government spends forty billion on pedagogical education and only rare graduates go to work in schools. More than a billion dollars is spent on pedagogical education, actually. But there is no return. So, it looks stupid [Rus. *nelepo*]. The state spends money, but the return is minimal. Here I see a fiscal reason [for the reform]. And they say that the numbers should be reduced because more teachers graduate than there is need for in the regions. In most regions. So they could reduce the target admission numbers, right? But when I participated in these conversations, I told them, 'You see, you have a leaky bucket here. You cannot keep up the level of water in it, if you stop adding water to it'" (Interview 43, January 2014).

Oleg Victorovich's explanation laid out the role of the reform: to reduce the state's expenditures on pedagogical education by reducing its scale. If the number of "budget" students—or students who received higher education with the help of state subsidies—was reduced, the state might save money. But then pedagogical universities would lose a major source of their funding and would not be able to survive. This is important for considering the incongruence between the title and the role of the policy: "support" in the title could create drastic funding cuts in reality. In fact, a year after the policy was discussed I received an email from one of the teacher education faculty describing the critical condition that the university was in because of the precipitous fall in federal funding. The benevolent mask of "support for development" disguised the state's move to defund teacher education institutions.

To justify defunding, Anton Mikhailovich often made an argument that decreasing the number of students would improve their quality. Tatyana Borisovna, in support of this position, argued that this way "only the best will become teachers." This position emerged in the policy as several obscure statements about more stringent requirements for pedagogical education than for other majors. Maksim Davydovich, as the only administrator of a teacher education university in the core group, saw a major contradiction in this position: "Personally, I am not fully convinced that this can be an effective mechanism of improving the quality of students. . . . The ministry thinks that because such a small number goes to work in schools and the scale of teacher preparation is such that it is possible to painlessly reduce [the numbers]. They think that if they reduce the number of students, then applicants with higher scores will apply. But in reality, we tried to calculate whether that might be the case. If we had fifty spots and one hundred people applied, and we create an exam score benchmark, would that change if we turn those fifty spots into twenty-five? Will we get students with a much higher score on the Unified State Exam? To tell you the truth, it did not work out that way for us. In other words, in a concrete case of a concrete program in a concrete university, it did not work. Reducing the number of students did not allow us to drastically improve the quality of students" (Interview 49, February 2014).

Maksim Davydovich's concern that decreasing numbers of students did not necessarily lead to the increased quality of applicants revealed one of the contradictions in the policy covered up by the mask of the name. The mechanism proposed by the policy had not been tested before and there was no evidence that it was likely to produce desired outcomes. But most reformers disguised the untested theories behind this proposal by the simple logic that fewer available spots for teacher education students would increase the prestige of pedagogical education and attract "the best" students.

The Mask of Intentions

The mask of the name was connected to the mask of intentions. This mask worked on a particular optical illusion—a tromp l'oeil—when the stated goals did not match the intended outcome. The way goals were presented in the text, however, tricked the audience into imagining the measures they hoped to see rather than the measures the text intended to introduce.

On the third page of the Concept, set in bold and positioned almost in the middle of the page was the following statement:

> **The main goal of the program lies in <u>increasing the quality of preparation of the teaching force</u>, aligning the system of pedagogical education with the teachers' professional standards and federal standards of general education, as well as overcoming the "double negative selection."** (Concept of Support for the Development of Teacher Education 2014)

The textual presentation of the goal—bold, with one key phrase underlined, almost in the middle of the page, and with an entire paragraph set aside just for this one sentence—attracted the reader's attention to the message that was hard to argue against. Who would not want to improve the quality of the teaching force, whatever that might mean? It is difficult to imagine anyone who might oppose such a goal. If one wants a car of higher quality, a house of higher quality, clothes of higher quality, a vacation of higher quality, how could one not want a teaching force of a higher quality?[4] The same applied for aligning pedagogical education with the teachers' and schools' standards. Those were legally binding documents, not necessarily for pedagogical education itself but for the teachers that pedagogical education prepares. Why would anyone argue against that which was already signed into law? It was not reasonable to do so. The only part that might raise an eyebrow was the concluding phrase—"overcoming the 'double negative selection.'" This was a construction that was continually contested, particularly by those who occupied spaces associated with teacher education (more on that in chapter 4). But tucked away, at the end of the sentence, with so many other things that one should not argue against, it presented a lesser threat than if it appeared earlier.

What followed this goal were the "tasks" for this program: "improving the quality of students," "changing the contents and technologies of teacher education programs," "increasing the effectiveness of the existing programs," as well as "creating and testing of an independent system of professional teacher certification." All these tasks appeared as a bulleted list, the phrases themselves appeared in bold, and were followed by an explanation and an elaboration of what these tasks might entail.

The most important thing about this list was the statement that appeared right after it: "In the process of Concept implementation a new system of pedagogical education must be created." Not set in bold. Not underlined. Not framed as an independent paragraph but rather as a statement that introduces the new principles for the new system. Located in the middle of the page, but buried in the middle of the text. This statement was followed by a list of ten elements that the new system would be based on (see Appendix A, page 237). The next section of the text proposed to use seventeen to twenty-five institutions as platforms for the pilot project of the Concept implementation, but there were officially only forty-four pedagogical universities left in the country. That meant that about half of the institutions were expected to participate in the pilot. By 2017, the entire system of Russian teacher education was expected to transition "to the new models." When combined with other statements regarding the introduction of "new ideology and technology" as well as the spread of the new model throughout the entire system of teacher preparation, the gap between the policy's directly stated goal of quality improvement and the policy's intentions of creating a completely new system widened.

This outcome of the Concept implementation did not seem to match either the stated goal that so cleverly caught the reader's attention or the title of the Concept that promised support for development. But this statement did match the contents of the text that focused on the destruction of the old and the creation of the new system of professional preparation. The measures of improving the quality of the teaching force demonstrated this point as they reflected new ideologies and new mechanisms of transforming the teaching profession.

New Ideologies for Improving the Quality of the Teaching Force

In light of the text's promise to improve the quality of the teaching force, it is important to explore how it intended to accomplish it. Several elements appeared throughout the text, reformers' presentations, and their publications: reducing the scale of pedagogical education (as stated), increasing the amount of practical preparation, as well as opening entry into teaching for those without pedagogical education. In what follows, I explore how the mask of intentions covered contradictions in these proposals and how the reformers navigated the spaces of these contradictions.

Increasing Practical Preparation

Apart from promising to improve quality by reducing the number of students, the policy also reoriented teacher education toward more practical preparation. This new practical focus was reflected in proposals to decrease the number of theoretical courses, introduce "a branched-out system" of practical experiences, move a significant proportion of teacher preparation to schools, and make an "applied bachelor's degree the main model of teacher preparation." The word "practice" and its derivatives appeared in the text sixteen times, often in sections on solutions.

It is important to consider how the interplay between theory as problematic and practice as promising affects the construction of teaching. All reformers agreed that theoretical courses were problematic and that the only way to improve teacher education was through increased practice. For example, speaking of pedagogy textbooks, Vadim Alekseyevich described their main message as: " 'It is necessary to teach a teacher to give his heart away to children.' But what the point of giving away this heart is and what they are going to do with it—all of this is not clear" (Interview 55, February 2014). Theoretical courses allegedly had nothing to offer their students and were perceived as problems that impeded quality. Practical school-based teacher education was supposedly able to fix these problems but required a major change in philosophical and methodological understandings of how teachers were prepared. This is how Maksim Davydovich explained the need for this change: "It is necessary to reconsider how practical preparation is provided. This requires changes in methodology and philosophy of teacher education because according to the current philosophy everything necessary for the future professional preparation is created in the university classroom during the interaction between the university professor and student. We believe, I believe and I think my colleagues agree, that this is completely wrong. We are not proposing anything new because Ken Zeichner's and Darling-Hammond's works are all about the same thing that in actuality the pedagogue's profession is *tacit knowledge. It is a profession connected to the knowledge in hands, it is a *craft. It is mastery rather than science-based professional activity. That is why the sources of this knowledge, or at least examples of this professional activity, are not in the university classroom but in schools where the children and teachers who have these competencies are. That is why school becomes the center of preparation—a model school, a base school, et cetera. And here we are not speaking about twenty weeks of practice instead of ten, but rather about what becomes the center, the source of knowledge and necessary competencies. And school becomes this center" (Interview 49, February 2014).

As the quote indicates, the call to increase the practical component in teacher education was not new. In the United States, the work of the Holmes Group (1986, 1990, 1995) as well as the ensuing pursuit of increased professionalization represented by Darling-Hammond's work did indeed emphasize the need to strengthen the relationships between university-based teacher education and schools. But there was one fundamental difference between the proposals of American scholars and Russian reformers—how the construction of teachers' knowledge was used to construct the teaching profession. "Teachers' knowledge lives in their hands . . . It is more like a *craft," said Maksim Davydovich as he tapped his fingers one against the other. This construction moved away from the Soviet legacy of viewing pedagogy as the scientific foundation for teaching and teaching itself as scientifically based. It also moved away from appreciating teaching as an art form (Alexander 2000). But more importantly, this construction presented teachers as "craftsmen" rather than professionals. As Anton Mikhailovich proudly stated during the group interview, "Teachers are not professionals; they are practitioners." When practice was positioned *in opposition to* a profession, rather than as its constitutive part, major questions about the policy's intentions to improve the quality of teaching emerged.

This construction of teaching as the work of practitioners rather than professionals emerges most clearly in the policy proposal to introduce an "applied bachelor's" degree as "the main model of teacher preparation." On the one hand, the "applied" aspect of these degrees captured the commitment to practical orientation of teaching. Thus, reformers argued that all teacher education graduates should receive "applied bachelor's degrees." But backstage reformers also shared observations that clearly underscored how much this degree would reduce the status of teachers and the teaching profession. When I asked Joseph Abramovich about these degrees, he explained, "This is *a second-rate* higher education degree. Everyone wants higher education, but not everyone should get it. So they will get an applied bachelor's degree instead" (Interview 47, February 2014).

Anton Mikhailovich shared with me how teacher education institutions came to be viewed as second rate throughout the twentieth century: "You see, they are second rate in their heads. There might be some strong specialists, but for everyone who works there or studies there, pedagogical universities are second rate. *Ped-ulishche* [*he pauses*]. I am serious. I mean—pedagogical college [Rus. **Ped**agogicheskoe u*chilishche*]. That is how you get *ped-ulishche*. In Russian education, there used to be teachers institutes, right? They were second-rate institutions that were not quite higher education. Something like an applied bachelor's."

As usual, Anton Mikhailovich was inserting his caustic jokes about teacher education. This time it was a portmanteau word *ped-ulishche*, coined out of the term "pedagogical college." When Anton Mikhailovich said it, he paused for effect—*ped-ulishche* sounded like "pedagogical backside," which metaphorically connected teacher preparation institutions with the lower part of the human body. It was in the context of this metaphor and in the explanation of teachers institutes as "second-rate institutions, not quite higher education" that the reference to an applied bachelor's emerged. In this context, the mask of intentions was covering a contradiction between quality improvement, practical focus of preparation, and the decrease in teachers' status that some of the reformers were pursuing. This contradiction was particularly palpable when compared with the intentions of attracting "the best" into teaching. How is it possible to attract the "most talented" or "most motivated" into teacher education when degrees associated with professional preparation for teaching were consistently referred to as "not real higher education" or "second-rate degrees"? One way to do that was to bypass teacher education altogether by attracting into teaching those who were trained for other professions. This area will be examined next.

Opening Entry into the Profession

The policy proposed to improve students' quality by "creating conditions for free 'entry' into the programs of pedagogical education" and into teaching for professionals in other areas. Of the ten elements that the new programs should be based on, three addressed those who did not have pedagogical education. Tatyana Borisovna explained this measure in the following way: "The first task is to expand points of entrance and exit. Our government has made an effort to make teachers' salary more competitive. It has reached the average for regional economies. In connection with that, teachers' work is becoming more attractive. Schools have a deficit of IT teachers. So, they try to get engineers who have IT education. But to move up the career ladder, these people need to have pedagogical education. They have to enter courses of professional retraining. That's a serious program. Five hundred hours and it lasts more than two and a half years. An engineer is not very inclined to do that because he already knows his subject and he does not want to study for two more years. So, the working group members proposed that there should be short courses of preparation and then there should be certification of graduates of these courses the way it is done in the Western countries. So, there should be certification for entering the profession. This way we get multiple channels of entry into the profession. Fast-track preparation, then certification. This way we can expand the means of getting into the profession" (Interview 41a, January 2014).

Yet when I asked her if there were significant numbers of those who wanted to work in schools, she admitted that the reformers had no such data. It was not simply the absence of data but a lack of likelihood that there were many of those who wanted to work in schools that raised questions about this proposal. According to Tatyana Borisovna herself, this was an area in which reformers received major push-back at the Ministry of Education. But they still hoped that if this measure was created, more people would be interested in becoming teachers.

It is not only the overt commitment to allowing other professionals to become teachers that is worth considering. Throughout the text and reformers' other public engagements emerged an implicit unfavorable comparison between those who held other jobs and those who chose teaching when they entered higher education institutions. This implicit comparison was most clear, for example, in an article about the Concept based on the interview with the core group. In the following quote, the journalist used "an almost fictional" example of himself to explain how the Concept would work for those without pedagogical education who wanted to work in schools: "An almost fictional Grisha works as a journalist. . . . He reaches the stage of the middle-age crisis and wants to sow the seeds of intelligence, kindness, and something else.[5] He is drawn to school. The knowledge and experience he has are enough to teach, for example, social studies. In some sense, *he is better than a typical teacher*—he has seen a lot, he has interacted with a lot of people. During his presidency, Dmitriy Medvedev from time to time put out calls to 'attract people from other professions to schools,' but to tell you the truth these calls did not turn into anything concrete" (RR 2014, emphasis added).

Note how Grisha was described as "better than a typical teacher" because "he has seen a lot, he has interacted with a lot of people." The reformers' explanation of why other professionals should be allowed to become teachers and how the Concept would facilitate it made its way into this article. The only person who did not support this position was Maksim Davydovich, who believed that those who entered universities to become teachers should not be penalized for their choices.

In the preceding quote, the journalist referred to President Medvedev's calls "to attract more people from other professions into schools." This is a reference to Our New School—the policy that first introduced this new ideology into the Russian context: "It is a separate task to attract to school those who do not have pedagogical education. After receiving psychology and pedagogy training and having learned new educational technologies, they will be able to demonstrate to the children—first of all to the high school students who choose a specific specialization—*their rich professional experiences*" (Our New School 2010, emphasis added).

Both the Concept and Our New School implicitly positioned those who were trained as teachers as inferior to those who were trained for other professions. Our New School suggests that those who did not have pedagogical education had "rich professional experiences," as if those who were trained as teachers did not have them. Those without pedagogical education were believed to have more to offer to their students. This unequal positioning raised important questions about improving the quality of the teaching force that the Concept would facilitate. It revealed that hidden under the mask of intentions was an agenda that deprofessionalized teaching by valorizing personal and professional experiences of those who were not associated with the field of education. This approach placed more value on forms of knowledge different from the knowledge accumulated by the teaching profession and teacher education institutions.

This devaluing of professional knowledge in pedagogical education was common among reformers and experts in their networks. For example, during LEU's conference for master's students, Anton Mikhailovich referred to a doctor of methodological sciences as a "methodological tractor-woman." When the professional development seminars for the Concept implementation began at LEU, one of LEU's experts told a room full of teacher educators, "No offense, but I don't think that pedagogy is a science. I have a degree in psychology. That is science. Pedagogy is snot covered in sugar." Finally, during an interview Yelena Vasil'yevna—LEU's expert in the reformers' network not actively involved in the creation of the Concept—described faculty at pedagogical universities: "They are nobodies but they so arrogantly think that they are the best" (Interview 50, February 2014). Given this general sentiment toward pedagogical universities at LEU, it becomes clear why reformers perceived those without pedagogical education as better candidates for teaching. In the words of Yelena Vasil'yevna, uttered in praise of a presenter during the master's students' conference, they were "not contaminated by any of this pedagogical nonsense" (Field Notes, February 2014).

This contempt for pedagogy and knowledge production in education made its way into the World Bank reports that reformers coauthored with other experts. For example, a 2004 World Bank report on Russian research in educational sciences was described this way: "Most [educational] studies do not meet modern requirements. They lean toward 'conversations' about politics in education, and not toward action and its practical implementation, are rarely built on reliable empirical data, and have limited application for solving new problems in Russian education" (Canning et al. 2004, 13).

Decreased Authority of Pedagogical Universities

Improving the quality of teacher education, according to the policy, requires a major change in the contents, methods, and technologies used in pedagogical universities. Because reformers saw those universities as a monopoly, they believed that it was necessary to break that monopoly apart to introduce change. In a report describing international experiences prepared by the LEU team for the ministry, the following statement reflected this sentiment: "In

Russia a radical reform of teacher preparation has not yet started. Being isolated not only from the school but also from the system of higher pedagogical education, it is not expecting and cannot expect reforms, because the upcoming changes *cannot but take away autonomy* [or independence, Rus. *samostoyatel'tnost'*] from the system of pedagogical education" (International Report 2014, 21, emphasis added).

During my interviews, I learned that the group wanted to use the Concept to allow any organization to conduct teacher preparation. Oleg Victorovich cautioned against it by saying that without a system of quality control, any "vagabond will be churning out teacher graduates." While LEU's goal of allowing anybody to train teachers may have been stalled to a degree, it generated interest among actors typically perceived as disinterested outsiders in the field of teacher education. At the time when I first started fieldwork in Lyutvino and the Concept just appeared on the ministry's website, one of the experts told me that Russia's largest educational publishing house, Prosveshchenie,[6] showed keen interest in the Concept. Surprised, I asked why they should even care. "There is a lot of money that they can get their hands on, if they get involved," was the response I was given. My growing interest in the matter ended the conversation.[7] But the fact that experts working for Prosveshchenie were closely monitoring the reform suggests that the private sector received clear signals about the policy's intention to reduce pedagogical universities' authority over teacher preparation and hoped to grab its share of the market at the opportune moment. Under the guise of improving the quality of the teaching force, the policy attempted to create conditions for deregulating teacher preparation. The mask of intentions left this area of the policy invisible to most people outside reformers' networks.

Mask of Origins: New Words, New Worlds

One way in which the text constructed a new reality and created a new system, rather than supporting the old one, was through the introduction of ten new principles. Using the mask of origins, the text presented these new principles with the help of Russian words in ways that disguised the foreign origins of the ideas presented in the Concept or created a distance between the new measures and the practices already in use in the Russian context.

The case of liberal arts degrees demonstrated how reformers used the mask of origins. Because the notion of liberal arts lacked a Russian counterpart, reformers were attacked for trying to turn teachers into "free artists."

To address that notion, reformers coined "universal" and "broad bachelor's" as an "analogue of the *Liberal Arts Bachelor's" (Concept 2014, 4). Fedor Aleksandrovich, who favored the liberal arts model, later explained that "if the term 'universal bachelor's' gets accepted, we would have to take the words 'liberal arts' out and only use them as a reference to a precedent that exists in the world simply because the ideology now is such that it is impossible to use foreign words to name mass movements" (Field Notes, June 2014).

To describe other principles, reformers used familiar Russian words to denote new practices that also came from foreign sources—their counterparts in Russian practices were either named differently (and thus carried different connotations) or had no analogous constructions (table 1). For example, "partner schools" has a historical Russian antecedent—"base schools," or training schools for teacher education students during the Soviet era. Their use diminished because of the differences in financing and accountability that were applied to institutes of higher education and schools (discussed in more detail in part 1). The use of "partner" in this phrase connected this text to the National Council for Accreditation of Teacher Education (2010) report on clinical practice that prioritizes teacher learning through "partnerships with school districts." The applied bachelor's reflected practical focus and drew on the European model of applied degrees that resemble higher education diplomas but are intended for those who work in applied fields. Applied bachelor's degrees, similar to "universal" or "broad" bachelor's degrees, had no Russian counterparts—there was no concept or practice to connect them to in order to make sense of this proposal.

Students' internship, on the other hand, was presented in the text with the common Russian word *stazhirovka* that was often used to describe practical training for representatives of different professions, but not teachers.[8] For example, my presence in all three institutions where I conducted my research was framed through this term, as I was believed to be receiving practical training on how to be a university professor or a researcher. My mother—a railroad engineer—was sent on *stazhirovka* trips every five years. Practical training in teacher preparation, on the other hand, had been traditionally referred to as *praktika*—or practicum—that always occurred before one completed the initial degree. Proposals to add practical training after the initial degree were usually promoted with the calque of the English word internship—*internatura*. Even though reformers and experts used this word in their conversations and explanations, including this word in the policy could give away the process of borrowing involved in introducing this approach into Russian pedagogical universities. Thus, the Russian word was used instead, even though its use was more problematic from the perspective of its semantic appropriateness.

Even more baffling was the phrase "accompanying the beginning teacher" that was listed as the eighth element of the new system. Was it about going with them somewhere? The calque of the English word "mentoring"—*mentorstvo*—immediately evoked the necessary meanings and connotations, but putting an English word in the text would connect it with practices used internationally. This could potentially put the text in jeopardy if the audience was less inclined to accept international approaches as better than national practices. The Russian counterpart for this practice—*nastavnichestvo*[9]—would have gotten to the notion of mentoring more easily, but because it had a more traditional and outdated feel to it, it did not match the policy's intention of creating new models and new forms.

In another case, a Russian phrase—"qualification exam"—emerged as a problematic area for a completely different reason. The notion of "qualification exam" already existed in Russian education. In 2010, a new system was instituted for teachers moving up in the career ladder—qualification categories. There were three different categories: second category for beginning teachers who had to prove that they were fit for working in schools; first category for those who were ready to assume a full professional status; and the highest category for those who deserved to be recognized for excellence in teaching. Different regions awarded these categories differently but many used "qualification exams." These exams tested practicing teachers' knowledge of pedagogy, subject knowledge, or information technologies to determine whether they should receive a higher category than the one they held. Thus, the notion already existed but it denoted a practice that was used to allow teachers to move up the career ladder rather than prove that their degree has equipped them with the competencies necessary to enter the profession. In interviews, reformers commented how this exam was similar to the licensing exam used in Western countries, but the policy text used an existing Russian term instead, causing confusion among the audience.

The use of these words distanced the policy both from the foreign origins of these ideas and from their antecedents in the Russian past. This mask of origins—creating something new without help from the West or from the national past—protected the policy from accusations of Westernizing Russian teacher education or reinventing the wheel. Inadvertently, this mask performed another function. By making this text more challenging for the audience to understand, it diffused the audience's critiques. Thus, critics focused either on the parts that were more easily comprehensible

Table 1. Policy Words and Their English and Russian Counterparts

Russian Words/Phrases That Appear in the Policy	Translation	English Counterpart	Historical Russian Antecedent or an Existing Foreign Calque
prakticheskie kompetentsii (практические компетенции)	practical competencies	practical competencies	*prakticheskie navyki* (практические навыки)—practical skills
shkoly-partnery (школы-партнеры)	partner schools	partner schools, professional development schools, lab schools	*bazovye shkoly* (базовые школы)—base schools
prikladnoy bakalavriat (прикладной бакалавриат)	applied bachelor's	applied bachelor's/associate degree	—
universal'niy bakalavriat (универсальный бакалавриат)	universal bachelor's	liberal arts bachelor's	—
shirokiy Bakalavriat (широкий бакалавриат)	broad bachelor's	liberal arts bachelor's	—
kvalifikatsionny ekzamen (квалификационный экзамен)	qualification exam	license exam	*kvalifikatsionny ekzamen* (квалификационный экзамен)—qualification exam (that confirms a practicing teacher's qualification category—second, first, or highest)
soprovozhdenie nachinayushchikh pedagogov (сопровождение начинающих педагогов)	accompanying of beginning teachers	mentoring of beginning teachers	*nastavnichestvo, mentorstvo* (наставничество; менторство)—overseeing, mentoring
stazhirovki studentov (стажировки студентов)	students' internship	internship	*internatura* (интернатура)—internship

(i.e., not lost in translation), such as an increased practical orientation, or they blamed the authors of the Concept for proposals that were not quite there, such as shortening the length of teacher preparation (Privalov 2014).

Mask of Uncertainty: Concrete Models or Abstract Proposals

Another mask worth consideration is the mask of uncertainty. While LEU's earlier version of the policy contained an additional page describing concrete models to be tested during the Concept implementation, the ministry's final version of the policy text did not include them. For example, in relation to the bachelor's programs, the LEU version provided the following suggestions: "Bachelor's programs should be oriented toward a broad general humanities preparation of first- and second-year students. Starting with the third year it is necessary that students have a specialization, during which students can choose either a pedagogical specialization [Rus. *profil'*], or other specializations ["humanities, sciences, anthropology," etc.]. With that, the best students who have the inclination toward pedagogical work and have some experience in it, should be offered precisely the pedagogical specialization" (LEU's version of the Concept).

This explanation described the model promoted by Joseph Abramovich and Vadim Alekseyevich: general preparation during the first two years and teacher education specialization only for the best students beginning with the third year. This was the model they created during their time in Fevral'sk as a result of participating in several of Shchedrovitsky's seminars. But in the "cleaned-up" text that appeared on the ministry's website, this model was only briefly mentioned as one of the ten principles for the "new teacher education" but was removed from the other sections of the Concept. Together with it, specifications for the amount of practice that pedagogical students should have disappeared—LEU's text suggested no fewer than one thousand hours. Other missing parts included different types of master's programs (fast-track degrees for those who came with bachelor's degrees in nonpedagogical areas; research master's or master's degrees for those who needed training in specific areas of education; and finally, master's degrees for those who were engaged in education outside of educational institutions [museums, libraries, etc.]). All of these provided concrete models that had to emerge out of the Concept's implementation, yet they were removed from the final version of the policy.

Comparing different versions of the text helped me see how the removal of specific model descriptions made the policy sound vague and abstract. Those who discussed the policy reacted strongly against this uncertainty in the policy. Many readers criticized the Concept for a lack of specificity in it. For example, during the debate at the Committee on Education at the State Duma,[10] one of the participants stated that the Concept should not be submitted for public discussion because of its vagueness.

Yet this mask of uncertainty reflected a strategic move that allowed reformers to cast this policy as an open stage of experimentation and exploration of more abstract ideas. To address the criticism unleashed against the Concept, Dmitriy Grigoryevich explained why this uncertainty was necessary: "Right now, the discussion of the Concept is going on. It seems to me that people are discussing it without fully realizing that it proposes to develop some models. Some look at it as if it were ready for implementation. And then they criticize it because it has not been fully thought through. What they don't realize is that it was done on purpose. It is intentionally presented as not fully thought through because we need to test it out and see how it will work out" (Interview 45, February 2014).

Dmitriy Grigoryevich responded to the critics by suggesting that abstract ideas of the final text should be approached as an opportunity to try out different ideas to see which ones would work. Because the policy came with a proposal to run a pilot program first, his explanation matched how the policy was framed by the Ministry of Education. Dmitriy Grigoryevich also noted that what distinguished this policy from previous attempts to reform Russian teacher education was the money that universities would receive to test these ideas. "This program needs to be tested to find optimal solutions. So, the proposal is to give money to different universities that will put forward these proposals. They will research those and propose solutions. That is why this new Concept gives money for testing out several models, which we believe is more sustainable than just writing the Concept and passing it on for someone to implement" (Interview 45, February 2014).

This process was described to me in several different ways at LEU. Tatyana Borisovna explained that once the ministry ratified the Concept, it would announce a grant competition for different universities to develop new models. They would compete, the best ideas would receive money, and different universities would be responsible for developing different aspects of the new teacher education model. The problem was that even though the Concept now had only descriptions of abstract ideas, the competition was announced for the concrete models that were identified in LEU's text. That meant that only those who belonged to the reformers' network could submit competitive proposals for this grant. For other universities participating in the competition, the Concept was not a helpful guide for developing proposals. Those groups were out of the running even before the competition began. The mask of uncertainty disguised the concrete models that were supposed to be tested out during the pilot stage, making resources available only to like-minded actors (more on that in chapter 6).

Mask of Evidence

The final mask that I will describe is the mask of evidence—or the misuse of statistical data to support policy's claims. One of the key claims made by the policy stated that "a significant number of graduates from teacher education programs do not get jobs in education or in the social sphere." In the policy text, a diagram was provided as evidence for this claim (fig. 4). The diagram was described in the following way: "the change in attitude of teacher education students toward working in schools." A sociological study of teacher education students conducted by Sobkin and Tkachenko in 2007 was identified as the source of this diagram. Each column was a year in teacher education program: 22.3 percent—first year, 12.3 percent—third year, and 10.1 percent—fifth year. The diagram underscored that state resources were not used efficiently because of the decline in numbers. Careful readers of the paragraph and of the diagram might ask: But what can percentage points from different years in a teacher education program say about employment after graduation?

The answer to this question was actually nothing. The sociological study in question examined "students' plans for future employment"—as the title of the figure in the original source stated (fig. 5). This was a study based on questionnaires with students at a pedagogical university about their *plans* after graduation. The study showed that those plans changed throughout the years in the program. But it actually said nothing about graduates' eventual employment because it did not follow graduates into the field.

The original diagram in the sociological study presented a more complex picture of teacher education students' aspirations for their future careers than what the policy suggested. First, the diagram showed that by the fifth year a quarter of the students planned to go to graduate school. This observation undermined reformers' claims that "not the best students" chose pedagogical education. If all students were academically weak, they would be unlikely to show interest in advanced degrees. Second, the diagram showed that by

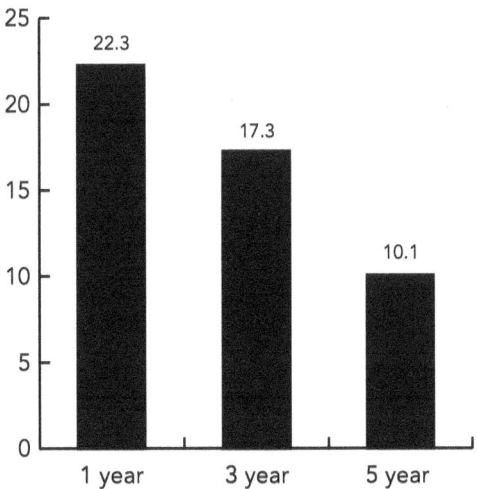

Figure 4. Diagram from the policy text. The original caption stated, "Dynamics of change in orientations towards work in school among students from pedagogical universities (%, in 2007)." Reprinted from the Concept of Support for the Development of Teacher Education with English translation.

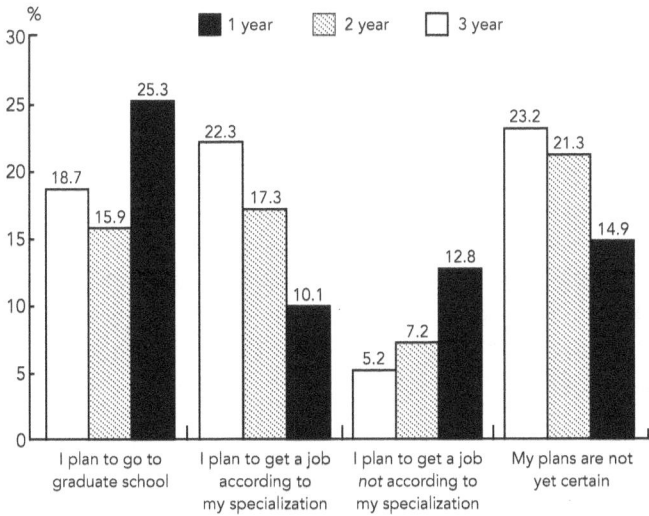

Figure 5. Diagram from the original study. The original caption stated, "Dynamics of change in educational and professional plans among students in pedagogical universities." Reprinted with English translation from Sobkin and Tkachenko (2007), *Student Pedagogicheskogo VUZa* [A student of a pedagogical university] published by the Russian Academy of Education. Image 25. Numbers represent percentages.

the fifth year, 14.9 percent were uncertain about their plans. Those who planned to work according to their specialization comprised 10.1 percent, but those who did not plan to work according to their specialization were 12.8 percent. In other words, the difference between different groups of students was not large. If nothing else, the diagram captured graduates' uncertainty about future employment. Third, the statements to which students had to respond focused on "specialization," which could be interpreted widely without a necessary connection to a school. In other words, the survey did not ask students if they were planning to work in schools. It only asked if they were planning to find employment according to their major. That opened more possibilities for imagining future employment than just education or social sphere. Not to meddle with the policy's main claims, only the second cluster of the original diagram that promoted reformers' agenda was inserted into the policy text.

The mask of evidence fit the "crisis" narrative and disguised the absence of relevant data on the conditions of the job market. The situation in Russia was such that nationwide statistics for recent graduates' employment were not available. This point was not lost on reformers. Larisa Nikolayevna explained it to me this way: "No, there aren't [any large-scale analyses of labor market trends]. We ran into this exact problem . . . when we started collecting data. We started analyzing the situation. We wanted to see where [graduates] are employed, what the ratio of employment is. So, one hundred percent graduated, but where did they go to work? But it was impossible to analyze the labor market because there was no official data" (Interview 59, March 2014).

While there was no data about recent graduates, 83 percent of the teaching force held degrees from pedagogical universities (Ministry of Education Memo, 2014). It is possible that despite students' plans to pursue other careers, many of them still ended up in schools. The mask of evidence eliminated such possibilities and focused the audience's attention only on the data that supported the construction of a crisis narrative around teacher education.

There was another twist in the story of graduates' employment. When the Concept was introduced, there was either no shortage of teachers or in some parts of Russia this shortage was minimal. Joseph Abramovich and Maksim Davydovich referred to this as "an oversupply of cadres." That meant that even if pedagogical university graduates wanted to find teaching jobs in schools, they were not always available to them. The problem of graduates' employment then not only lacked evidence to back it up but also was not a problem after all because most schools were fully staffed.

Despite its shakiness, the problem of graduates' employment was used to demonize pedagogical universities. Anton Mikhailovich and Vadim Alekseyevich argued that graduates' choice of employment did not rest on the labor market dynamics or other affective factors but rather on pedagogical universities' inability to train teachers to work with real children in real schools. In an academic publication, Vadim Alekseyevich developed this point more extensively: "The real situation is such that most pedagogical education students announce that they don't want to work in schools when they are in the second and third years. The number of such students increases as they move through their educational programs. We can confidently assume that this situation is created by the organization and the quality of the teacher education that these students are receiving. So, we have to completely change the pedagogical and psychological components of teacher education" (DSH 2012).

Implicitly referring to the same diagram, Vadim Alekseyevich argued that students' lack of desire to work in schools could be "confidently assumed" to be the result of the low quality of instruction students receive. The original study made no such claims. This time the mask of evidence was used to advance reformers' predetermined agendas to demonize pedagogical universities in order to transform teacher education (see chapter 4).

Concluding Thoughts

In this chapter, I have analyzed how the policy's masks disguised its intentions and contradictions. Even though the policy text contained no references to global policies targeting teachers, reformers underscored similarities between their proposal and international practices. Indeed, teacher education in the United Kingdom has multiple options of entry into the profession, many of which are school based (Maguire 2014). The understanding of teaching as a craft learned by doing, theory as dangerous, and educational research as useless took root in England in the nineties (Furlong 2013; Hilton 2012; Judge et al. 1994) with drastic consequences for university-based teacher education that is now on the brink of extinction (Beauchamp et al. 2016; Ellis and McNicholl 2015). In the United States, conservative think tanks, such as the Fordham Foundation, and a number of influential economists valorized the strengths and advantages of those who were not trained to be teachers. Their argument was that teacher quality would improve if teaching was open to graduates from other majors or if organizations other than university-based teacher education provided training (Hanushek and Rivkin 2004; Hess 2002; Kanstoroom and Finn 1999). The rise in the number of alternative providers coincided with the decrease in the number of college students choosing education as their major. These changes do not bode well for the future of university-based teacher education in the United States. Both the UK and US cases reflect transnational trends of producing "a global teacher," with "the emphasis on compliance with competencies rather than thinking critically about practice; focusing on teaching rather than learning; doing rather than thinking; skills rather than values" (Maguire 2010, 61). The Concept leaves out these connections, but reformers' conversations about their proposal backstage echo these discourses and foreshadow the demise of Russian pedagogical education.

Revealing these connections and stating these intentions publicly was dangerous. Creating a policy text more palatable to the opponents of the reform would have decreased the binding power of the Concept to create a new system. So, through some rhetorical and visual twists, the text's masks disguised the changes that the policy was intending to introduce. Masks helped obscure not only the intentions of reducing the scale of teacher preparation or deprofessionalizing the teaching profession, but also the connection of these ideas with globally circulated policies. It is likely that some of these masks, such as the mask of uncertainty, also precluded the Concept from gaining wide support. After all, it was never signed into law. Despite this fact, masks deployed allowed the experiment based on this Concept to start by the end of June 2014.

Studies drawing on the construct of educational spectacle often note the gap that exists between the policy's rhetoric and its implementation (Gonzalez and Carney 2014; Koyama and Bartlett 2011; Wright 2005). This analysis underscores the ways in which powerful actors use masks to manage policy reception, manipulating the text itself long before the policy's implementation. Smith et al. (2004) observe that "education policies in the political spectacle serve the special interests of the few . . . and hide behind a mask of common sense and the common good" (37). This chapter extends this observation by showing that policy masks perform the complex work of managing the audience's perceptions by disguising the aspects of the policy that are more likely to unleash opposition or reveal the shakiness of policymakers' arguments. The use of masks becomes visible in the differences between the official and unofficial presentations of the policy. The next chapter will examine the discrepancies in timelines of how the policy was developed in order to understand how reformers produced an illusion of democratic participation and diffused responsibility for policy formation.

3

Dress Rehearsals and Missing Directors

Researchers who conduct policy analysis, particularly in international settings, often make assumptions about key actors of policy formation. Particularly in Russia, researchers and research participants often focus on the *institutes of power* (Rus. *institut vlasti*)—the president, the parliament (called the State Duma), different government offices, or various ministries—as the authors and initiators of reforms.[1] The president is often believed to be in charge of choosing directions for reforms and steering the policy formation processes to accomplish the goals he identified. This assumption is supported by the phrase often used to describe President Putin's rule as "manual control" (Ledeneva 2013). While there might be various readings about how policy formation proceeds, most people assume a relatively linear process in which the Ministry of Education proposes a reform, which then becomes ratified by the parliament or the president, and then gets implemented by higher education institutions.

In this chapter, I show that the notion of a production sequence can be helpful for disrupting these assumptions about key actors and main processes in policy formation.[2] Production sequence represents the steps of putting together a theater performance (Gillette 1997). First, the director selects a script. Next, the director holds auditions and selects actors to play different roles. After the stage is set, rehearsals ensue. Throughout this process, the director coordinates "all design and production elements into a unified performance" (Barranger 2006, 235). As the performance appears onstage, the director steps back and the actors take over the production. This process is important not only as a sequence of events but also as the procedure of role allocation because different participants of the play step in at different times to fulfill their specific functions.

To disrupt assumptions about policy formation through the lens of a production sequence, I analyze two timelines: the official and the unofficial. The official timeline of policy formation creates a narrative of a participatory process in which different actors have a say. But when the official timeline of policy formation is juxtaposed against the unofficial timeline shared by the reformers during interviews, discrepancies emerge. These discrepancies reveal that the phase of policy deliberation was in fact dress rehearsals of a ready-made script, leaving those participants who believed that their input mattered betrayed by the performance. These discrepancies also show the complex inner workings of power, in which reformers push through their ideas but place the responsibility for these ideas and their outcomes on the characters representing institutes of power—the president or the Ministry of Education. Ultimately, reconstructing policy formation as a production sequence affords a unique opportunity to examine how roles are reshuffled in such a way that it is no longer possible to identify who performs the role of the director offstage. This reshuffling diffuses responsibility for the resulting policies, leaving no one accountable for outcomes.

Official Timeline

On January 14, 2014, the Ministry of Education displayed the Concept of Support for the Development of Teacher Education on its website for public discussion. It was accompanied by a letter addressed to the Minister of Education that opened with the following statement: "In November of 2013, the working group for the pedagogical education reform finished its work on the development of the concept of the program for the support of development of pedagogical education [sic] in Russia. The document that was developed was agreed on by the members of the working group. According to your order, public discussion of the Concept was organized. It is necessary to acknowledge that discussions of prior versions of the Concept took place from March to October 2013 using different discussion platforms in fifteen regions of Russia. More than 3,000 people—university faculty, teachers, and administrators of educational systems—participated in those. . . . The final version of the Concept was developed based on these discussions."

The letter listed different conferences and other events where the Concept was discussed. It included brief statements of approval that participants of these events allegedly shared about the Concept, noting that "requirements [listed in the Concept] match the requirements of the Federal

Standard of General Education" and that they represent "systematic approach to solving the problems of pedagogical education." The letter concluded with the motion put forward by the assistant to the minister of education to approve the Concept.

This letter became a public passport of this policy, describing how it was developed and asserting its legitimacy as an expressed wish of the teacher education community. Whether at times when the Concept became the subject of severe public criticism or when it became accepted as a de facto reform of teacher education, ministry officials used the language drawn from this letter to argue that the proposed measures emerged out of widespread consensus. During my fieldwork I learned that it was Tatyana Borisovna who prepared the letter and submitted it to the ministry (this substitution of actors is one manifestation of role reshuffling that will be discussed in the last section of this chapter). Regardless of its authorship, the letter is worth a closer look.

Working Group

The letter stated that a working group developed the policy. But neither the letter itself nor the Concept included the list of those who belonged to the working group. Most of the public releases that followed had no names that identified the "authors" of the text either. This was not typical as other policies that were developed at the same time often included the names of those who worked on them.

Only through a fortunate event did I stumble on the MOE decree that created the working group on February 22, 2013, signed by the same MOE official who approved the Concept in the letter. Titled the Working Group on Institutional Transformations in Teacher Education, it consisted of twenty-two members. Among them, there were Anton Mikhailovich, Maksim Davydovich, Vadim Alekseyevich, Joseph Abramovich, Sergey Valdisovich, and Larisa Nikolayevna (see chapter 1). Seven participants represented pedagogical universities, including Ognensk State Pedagogical University, Lyutvino Pedagogical University No. 1, Lyutvino Special Education University, Nikitinsk State Pedagogical University, Mirotropl' State Pedagogical University, and others. Other members included two school principals, one administrator from a professional development institute, director of a teacher education research institute, and representatives of the informal education sector. Four members of the group were affiliated with LEU. Not a single teacher was included in the working group.

Apart from granting anonymity to the Concept's authors, the letter emphasized the participatory and democratic nature of policy development: various stakeholders participated in the discussions that shaped the final version of the text. These discussions took place during four major events: a conference at Lyutvino Social Sciences University in February 2013, a conference in Mirotropl' in April 2013, a conference in Fevral'sk in April 2013, and a seminar at LEU in October 2013. In what follows, I describe how these events served as dress rehearsals of an existing script and were used to produce an illusion of dialogue, consensus, and wide participation.

First Meeting of the Working Group: February 2013

On February 20–21, before the working group was officially formed, Lyutvino Social Sciences University held its annual educational research conference with a provocative title: Do Cadres Determine Everything? This conference attracts about five hundred participants, many of whom are LSSU graduates or members of reformers' networks. Out of twenty-two sessions, seven focused explicitly on pedagogical education and its modernization. Vadim Alekseyevich chaired two roundtable sessions under the title the Development of Pedagogical Education in Russia that lasted a total of three hours. According to Larisa Nikolayevna—the working group's first secretary responsible for "keeping track of everything, collecting information, and coordinating the work of this group"—this was the first time the working group came together.

Larisa Nikolayevna described what happened at that conference in the following way: "The members of the working group were present there. And that was the place where we had the first working meeting of the working group. There, during that meeting, we discussed the plan of work, identified directions, and split ourselves into subgroups, but officially the working group membership was not yet confirmed. . . . On the twenty-first the conference ended and on the twenty-second, possibly after seeing that the group is working, that people are motivated, Sergey Valdisovich reported to the minister of education's assistant and on the twenty-second they signed the decree. After that, the work proceeded in two directions. Because small groups were created dedicated to specific directions, group leaders focused on these directions. That is, they developed proposals to add to the plan of pedagogical education modernization. That was one direction. The other direction was internal, substantive."

According to Larisa Nikolayevna, working group members who came to this meeting had an opportunity to contribute to the development of this policy by joining different subgroups and working on the aspects assigned to those subgroups. The core group, however, was proceeding with "internal, substantive" work. This work included a study of international experiences in reforming teacher education conducted by the LEU team that included Anton Mikhailovich, Larisa Nikolayevna, Tatyana Borisovna, and several other experts. It also included the development of guidelines for how the Concept can be implemented through an experiment.

While transcripts of the roundtable session were not available publicly, some participants shared their observations about that meeting online. A higher education faculty who attended the roundtable summarized the key points discussed there on her blog: "The monitoring showed that most pedagogical universities are ineffective. Pedagogical education can be improved with the help of such measures as variability in professional preparation, introduction of professional qualifications exam, strengthening of psychology and pedagogy components in teacher education, introduction of internships, carrying out statistical analysis of the labor market, and strengthening collaborations in pedagogical universities' network."

This list bears an uncanny resemblance to many of the ideas that appeared in the final version of the Concept (chapter 2). This participant's description points to the first discrepancy: How is it that some of the Concept's main points were presented at this conference, if the group that the ministry organized to develop this policy met at this conference for the first time and only began to identify the directions for future work?

Mirotropl' Conference: April 2013

Another discussion of the pedagogical reform happened during a conference held in Mirotropl' and cosponsored by LEU. The conference had about 250 participants. Vadim Alekseyevich, Dmitriy Grigoryevich, Fedor Aleksandrovich, and Joseph Abramovich alongside a colleague from abroad were plenary speakers. Joseph Abramovich and Sergey Valdisovich chaired a four-hour roundtable titled Pedagogue in the System of Modern Challenges where the large working group came together again. The program included three key points for discussion that captured some of the Concept's key principles: "the network of pedagogical education institutions—perspectives for change; variability in teacher preparation trajectories; teacher preparation—possibilities of collaboration between universities and schools."

The roundtable consisted of several parts and, unlike other events organized by the group, included presentations of three other working group members. The presentations were followed by a little over an hour and a half of discussion. Two of the speakers from pedagogical universities had gone through Skolkovo's 100 Rectors program. Larisa Nikolayevna spoke very highly about the speaker from Nikitinsk State Pedagogical University, calling him "young, creative, deep, and very competent." He argued that "pedagogical education is a form of governing the future," which is achieved by "creating the desired future by creating a desired human being." This framing of the significance of pedagogical education resonated with the reformers' vision for teacher education modernization (chapter 4). He also underscored the importance of international experiences in conceptualizing change—a stance uncommon among the leadership of pedagogical universities but typical for the reformers and experts in their networks. Overall, his example showed that those who were invited to present during these events promoted reformers' ideas.

Fevral'sk Conference: April 2013

According to the ministry letter, the next meeting of the working group took place in Fevral'sk. It happened during an annual conference organized by Matvey Yakovlevich—Vadim Alekseyevich and Joseph Abramovich's colleague and close friend, also a member of the working group. That conference brought together about five hundred participants.

Larisa Nikolayevna spoke about the events in Fevral'sk as follows: "The most significant event was in Fevral'sk. There, at the end of April, a large international conference dedicated to the practices of development took place and we organized a roundtable with involvement of Fevral'sk TV, in Fevral'sk State Pedagogical University. Then we gave a presentation of the most important ideas of the Concept and the plan of reform activities. Anton Mikhailovich gave a talk, and rectors and pro-rectors from [several] pedagogical universities gave talks as well. And there we also organized a foresight session that Matvey Yakovlevich moderated, also dedicated to the main directions of pedagogical education modernization.[3] We were trying to look ahead, asking ourselves a question, what would happen by 2020 if we implemented the measures that we are discussing. These roundtables gave us a chance to hear the pedagogical community."

Similar to the event in Mirotropl', representatives of pedagogical universities were given an opportunity to speak, but the cast of characters did not change much from the previous conference—it was the same people who spoke before and who expressed ideas that the core group was promoting.

Furthermore, Larisa Nikolayevna's description captured another discrepancy: "There we gave a presentation of the most important ideas of the Concept and the plan of reform activities" at the same time as we had "a chance to hear the pedagogical community." This deserves more attention.

Anton Mikhailovich gave a presentation that captured "the most important ideas of the Concept." He discussed the problem of "double negative selection," "ineffective pedagogical universities," and insufficient preparation in the practical skills of teaching that pedagogical universities offered. To describe solutions to these problems, he suggested that there should be more points of entry into and more points of exit out of pedagogical education. He also spoke at length about the changed nature of teachers' work because of the new professional standard that no longer required a subject specialist. Because of this change, future teachers should spend more time learning in schools, rather than in universities. These ideas, yet again, reflected the final text of the Concept.

The Q&A sessions after Anton Mikhailovich's and other reformers' presentations had fiery exchanges about "the contents of teacher education preparation," "the place of subject area specialization," the challenges of "quantitative measurements of teacher competencies" (i.e., qualification exams), as well as the dangers of increasing practical preparation at the expense of theoretical grounding. Even though conference participants voiced concerns that resonated for months and years ahead, their contributions were not reflected in the final policy text.

October Seminar at LEU

The final event identified by the ministry letter was one of the regular LEU seminars that in the middle of October was dedicated to the presentation of the Concept. This seminar, open to the public and usually attended by about fifty people, served as a hub for the expert community in Lyutvino and many noted that it was the gathering place for many in the reformers' networks. Anton Mikhailovich gave his presentation; Dmitriy Grigoryevich and Fedor Aleksandrovich were his discussants. Anton Mikhailovich outlined the problems that existed in pedagogical education: "double negative selection," "ineffective pedagogical universities," oversupply of teacher candidates, as well as graduates not going to work in schools. He noted that most countries of the world had already reformed their systems of teacher preparation. Based on a study of international experiences, he proposed the following reform measures: increase in the number of points for entry into and exit out of teacher education; screening measures to select the best students for teaching; increase in the practical component of teacher education; a network of university-school partnerships; and an internship as a required component of a teacher education degree. One idea dominated the concluding segment of Anton Mikhailovich's presentation—it is necessary to break up the monopoly of pedagogical universities. This presentation laid out the problems and solutions that became reflected in the final text of the policy and shed light on reformers' backstage commitments.

When the audience raised questions and concerns about these proposals, Joseph Abramovich noted that the policy's key point was to create a variety of paths into teaching. Dmitriy Grigoryevich and Fedor Aleksandrovich took the floor as representatives of the pedagogical universities in this debate. Counter to the expectation that they would challenge this proposal because it deprofessionalizes teaching and because that is what discussants usually did at these seminars, they pointed out some minor flaws but then enthusiastically supported the policy and expressed interest in implementing it. Fedor Aleksandrovich elaborated that the Russian system of education should offer liberal arts degrees and that his pedagogical university already began developing such programs. The debate that followed was charged and the room often erupted into loud chatter. Vadim Alekseyevich, who chaired the seminar, several times made announcements that those who needed to talk should step out of the room.

This seminar concluded the list of events that were used to facilitate discussions of the policy. Larisa Nikolayevna repeatedly emphasized the importance of this stage during our interview: "All of these roundtables and presentations allowed us to hear the community. . . . If I could give a summary, we saw the relevance of and the interest in our reform measures. We saw that people accept the key tasks that we have conceptualized and the directions we are proposing. We saw that we did not make many mistakes or inaccuracies. This was a very important stage . . . It allowed pedagogues, the representatives of the pedagogical community, to see themselves, to take ownership of the reform, to perceive themselves as active subjects of pedagogical education reform. I mean it did not fall on them from the top" (Interview 69, March 2014).

The use of "we" in the preceding statement suggests that it was the reformers who selected reform measures and created the policy text. A close look at the proposed measures and their consistent reemergence from one event to another demonstrates that the policy did not undergo any major transformations from the time it was first presented in February 2013. The only exception to this is the statement about "points of exit." Even though the reformers continued describing it as a part of the reform, all references to it were removed from the final text of the Concept. Coupled with other factors that will be discussed later, this suggests that the script for performance was agreed on before the working group was created by the ministry, making this conference season less of a participatory policy deliberation process and more of a dress rehearsal for the final release of the policy. As Larisa Nikolayevna acknowledged during our interview, when Anton Mikhailovich gave his first presentation in February, most measures were already decided on.

While the question of a script will be discussed in more detail later (chapter 5), I want to briefly examine how the teacher education community attempted to participate in the development of the policy. To do that, I will explore an event that took place in Ognensk State Pedagogical University in spring of 2013 but was omitted from the ministry's timeline.

Seminar at Ognensk State Pedagogical University: March 2013

"In March of 2013, 29 and 30 of March, there was a huge event in Ognensk State Pedagogical University. The key person there was Pavel Bogdanovich. They prepared very interesting experts from their side. We discussed the key directions." This is how Larisa Nikolayevna described the seminar at OSPU to me. In fact, she was the only person who spoke about that seminar from a substantive viewpoint. Sergey Valdisovich mentioned it only when I asked about financial support for the policy development. He explained that the only money that the ministry spent on developing this policy was to pay for this event. In the photos of that event in the OSPU newspaper only Larisa Nikolayevna and Sergey Valdisovich were present from the reformers' core group. This might explain why other members did not discuss this event and why it was not included in the letter to the ministry.

This event was the only discussion of policy that happened at a pedagogical university—other events described earlier occurred at conferences that generally brought together those who belonged to reformers' networks. Ognensk was different. This was not just any pedagogical university, but one of the leading universities in the country. Pavel Bogdanovich—one of OSPU's pro-rectors—was included in the working group in recognition of the university's standing. Seeing the proposals that LEU prepared, he created a team at OSPU that was working on an alternative proposal for teacher education modernization. From my interviews with different members of OSPU's team in the fall of 2013, I learned that the OSPU team working on this proposal defined themselves in opposition to the core group of reformers and looked for ways to counteract the Concept's measures. Even though some aspects of it were perceived as positive developments for teacher education, there was a general sense of concern that the Concept did not address actual problems that teacher education, underfunded and lacking prestige, was facing.

The article dedicated to this event in an OSPU journal stated that the goal of this seminar was to allow different representatives of the educational system to discuss problems in teacher education and their solutions. The quote from Sergey Valdisovich's introductory statement, however, sheds a different light on this goal: "The working group has created a general vision, has determined some general directions that we believe are priority areas for solving the problems of pedagogical education. But this does not mean that we are not ready to change them, *if we hear anything important*" (OSPU Journal 2013, emphasis added). This statement suggests that to be heard, the pedagogical education community had to have something worthwhile to say. Only then could their suggestions be incorporated into the policy proposal.

Sergey Valdisovich proceeded with the presentation of the policy: "If we (pedagogical education) do not prepare cadres for education, then the question is why we prepare them at all. . . . The monitoring of higher education institutions' effectiveness. Three-quarters of pedagogical universities have indicators of ineffectiveness. . . . The percentage of population growth shows that the teaching profession has to become renewed. . . . The task of the working group is to propose simple solutions that any bureaucrat can understand . . . to propose easily understandable solutions, which could be implemented. . . . We focused on four types of changes: flexible entry into the profession, a mechanism of renewing the teaching profession, modernization of the preparation contents; motivation of talented and energetic [young people]. . . . The last position that is firm is the introduction of a professional exam" (OSPU Journal 2013).

Sergey Valdisovich's speech bore a heavy resemblance to the ideas presented by Anton Mikhailovich and by the Concept itself, demonstrating that the script remained relatively consistent throughout the policy formation stage, even when presented by different members of the core group. This shows that reformers came not to discuss potential measures and hear the teacher education community but rather to state what they already chose as the path for reform.

One final note is worth consideration. The OSPU rector's and Pavel Bogdanovich's overview of the seminar published in the same journal showed support for some of the Concept's measures, such as the introduction of internships or the improvement of school practicum experiences. Yet the definition of the problem—that pedagogical universities are not effective or that their graduates do not work for the educational system—was questioned. For example, responding to the reformers' claims about graduates' work, the authors of the article noted, "This approach does not include the employment of those who become employed in preschools and kindergartens, organizations of additional and informal education, psychological and social services, etc." The construction of pedagogical education as responsible for economic development was also problematized: "A no less important factor of educational system development is the worldview-determining role of pedagogical education that must shape the continuity of national consciousness and foundational constants of the national culture." These challenges did not make it into the final text of the Concept, even though Pavel Bogdanovich was a member of the large working group and had attended most of their meetings.

During my fieldwork at OSPU in the fall of 2013, the OSPU team members still hoped that their alternative proposal challenging the Concept would make a difference. They believed that if it was submitted to the ministry by the end of December, their voices would be heard. But as the ministry's letter indicated, work on the Concept was finished by the end of November. At the end of December 2013, the ministry was already advertising grant competitions for reform implementation based on the Concept. Even if the OSPU team had "something important to say," their report arrived at the ministry too late to influence the policy.

There are several reasons why I went into such detail describing what happened during the conferences highlighted in the official timeline or omitted from it. Sergey Valdisovich, who moderated work on the Concept, emphasized that one should not treat it as a text created by a group of authors—it was a product of a collective effort. Larisa Nikolayevna similarly emphasized that the pedagogical community were active participants in this policy formation. This point is emphasized across different contexts, as the ministry's letter in the beginning of this section so aptly shows.

Yet as one traces these events, several things become apparent: neither the time nor the structure of conference roundtables or seminars allowed for significant input from the members of the pedagogical community. Apart from the seminar at OSPU, the sites where the Concept was discussed were not typical conferences that members of the pedagogical communities would attend but rather conferences organized by participants in the reformers' networks. They were also too small to solicit perspectives from the educational community. The working group created by the ministry to develop teacher education reform came together only five times. Most of these meetings lasted about three to four hours, which was not enough time to make substantive contributions to policy proposals. Many of those meetings were structured around presentations and talks given by the reformers themselves or the working group members who had gone through Skolkovo's 100 Rectors program. This suggests that ideas to be presented at these meetings were carefully screened to allow only like-minded participants to share presentations that would extend support for the reform measures.

The event in Ognensk, where opposing views were shared, was either downplayed or dropped altogether from the reformers' timeline of events. The views expressed by OSPU's leadership did not make it into the final text of the Concept. Thus, despite the apparent participatory framing of this policy's development, members of the pedagogical community were led to believe that their voices mattered, but the dress rehearsals they were participating in were based on the ready-made script. The illusion of dialogue and democratic participation (Smith et al. 2004; Wright 2005) around this policy obscured the fact that they were afforded only the role of an audience for reformers' performances. In the next section, I will explore aspects of the unofficial timeline to demonstrate that the script was selected before the large working group got together and that the formation of the large working group was a symbolic act of promoting the Concept's legitimacy.

The Unofficial Timeline

The official timeline of policy formation is not the entire story of how this policy came to be. In what follows, I reconstruct a different timeline shared only within the reformers' network. This unofficial timeline sheds light on the ready-made script and the role of the working group's other participants. The significance of this timeline lies not only in disrupting the official representation of the policy formation processes but also in shedding light on the role reshuffling that obscures responsibility for policy formation, which will be discussed more fully in the last section of this chapter.

Larisa Nikolayevna once again helped me understand the process: "The work actually began in October 2012. At the beginning there was this small group: Alexander Dmitrievich, the rector of the Lyutvino Special Education University; then, there was Anton Mikhailovich, Joseph Abramovich, Maksim Davydovich, and I. This small group was busy thinking through what needs to be done, how to organize the work of creating the Concept, and how to design the program of pedagogical education modernization."

Of note here is the difference between the official start of the work—February 2013 when the ministry decree was signed—and the unofficial start in October 2012 when the small group of reformers started holding regular meetings. Other reformers similarly identified October 2012 as the beginning of the work on this policy and named the same actors as those who participated in this work. Some added Vadim Alekseyevich and Sergey Valdisovich to this list. Larisa Nikolayevna continued, "The first thing that we collectively realized was that this was yet another attempt to modernize pedagogical education. I personally counted: from 2003 there were at least three such attempts. And not a single one of them ended successfully. All the time they would try to modernize pedagogical education, but they did not take a systematic approach. There were no concepts or programs signed into law that would encompass all of pedagogical education" (Interview 59, March 2014).

All of the reformers shared the same observation that this was not the first time that pedagogical education was a target of modernization reforms. The commonality of this observation is not surprising, given that it was reformers themselves who often participated in prior attempts to modernize teacher education. Vadim Alekseyevich was involved in developing the Program of Pedagogical Education Modernization in 2003; Dmitriy Grigoryevich participated in developing Measures for the Renewal of Teacher Education in 2009 and Our New School policy in 2010; Vadim Alekseyevich, Joseph Abramovich, and Anton Mikhailovich in 2011–2012 worked on developing policy proposals for educational modernization that was a part of Strategy 2020. All of these policies and policy proposals included measures targeting pedagogical education.

It is not simply that these characters participated in earlier attempts to modernize teacher education; they also had been working with a consistent set of ideas throughout most of this time. The first Program of Pedagogical Education Modernization emphasized the need to increase the practical orientation of teacher preparation. In 2009, the Measures for the Renewal of Teacher Education included the same emphasis on practical preparation and suggested the introduction of an internship. That proposal also suggested that those who want to work in schools should pass "certification exams." Similar to the current Concept, it stated that "teachers at all levels of education should receive a high level of psychology-pedagogy training" (UG 2009). Our New School for the first time introduced the idea that those who are trained for other professions should be encouraged to work in schools. Strategy 2020 argued that teacher preparation should be moved from pedagogical universities to other universities. It also suggested a yearlong internship for preservice teachers and a qualification exam for those who want to work in schools but were not trained as teachers.

When this consistency of characters and measures proposed during different waves of teacher education modernization became apparent to me, I asked my participants whether there were any connections between Our New School, Strategy 2020, and the Concept. I received an affirmative answer from most of the reformers. Sergey Valdisovich elaborated on this point in ways that echoed other explanations I heard: "Of course, these are all connected. Because people who participated in developing Strategy 2020 . . . The Strategy had a really good section dedicated to school . . . Of course, all of this is connected. People are the same and these ideas are theirs . . . Since these ideas have not been implemented, they remain. [*He laughs.*] If these ideas were implemented, we would know whether they were good or bad, we would test them somehow. But they have not been implemented, so they remain. People are the same. Ideas are the same. Of course, changes happen and the international experience is moving forward. But the main directions, the key substantive aspects, they remain unchanged" (Interview 44, February 2014).

Sergey Valdisovich confirmed my observations—the development of this policy did not start in February 2013 when the ministry issued the decree; it did not start in 2012 when the small group got together. Instead, it actually started in 2003, at the latest, when the first program of teacher education modernization began to evolve. Since that time, there was a search for solutions and an accumulation of possibilities that were already put together by 2009. Ironically, the solutions became most clearly defined after Michael Barber and Mona Mourshed's report *How the World's Best-Performing School Systems Come Out on Top* was translated into Russian and published in LEU's educational journal in 2008. The report became the script for the reformers' proposal because it comprised "simple solutions that any bureaucrat can understand" and "easily understandable solutions, which could be implemented" (more on that and Barber's role as a playwright in chapter 5). Since 2010 when Our New Policy emerged, it became a matter of translating the rest of these ideas into practice. Strategy 2020 was supposed to carry out that function but the government's final approval of it stalled because of widespread resistance to it. The Concept incorporated most of these ideas and moved them forward toward implementation.

Interestingly, when Michael Barber visited Russia in September 2012, he gave a presentation at LEU on the need for a revolution in education to secure leadership positions in the world. At the end of his presentation he mentioned that he had the privilege of reading Strategy 2020 that his friends had developed but was concerned that the steps identified in it lacked the specificity to be implemented. The small group started meeting regularly in October of 2012. The text that emerged out of that work is a more fleshed-out version of Strategy 2020's proposals.

Next, I explore how the large working group was put together. This will show both the symbolic significance of the working group and the symbolic nature of the ministry's involvement in this work.

Auditions, or Recruitment for the Large Working Group

"October, November, December we worked in this small group. Then Joseph Abramovich gave me a task: to draft a possible composition for the working group. Not even the working group. We were planning to organize a roundtable dedicated to pedagogical education modernization.[4] We had it January 19, 2013, at Lyutvino Special Education University. We invited some people there. I don't know whether by accident or not, but some people knew some people, some people worked on projects together. So, we invited rectors, assistant rectors, school principals, higher education faculty, MOE representatives. It was a very interesting format—a business game.[5] That's how we initiated the process. We held a roundtable that looked like a business game where the key problems of pedagogical education in Russia and some approaches, some understanding of approaches of modernizing pedagogical education, were discussed. Figuratively speaking, we talked of that which was causing pain [Rus. *O nabolevshem*; Russian idiom—"whatever causes you pain, that you talk about"].[6] So, January 19, there was no working group yet. We just invited some experts to contemplate and think about it. It was a problem-posing seminar [Rus. *problemny seminar*] . . . But to tell you the truth, it was a matchmaking event [Rus. *smotriny*]. We needed to create a group, but to do that we needed to look at the people" (Interview 59; March 2014).

Larisa Nikolayevna's explanation reveals that it was Joseph Abramovich who gave her the instructions to begin drafting a possible list of names. This is an important aspect to consider because the ministry's order initiating the work of the group produces the impression that the ministry was in charge of bringing together the people to design this policy. Larisa Nikolayevna's explanation suggests that this may not have been the case.

Another interesting aspect of Larisa Nikolayevna's explanation is how she described the event as *smotriny*—a matchmaking event in which a groom selects a bride. The game was organized to select those who would be a good match for the small group and the script that they agreed on. This description resembles auditions when directors match "an actor to a role" in putting together theater performances (Barranger 2006, 235). Sergey Valdisovich's explanation renders support for this observation. When I asked him how the people for the large working group were selected, he at first hesitated to answer, but then shared the following: "Based on their expert noticeability. That is people who position themselves as experts in different questions, they are visible, they participate in discussions, they meet with each other, they know each other . . . That is the principle of selecting members of the group. Of course, there is a degree of subjectivity. For example, I started working with the Skolkovo program Russia's 100 Rectors. It was a program designed to provide training for rectors and pro-rectors to create a leap into the future, so that it would be possible to discuss with these people a reform, a move, changes in Russian education, so that these people would become agents of these changes. That is the idea of this program. And in it, there was a group of pedagogical university rectors, about ten or eleven at the beginning, then the group became smaller. There were four pro-rectors in the end. I was the moderator for that group. When I started working with them, I invited two people from that group. You could say that it was a subjective element. I saw that those were rectors from the Russian regions, thoughtful, understanding, with a desire to change something. At the same time, because they don't publish in this area, they are less visible in the field. So I invited them. Other people invited other people, they recommended each other. That's how the group was formed" (Interview 44, February 2014).

Sergey Valdisovich's explanation reveals one of the criteria for selecting group members—they had to have "a desire to change something." Also, having gone through Skolkovo's 100 Rectors program, these participants were trained in new ideologies. As Victor Anatolyevich, who was involved in administering that program, explained: "The goal of the program is to change the present and future rectors by changing how people think about running a modern university" (Interview 51, February 2014). For that program, rectors of pedagogical universities designed a teacher education reform that included such elements as "pedagogical internship," "professional exam," and "base centers for students' practical training" (100 Rectors program, Group 11 Presentation, September 2013). These were the same rectors who presented their vision for reforms during the conference season. So, some people were invited to be a part of the group because they adhered to a similar ideology of change.

Sergey Valdisovich also shared that there were those who were invited because of their "visibility." Joseph Abramovich elaborated on this point further, "The group was created, as everything that is done in these cases, as a compromise between content and political demands. On the one hand, there were experts that the ministry trusted, and on the other hand there were experts without whom the legitimacy of the material, the public legitimacy of the product, would have been insufficient. That is why the ministry invited their own [Rus. *svoi*] that it trusted and then added a couple of other politically significant personas" (Interview 47, February 2014).

Joseph Abramovich indicated that the ministry trusted "experts"—that is him and his small group. So, they became a part of the working group. But the ministry also needed those "experts without whom the legitimacy of the material . . . would have been insufficient." That is how one of the OSPU rectors and the director of a teacher education research institute appeared on the list. They were known in the country as some of the key representatives of the pedagogical community; they were also strongly opposed to the Concept. Co-opting them into the production of the Concept would add legitimacy to the final product. Thus, the large working group was created not to develop a policy but rather to legitimize it.

Joseph Abramovich's explanation, however, provides another insight into the policy formation processes. Note how he positioned the ministry as the agent of reform action: "the ministry trusted," "the ministry invited," and "the ministry added." Joseph Abramovich presented the process of policy formation as if it was initiated by the ministry. In this scenario, his responsibility was only to carry out the orders that he was given by the ministry because he was one of the people that the ministry trusted. But remember that when Larisa Nikolayevna described how the group was formed she noted that it was Joseph Abramovich who asked her to draft the composition of the group. It is possible that the ministry gave Joseph Abramovich the order to organize the group and he just passed that order to Larisa Nikolayevna. But given the fact that by that point the reformers had been attempting to introduce teacher education modernization for at least twelve years, questions emerge about how the institutes of power, such as the Ministry of Education and the president, were used in reformers' performances. This will be examined in more detail in the next section.

Discrepancies in Timelines and Inner Workings of Power

During the interviews I regularly asked, "What served as the stimulus to begin the work on the Concept?" Two patterns of responses emerged. Most of the core group members identified the monitoring of the higher education institutions as the starting point for their work. According to those answers, the ministry realized that so many pedagogical universities were ineffective, so it became necessary to do something about them (more on the monitoring in chapter 4). The only trouble with this is that the small group started their work in October, and the monitoring was initiated in September. According to the Ministry of Education's reports, most of the committee meetings making decisions based on the monitoring data happened in November. Given the size of the Russian bureaucratic machine with all of its many agencies that are involved in collecting, collating, and analyzing the data, it seems that in October there would have been very little reliable evidence that would allow the ministry to act. The time span between the monitoring and the beginning of the core group's work seems to be too narrow to be plausible. It is, however, important to point out that the ministry was regularly identified as one of the initiators of reform activity. The second pattern of responses, however, assigned that role to the president.

The President's Speeches

Many interviewees mentioned specific speeches that the president gave as the impetus for reform: the president's address to the Federal Assembly in 2008 and in 2009. When I created the chart of the Concept formation to check whether I understood the process correctly and showed it to several core group members, all indicated that the president's speech mattered. Most people were not sure which one or where I could find it, but they emphasized that "the president spoke about it."

My exchange with Larisa Nikolayevna on this matter was particularly interesting. When I asked her about the starting point of this work, her answers became more tentative and ambivalent: "Oh, I don't know. You should ask Joseph Abramovich about it. It is like the push leg for a runner. Who knows which push leg it was here. I know my right leg is my push leg. If I could guess, I would say it was Putin's decree. I have a quote saved from his speech from November 2012 when he talked about pedagogical education. That might have been it" (Interview 59, March 2014).

I find it interesting how Larisa Nikolayevna, who was very careful to give me the exact dates of events and the exact order of all the conferences, would all of a sudden flip the order of events. What started the work of the group in October 2012? The speech that the president gave in November 2012.

But there is one aspect in which Larisa Nikolayevna is right. Indeed, President Putin had a meeting with several of the ministers to discuss how modernization of general education was proceeding on November 7, 2012. During that meeting, of the four areas that deserved attention, President Putin named pedagogical education, which appeared last on his list: "We have to very seriously look at our pedagogical education. Here we are speaking about both the preparation of students and teachers' professional development. What points I consider to be important here: future teachers need a strong fundamental (theoretical) education, that is why we should use more broadly the resources available at classical universities for the preparation of school teachers. In such a sphere as education, it is impermissible to have hesitations, contradictory steps. All the leadership decisions have to be explained to people, arguments should be presented clearly. . . . When people don't understand what is happening, mistakes occur in general work, and society's misunderstandings are a very painful thing. It is necessary to constantly participate in an open dialogue with citizens, with the professional community. This applies to all levels of power. Regional authorities should determine exactly how many teachers and for which disciplines schools need and based on these needs determine the number of specialists higher education institutions should prepare."[7]

This call for action is both sufficiently specific and sufficiently vague. The emphasis on increasing the role of classical universities in teacher preparation reflected the proposal that appeared in Our New School and was about to be applied to address the problem of "ineffective institutions." When the results of the monitoring were released in November 2012, the ministry announced that ineffective pedagogical universities would be closed or merged with classical universities. But the next part of his quote that focused on the labor market analysis and the distribution of pedagogical education applicants based on that analysis became reflected in the Concept. Given the fact that this speech took place a month after the core group started their work but two months before any official meetings started, I read it as a commentary of a person who was informed that some efforts were already under way. He was explicitly addressing those he was meeting with and implicitly those who were already engaged in this work. This became a retroactive blessing of sorts.

Larisa Nikolayevna's reference to this speech is helpful for revealing another discrepancy in the timelines. The president's speech mattered for the beginning of this work, only it happened after the work began. This discrepancy sheds light on the role reshuffling that occurs in Russian policymaking, in which reformers push to introduce policies but cast the representatives of institutes of power as the initiators of change. During my time at LEU, I once participated in an enlightening exchange on this matter.

Tatyana Borisovna was leaving the office closer to the end of the day. Another woman who shared the office with us asked her where she was going. Tatyana Borisovna answered, "To the ministry." Then she turned to face both of us and said, "You know what I realized recently. We should all create a little library of the president's speeches and quotes. Without those there is not much you can do with any proposal. We sent some documents to the ministry. They returned them to us with corrections. The person who did the corrections inserted Putin's quotes everywhere" (Field Notes, February 2014). This description of the situation reminded me of the Soviet past where references to party orders and decrees had to be inserted into various texts.

This exchange revealed that in order to justify or legitimize a policy, it had to look as if it was initiated by the president. It did not have to come as an order from him; it was sufficient to include quotes from his speeches to make it appear as if it was bearing the stamp of his approval. In the next section, I will present an analysis of presidents' decrees and transcripts of officials' meetings with them to demonstrate the presidents' limited interest in pedagogical education reform, which stands in stark contrast with the reformers' passionate stance that it has to change dramatically.

Pedagogical Education Reforms in Presidents' Decrees and Roundtable Discussions

The most immediate and binding of all of the president's speeches around 2012 were the decrees of May 2012. In fact, when Lyutvino had their final seminar of the year in 2014, May decrees were on the agenda to be discussed—their implementation was very important. But pedagogical education was not included in those decrees. It was not on the list of tasks that the government or the ministry had to carry out.

In August 2011, President Medvedev held a meeting with representatives of the education sector and ordered that the program for pedagogical education modernization must be created by December 1, 2011.[8] Even though the order appears stern in its wording,[9] the report on fulfilling this order that came out on January 19, 2012, stated that the measures of modernizing pedagogical education would be developed as part of the Federal Program of Educational Development for 2011–2015.[10] Nothing came out of Medvedev's orders and they were quietly archived away as fulfilled.

So, neither one of those seemed to matter in actually initiating teacher education modernization reform.

In my search for the initial spark, I came across the transcript of President Medvedev's meeting with representatives of the educational sector that took place in April of 2012.[11] Medvedev framed the discussion as a free-flowing conversation and tried to stop those who were trying to give formal presentations. In his opening comments, he gave general descriptions of the educational systems and highlighted several priorities for reform. Pedagogical education did not appear on his list. The roundtable participants raised different issues that they thought the government had to address in education. The rector of LEU brought up the quality of teachers and suggested that teacher education had to drastically change. The rector of OSPU, who was also a participant in this discussion, tried to defend pedagogical education as the "valued resource of our society." Joseph Abramovich spoke up. Emphasizing the objectivity of statistics, Joseph Abramovich explained that pedagogical education suffers from "double negative selection" and that President Medvedev's orders to create a program of pedagogical education modernization of 2011 had no "observable effects."

"You see, Singapore and Finland took a very specific position: they take very few people for these programs, but these are the best people, they are given high enough scholarships. But the principle that [the system is based on] of taking more students with the hope that a fraction of graduates will go to schools does not work. And here, I think it is important to return to that president's order, look at that program one more time, and take more bold steps. No one is saying that any university needs to be immediately shut down. But I repeat, as [the rector of LEU] said, here we need not improvement, but change."

This exchange is illuminating because it is clear that the president of the country does not have much to say on the matter, but the reformers do. They are the ones advocating for a major reform of teacher education.

Note how this reform was framed—"not improvement, but change." This framing is important to remember in light of the Concept's masks (chapter 2). Both LEU's rector and Joseph Abramovich had been advocating for the radical transformations of pedagogical education at least since 2005 when the first roundtable dedicated to this topic was held at LEU. The president did not seem that interested in this topic either before or after this comment, but in his closing remarks he supported Joseph Abramovich's suggestions and told OSPU's rector that the system of pedagogical education needed to be optimized and reorganized, or changed dramatically.

Of the publicly available materials of presidents' speeches and meetings, the events I have described are the only times when the president discussed pedagogical education close to the time of policy formation. This suggests that while reformers state that the president's speeches matter for initiating reforms, those speeches took place long before or long after the work on the reforms was initiated. After all, the aforementioned conversation happened in April 2012; May decrees of 2012 made no mention of pedagogical education; the work of the group started in October; the president identified pedagogical education as an area that needs to be reformed in November. Discrepancies in these timelines reveal a peculiar role the president plays—his quotes were necessary for the proposals to be seen as legitimate and his approval could potentially justify reformers' proposals, but he himself could not care less about these reforms.

Ironically, when I asked Oleg Victorovich why this wave of teacher education modernization started, he responded, "One of the speech writers stuck it into Putin's speech. Well, once he said it, something had to be done about it. That's how things are usually done in Russia" (Interview 43, January 2014). This brings us full circle. How does reform start? The president says that it has to happen. How does the president decide that a reform has to happen? Someone writes it in his speech. This is hardly a description of the president who initiates change or identifies the directions for development but more of a character that is called out on stage and told what to say.

The process of assigning a role to the president or to the ministry takes place backstage—the area researchers often cannot access. But discrepancies in sentence or narrative structures can reveal the inner workings of this power backstage. For example, Joseph Abramovich in his interview used a curious turn of phrase: "There was this idea that someone inserted [Rus. *vlozhil*] into President Medvedev's head when he was still a president that those should be large transregional complexes, that teachers should be prepared in classical universities. He even spoke about it, there was a decree, but then nothing came out of it" (Interview 47, February 2014). Addressing the Federal Assembly in 2009, President Medvedev stated that "pedagogical universities should be gradually transformed either into large base centers of teacher preparation or into the departments of classical universities."[12] The same idea appeared several months later in the policy Our New School under the call "to modernize the system of pedagogical education."[13] As someone who had backstage access, however, Joseph Abramovich knew that this was not the president's idea but rather something "inserted" into his head.

Most people assume that reforms and policies emanate from the institutes of power or their representatives—those who are believed to be the directors of the performance. But Joseph Abramovich's short phrase "someone inserted it into the president's head" challenges those assumptions. What it points to instead is a reshuffling of roles in which reformers select scripts for reforms, add a representative of an institute of power that is assumed to perform the role of the director for staging the performance based on those scripts, but continue running the performance themselves. Those who represent the institutes of power do not always live up to reformers' expectations because occasionally reformers complain that the ministry did not publicize the reform enough or did not release the policy with enough positive fanfare. So, this relationship is never easy and straightforward. But it obscures a complex inner working of how power is shared in the policy formation process in ways that diffuse the responsibility for policy implementation or its outcome.

Concluding Thoughts

Policy formation is traditionally analyzed from the perspective of policy windows—or "opportunities for action on given initiatives" (Kingdon 2011, 166)—that open when administrations change and political priorities realign. Policymakers are believed to "slack off" when policy windows are closed as they are "unwilling to invest their time, political capital, energy, and other resources in an effort that is unlikely to bear fruit" (167). The timelines analyzed in this chapter raise questions about the universality of these assumptions. Not only did Russian reformers persistently pursue change in teacher education for over twenty years, they did it without much regard for political regimes or reigning ideologies. After all, when reformers first started redesigning teacher education, the Soviet Union was still a superpower that many expected to endure. The core group of reformers did not wait for policy windows to open up—they worked hard to create these policy windows at every opportune moment. Their efforts were a gamble as their previous attempts of reform did fail. Nevertheless, each moment of failure became an opportunity to learn how to edge closer toward success.

Most importantly, Kingdon (2011) states policy windows most often occur when administrations change. This statement aligns with a commonly held assumption that actors who hold power determine directions of reform. Just like the governor of Ognensk who told the participants of OSPU's educational conference that it was important to carry out the tasks set by the country's leaders in the policy Our New School, many researchers and educators assume those in power to be in charge of reform efforts. But these assumptions are no longer viable. The case of policy formation analyzed here demonstrates that those who hold power are only brought in to justify or legitimize reforms that have already been conceptualized by reformers. Similarly, in the United States philanthropic organizations have a much greater influence on setting the agenda for education policy than the federal government itself (Owens 2015; Tompkins-Stange 2016). In the United Kingdom, lobby groups influence not only which reforms become ratified but also how they are covered by the media (Cave and Rowell 2015). The Russian case, yet again, points to a global trend of refashioning the relationship between those in power and those who conceptualize reform but remain in the shadows of the networked governance (S. Ball 2012; S. Ball and Junemann 2012; Wedel 2009).

More specifically, discrepancies in timelines reveal how reformers allocate the role of the director to the president or to the Ministry of Education but themselves select the scripts for the performance and orchestrate its production. Reformers appear as actors on stage who dutifully carry out someone else's orders, just as they produce those orders and insist that they should be carried out as soon as possible. This reshuffling of roles diffuses their responsibility for the proposals. This diffusion leaves no one truly accountable for the directions of reforms—the directors of the performance are missing. The president gets ideas "inserted into his head" and words "written into his speech"; reformers say that it was a higher authority that made these decisions or identified these directions for change. The inner workings of power are obscured; the sources of ideas are made invisible. Those who experience those reforms blame the president or the ministry for their misfortunes, as if they were the actual directors of the dramas of their professional lives. Furthermore, the illusion of democratic participation allows authorities to put the blame back on the educational community. If questions arise or complaints mount, policymakers present the record of all the discussions of the policy that were held to argue that consensus was indeed reached through these conversations.

Looking closely at the composite timeline of events (see below), one will notice that some of the members of the core group engaged heavily with the media, gave regular interviews, and participated in public chats. This might lead to a reasonable question: Does this not suggest that they are taking responsibility for this reform? I believe that their involvement in these activities was about promoting a certain ideology, as they themselves would say. It was not about claiming full authorship rights or being accountable for the outcomes of the reform that was about to be rolled out. Rather, it was about playing the part of a character on stage and perpetuating the myth that the director is someone else. This allows only those who are a part of the production to know who they should be taking cues from. The audience, however, is left with the assumption that the character who plays the president's or the ministry's parts is the actual director of the play. When presidents change or new ministers are appointed, the audience sighs in relief that change is coming. But what they get instead is more of the same reforms that they have been battling before. The change in US administrations is a case in point. George W. Bush's No Child Left Behind wreaked havoc in the public school system. When Obama was elected president, many hoped for a change in educational policies, but Race to the Top issued by his administration only further intensified the measures laid out in NCLB (Ravitch 2011, 2013). In the case of Russian teacher education, despite the multiple changes in individuals who represent institutes of power, reformers pursued the implementation of ideas put forward in the Program of Pedagogical Education Modernization of 2003, the Measures for the Renewal of Teacher Education of 2009, Our New School, and Strategy 2020. That is how the Concept of Support for the Development of Teacher Education emerged.

A Composite Chronology of Policy Formation Events

April 2003 The Ministry of Education issues a decree initiating the Program of Teacher Education Modernization.

March 2004 Andrey Fursenko is appointed Minister of Education and Science of the Russian Federation.

September 2005 LEU holds the seminar "Can Education Manage without Pedagogical Universities?" LEU's rector and Joseph Abramovich chair the seminar. Participants include Vadim Alekseyevich and fourteen others from the

	reformers' network. Conversations focus on the low quality of preparation offered by pedagogical universities and of their graduates. Some participants argue that pedagogical universities should be shut down.
March 2008	Dmitriy Medvedev is elected President of the Russian Federation.
July 2008	Michael Barber and Mona Mourshed's report *How the World's Best-Performing School Systems Come Out on Top* is translated into Russian and published in one of the leading educational journals in Russia.
November 2008	President Medvedev in his address to the Federal Assembly mentions the need to attract talented people "not necessarily with pedagogical education" into schools and orders the development of a new initiative, Our New School.
January 2009	A press release covers the policy proposal Measures for the Renewal of Teacher Education. The policy does not become signed into law.
November 2009	President Medvedev in his address to the Federal Assembly proposes to modernize pedagogical education by "merging pedagogical universities with classical universities" as part of the new initiative Our New School.
February 2010	President Medvedev signs Our New School into law. It emphasizes the need to create "the school of the future" and introduces the transition to the new school standards. Pedagogical universities are supposed to be modernized by being transformed into "large base centers" or attached to classical universities as departments of pedagogy.
February 2011	Mona Mourshed, Chinezi Chijioke, and Michael Barber's report *How the World's Most Improved School Systems Keep Getting Better* is translated into Russian and published in a leading Russian educational journal.

August 2011	President Medvedev holds a meeting dedicated to national priority projects and emphasizes the need "to seriously modernize the network of pedagogical universities."
September 1, 2011	New Federal School Standards take effect in elementary schools.
January 2012	A report is filed that pedagogical education modernization will become a part of the program the Development of Education for 2013–2020.
March 2012	A final version of Strategy 2020 is released. Proposals include modernizing pedagogical education through demonopolization and deinstitutionalization, an internship year, and a qualification exam for anyone who wants to work in a school.
April 2012	President Medvedev holds a meeting dedicated to the problems in K–12 education. LEU's rector and Joseph Abramovich emphasize the need to "drastically change pedagogical education."
May 2012	Vladimir Putin is elected president.
May 2012	Dmitriy Livanov is appointed as the new minister of education.
September 2012	Michael Barber presents his new book *Oceans of Innovation* at one of LEU's seminars.
October 2012	The core group of reformers starts weekly or biweekly meetings to develop reform measures for modernizing pedagogical education.
November 2012	President Putin holds a meeting where he underscores the need to reform pedagogical education to match the needs of the labor market.
January 19, 2013	The first meeting is held to select members for the large working group. The meeting takes place in Lyutvino Special Education University (LSEU).

February 2013	The large working group comes together for a conference at Lyutvino Social Sciences University, cosponsored by Lyutvino Economics University. Vadim Alekseyevich chairs a two-part roundtable entitled "The Development of Pedagogical Education in Russia."
February 22, 2013	The ministry issues a decree stating the large group membership and marking the beginning of their work.
February 2013	Multimedia roundtable with RIA NEWS: "Does Pedagogical Education Have Any Chance?" Participants are Vadim Alekseyevich, Alexander Dmitrievich, Fedor Aleksandrovich, and two others from their network.
March 25, 2013	The minister of education holds a combined meeting with the group that designed the new teachers' professional standards and the group working on institutional transformations in teacher education.
March 2013	A seminar is organized at Ognensk State Pedagogical University (OSPU).
April 2013	The group meets at a conference in Mirotropl', cosponsored by Lyutvino Economics University. They hold a roundtable discussion. The conference receives media attention.
April 2013	The large group meets at a conference in Fevral'sk. A professor from Fevral'sk conducts a foresight session during which Anton Mikhailovich lays out the principles of the changes required in teacher education for it to serve the future.
July 2013	The group meets with the minister to discuss a draft of the Concept.
July 2013	Dmitriy Grigoryevich is appointed rector of Lyutvino Pedagogical University No. 2.
August 2013	The Ministry of Education appoints Fedor Aleksandrovich as a new rector of Lyutvino Pedagogical University No. 1.

October 2013	Anton Mikhailovich presents the Concept during an LEU seminar. Dmitriy Grigoryevich and Fedor Aleksandrovich are discussants.
November 2013	The Concept is discussed at the curriculum meeting in pedagogical education.
December 18, 2013	The new Teachers' Professional Standards are signed into law.
December 2013	The Concept is discussed at the curriculum meeting on pedagogical-psychological education housed at LSEU. The Concept is approved.
December 2013	The Concept is discussed at a public chamber meeting.
January 14, 2014	The Concept appears on the website of the Ministry of Education "for public discussion," together with the letter to the minister stating that the Concept has been discussed at several conferences, meetings of curricular and methodological councils, the public chamber, and other professional meetings. Several pedagogical universities display the Concept and the letter on their websites as well.
January 15, 2014	The Ministry of Education holds a meeting of the joint commission on improving the professional qualifications of pedagogical workers of educational establishments, which includes members of three working groups: teachers' professional standards, teachers' merit-based pay, and modernization of pedagogical education.
January–February 2014	Newspapers and online communities erupt with criticism of the Concept. An article written by Privalov in Ekspert runs under the title "The Reform of Education Will Give Us Community Colleges with Poorly Prepared Graduates Instead of Universities." Reformers invite a journalist to conduct a group interview with them to rebut this critique.
February 2014	The development of pedagogical education and the Concept are discussed at a curriculum committee meeting at one of Lyutvino's pedagogical universities.

February 6, 2014	The Concept is discussed by the State Duma Committee on Education. The discussion is heated. The resolution is mild, but the State Duma Committee does not support the Concept.
February 14, 2014	The Concept is supposed to be discussed at the Ministry of Education's College Meeting (the governing body) to get signed into law and gain official status. The Concept is removed from the agenda and is not discussed. Participants from the teacher education community share that they have managed to block the Concept.
February 28, 2014	The Ministry of Education holds a meeting of the joint commission on improving the professional qualifications of pedagogical workers of educational establishments, which now includes four groups: teachers' professional standards, teacher education modernization, effective contracts (merit-based pay), and "improving the status and prestige of pedagogical workers." The pedagogical education modernization group is tasked with revising the Concept by June 1, so that it could be signed into law by the president's decree.
March 3, 2014	A second meeting dedicated to teacher education reform takes place in the State Duma.
March–May 2014	The group members give interviews and participate in public events dedicated to the Concept of Teacher Education Modernization and to the changes in educational ideology and systems in general.
March 2014	Lyutvino Special Education University, among four contenders, wins the bid for the supervision of the experiment on teacher education modernization reform. It is awarded 86,000,000 Russian rubles (about $2,800,000). Lyutvino Economics University becomes a comanager of the project.
April 2014	The competition for participation in the experiment is announced for other institutions to be awarded approximately 17,000,000 rubles (about $500,000) each.

May 28, 2014	The Ministry of Education signs a decree initiating a Comprehensive Program of Improving the Qualifications of Pedagogical Workers. The program has four strands: teachers' professional standards, teacher education modernization, teachers' merit-based pay, and increasing the prestige of the teaching profession.
June 2014	A public chat is organized by a liberal newspaper at a restaurant in Lyutvino. Participants include Vadim Alekseyevich, Dmitriy Grigoryevich, Victor Anatolyevich, and several others, including a representative of McKinsey. Participants argue that real reforms that would drastically change the system have not happened and that modernization has to go on.
June 2014	Professional development courses for the faculty from universities that have won the competition for the experiment grants are held at LEU and LSEU. Faculty are told to design modules for new programs. The experiment has officially begun.
June 2014	The ministry holds a meeting dedicated to the principles of the Concept and the experiment based on it.
June 2014	During the final seminar at LEU, the topic of teacher education modernization is voted the most pressing topic in Russian education. Alexander Dmitrievich and Anton Mikhailovich outline the direction for the future steps of implementing the Concept and discuss dangers of expecting too much to happen too soon.
June 2014	A petition on change.org is addressed to the President of the Russian Federation asking him to prevent the destruction of a pedagogical university and pedagogical education in general. By October 2014, the petition has almost ten thousand signatures. It receives media attention and causes the second information splash around the Concept. The ministry states that the process of Concept creation was participatory and vows to investigate the problem.

September 1, 2015	New school standards take effect for grades 5–9.
June 2014–November 2015	Teacher education reform based on the Concept is implemented in forty-four universities across the Russian Federation.
November 2015	A cumulative conference on the results of the first stage of the experiment is held at LSSU. Teams from participating institutions describe the aspects of the reform they developed to MOE officials and other academics.
December 2015	The second stage of the experiment receives funding from the Ministry of Education.

4

Light and Shadows

"If the quantity of fluid passing through a pipeline per unit of time remains static or increases only in a linear progression," my physics teacher was fond of intoning during lessons, "it is only logical to assume that it will take a long time for the number of people with access to the pipeline to increase."

—Victor Pelevin, *Empire V*

Lighting plays an important role in theater productions: it "create[s] a selective visibility that subtly directs the spectators' attention" (Gillette 1997, 289). In political spectacle, social constructions of problems similarly receive different amounts of attention—that which politicians construct as a problem may in fact not be perceived as such by a majority of the population (Edelman 1988). What gets pushed into the spotlight becomes the material for constructing the problem and for rallying reform efforts to address it; what gets obscured by the shadows goes unnoticed by the audience. In this chapter, I explore problem constructions that Russian policymakers put forward and explore answers to the following questions: In constructing the problem of Russian teacher education, what is made visible and what is not? What is revealed and what is (un)intentionally obscured?

To explore the answers to these questions, I examine how reformers drew the audience's attention toward failing teacher education by focusing on the "low quality" of students attending these universities and on the ineffectiveness of universities themselves. This problem construction was not used to suggest improvement but rather to call for the elimination of pedagogical universities. The focus on pedagogical universities' failures distracted the audience from the way education was reoriented to serve the economy. Among the actors who stood to benefit most from such transformations were corporations whose involvement in directing educational reforms were left obscured by the shadows.

"Double Negative Selection"

One problem in teacher education that most reformers consistently discussed was the problem of the low quality of its students, dubbed "double negative selection." Some of them were prepared to say it as soon as we started the interview; others paused, as if they were wracking their memories for that one term that so perfectly described the problem. For example, Joseph Abramovich brought it up in the first two minutes of our interview: "It turned out that in these institutions there is double negative selection, meaning the worst [students] go there and then the worst of their graduates go to work in schools, statistically speaking" (Interview 47, February 2014).

Tatyana Borisovna explained this problem to me during our first interview in the following way: "Pedagogical education in Russia is characterized by double negative selection. What this means is that according to the Ministry of Education's monitoring of higher education institutions, applicants with not a very high score on the Unified State Exam go to pedagogical universities, and the graduates of pedagogical universities do not look for employment not only in schools but also in other social spheres. Not the best graduates go to work in schools. That is why you get a double negative selection at the entrance and at the exit points from a pedagogical university" (Interview 41a, January 2014).

LEU's earlier version of the Concept contained a chart that showed this tendency: several specializations were ordered based on the descending average scores on the Unified State Exam: international affairs—86.4; law—79.6; economics—75.3; nuclear physics—73.5; management—72.8; psychology—68.9; pedagogical education—65.2. Listed last in the chart with the lowest average score, pedagogical education appeared to have the "worst" students. Yet, similar to the chart used in the policy (fig. 4), the data in its original context captured a slightly different story. In the report where this data came from, sixty-five specializations were listed in a similar order: from the highest scoring to the lowest scoring. Pedagogical education did not appear at the end of the list, but rather closer to the middle—as number 40.

Most importantly, however, a rupture in this construction occurred when presenters at an LEU seminar showed that the Unified State Exam was not designed to allow comparisons of average scores between different subjects. An analysis conducted by Bochenkov and Val'dman (2013) showed that exams in different disciplines were normed differently: exams in natural sciences had higher average scores than exams in social sciences. Because students who chose physics or medicine as their college majors had to take science exams, their average scores appeared higher. Those who chose pedagogical education had to take social science exams, thus their average scores were lower. This pattern was not a function of student quality (even though that might be a factor as well), but rather a function of the exam design.

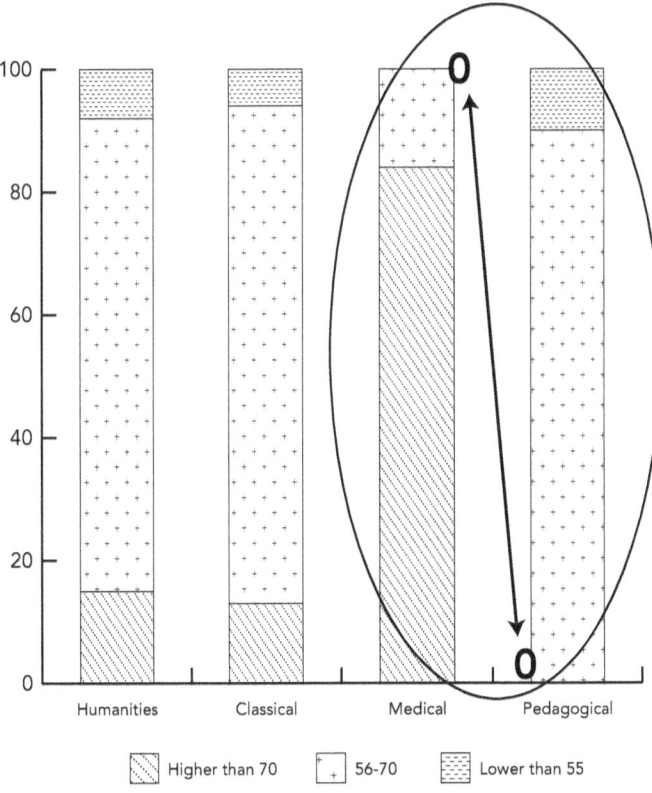

Figure 6. Representations of pedagogical university applicants' performance on the Unified State Exam in reformers' presentations. Reprinted with English translations. Data provided without year of collection.

Despite this discrepancy, one diagram was commonly used to prove the point of "double negative selection" in reformers' presentations of the Concept (fig. 6). Based allegedly on the monitoring of higher education institutions' enrollment data, the diagram showed that 84 percent of medical universities' applicants had scores higher than 70, whereas pedagogical universities had 0; 10 percent of pedagogical universities' applicants had scores lower than 55, whereas medical universities had 0. Zeros played a dramatic role in this representation. They visually dominated the space between the two types of universities, drawing the audience's attention to the emptiness and absence that they represented: the absence of low-performing students in medical universities and the absence of high-performing students in pedagogical universities.

The diagram constructed an optical illusion of sorts. Historically in Russia, pedagogical universities were never compared to medical universities. Their closest counterparts were classical universities. Imagine the second (classical universities) and the last column (pedagogical universities) side by side. You will notice that the drastic difference dissipates. Both groups have low-performing students; both groups have a large number of mid-range students. It is true that pedagogical universities here do not have top-scoring students, but that might be the function of the year when the data was collected as this was not a persistent trend.

Furthermore, available reports from years 2011 to 2013 on students' admissions scores did not match any of the statistics provided in the diagram (fig. 6). For example, table 2 shows that in 2012 when pedagogical universities had no high-performing students, medical universities had 76.5 percent high-performing students, not 84 percent as the diagram suggested. That was also the year when medical universities admitted some low-performing students. Even if we assume that reformers' diagram was based on real data, it did not account for the fluctuations that commonly occur in admission standards from year to year. In 2012 the fewest number of students applied to universities because of demographic decline. This had a profound effect on the admission standards across all sectors. Not considering these factors was a significant omission.

Table 2. Comparison between Pedagogical and Medical Universities in the Number of Students with a Unified State Exam Average Score Higher Than 70

Type of University	2011	2012	2013
Pedagogical Universities	1.6%	0%	10%
Medical Universities	74.5%	76.5%	91.7%

Another factor that needs to be considered is that medical universities did not always receive top applicants. Responding to Anton Mikhailovich's presentation that contained this diagram, Dmitriy Grigoryevich explained that it was nothing more than a fluke that medical universities had such high-scoring applicants: "In the ministry we analyzed why more students started applying to medical universities. We found that a major influence was *Doctor House*[1] and *Interns*.[2] The year when these shows were originally broadcast very abruptly the admission [average] scores started going up. That's when the strong children went there. It got to them somehow" (Video, LEU seminar, October 2013).

This moment of rupture showed how the hard evidence, scientific-looking charts, and ironclad arguments could melt into thin air when alternative explanations revealed cracks in the problem construction.

Despite all the discrepancies, ruptures, and inconsistencies, reformers continued to call pedagogical university students "the weakest" students, "the least qualified" pedagogues, "the dumbest applicants," and "the worst" students. With their derogatory appraisals, they supported and strengthened the narrative circulated in society that someone went to a pedagogical university only because she or he failed to get into other universities. Anton Mikhailovich shared that the notion of "double negative selection" came from the 2007 study by Sobkin and Tkachenko—the same book that served as the source of the graduates' employment diagram (see fig. 5).

Based on survey results from over two thousand students in a large central city, Sobkin and Tkachenko argued that the positive feature of pedagogical education was that it functioned as a mechanism of social mobility for students from lower social strata. Its negative feature was that there seemed to be a "double filter" where "weaker" students ended up in pedagogical education and in schools.[3] The authors noted problems in the contents of pedagogical education: students had few opportunities to engage in research and coursework was often outdated. But they also reflected on positive aspects: students were taught to treat their students with respect, knew their subject well, and could explain their subject matter in an accessible and engaging manner. There was hope, the authors concluded, that the graduates of pedagogical universities were ready to become "new pedagogues" in more humanistically oriented Russian schools.

That hope dissipated by 2010 when Our New School appeared and suggested that pedagogical universities need to be closed or combined with classical universities because they do not prepare teachers "fit enough" for the "new school." The neutrality of the term was lost by the time it reached Strategy 2020 and the Concept of Support for the Development of Teacher

Education: "a double filter" that caught "weaker" students in the sociological study became "a double negative selection" sorting out the "worst" of all for work in schools. The transformations of the terminology used to construct the problem of teacher education seemed to reflect the intensifying push to get rid of the universities that prepared teachers.

Overall, this analysis reveals important aspects of reformers' performance. Similar to reformers in other contexts (see Berliner 2006; Berliner and Biddle 1995; Ravitch 2011, 2013; Smith et al. 2004), they manipulated data to manufacture a crisis in order to accomplish their agendas. The focus on pedagogical universities exaggerated their weaknesses and downplayed their strengths.

The Ministry of Education's Monitoring of Higher Education Institutions

Ineffective Institutions

When I was conducting interviews with reformers, I regularly asked what served as the stimulus for reform. As I mentioned in chapter 2, most of the time I received a response that was consistent with the framing of the problem in the text of the Concept: the monitoring of higher education institutions' effectiveness (Rus. *effectivnost*) revealed that most of the pedagogical universities are ineffective.[4]

The Ministry of Education started this monitoring in 2012 and used five indicators to evaluate performance of higher education institutions: 1) "educational activity" measured by students' scores on the Unified State Exam; 2) "scientific activity" based on research output of the universities' employees (which originally meant R&D and in 2013 included the ability to secure grants and publish in journals indexed in SCOPUS and Web of Science); 3) "international activity" judged by the number of international students; 4) "financial and economic activity" evaluated based on universities' ability to generate revenue; 5) "infrastructure"—universities' assets measured by the area of classroom facilities per student. In 2013, students' ability to find employment was included as the sixth category—"graduates' employment." This was a particularly problematic indicator because it was based on the numbers of those who applied for assistance at job placement agencies and on the numbers of those who were reported as unemployed by those agencies. Even though some of these indicators were used widely outside of Russia, their introduction in the Russian context became quite contentious (see the following discussion). The benchmarks for being judged "effective" set by the ministry seemed to be arbitrary and set unrealistically high (Smolin 2012).

Explaining the role of the monitoring in initiating teacher education reform, Sergey Valdisovich described the situation in the following way: "The ministry carried out the monitoring of higher education institutions, which showed that a quarter of universities have indicators of ineffectiveness. This proportion of 75 to 25 was true across all types of universities. And only among those universities that called themselves pedagogical universities was this proportion flipped—75 percent had indicators of ineffectiveness and 25 percent indicators of effectiveness. Well, without indicators of ineffectiveness. But that nevertheless tells you a lot" (Interview 44, February 2014). What Sergey Valdisovich pointed out here was that when higher education institutions were evaluated based on the five or six indicators of effectiveness, they were labeled "ineffective" if they failed in four or more categories.

Based on the publicly displayed monitoring results from 2013, the pedagogical universities tended to do poorly in three areas. Only 23.53 percent of institutions were found effective in infrastructure, 41.17 percent in financial and economic activity, and 58.82 percent in graduates' employment (see fig. 7).

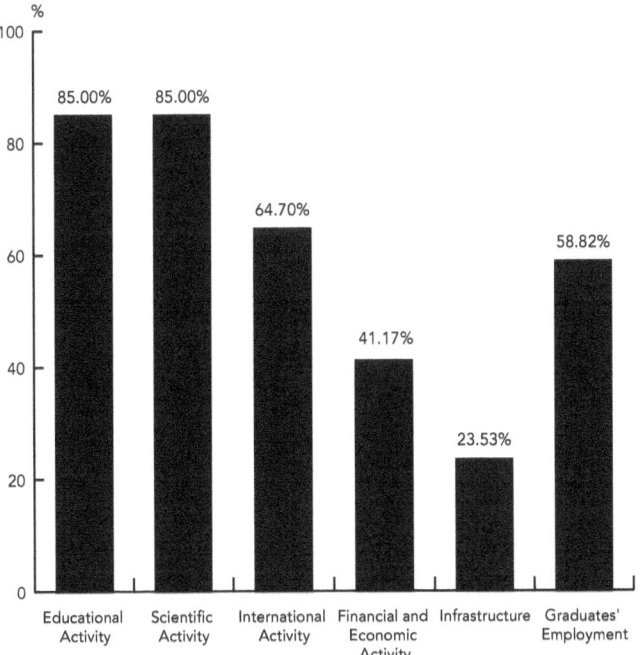

Figure 7. Percentages of "effective" institutions among pedagogical universities based on MOE criteria. Data obtained from http://miccedu.ru/monitoring/2013/.

The history of these institutions as mass institutions by design provided partial explanation for their poor infrastructure, or a lack of facilities (see part 1). The nature of their work—they served schools and other institutions in the social sphere—pointed to the reasons why generating revenue might be a challenge. Reformers, however, never focused on any of these details and, as Sergey Valdisovich's explanation showed, tended to lump institutions together under the label "ineffective." In society at large, however, it was the monitoring itself that was considered "ineffective"—the point to which I turn next.

"The Ineffective Monitoring of Effectiveness"

When monitoring results were first released in 2012, a series of scandals erupted because they labeled many famous and powerful institutions in the country as ineffective (Vazhdaeva 2012). The ministry also appointed a committee to determine which "ineffective" universities should be reorganized, merged, and closed. Newspapers that covered the results of the monitoring called the monitoring itself "ineffective" (Dmitriev 2012) and the day when the results were announced "the end of the world" (Lemutkina 2012). Some stated that "experts believe that the criteria that were not thought through were to blame for the results of the monitoring" (Vazhdaeva 2012). Faculty and students staged protests against the closures of their universities; the rectors' union called the results into question. All of this was to no avail: the measures were presented as objective because they emerged out of "an established procedure" (Lemutkina 2012). Overall, however, monitoring served an important function. Reformers argued for several years that the Russian higher education system was too large to maintain quality and that at least 30 to 40 percent of the universities should be shut down. The monitoring allowed the ministry (and the reformers) to push through the very unpopular measure of reducing the size of the higher education system overall.

Importantly, media coverage of the results did not blame higher education institutions for their ineffectiveness. Most journalists and experts acknowledged that specialized higher education institutions serving such diverse areas as education, arts, agriculture, and industry cannot be evaluated with the same measures as the rest of the system. Instead, it was the Ministry of Education that was blamed for its own incompetence (Dmitriev 2012). One of the articles ran under the title "The Ineffective Monitoring of Effectiveness," which communicated a pervasive sense of contempt and disdain for the ministry's actions.

"Bringing Down" Pedagogical Universities

Regardless of the problems inherent in the design of the monitoring exercise, the data it produced provided reformers with the "evidence" that pedagogical universities should be closed. Anton Mikhailovich had the most to say about the usefulness of the monitoring results: "Whether it is good or bad but a year ago, the Ministry of Education started conducting the monitoring of higher education institutions. So, attempts to bring down teacher education . . . to do something with teacher education happened before. Many times. Each reform touched teacher education in one way or the other. But teacher education is hard to bring down [or destroy, Rus. *svalit'*] because their graduates occupy all the key positions."

I was sincerely surprised, "Really?" This seemed to contradict the logic of the weakest students entering the weakest institutions that reformers so neatly packaged under the problem of "double negative selection," but I did not say anything about that.

"Of course. What other institution . . . Imagine some regional city. They have a forestry institute, a medical institute, and a pedagogical institute. Who will become the secretary of the regional [Communist] party office? It is going to be the graduate of the history department of the pedagogical university. They were very strong. In the central cities, pedagogical universities didn't play a significant role. But in the regions, pedagogical universities most often prepared key administrators. That's why it was hard to do anything about them. The universities in the central cities would block all attempts at reform. In the regions, graduates of pedagogical universities also blocked reform efforts.

"And then the monitoring was introduced. It could have been good. It could have been bad. It does not matter. Probably, it was worse, not better, because indicators were not the best. But they were nevertheless there. Based on these indicators it turned out that pedagogical universities are in deep crisis compared to universities of other types. Well, you can't fight with the thermometer. If it registers fever, you gotta do something about it. They figured out that there is no one to turn to. Those who work inside this system, what, are they going to change themselves? So, they put together a team that is related to education but is not located inside the system" (Interview 48, February 2014).

Anton Mikhailovich's explanation provided insight into the role of the monitoring in the construction of crisis around teacher education. Before there had been numerous attempts "to bring teacher education down." The verb that Anton Mikhailovich used is the verb that in Russian describes the act of overpowering a strong opponent in a physical fight. Joseph Abramovich tellingly described pedagogical education as that which "*should have been destroyed* long ago." That sentiment was expressed as early as 2005 when Lyutvino conducted a roundtable discussion—Can Education Manage without Pedagogical Universities?—chaired by LEU's rector and Joseph Abramovich. At that time one of LEU's professors described the contradictions that emerged in Russian teacher education and concluded with the following statement: "What should we do if the quality of the cadres does not meet the requirements of the time? We have multiple alternatives. The first one is simple but attractive: 'down to the foundations, and then . . .'⁵ I like this option best. We know examples of such painful destruction of a worn-out social institution to the foundation, to the roots, and then building a new one from scratch, according to the new plan. According to the plan that will match the requirements of this half of a century" (VO 2005).

The quote the speaker used came from the Russian version of the "International Anthem of Socialism": "We will destroy this world of violence / Down to the foundations, and then / We will build our new world." The social institutions referred to here might be the centrally controlled economy of the Soviet Union destroyed through the introduction of market economy. This was accomplished through the shock therapy advocated by Western advisors and often carried out under the supervision of LEU's professors and experts. It is likely that the radical transformations of the nineties were referenced here as the preferable path for reforming teacher education. This refrain came to represent the reformers' stance on problems in teacher education, and Anton Mikhailovich's description of the problems fit well with this agenda.

The monitoring then provided data to prove the existing point—something had to be done with teacher education. It drew the ministry's and, supposedly, the public's attention to the problem of Russian teacher education, giving the reformers justification to "bring it down." It is interesting that Anton Mikhailovich drew on the metaphor of sickness: the monitoring was a thermometer; the data it generated revealed "high temperature." This metaphor appeared in several other interviews among those who belonged to their network. This metaphor did important work: it allowed Anton Mikhailovich to justify the appearance of reformers as those who could act as doctors. Acting as an external authority that the ministry could trust because they are "related to education but are outside of the system," reformers could now perform the treatment. The question was what they wanted this treatment to accomplish.

Technically, some of that treatment was initiated earlier. As I mentioned in chapter 3, in 2010, Dmitriy Grigoryevich introduced Our New School, which stated that pedagogical institutions should be merged with classical universities. This suggests that these institutions were targeted for closure even before the monitoring exercise; the monitoring exercise took away institutions' power to bargain and to fight for their survival. That is when the numbers started dwindling—from seventy institutions in 2008 to forty-eight in 2013 ("or forty-four, or thirty-three, or maybe even twenty-five"—as my participants from pedagogical universities joked). The Concept alluded to this change by saying that "the number of pedagogical universities is declining." Dmitriy Grigoryevich described this process in a very naturalizing and neutralizing way: "When competition between institutions started in the nineties, citizens preferred classical over pedagogical universities. And tried to get there. Better faculty moved from pedagogical universities to classical universities. So, subject preparation in pedagogical universities became of lower quality. . . . About seven years ago there were about seventy pedagogical universities. Then many pedagogical universities started 'clinging' and merging with other universities. So, there are not many of them left" (Interview 45, February 2014).

The light pointed on stage concealed substitution of actors—not the ministry issuing decrees of closure, potentially under reformers' suggestions, but pedagogical universities pursuing mergers themselves. This allowed Dmitriy Grigoryevich to normalize the ministry's actions. His account of how the system of pedagogical education had been transformed supported the construction of the problem promoted by reformers: teacher education was of such low quality that everyone recognized it and tried to address it, either by mergers or by sending children to other institutions.

"Defended, Not Surrendered"

However, what I saw in 2012 and in 2013 were institutions under threat that were preparing to fight tooth and nail to survive. OSPU's education conference that I described in the introduction was one such example. Another example came from my trip to Fevral'sk, where a new rector was trying to revamp the pedagogical university into a school of social work and special education studies with the help of the team from LEU. There I was told a story about what happened when Fevral'sk State Pedagogical University was declared ineffective based on the ministry's monitoring. A university faculty took me on an impromptu tour of the town in a university car driven by the university driver. I asked about higher education institutions in the city and they told me that several were merged into a federal university; but the pedagogical university "was defended, not surrendered, and left alone." How, I wondered. The driver embarked on his story.[6]

"We used to have a governor. He kept threatening to merge the pedagogical university with the classical university in town. Our rector had a lot of connections, everywhere. He made a whole bunch of phone calls and people from all over the world started calling our governor telling him to leave our pedagogical university alone. Politicians, governors from Germany, from America, from Canada. Then our rector took a bottle of whiskey and went to talk to our governor. I took him there myself. We arrived at eleven at night and until six in the morning they were 'talking.' Our rector got out of there smashed, but the governor afterward said, 'No one should touch the pedagogical university. It must have its own life.' Of course, all these people got to him, calling all the time. He did, though, leave the governor's post here, moved somewhere close to the Caucasus, and merged universities there. These mergers, they are bad. Nothing good ever comes out of them" (Field Notes, January 2014).

The monitoring of higher education institutions and its consequences for pedagogical universities were a contentious matter. The language used by teacher education participants to describe these was the language of war and battle, not the language of sick patients who needed professional help. Reformers used the monitoring to exaggerate the weaknesses of pedagogical universities and to construct the image of failing institutions that could do nothing to fix themselves. This construction facilitated rapid closures and mergers of half of those universities. It was also used to justify the reforms introduced by the Concept. The inconsistencies in the construction of the problem, the fictionalized data, as well as the contradictions between problems and solutions, however, raised questions about that which remained in the dark. In other words, if the audience's attention was directed toward the weak and failing pedagogical institutions, what remained obscured by the shadows? To the exploration of this question I turn next.

Building a New World: New Schools, New Teachers, and New Subjects

As I proceeded with my fieldwork, I became increasingly aware that there was more to this drama than just the urge to fix failing institutions. Elimination of pedagogical universities was necessary to create new institutions. As Sergey Valdisovich explained to me, "the work [on the Concept] started because there emerged a need . . . to change teacher preparation so that [teachers] would match . . . so that they could prepare children that match the modern world, the life around us, the economy . . ."

As we proceeded with the interview, he elaborated on these points: "Many of the ideas come from the 2000s, when it became clear that many countries are reforming their pedagogical education because it is an important stage in transforming the economy. If we want to talk about innovation, or about a postindustrial society, about economy that does not rely on natural resources, we should be talking about people who can work in new ways. Live and work in new ways. And we arrive at a school, we come to the teacher" (Interview 44, February 2014).

Sergey Valdisovich, similar to other reformers, suggested that to create a new economy, schools and teachers should produce new people. His answer showed that reforms of teacher education were not only about tearing an old world "down to the foundations" but also about building a new world—the type of new world envisioned by the term "modernization" that accompanied attempts to change teacher education since the early 2000s. Most overtly, discussions about modernization happened when Strategy 2020 was being prepared. As one of the members of the working group Our New School noted, "modernization should be not economic and technological, not political, but first and foremost sociocultural."[7] To accomplish sociocultural modernization first, so that economic modernization could follow, it was necessary "to change values," which could only be accomplished by creating new educational institutions. This vision redefined purposes of schooling and reoriented teachers' work, positioning them at the service of the economy rather than cultural continuity, social cohesion, or development of democracy. In the next section, I explore these transformations in more detail.

New School Producing a New Subject

Both the 2010 policy explicitly titled Our New School and the section "New School" in Strategy 2020 demonstrated this pursuit of new forms. The creation of the new school was based on the globally circulated discourses of human capital and knowledge economy. Many in the reformers' network argued that future generations needed to be prepared "to work with their heads, not their hands." In an article dedicated to the argument in favor of a new type of school, one of the experts wrote, "From the perspective of global trends in social development, the deciding role in the life of society in the twenty-first century will be played by people of intellectual labor [Rus. *umstvennogo truda*] who are set apart by their ability to see a problem and find a solution for it" (VO, 2013).

Like many other aspects of my story, this argument was not without its own paradoxes. Even though the new school was supposed to help Russia develop a knowledge economy and prepare students for innovation, many experts insisted that it should *not* have "scientific foundations" or the disciplinary orientation that Russian schools inherited from the Soviet past. Rather, reformers claimed that schools should focus on "socialization."[8] Vadim Alekseyevich contended that society wanted schools to provide socialization more than anything else: "There have always been and always will be parents who will say, 'Listen, do whatever you want with him. Don't bother me with my child's problems.' There have been and now there are more parents that have begun talking about socialization of their children. It is connected to the Internet . . . to drugs . . . to a lot of examples of asocial behavior . . . 'We want socialization.' Grandmas and grandpas remember their pioneer and Komsomol units and say, 'There used to be socialization. But what is left now? The street?'" (Interview 55, February 2014).

In the policies they proposed, reformers replaced knowledge transmission with socialization as the primary role for schools. For example, Our New School referred to schools as institutions that should guarantee "successful socialization" of all students. Strategy 2020 spelled out two main purposes of this socialization: "ensuring school graduates' readiness to continue learning" and helping "school graduates achieve high levels of social competencies and civil positions" (Strategy 2020 2013, 344).

In their writing, reformers and experts in their networks presented qualities that graduates should have as "behavioral archetypes" that should serve as "vectors of children's socialization."[9] For example, in an interview for an educational newspaper, one of the experts shared the following list of qualities that schools should develop in children: "adaptability, responsibility, ability to choose, ability to learn on one's own, the skill of self-development, ability to keep one's word, ability to work in networks and teams, creativity, critical thinking, ingenuity, value-based structure of a person—his/her value system; loyalty to the organization (class, school, state, region, firm/company)" (UG 2009).

Many items on this list are familiar to readers from a variety of contexts—discourses of knowledge economy and innovation circulate around the world a relatively standard list of desired qualities that schools should develop in their students (Lauder et al. 2012). This list, as the interviewee acknowledged, was based on his knowledge of educational scholarship published in the West. These qualities were supposed to characterize a New Subject for the innovative economy. Many of these qualities have also become synonymous with neoliberal ideology and the construction of a neoliberal subject—an individual driven by responsibility, choice, and self-advancement (Ong 2006). Particularly striking on this list is the last item both because it emphasized "loyalty" that schools should develop and because it included "firm" and "company" as the institutions that individuals should feel loyal to.

Many of these qualities appeared in the new standards for general school that went into effect September 1, 2011. The standards were "oriented toward the development of students' personal qualities" (Federal Standards for General Education 2012, 4) captured in the "graduate's portrait" (fig. 8). Some items

> 1. Loves his local area and his Motherland, respects his people, their culture, and their spiritual traditions;
> 2. Knows and accepts traditional values of family, Russian civil society, multicultural Russian society, humanity. Recognizes own role in the fate of the nation;
> 3. Creative, critical thinker, active and purposeful in learning about the world. Recognizes the value of education, science, labor, and art for a person and for society;
> 4. Possesses the skills of scientific methods of inquiry of the world;
> 5. Motivated for creativity and innovative activity;
> 6. Prepared for cooperation; able to engage in learning and research, project, as well as information retrieval activities;
> 7. Recognizes self as a person; socially active; respects law and order; recognizes responsibility for the family, society, state, and humanity;
> 8. Respects other people's opinions; able to carry out a constructive dialogue, to reach mutual understanding and to cooperate successfully;
> 9. Consciously following and advocating for the rules of a healthy, safe, and ecologically sound lifestyle;
> 10. Prepared for a conscious choice of a profession; understands and recognizes the significance of professional activity for a person and for society;
> 11. Motivated for life-long learning and self-education.

Figure 8. Portrait of a graduate (Federal Standards for General Education 2012, 3–4).

on this list were rooted in Russia's recent struggles. For example, the love for the Motherland was a legacy of Soviet educational policies brought back to combat high numbers of emigrants who allegedly left the country because they lacked patriotism (Aydarova 2017b). Focus on a healthy and safe lifestyle revealed the state's attempt to address Russia's recent demographic challenges: high mortality rates; rapid decline in life expectancy, especially among males; and low fertility rates leading to "demographic pits" (Rus. *demographicheskaya yama*).

Apart from qualities that emerged in response to national struggles, there were also those that represented global flows of educational transformations. Items 3, 5, 6, 9, and 11 echoed qualities and traits that can now be found in standards documents of nations across the globe: cooperation, creativity, and critical thinking became the buzzwords associated with twenty-first-century competencies. Those were believed to be necessary for the creation of a knowledge economy and for securing a nation's competitiveness. In a way, the standards set the agenda for creating universal neoliberal subjects—subjects whose qualities made them indistinguishable from subjects in China, India, or the United States because similar qualities were promoted as targets for educational systems around the world.

Russia's attempts throughout the Soviet era to create a distinct subject—different from those produced by capitalist educational systems—became erased with the push for universal "soft skills" allegedly necessary for the participation in the global economy. This erasure demonstrated most clearly the change in the purposes of schooling. For decades before this, standards documents, along with textbooks in pedagogy or curriculum guides, included the statement "A graduate should know the scientific, literary, and artistic accomplishments of humanity and his/her society." This phrase harkens back to the Soviet conception of encyclopedic knowledge that schools should transmit to students. In their evaluations of the Russian system, international organization reports described this conception as a deficiency (Canning et al. 2004; OECD 1998). In the new standards, this aspect was missing. Instead, "an appreciation for science, education, labor, and art" appeared. No longer responsible for knowledge transmission, schools had to facilitate students' "personal development," the parameters of which were predetermined as a set of qualities necessary to live in "the modern world." Those qualities set the parameters for specific "behavior archetypes," foreclosing possibilities of open-ended human becoming.

Discussions of the new standards caused an uproar in society. Their introduction did not create the change desired by policymakers. Teachers and schools put on a performance of having complied with the new standards without really changing much in their daily teaching (Aydarova "Fiction-Making"). Thus, a new slogan emerged—that a new school needed a new teacher.

New Teacher: Not to Enlighten or Educate, but to Develop and Regulate

Russia inherited from the Soviet Union the system of itemizing job responsibilities, knowledge expectations, and minimum qualification requirements for a wide range of professional and workers' positions, known as the *Unified Qualification Manual for Administrators, Specialists, and Workers*. Teachers and other professionals working in schools were also included in the system. Teachers' qualification characteristics listed in this manual were extensive. The teacher was responsible for teaching, upbringing, "supporting the formation of individual's culture" (Rus. *kul'tura lichnosti*), socialization, and assisting students "in a conscious choice of individual learning trajectories." Interwoven throughout job responsibilities were expectations placed on teachers in helping students develop knowledge, skills, and abilities, at the same time as they "protect students' rights and freedoms . . . respecting their human dignity, honor, and reputation." Nowhere on this list appeared references to students' behavior.

In May 2012, President Putin allegedly ordered the development of new professional standards. Similar to the process of Concept development, it is quite likely that reformers pushed for this idea backstage. A 2012 book written by a journalist who often supported and promoted reformers' efforts outlined the direction that the new standard would take: "A new pedagogue is needed for the new model of education in innovative economy. It must be a person who likes teaching, who tries to facilitate people's growth and gets satisfaction from people acquiring new competencies."

A working group of eleven educators prepared teachers' professional standards. Fedor Aleksandrovich and his wife were on this team, along with a professor from the Lyutvino Special Education University (who was later involved in the Concept implementation). The work was headed by a renowned educator closely associated with the reformers' network and Anton Mikhailovich's good friend. The first draft that the Ministry of Education shared with the public stated that a changing world required a new teacher whose main quality was "the ability to learn." The old detailed qualification characteristics were described as "cumbersome" and "constraining teacher's initiative." The new standard was supposed to "liberate a pedagogue, give a new impetus for his development."

The new professional standard for teachers that reflected this vision was signed into law in December 2013. It constructed the role of a teacher as someone who facilitated development rather than participated in enlightenment or knowledge creation (table 3). Similar to the standards for general education, teachers' professional standards had little engagement with the question of knowledge. Anton Mikhailovich in his presentation of the early version of the Concept emphasized the move away from the teacher as a subject area specialist: "If you read the professional standard, you will realize, it practically has nothing to say about subject knowledge." He paused and he looked at the audience. Then he slowly repeated, "It practically has nothing to say about subject knowledge. We can have different attitudes about it. I think it is an unrealistic standard, I think no teacher can ever achieve it . . . But the reference point, or I would say the emphasis, lies outside of this subject knowledge" (Video, Fevral'sk Conference, April 2013). Media coverage of the new standards explained this point by stating that teachers' knowledge of the subject matter should not exceed school curriculum.

Unlike prior qualification characteristics, the new standard focused more on teachers regulating students' behavior and managing students' development (table 3). Of particular interest is a line that appears both in columns B (item 10) and C (item 9). It states that a teacher was responsible for the "development of students' learning activity, independence, initiative, creative abilities, civil position formation, ability for labor and life in the conditions of the modern world, shaping students' culture of a healthy and safe lifestyle." These qualities reflected the parameters for students' development set by school standards. This appeared to be a significant departure from the prior frameworks that held the teacher responsible for protecting students' freedom, dignity, and honor and for developing students' individual cultures (Rus. *kul'tura lichnosti*) that had no predetermined outcomes. These transformations in how teachers' work was conceptualized were significant in light of another concurrent change—the introduction of performance pay, or "effective contract." The new professional standard was supposed to become the foundation for evaluating teachers' performance and merit-based pay.

Reformers promoted the changes in teachers' professional standards; they also realized that those changes were not widely supported. This realization prompted them to alter their performance, so that the new ideologies they were promoting would not always be visible to the audience. For example, during the group interview, Vadim Alekseyevich explained to a journalist that the new teacher should be "a facilitator, a tutor, an organizer of the learning process." When several minutes later it turned out that the jour-

Table 3. Teachers' Labor Functions According to the New Professional Standards (emphasis added)

A. General Pedagogic Function/Teaching	B. Upbringing Activity	C. Developing Activity
1. Development and implementation of curriculum within the frame of general education curriculum	1. Regulating students' behavior to create a safe educational environment	1. Identifying in the process of observations students' behavior and personality problems connected to their developmental stage
2. Carrying out professional activity in accordance with federal state educational standards of preschool, elementary, general education	2. Implementation of modern upbringing approaches, including interactive forms and methods, their use in class and during extracurricular activities	2. Evaluation of parameters and design of psychological safety and comfortable educational environment, development of programs that prevent different forms of violence at school
3. Participation in developing and implementing of the educational organization's program of development	3. Setting upbringing goals that foster students' development regardless of their abilities and character	3. Using instruments and methods of diagnosing and evaluating the level and dynamics of child development
4. Planning and carrying out lessons	4. Setting and accepting clear rules of students' behavior in accordance with the educational organization's handbook and internal rules of the educational establishment	4. Use and application of psychological and pedagogical technologies (including inclusive) necessary for targeted work with different types of children: gifted children, socially vulnerable children, children in difficult life circumstances, migrant children, orphans, children with special needs (autistic children, children with ADHD, hyperactive children), children with disabilities, children with behavioral deviations, children with addictions
5. Systematic analysis of lessons' and educational approaches' effectiveness		
6. Organization, control, and assessment of students' ongoing and final mastery of educational programs	5. Designing and implementing upbringing programs	
7. Formation of universal study actions		

ciontinued on next page

Table 3 (continued)

A. General Pedagogic Function/Teaching	B. Upbringing Activity	C. Developing Activity
8. Formation of information information communication technology skills	6. Drawing on upbringing capabilities of the child's different activities (study, play, labor, sports, art, etc.)	5. Giving students targeted assistance
9. Formation of motivation for learning	7. Designing of situations and events that develop students' emotional and value-oriented environment (the culture of feeling and value orientations of a child)	6. Interacting with other specialists within the framework of psychological-medical consultations
10. Objective assessment of students' knowledge based on tests and other methods of control/assessment	8. Help and support for the organization of students' self-governance	7. Development (together with other specialists) and implementation together with parents (legal guardians) individual program plans for child's development
	9. Creation and support for the organization, atmosphere, and traditions of the educational organization's life	8. Learning and appropriate application of special technologies and methods that allow correctional and developmental work to be carried out
		9. Development of students' learning activity, independence, initiative, creative abilities, civil position formation, ability for labor and life in the conditions of the modern world, shaping students' culture of healthy and safe lifestyle
		10. Formation and implementation of programs that develop universal learning actions, models

10. Development of students' learning activity, independence, initiative, creative abilities, civil position formation, ability for labor and life in the conditions of the modern world, shaping students' culture of healthy and safe lifestyle

11. Formation of tolerance and the skills of behavior in a changing multicultural environment

12. Using parents' (legal guardians') constructive upbringing efforts, helping the family solve problems in bringing up a child

and values of social behavior, the skills of behaving in the world of virtual realities and social networks, formation of tolerance and positive models of multicultural communication

11. Formation of students' behavior and activity regulation

nalist himself worked as a teacher in school but illegally because he had no pedagogical education, Maksim Davydovich started laughing. "Listen," he said in between laughs, "we won't tell anyone that you have no right to work at a school and you don't tell anyone that we want to turn all teachers into facilitators, alright? Because otherwise, the discussion of our Concept will be over." The word "facilitator" did not appear in the final text of the article. Maksim Davydovich was right, however. The word "facilitator" was not popular in the pedagogical community. During a methods class I observed in Ognensk, the professor asked the students if they knew what they would be called based on the new policies. When she told them that they now would be "facilitators," the class erupted in angry laughter (Field Notes, October 2013).

Despite its problematic reception, the reorientation of teachers' work manifested in the new professional standards was soon translated into the new expectations for teacher preparation. During our interview, Vadim Alekseyevich explained, "We managed to explain to Minister Livanov that if we want to transition to the new standards, teacher education must change" (Interview 55, February 2014). The change entailed reducing subject knowledge preparation and increasing the psychology and pedagogy components. In an article describing the Concept, Vadim Alekseyevich wrote, "The modern school does not require a teacher with (subject) knowledge preparation, as it used to do, but serious *psychological and pedagogical training* without which the teacher will not be able to handle school standards" (OP 2012, emphasis added). The connection of this shift to the school standards indicated that teachers should be skillful users of new psychological methods and approaches in order to develop new subjects.

In itself, the focus on pedagogy and psychology may not appear harmful. In the United States, debates about knowledge for teaching occur between those who argue that subject knowledge is enough to be a good teacher (Gladwell 2009; Hanushek and Rivkin 2004; Hess 2002) and those who claim that to be a good teacher one needs to know pedagogy, psychology, and teaching methods (Darling-Hammond and Bransford 2005). The reformers' position appears to align with what teacher education communities in many parts of the world, including the United States, might support. The trouble lies in the roles that teachers are expected to play in the new economy. Disciplining students' bodies and minds with the tools of pedagogy and psychology are given more attention than teachers' role in imparting to students the knowledge necessary to create, innovate, or imagine alternatives. According to reformers, these standards set out "to adapt children to the modern world" rather than teach them how to transform it. In 2007, a Russian minister of education explained it this way: "The downside of the Soviet educational system was its attempt to produce a Creator, but now the task is to produce a well-trained consumer who knows how to use products that result from someone else's creativity."[10]

Most importantly, the standards and the reformers' designs for teacher education depoliticize teaching. As Zeichner (2009) observed in an "unequal and unjust society . . . teacher educators are morally obligated not only to pay attention to social and political issues in the education of teachers, but to make them central concerns" (54). Issues of inequality and injustice are absent from the policies that are reorienting teachers' work in Russia.

Guy Debord (1998, 22) makes an important point about the relationship between knowledge (the role of which is downplayed both in school and in teachers' standards) and a subject's social position: "The spectator is simply supposed to know nothing and deserve nothing. Those who are always watching to see what happens next will never act: such must be the spectator's position." In chats, in offhand comments during presentations, or in quick statements during our interviews, referring to the events in Ukraine in December of 2013 when protesters occupied Madison, the central square of the capital, until the government stepped down, reformers said, "We don't need another Maidan." Reflecting a similar ideology, Vadim Alekseyevich explained to me during the interview that the civil rights struggles in the United States happened because of protesters' lack of education. Were they better educated, they would not have taken to the streets. Together these comments revealed reformers' general orientation against social protests and their belief that teachers were responsible for preventing those from happening. Thus, the new standard became the foundation for conceptualizing the work of a teacher as both "the manager of human capital" and a regulator of students' behavior who prevents social unrest. Or, as Debord would argue, a new teacher is a producer of spectators.

Shchedrovitsky Connection: Pedagogy to Blueprint New Subjects

The new framing of teachers' work was connected to Shchedrovitsky's writing on the role of pedagogy in society. Connections between reforms and Shchedrovitsky's philosophy were rarely discussed voluntarily with me. Only Vadim Alekseyevich explained to me that the current wave of pedagogical education reforms dated back to the 1980s when he and several other reformers participated in a seminar organized by Shchedrovitsky. In preparation for that seminar, Vadim Alekseyevich read Shchedrovitsky's *Logic and Pedagogy*. That book was helpful for his doctoral dissertation on pedagogical education modernization and for designing his own approach to preparing teachers. Partly, it was this approach that was being reproduced through the Concept.

Before I delve further, I want to note that Vadim Alekseyevich's observation is important not only for his personal case, but for the team of reformers in general. As I showed in chapter 1, many of the reformers had connections to the Shchedrovitsky network. When I realized these connections, I attended a conference organized in Shchedrovitsky's memory. It was there that I saw Sergey Valdisovich and Zinaida Vladislavovna strolling casually through the halls of the expensive hotel where the event was held. It was also there that I had an eye-opening exchange with the organizer of the Pedagogical Olympiad at one of Lyutvino's most prestigious universities. As we were grabbing our food during a break, I asked him what he thought of the presentations. He smiled and said, "The most important part is what happens behind the curtain [Rus. *v kuluarah*]." "But how does one get behind that curtain?" I asked wide-eyed. "Behind the curtain is here. Right in this hall" (Field Notes, February 2014).

Even though education was not of primary interest to Shchedrovitsky, according to Joseph Abramovich, his book *Logic and Pedagogy* (1993) focused on the purposes and methods of education. In the opening of the book, Shchedrovitsky lamented the fact that Soviet pedagogy prioritizes the contents of education over its methods and argued for the need to redesign the relationships between science and pedagogy. Later in the book, he employed the language of engineering to speak about designs for human beings that the society or economy would need in the future. According to his explanation, it was necessary to identify the niches that these human beings would occupy, identify the type of activity they would carry out, and then develop pedagogy as the science that allowed these blueprints to be reproduced in individual children. "From the system of pedagogy emerges the unique specialization of educational blueprinter, who develops the model and blueprint for a member of the future society" (qtd. by Kukulin 2011, 78).

In the text, Shchedrovitsky acknowledged that some of his audience might be appalled at such a cynical reading of education, but he dismissed the thought by saying that every society was doing it anyway. All he was allegedly proposing was the technological clarity that should guide this process. Kukulin discussed Shchedrovitsky's ideas as an "alternative social blueprinting . . . for a transformed human nature" (54). Shchedrovitsky's writing emerged during Soviet times and echoed much of the Soviet ideology surrounding education: schools were expected to produce the New Man based on the official state ideology. The modern-day reappearance of this theory represented an ironic continuity between the Soviet past and the neoliberal present. Yet it was also markedly different because of the new corporate actors involved in shaping the new subject—a point I will explore in more detail later.

Vadim Alekseyevich, as one of Shchedrovitsky's disciples, in his doctoral dissertation put forward the blueprint for a reflexive agent, responsible for self-construction and his life position. In this framing, the educational system was supposed to produce "a free man, a cultural subject of his own activity, consciously and responsibly making decisions based on specific cultural and historical antecedents." Referring to Vygotsky, Elkonin, Davydov, and Shchedrovitsky (the latter did not appear in the reference list for political reasons), Vadim Alekseyevich rejected the knowledge-based paradigm of education and proposed a new paradigm for teachers' work: "Know what is developing in your student and support it with the tools of the subject you are teaching." In his interview, however, this became translated into a less idealistic dictum: "Children from the part of town where alcoholics live don't need advanced mathematics and knowledge of algebraic functions. The teacher should use math to develop them as people" (Interview 55, February 2014). As someone who grew up "in the part of town where alcoholics live," with an alcoholic father, I was shaken when I heard this statement. Without "the advanced mathematics and knowledge of algebraic functions" that I was taught at school, I would never have been able to take the GRE and end up in a graduate school in the United States. The theory translated into a model where elites deserved the education they needed for access to higher education and the rest of the children received education that kept them "well adapted to the changing world" (the phrase often repeated in the reformers' network and in the McKinsey report—a connection that will be discussed in the next chapter).

Shchedrovitsky's methodological tools were often used for subjects' "adaptation" in the corporate world. Many among those who left the Shchedrovitsky network shared that they were uncomfortable with the manipulation of human consciousness that Shchedrovitsky engaged in during the games he organized. Those who identified with his ideas boasted about the corporate use of Shchedrovitsky's games and other tools to foster "ideological alignment" among a corporation's employees. During a Shchedrovitsky conference, one of the panels spoke about the project they conducted for a

Russian corporation where they "adjusted workers' thinking to achieve the corporation's plan of development." One of the speakers described the role of the "anthropotechnician" in developing a corporation—he changed people by changing their thinking or changed people by firing them and hiring new ones. "People should be grown or developed for specific positions," she explained to the audience.

After the presentation, an audience member raised questions about the (im)morality of manipulating human consciousness that was involved in "changing people's thinking"; the question was quickly dismissed. Zinaida Vladislavovna—a member of the working group on teacher education modernization from the reformers' network—asked whether there should be an actor who could monitor and limit the influence of an anthropotechnician. "No, the corporation is the only body that can set the limits for what can and cannot happen" was the presenter's answer.[11]

This presentation and the exchange that happened after it troubled me for a long time. The elimination of human freedom (in humanistic, not in a neoliberal sense) that such "adaptation" pursued and the normalization of manipulation it entailed revealed a treacherous path for the future of education. The presence of at least two working group members and the minister of education's advisor in the audience made me wonder about the impact of these conversations on educational developments that reformers and experts pursued in their work. During my interview with the MOE advisor that happened right after the conference, I asked if the minister of education supported Shchedrovitsky's approaches. "Shchedrovitsky's son and I had a lengthy conversation with the minister recently where we discussed the future of education and, of course, we spoke about the ideas that were discussed here. What concept of the world, what form of thinking, what worldview will be the leading forms . . . Of course we referred to Shchedrovitsky, his school, his writing on systems thinking . . . ," he explained.

I asked what the minister's response to those ideas was.

"He managed to set aside three hours for a conversation with us. I think that shows that he is interested in seeing what this approach has to offer" (Interview 51, February 2014).

Corporate Connections: Shadows in the Dark

The reformers' connections to the Shchedrovitsky network and to the corporate sector revealed the outlines of the shadows lurking in the dark.

Sometimes the corporate presence in educational reforms became visible only in offhand comments or indirect observations that participants made. Corporate influence also appeared in experts' and reformers' framing of educational reforms in general and teacher education modernization in particular. But my ability to explore and analyze this influence was limited because participants often evaded answering questions on this topic. What I present here is a tentative exploration of the connections that emerged despite these limitations.

An exchange with a participant from outside the reformers' network first pointed me to the question of corporate involvement in educational reform and revealed how roles in setting agendas for social transformations had been reconfigured. At the end of my interview with an OSPU faculty member who was actively involved in discussions of the Concept, I asked him about the state demands for the production of citizens. I was curious how the changes that were happening would allow the state to have the citizens it needed. His response left me speechless for a minute.

"Is there a state demand for ecological disaster?"

"No," I mumbled in response.

"But we have it . . . We understand perfectly well that in Russia the state demand [Rus. *zapros gosudarstva*] is dictated by the corporations' wishes. What do corporations need? A citizen or a consumer?" (Interview 6, November 2013).

A former military man, he responded to my question with another question. Russia and many countries around the world watched how corporations pursued higher profits through excessive extraction of natural resources, pollution, and deforestation (Davidov 2012; Tsing 2005). This corporate demand for higher profits created ecological disasters that occurred regardless of what state demands might be. This twist in the conversation revealed how naïve my assumptions were. By looking at the state, its demands and its responsibilities, I was unable to see other more powerful actors involved in shaping educational agendas. Similar to other observers of educational reforms in Russia, I focused on what was most visible—failing pedagogical universities, the ministry, the president, and the state. But I missed that which was obscured by the shadows. Intrigued by this revelation, I asked him whether he could name the corporations involved in Russian education reforms. He refused to answer.

In other contexts, my questions about corporate involvement in any spheres of Russian education were met with similar walls of silence. Private sector actors interested in the rollout of Russian educational reforms remained obscured by the shadows when all the attention was directed at failing state institutions. Perhaps, the fear of possible repercussions of conversations about them also added to this effect.

One way in which corporate influence on the framing of educational reforms was made visible was through reformers' desire to emulate corporate practices in education. One of the LEU experts shared her vision for higher education and teacher education reforms that aligned with the work of Shchedrovitsky's followers in "developing and growing people into positions." She was so inspired by the Russian internet company Yandex that she regularly arranged tours for her LEU students to visit this company. During our interview, she shared with me the model that Yandex used to identify and train "the right people" for their jobs.

"They don't walk in the streets like investors. The people who are motivated to solve complex problems [that they need] don't walk in the streets either. It is not written on their forehead. They have to be found. So, they understood that it is pointless to look for those people in higher education. Too late. It is necessary to look for children who are twelve, who are interested in this. And then to accompany them the entire time, to escort them through all levels of education, but most importantly to motivate them. This idea of looking for motivated people and to invest first of all into these people. That's why it is necessary to find them at the youngest age possible, to grow them, to make them, and so on. They should become my . . . What's the word that I need here? [Like-minded person, I realize later.] They should share my ideas and my vision for the future. It is necessary for them to want to live in the future that we together will design and produce. I have to make people that will want to be my coparticipants, people who share my values, so to speak" (Interview 58, March 2014).

This description of one corporation's pursuit of workers "from a very young age," so that they could be molded, "grown," and "developed" into shared values and into a shared vision of the future resembled the construction of learners in the new educational standards and new teachers' professional standards. All of those foreclosed possibilities of open-ended human becoming and instead pursued a production of a particular subject that could fulfill a particular function in the corporate structure. Corporate influence here emerged in colonizing the imagination of the experts themselves; instead of envisioning multiple forms of education and selecting among alternatives, only the blueprint provided by a corporation appeared to be a viable option for the educational system to emulate.

Another way in which corporate influence on the framing of educational reforms was made visible was when experts commented on the educational system's failure to meet the needs of businesses and corporations. After the Shchedrovitsky conference, I managed to interview Victor Anatolyevich—a former Skolkovo administrator who at that time served as an advisor to the minister of education. I was trying to understand the reasons for implementing such programs as 100 Rectors. Victor Anatolyevich explained to me that those were supposed to create "new people with a new type of thinking" and "a new class of leaders in higher education." I kept wondering why these new people and new educational institutions were needed. After all, it seemed that most people in society did not feel this need. Eventually, my interviewee noted, "I can tell you that all of these reforms are necessary because businesses and corporations need new people, engineers with modern preparation for space exploration, for nuclear programs, and so on. But that is self-evident" (Interview 51, February 2014). For him, businesses' and corporations' needs went without saying, which was not the case for me.

Victor Anatolyevich was not the only person in the reformers' network who wanted to change the educational system so that it would supply the workers that corporations needed, nor was this message directed specifically at me as a researcher from the West. During a Pedagogical Olympiad I attended, I observed a lecture given by Il'ya Markovich—a professor from Fevral'sk State University—on the use of Shchedrovitsky's organizational games in teacher education. He belonged to the Shchedrovitsky network and was closely connected to Joseph Abramovich and Vadim Alekseyevich—connections that became clear to me only after the lecture. Addressing university students from across Russia who came to compete in this teaching contest, he spoke about the problems in Russian schools and the need to reform teacher education to address these problems. According to him, schools that acted as mere "luggage storage facilities" were to blame for the nation's poverty and people's inability to find jobs. Consistently sprinkled throughout this lecture were references to corporate practices and business needs. "Modern business needs one set of qualifications, one set of competencies, but both the school and the university are too far away from giving students these competencies," he noted in the middle of the lecture. "Businesses are saying, 'You just hold them a little longer for us, but then we will have to train them ourselves.'" His main point was that schools should allow children to produce knowledge but this process should be organized the way it was done in the corporate world.

"There are two types of knowledge production in corporations. Top-down and bottom-up. A worker knows his job like no one else. Better than any professor would. When someone comes to this worker and asks, 'How are you doing this?' he will just mumble in response. It is one thing to do it, but it is another thing to talk about it. So someone has to come in, study it, summarize it, and make it generalizable. To see new methods and new means, then spread those across this corporation. That's how global corporations are organized. But not schools and universities. And that's a problem. Scientific knowledge is useless on its own. It needs to be reshaped and reformatted to be applicable in work settings. Recently I attended a seminar on TRIZ [the theory of solving inventive and creative tasks]. It was designed in the Soviet Union. It is not used here but is used in Samsung. Why? They are a Korean firm. They use TRIZ and they use *kaizen* [a system of continuous improvement]. When new people are hired, they undergo ideological treatment, so that they would be committed to work for the benefit of the company, for the improvement of the company. From the very beginning they are subjects, they are workers like you. If they have ideas, TRIZ is used to test those ideas and spread them throughout the corporation."

The knowledge production that the speaker wanted the schools to emulate appeared limited in its function. It was not new inventions, new discoveries, or pushing new frontiers in sciences or humanities. It was not the kind of knowledge production envisioned by progressive educators when students "try on" identities of scientists (Gee 2004) and immerse themselves in the disciplines' way of thinking. It was certainly not the kind of knowledge production promoted by critical scholars, which was supposed to liberate individuals and transform societies (Apple 2013; Freire 1970; Gramsci 1971). Rather, it was knowledge production targeted to improve the functionality, cut costs, or increase efficiency of production. The value of workers' contributions was not measured by their ability to improve humanity's condition but rather by the usefulness of their ideas for the corporation's development. To increase workers' commitment to the corporation, they had to undergo "ideological treatment"—the kind of work that in the Shchedrovitsky network anthropotechnicians were hired to do. Together these measures set the parameters for human becoming, for the worth of produced knowledge, and for the value of a human life. This vision of corporate dystopia became the blueprint for reformed educational institutions.

After the lecture, I approached Il'ya Markovich with a clarification question. I asked what types of workers he thought schools should produce and what types of knowledge these workers were expected to generate. I did not get a chance to introduce myself, and because this was a Pedagogical Olympiad he assumed that I was one of the teacher education faculty who accompanied the students. He raised his voice as he spoke to me, "Why is the country so poor? Because there are no people. Business is asking for people. Industry is asking for people. But there are no people. And it is *your* fault. You have not prepared those people" (Field Notes, January 2014). At first, I was shocked by this accusation: I—an outsider—became responsible for business' inability to get the workforce they needed. But I was also shocked by the justification for reforms that his statement represented. Public discussions of educational reforms rarely included considerations of businesses and corporations. But reformers' and experts' comments seemed to indicate that those had become key actors whose interests determined the directions of reforms, even as the public or other educators remained oblivious of their involvement in education policy.

In my interviews with those outside reformers' networks, I saw a counternarrative: schools supply well-prepared graduates. For example, according to Konstantin Mikhailovich, a seventy-year-old former assistant to the minister of education, the problem was that there had been no investment in developing knowledge economy or national innovations. Konstantin Mikhailovich analyzed trends in the national economy and showed that there were well-trained people but industries and businesses were not utilizing their talents. After Konstantin Mikhailovich wrote about this mismatch in a *Federal Collection of Essays* for the State Duma, he was never asked to submit another essay for them. After my interview with Konstantin Mikhailovich, I wondered whether the issue was not so much graduates' lack of preparation but rather their insubordination or lack of conformism. Viewed from this angle, it becomes clear why businesses and corporations are interested in educational reforms. They are likely to benefit from the production of more docile bodies and minds intended by the new school and teachers' standards.

Concluding Thoughts

Political constructions of policy problems are not unique to Russia. Educational crises are manufactured through "misleading methods of analyzing data, distorting reports of findings, and suppressing contradictory evidence" (Berliner and Biddle 1995, 4). In the United States, policymakers constructed images of failing public schools to pave the way for their elimination and privatization through No Child Left Behind and the Every Student Succeeds Act (Granger 2008; Koyama 2010; Mathis and Trujillo 2016; Owens 2015; Ravitch 2011, 2013). American teacher education has undergone similar processes of dismantling. Arthur Levine's (2006) report *Educating School Teachers* presented a scathing portrayal of university-based teacher education. The report was neither methodologically sound nor consistently accurate (Zeichner and Conklin 2016). Several years later, the National Council on Teacher Quality issued *Teacher Prep Review* (2013), which assigned failing grades to many top teacher education programs using "shaky methods" and inaccurate evidence (Fuller 2013). Despite glaring problems, these reports became a rallying cry for American reformers seeking "to create revolutionary change" (Duncan 2016) in teacher education. What the focus on the failing teacher education programs obscured, however, was corporate and philanthropic involvement in a growing privatization of the field (Zeichner and Conklin 2016). The number of alternative teacher training providers is rising and the quality of training they provide is uneven, but those processes remain outside of the public's purview.

Other scholars noted that US policymakers persistently focus on failing schools and failing teacher education to move the audience's attention away from the effects of poverty and growing inequality on students' educational outcomes (Berliner 2006; Berliner and Biddle 1995; Granger 2008; Ravitch 2011, 2013). The case of Russian reforms shows that new policies do not just direct the audience's attention away from poverty; they normalize unequal educational attainment among different social groups as part of a natural hierarchical arrangement in a capitalist society. This normalization is particularly detrimental for students from marginalized and underserved communities because the socialization they will receive in schools will not help them pursue social mobility or equip them for democratic participation in society.

The Russian case also extends these observations further. It shows that the selective focus on failing pedagogical universities obscures reformers' pursuit of larger sociocultural change. Even though the change is allegedly necessary to create new subjects for the knowledge economy, knowledge seems to be significantly downplayed in new school standards, new teacher standards, and designs for new teacher education. Instead, the focus on "soft skills," character traits, socialization, and regulation of students' behavior permeates new policies. With some variation (Busemeyer and Vossiek 2016), this focus on skills and character traits drives curriculum reforms around the world due to the "corporatization of future workers" that attempts "to shape their character traits, knowledge, and skills to meet the needs of the global labor market and the desires of multinational corporations" (Spring 2015a, 5). International organizations promote reforms that will produce "flexible and adaptable individuals" (OECD 2001, 17) with a highly valued "ability to adjust to change" (World Bank 2002, 30), so that global corporations and businesses can receive the workforce they need (Spring 2015a). In the end, the problem is not that pedagogical universities are of low quality, but that businesses and corporations want schools to produce different people—loyal, compliant, and docile. In the political theater of teacher education reforms, schools have to produce spectators willing to adapt to the world rather than actors committed to transforming it.

5

Props, Scripts, and Playwrights

In mid-October 2013, Anton Mikhailovich was giving a presentation on the Concept of Teacher Education Modernization at a weekly LEU seminar. When the camera zoomed out to focus on the next speaker's face, I caught a glimpse of a packed room. There were numerous questions from the audience that quickly turned into heated arguments. Closer to the end, the seminar organizers took several minutes to allow those who were participating online to raise their questions. Tatyana Borisovna turned on her microphone, "We have an interesting question from an online participant." She twitched her nose a bit. "Alexander is asking, 'Is there anything non-Western in your proposals?' Yes, such an interesting question."

A faint murmur filled the room. Vadim Alekseyevich turned on his microphone: "Anton, I will answer that. What is Western? There is no such thing as Western. Each country has their own system. France prepares their teachers one way. Finland another way. We looked at what other countries were doing and we proposed our own plan."

The room was galvanized for a minute. The question that the online participant asked was not simply a question, it was an accusation. To get the seminar back on track, Vadim Alekseyevich asked those who wanted to continue their discussions to step out of the room. Eventually, the conversation moved on to another question. I was watching it online, but I could still sense the tension when someone made a comment and the room erupted in an angry whisper. The debate was heated and the conversations were uncomfortable. Vadim Alekseyevich repeated multiple times that those who wanted to talk should step outside and not interrupt the flow of the seminar. Several months later when I became a regular at these seminars, I realized that the room was rarely so packed and hardly ever did the organizers have to make announcements asking people to leave if they made so much noise. This meeting was different. It was one of the few times when the Concept of Teacher Education Modernization was presented at a public event and conversations about it quickly turned to questions about its origins.

In this chapter, I ask a similar question—Where did the script of the Concept come from? I examine international influences on Russian policy-making and trace discursive constructions of global transformations as props for Russian modernization dramas. Even though international assessments, such as PISA, had a role to play in reshaping Russian education, it was the McKinsey reports authored by Michael Barber (Barber and Mourshed 2007; Mourshed, Chijioke, and Barber 2010) that became the sources for the Concept's ideas. The traction occurred because reformers knew Barber personally and because these texts aligned with the ideologies and theories to which reformers subscribed. Even though the reformers saw the solutions offered in the script as universally applicable, reform participants did not share their convictions.

International Assessments

Reformers often used international assessments to construct a narrative of crisis in Russian education, even though Russia's performance on different tests was not consistent. On the 2011 TIMSS,[1] Russia ranked sixth on the eighth grade math assessment and seventh on the science assessment. It ranked second on the PIRLS[2] fourth grade reading assessment. In PISA,[3] however, Russia ranked thirty-seventh—with average scores being 482 in math, 475 in reading, and 486 in science. In contrast, top-scoring Shanghai had average scores of 613 in math, 570 in reading, and 580 in science. Of all these different results, reformers discussed PISA scores most often, downplaying achievements revealed by TIMSS and PIRLS.

This contrast was clear in Vadim Alekseyevich's article on "the low quality of pedagogical education": "The first thing we have to do is to analyze the results of our students' performance on international comparative studies in education. It turns out that Russian students steadily show good results in the international research PIRLS that examines literacy. . . . We have not bad results in international research TIMSS that checks mathematical and scientific literacy. . . . The results of TEDS-M[4] show not bad quality of mathematics teacher preparation. . . . And yet the results of international research of PISA regularly show that fifteen-year-old students perform poorly on the tasks connected with using school knowledge outside the classroom" (DSH 2012).

Reformers described top scores in some of these assessments with the help of evaluative adjectives "good" or "not bad" (Rus. *neplokhie*). But Russian students' poor performance on PISA was presented with the help of specific descriptors—the inability of Russian students to apply knowledge in new situations. A similar narrative structure appeared in other publications produced by the reformers. In Strategy 2020, after several brief nods toward students' performance on TIMSS and PIRLS, the authors noted that PISA could reveal whether students could solve the problems posed by the new technological order (Rus. *uklad*) or whether they were ready to participate in an innovation economy. This was where "Russian students are significantly falling behind their peers from most developed countries in the world" (Strategy 2020 2013, 333).

The OECD claims that PISA assesses students' competencies necessary for the knowledge or innovation economy. This assessment prioritizes economic productivity over democratic participation or other purposes of schooling (Labaree 2014; Meyer and Benavot 2013). In doing so, it aligned well with the reformers' agendas in reorienting Russian schools and changing teachers' work to serve the economy better (chapter 4). The association between education and economy is assumed to be so close that "PISA points are now equated with Gross Domestic Product (GDP)" (Gorur 2016, 601). For example, Hanushek and Woessmann's (2010) claim that there is a causal relationship between a nation's performance on PISA and its subsequent economic gains: if educational performance improves, economic growth will follow. International researchers dispute these claims, arguing that they are based on ahistoric and flawed analysis (Berliner 2015; Morris 2016; Ramirez et al. 2006; Komatsu and Rappleye 2017). Despite this ongoing criticism, however, these claims influenced Russian official government reports. The Federal Program of Educational Development for 2011–2015 (2011)[5] stated that as a result of educational modernization, Russia's PISA scores will improve and annual GDP growth will increase 1 to 2 percent.

Unlike other countries, however, Russia did not undergo "PISA shock" (Ertl 2006; Grek 2009). When PISA results were released, some news sources ran articles about them, but there was little interest in these tests either among the public or among the political elites. Commenting on a lack of response to international assessments results, Joseph Abramovich shared a story about PISA 2000 results: "I will never forget how a prominent specialist from the

Russian Academy of Education said that those data cannot be of interest to us because the very tasks of the assessment do not match our mentality" (VO 2008). Reformers and experts in their networks, on the other hand, organized seminars, gave TV and radio interviews, and published extensively on the need to improve the quality of education to raise PISA scores. They did not see any incongruence between PISA and Russian mentality.

The differences in responses to PISA revealed another chasm: polarization in appraisals of the Soviet school. While many in society kept the Soviet legacy in education in high regard (Aydarova 2015b), reformers did not. For example, in a radio interview in 2010, Anton Mikhailovich shared that PISA 2009 showed that a third of Russian schoolchildren leave school unable to read and count (which it did not). The radio host exclaimed that it was a catastrophe. Another guest fondly described her memories of the Soviet school and questioned the usefulness of PISA results for Russia. Anton Mikhailovich responded, "This is what this drama is about, that even in this studio, we cannot agree on one thing. Our school was great in the sixties, in the seventies. But it is wrong to teach now the way it was done in the sixties and seventies. . . . It was the time of industrial production. So, what used to be required of a person was a sum of knowledge, a sum of skills that allowed him to be successful throughout all of his life. . . . But today it is not enough. Today what a student learns in the engineering department during his first year is already outdated by his third year. We need new approaches" (EM, 2010).

Despite public indifference toward PISA results, reformers continued to call for new approaches, such as changing the contents of education, reducing the number of school subjects, and reorienting educational processes toward activity- and competency-based instruction (VO 2008). These calls were consistent with recommendations from international organizations: from the OECD's (1998) emphasis on competencies to the World Bank's (Canning et al. 2004) push for new outcome-oriented school standards. New school standards emerged in response to this activity. As Vadim Alekseyevich explained to me, they "were introduced under the influence of international assessments . . . and raised the question whether teachers can work according to them" (Interview 55, February 2014). In a domino effect, new school standards paved the way for the introduction of teachers' professional standards and teacher education modernization.

Without much consideration for other school or out-of-school factors (Berliner 2015; Perry and Ercikan 2015), particularly rising social inequality (Sellar and Lingard 2014), responsibility for students' performance on international assessments was placed on teachers. This allowed reformers to make conclusions about the state of teacher education. This is how Tatyana Borisovna explained these connections, "The working group suggested that the quality of pedagogical universities' graduates should be evaluated indirectly based on the results of such research as PISA or TIMSS, considering that the result of teachers' activity manifests itself in the students" (Interview 41a, January 2014). This evaluation appeared in a report on teacher education modernization that the core group submitted to the ministry in spring of 2014: "Russian schoolchildren's results on PIRLS, TIMSS, and PISA allow us to state that Russian teachers have subject knowledge of sufficiently high level but lack the skills of pedagogy and psychology." These international assessments did not evaluate pedagogy and psychology components in teacher preparation, but reformers still used them to bolster the reform proposals they had been working on since the 1980s.

There was, however, an international assessment that evaluated preservice teachers' pedagogy, psychology, and subject knowledge preparation directly. Russia participated in TEDS-M—the international assessment of mathematics teacher preparation in seventeen countries—and produced relatively high results. Yet when I inquired how those results might have affected the working group's decisions, Tatyana Borisovna explained, "You see. Our standards of general education are changing. The most important thing is that we are supposed to move from the knowledge paradigm to competencies, to an activity-based paradigm. It is a good thing that we have good results in TIMSS, but the image of the teacher that can prepare well for TIMSS but cannot prepare well for PISA is no longer relevant. But that's what the standard requires. And as we know, the standard is a normative document. That's why teachers should be prepared in the university in such a way that they can carry out practical work with students. Projects, for example. But right now, it is not happening because university standards do not support this type of work" (Interview 41a, January 2014).

According to Tatyana Borisovna, students' low performance on PISA showed that Russian teacher education was not preparing teachers well. She dismissed Russian preservice teachers' competitive performance in TEDS-M as no longer relevant because both PISA and new school standards required that teachers should be trained differently. The very framing of teacher preparation "for PISA" revealed a change in priorities pursued by reformers.

Anton Mikhailovich spoke about TEDS-M results during the conference in Fevral'sk in April 2013 in a similar vein. He noted that Russian students were ranked second or fourth in TEDS-M, but then quoted the report as saying that Russian students could carry out tasks to which they had been exposed before but were not able to find solutions to novel problems. Because Russian students did not do well on PISA for similar reasons, he noted that TEDS-M showed that teacher education had to change. When Anton Mikhailovich presented the Concept during a seminar in Lyutvino in the fall of 2013, he no longer included TEDS-M in his presentation, even though other aspects of his presentation were the same as the ones he used in Fevral'sk.

Overall, TEDS-M results revealed most strikingly the tendency among reformers and experts to selectively focus on the results of international assessments that best supported their reform efforts. Most reformers avoided speaking about it and focused on the results of PISA. If it was brought up, either voluntarily by them or with my prompting, the only finding that they addressed was that pedagogical university graduates were not trained to prepare students to do well on PISA or that they did not go into teaching after they graduate. Other findings of TEDS-M were often ignored or omitted.

Silence in regard to TEDS-M could not be explained by the absence of information. In a journal where many of the reformers published their work, an article by Russian experts presented the findings of TEDS-M. Titled "Pedagogical Universities Give High Quality Mathematics Preparation but Their Graduates Are in No Hurry to Work in Schools," the article showed that Russian preservice teachers in general demonstrated good results in subject knowledge preparation but slightly weaker results in the knowledge of methodology. Overall, Russian teacher education rankings were above international average: they fell between the second and the seventh positions. Some questions focused on perceptions of constructivist teaching and Russian students seemed to do well on those; others asked about their opinion of their education's and universities' effectiveness. The answers showed a high degree of satisfaction. The team of authors concluded the report with the following summary that demonstrated discrepancies between TEDS-M findings and the reformers' position: "The main result, from our point of view, was the answer to the question about the competitiveness of Russian university graduates, receiving the qualification of a primary or secondary school math teacher. Russian students' results were above the international average. The fundamental math preparation was the strong aspect of curriculum in Russian universities. More than half of Russian students received scores that exceeded the 'advanced level' benchmark set by the international experts. This result was unexpected because society has formed an opinion about the low quality of pedagogical education.

"The data obtained drew attention to the problem of educational system staffing. Why does the majority of well-prepared, according to the international standards, graduates of Russian universities not go to work in schools? What happens to the students who have shown the highest results and plan to dedicate professional life to teaching at a school after they have stepped inside a school? Why does society not see them? Why is the opinion that only 'losers' go to work in schools so widespread?" (Kovaleva, Denishcheva, and Sheveleva 2011, 146).

The questions that appear at the end of this quote spoke directly to the claims on which the reformers' position rested. TEDS-M challenged the claims that students who went to pedagogical universities were weak academically and were not prepared to be good teachers in schools. This contradiction was not helpful for the reformers' agenda. Similar to the results of TIMSS and PIRLS, TEDS-M results were either completely removed or discussed only in passing to demonstrate that they did not match the expectations placed on schools and on teachers in the new global economy.

To summarize, because PISA was a prominent international assessment where Russian students showed weak results, reformers emphasized it most in their performances. The negative picture that PISA presented fit well with the reformers' agenda—it allowed them to argue that the system is in crisis and it needs to be urgently reformed. Ironically, reformers recognized that PISA results did not produce a feeling of crisis in Russian society, but they continued to instigate it through their public engagements. As Maksim Davydovich noted in our final interview: "In Russia, there was no crisis around PISA. Ask anyone on the street what PISA is and they won't even know what it is. Most people certainly don't care. We just needed to have something to get the ball rolling. And it seems that it worked out" (Interview 78, December 2015).

Selective references to international assessments have been used in other countries to instigate crises and push for reforms (Grek 2009; Takayama 2008, 2010). Those reforms often reflected OECD's "soft governance" (Lawn 2006; Ozga 2012) because they aligned with the OECD's recommendations based on PISA results (Niemann, Martens, and Teltemann 2017) but were not legally binding. Andreas Schleicher's (2011) report *Building a High-Quality Teaching Profession*, published in a Russian education journal, used high-performing nations as references for teacher policy recommendations. Similar to the Concept, it advocated diversifying paths into teaching and offering master's degrees to those who wanted to switch careers. But apart from these two points, the Concept did not seem to have much in common with OECD policy prescriptions. PISA did not seem to provide a policy script, but its league-table format with "winners" and "losers" fit into reformers' constructions of Russia's failing positions in the "global education race," the point I explore next.

Global Education Race

Reformers often argued that change was necessary to "ensure Russia's global competitiveness in the future" (Strategy 2020, 327), deploying images of falling behind in the "global education race" or becoming isolated in an integrated world. For example, Victor Anatolyevich—one of the founders of the Skolkovo Moscow School of Management—explained his motivation for overseeing multiple projects of educational reform this way: "Russia must enter global education. It must compete. We were an *isolated country for seventy years. . . . We have a different institutional culture. There are a lot of things that we don't have . . . We have to acknowledge that in some areas Russia had high achievement in education, especially in *science, technology, and engineering. There we have nothing to be ashamed of. We have world-class accomplishments in those areas. But in other areas—in economics, in politics, in humanities, we have fallen far behind" (Interview 51, February 2014).

Our conversation was focused on Skolkovo's programs intended to increase Russia's global competitiveness and prevent it from falling behind by creating "a new class of people who think and act differently." Among other things, we discussed Skolkovo's 100 Rectors program that Sergey Valdisovich described as a starting point for bringing together like-minded rectors of pedagogical universities into the working group (chapter 3). As the person who organized that program, Victor Anatolyevich emphasized its role in "creating new people" (similar to schools, see chapter 4). In that moment, however, I wanted to understand why this change was necessary.

"Why is it necessary to have a class of people who think and act differently?"

"Because without it, nothing will happen. Everything will remain as it is. Period."

By that time, I had noticed that many people resisted change. "But there is a large proportion of the Russian population who would be happy for things to stay as they are, isn't there?"

"I don't care about that."

"But why change? What is the goal of the changes?"

"Because it is impossible to continue living this way. As I always say in my interviews, we will become a backward educational village [Rus. *obrazovantel'noy provintisyey*] that no one needs. I want to live in a great country, if I can use the language of values here . . . For that to happen, universities must change, they must change the programs, they must provide modern education" (Interview 51, February 2014).

This reflexive fear of isolation, peripheral position, and falling behind ran through several other interviews with reformers directly involved in teacher education reform. During the group interview, Oleg Victorovich noted that it is important for Russia not to fall behind in "the global education race." Maksim Davydovich concluded our interview by saying that the Concept was addressing the problems of today but, unfortunately, it was not radical enough for the future. Similar to several others in the group, he believed that traditional institutions of schooling would soon disappear and therefore teachers should be prepared to work with new educational forms. "Our project does not address that. But I don't think this has been developed anywhere else yet. At least, in this sense, Russia *has not yet fallen behind*" (Interview 49, February 2014, emphasis added).

The background of race in which Russia was falling behind was further intensified with the help of external actors. At the beginning of my fieldwork, I attended an international conference on higher education held in Russia where Simon Marginson gave a plenary talk entitled "Science and Higher Education in a More Global Era and How Russia Is Positioned." Drawing on dismal positions of Russian higher education institutions in international rankings, Marginson argued that Russia had potential but its research was too "inward-looking" and intellectual life too "isolated." To address these issues, he recommended that Russian higher education should internationalize and follow global standards. This plenary speech was soon published in English in a Russian education journal. Multiple tables, charts, and graphs demonstrated how Russia had "fallen behind" in global knowledge production and was "performing poorly" in global engagement. The metrics of English-language publications, citation counts, international collaborations, and research grants presented a dismal picture of a country that did little to play an active role in global science and global education.

Russia became positioned similarly "on the periphery" of global education in Michael Barber's lectures and interviews on his visits to Russia.

For example, in September 2012, right before work on the Concept began (chapter 3), Michael Barber gave an interview to the Russian RIA News Agency later published on the website of the President's Council for Economic Modernization and Innovative Development of the Country.[6] The main point of the interview was to emphasize Russia's failures and the urgency of reforms to address them: "Russia has an opportunity to approach the center of international research and science, but there are a number of decisions that have to be made to improve Russia's positions in this sphere and to move from the stage of learning to the stage of knowledge generation. If Russia is planning to return from the periphery to the center of global education politics, it has the potential and the people who are ready to make that happen."[7]

Across Michael Barber's talks and presentations, Russia's position on the global stage was framed relatively consistently along the lines of the preceding quote: Russia used to be a great country; it had been isolated for a long time; it found itself on the periphery of global education; to become a leader again, it needed to drastically reform its educational system. In short, to reclaim the position of a global leader, Russia needed an educational revolution—a message already packaged in Barber's publication *Oceans of Innovation* (Donnelly, Barber, and Rizvi 2012).

The imagery of center and periphery constructed the world as a series of concentric circles; international rankings of various kinds, including PISA, provided resources for easy positioning of countries in those circles. The threat of finding oneself on the periphery, away from the center, was used to create a sense of crisis, which could be avoided if educational reforms were introduced. This narrative aligned well with reformers' efforts to introduce sweeping changes into the educational sector, functioning as a useful prop for their production.

These narratives can be approached in multiple ways. Some argue that discourses of the "global education race" recreate neocolonial and neoimperial hierarchies (Nguyen et al. 2009; Shahjahan 2016; Takayama, Sriprakash, and Connell 2017). What is important for the current discussion, however, is the use of "falling behind," being "isolated," and finding itself "on the periphery" as the props for the modernization drama. The constructs of an outdated social theory promoted both by global and national actors make their way into consulting and policy circles. They are deployed to evoke fear and prove urgency of reforms. Ultimately, without the Other whom Russia has to fear, against whom Russia has to compete, and against whom Russia has to measure itself, the narrative of crisis collapses on itself.

Reforms in Other Countries

Discursive constructions of the global education race often emerged in tandem with descriptions of how other nations were reforming teacher education. In presentations, publications, and interviews reformers recounted that many countries were engaging in teacher education reforms, pulling details in support of their proposals from teacher education in England, the United States, France, or Finland. For example, Anton Mikhailovich during a conference presentation stated that "all countries around the world, including Brazil, Mexico, Japan, Singapore, and Finland, between the seventies and nineties carried out a radical reform of pedagogical education" (Video, Fevral'sk Conference, April 2013). In an article in one of the leading Russian educational journals, he argued: "In the last third of last century extensive transformations of pedagogical education have occurred in *almost all countries* of the world" (VO 2013, emphasis added). In the rest of the article, he described the "unchanged state" of Russian teacher education (itself a prop—see Aydarova 2014, 2015a, 2015b) and argued that it needed reforms to catch up with the rest of the changing world.

Other countries' experiences mattered beyond the claims about the reforms they initiated. What they did was also worth consideration. A week after Anton Mikhailovich presented the Concept at the LEU seminar, a popular educational newspaper published an anonymous article titled "How Teacher Education Is Organized Abroad and What Can Be Done About It in Russia." The opening paragraph stated the following: "There are different ways a strategy of reform can be selected. The first path is to look for one's own, unique, not resembling anything 'road to success,' study the processes that are happening in school, carry out research, discuss the results of that research, and issue a document that would either be self-contradicting, as a result of much compromise, or it would be morally outdated the moment it sees daylight. The second path is to remember that we—Russia—are a part of Europe and the world, that our government signed the Bologna Agreement, then look around and take the good road toward the new school through the reform of teacher preparation programs. We hope that sooner or later the position of those who choose the second path will overcome and this report 'will work,' will create real benefit" (UG 2013).

The article presented two choices: time could either be wasted on designing one's own reforms or it could be productively spent on remembering that "we—Russia—are a part of Europe and the world." The second position implicitly advocated adopting globally circulated scripts for reforming teacher education. The path of adoption was presented as more efficient and potentially more beneficial. The rest of the article was devoted to describing ways in which twelve other countries reformed teacher education by introducing measures that increased the prestige of the teaching profession and facilitated teacher retention. The quote itself and the analysis of reforms in different countries that became the foundation for this article came from "a study of international experiences" that a team in Lyutvino carried out allegedly to develop the policy proposal.

The Study of International Experiences

"Why reinvent the wheel when we can study the international experience of teacher education reform?" noted Sergey Valdisovich. Tatyana Borisovna and Larisa Nikolayevna elaborated on how the LEU team studied the international experience. They shared that in spring of 2013 a small team was put together headed by Anton Mikhailovich. Each person on the team was assigned one country to research—England, Canada, the United States, Finland, France, Singapore, and Japan. It turned out that most sources used in this analysis were open-access sources or materials published in Russia. When I heard about that, I became somewhat skeptical. A comparative study is difficult to execute; to draw policy-relevant conclusions from it requires a significant investment in empirical data collection. How can someone draw policy-relevant observations from open-access or locally produced sources? "We get visitors from other countries at LEU," Tatyana Borisovna assured me. "We can always ask them about how teachers are prepared in their countries."

But my growing skepticism did not dissipate after this comment. When I got hold of the 127-page report that the team prepared based on their comparative study, I became even more puzzled. The evidence seemed uneven. For example, the section on Canada started with large amounts of information about the country's population size, political organization, and the history of its settlement, without any explicit links to its teacher education system. The section on Finland started with the subsection that compared "differences in scientific approaches between the countries of the OECD and the USSR" (which among other things raised questions for me about its origin). Descriptions of country studies were not parallel. A large proportion of the section devoted to Japan focused on the historical trajectories of the educational system in that country, whereas the analysis of US experiences covered predominantly contemporary professional organizations involved in teacher education accreditation and their contenders (such as the National Council on Teacher Quality and Teach For America).

It was also important how the report treated the changes that occurred in those countries. Focusing on descriptive details of different systems, it omitted the conflicts, contestations, struggles, or problems unleashed by the described reforms. For example, England was praised for significantly diversifying its routes into the profession and decreasing the authority of traditional university-based teacher preparation. Arguing that this approach significantly improved the quality of teachers, the report eschewed any consideration of how these multiple routes led to the deprofessionalization of teaching (Furlong et al. 2000; Furlong 2013) and proletarianization of teacher education (Ellis and McNicholl 2015). Similarly, the section on teacher education in the United States mentioned Teach For America but omitted the struggles over the deregulation and professionalization agendas that its emergence represented. Deeply contested value-added modeling (Amrein-Beardsley 2014) was discussed as "a promising innovation in teacher education," without considering the problems that its application engendered.

I was not alone in my skeptical assessment of this report. Marina Vitalyevna, who identified herself as a comparative education scholar, gently commented on the quality of international research that went into the production of that report during our interview: "There are some things that I just find hard to believe. People at LEU are wonderful people; they adhere to the right principles. But they don't read in foreign languages. I don't know who tells them stories based on what they read, but they know a lot of things only from stories. I know Anton Mikhailovich. He is a wonderful man. There were several people who came and told him: this is what is written here, this is what is written there. But with that, it is hard to develop an understanding of what drives reforms in different countries. To tell you the truth, even when you read yourself it is hard to develop an understanding. You have to see it" (Interview 42, January 2014).

Most importantly, what struck me from the international report was that the descriptions of other countries did not match the proposals for reform in the Concept. Even though the Canadian and American experiences of using multicultural education in teacher preparation were identified as important lessons for Russia because of its cultural and ethnic diversity, these lessons were not included in the Concept—also a part of this report. Examples of Singapore and Finland recruiting top candidates into teaching resembled Concept proposals, but strong academic preparation with opportunities for preservice teachers to conduct research highlighted in the report were downplayed among the other measures that the Concept advocated. An uneven presentation of American, Canadian, English, Japanese, and Finnish experiences did not seem to connect to Concept proposals, even though one section of the report attempted to do that. The mismatch was not only conceptual, it was also chronological. As I mentioned in chapter 3, Concept proposals were identified by January 19, 2013, but the group started working on the international report only after February 22. That suggests that the team started working on the international report after most of the key Concept ideas were already selected.

Interview data revealed more discrepancies. For the most part, reformers in the core group rarely mentioned the international report in their interviews. Some aspects of what was covered in that report did appear in their publications, as the quote from the newspaper article indicates (even though the article appeared in press without an author's name). But other than that, only the working group secretaries and Anton Mikhailovich, who published an article based on some of the ideas in this report, seemed to care deeply about it. Even though the report was submitted to the ministry as a result of the group's work on developing teacher education modernization reforms, the study of international experiences did not seem to work as a script for the Concept.

Michael Barber and the McKinsey Reports

One phrase appeared consistently in reformers' conversations, interviews, and presentations—"the quality of an educational system cannot exceed the quality of its teachers." Sergey Valdisovich tweaked the phrase slightly when he mentioned it in the beginning of our interview; Anton Mikhailovich and Joseph Abramovich pronounced it faultlessly without much thought. Both of them spoke of it when I asked them about the source of ideas for the Concept. "The McKinsey report," they both said. That was a reference to Michael Barber and Mona Mourshed's report (2007) *How the World's Best Performing School Systems Come Out on Top* that was published in Russian in a leading educational journal in 2008.

After the McKinsey report came out, a steady flow of articles about the need to reform teacher education ensued. In November 2008, Marina Vitalyevna published an article in the same journal on the quality of teachers and education in general. There she referred to the McKinsey report in the following way: "In it, it is convincingly proven that the most successful countries achieve high results in learning with the help of three factors: attracting the most talented into teaching, their effective professional development that leads to the improved quality of education, and the politics of teachers attending to every child equally" (VO 2008). Anton Mikhailovich's article published in the same journal in 2013 cited the McKinsey report in discussing "32 ways one can become a teacher" in England (Barber and Mourshed 2007, 23) and in describing the ability of teacher preparation to respond quickly to labor market demands. These served as a corollary to the variability and flexibility proposed in the Concept.

Other experts referred to the McKinsey report in their discussions as well. For example, when Anton Mikhailovich gave a presentation in Fevral'sk in April of 2013, his colleague commented that the McKinsey report suggested that a better teacher is someone who knew "something else, not just how to teach" and asked how the Concept would encourage other professionals to choose teaching. Anton Mikhailovich was pleased with the question (Video, Fevral'sk Conference, April 2013).

But referring to the report was not all that happened. When one compares the language and the measures proposed by the Concept and the measures advocated by Barber's report, one is struck by their seeming alignment. For example, a heavy emphasis on the practical orientation in teacher preparation resonated across both texts. Only once did the McKinsey report refer to the "strong theoretical background" of teacher candidates in Boston residency programs. Other than that, theory was not included in any of the solutions or proposals for reform. Instead, it argued that in order to improve the quality of education, it was necessary to introduce "coaching classroom practice" and to move "teacher training to the classroom" (29). The text of the Concept made similar moves emphasizing the need to equip teachers with practical competencies through training provided in partner schools. Moreover, the argument that candidates for teacher preparation should be selected based on tests that evaluate their basic skills and motivation to teach resonated with the Concept's proposal to introduce "additional entry requirements" for those who chose pedagogical education. Throughout the Concept, multiple references were made to the "need to select those who are motivated to teach." Finally, even the equation between teacher quality problem and the problem of teaching as a mass profession became a point of connection between the McKinsey report and the reformers' work. The McKinsey report suggested that "failure to control entry into teacher training almost invariably leads to an oversupply of candidates which, in turn, has a significant negative effect on teacher quality" (21). As I showed in chapter 2, the reformers' proposal was to reduce the number of those who were allowed entry into teacher education as a way of improving teacher quality. A more extensive comparison of the two texts is presented in table 4.

These two texts shared more connections than just the measures they advocated. The McKinsey report provided the explanatory framework for the proposals unexplained in the policy. For example, the idea that people without pedagogical education should go to work in schools had little support in Russian pedagogical literature or the history of how the teaching force came to be defined. In fact, in the nineties those who lost jobs in other sectors and went to work in schools often failed as teachers. The Concept's proposal to attract more people from other professions into teaching was connected to the McKinsey report's claim that this would improve the quality of the teaching profession (19–20).

Even though the policy did have measures not suggested by the report, the two overlapped greatly. The intertextual connections between the McKinsey report and the Concept, suggest that it became a script for the latter. Reformers confirmed the McKinsey report's influence on their proposal during interviews. Maksim Davydovich even noted that earlier drafts of the Concept were organized based on the structure of the McKinsey report. Similar to theater directors, the reformers infused the report with their own meanings, reworked some of the proposals based on their own experiences, included ideas from their work for other international organizations (such as OECD, chapter 6) and presented the Concept as the result of their own creative work.

The McKinsey report provided reformers with what Sergey Valdisovich believed was so important for the work of the working group—"simple solutions that any bureaucrat can understand" and "easily understandable solutions, which could be implemented" (see chapter 3). It also gave the team of reformers a consistent message to share across different contexts and with different audiences. Barber's report worked well because it was allegedly based on research, even though some in the scholarly community questioned the soundness of its methodology and the warrants behind the report's claims (see Coffield 2012).

Michael Barber seemed to influence more than just how teacher education reform was conceptualized. When his second report *How the World's Most Improved School Systems Keep Getting Better* (Mourshed, Chijioke, and Barber 2010) was published in Russian in the same journal, Joseph Abramovich called it "the blueprint for reformers," saying that it should

Table 4. Comparison of the McKinsey Report Suggestions for Improving Teacher Quality and the Concept of Teacher Education Modernization Measures

McKinsey Report (2007)	Concept of Support for the Development of Teacher Education
Attracting talented and motivated people into teaching (16) Systemwide recruitment processes (19)	Attracting into teaching "the most motivated" or "the best" students
Using tests for literacy, numeracy, interpersonal and communication skills, a willingness to learn, and motivation to teach to screen candidates (17)	Creating additional entry requirements for teacher preparation, particularly assessments of motivation to teach
Oversupply of candidates has a significant negative impact on teacher quality (18)	Improving the quality of students [by decreasing the number of students who are admitted into teacher education programs]
Top-performing systems control entry so that supply matches demand through funding (18)	Annual monitoring of regional and municipal needs for teachers; the development of models of targeted contract preparation
Alternative pathways into teaching, recruiting representatives of other professions to improve the quality of teaching (19)	Program of preparation of students from nonpedagogical majors Practical master's for quick entry into the profession for those who don't have pedagogical education
Procedures to allow lowest-performing candidates to exit preparation programs	Flexible entry into and exit from teacher education [the latter clause deleted from the final version but preserved in the experiment]

continued on next page

Table 4 (continued)

McKinsey Report (2007)	Concept of Support for the Development of Teacher Education
Building practical skills during the initial training (28–29)	Practical competencies for teachers
	A system of supporting students' practical work in schools
	Independent practical work of students placed in schools
Coaching classroom practice (26)	Internship for beginning teachers
Screening processes to create selective entry into the profession	Certification exam to simplify entry into the profession (for those who do not have pedagogical education) and to ensure the quality of initial teacher preparation
—	Applied bachelor's degree as the main model of teacher preparation
—	Liberal arts bachelor's degrees
—	Master's degrees for administrators and teachers responsible for methods work

serve as a useful guide for how to enact change. One of the sections in the second report, with a telling title borrowed from the world of theater, "Entering Stage Right," provided guidelines for introducing reforms into educational systems. Those guidelines evoked the events that took place in Russia in the last two or three years. The report stated that a crisis is useful for initiating the reform and, as I discussed earlier (chapter 4), the monitoring of higher education institutions that showed a high proportion of ineffective pedagogical universities was used to fabricate a crisis around teacher education. Reformers also attempted to fabricate a crisis around Russia's low scores on PISA, just as the report recommended. The next step was to "change the leader." In Russia, a highly unpopular minister of education was removed from his post and a new minister appointed in May 2012. Then the reformers were advised to "appoint like-minded people in key positions." As I mentioned before, two rectors of key pedagogical universities in Lyutvino were removed from their posts and new ones were appointed in the summer of 2013, two months before the Concept was publicly announced as the next reform targeting teacher education. The two new rectors supported the reform throughout its inception and came from the team that was involved in developing it. Barber's ideas seemed to have a profound impact on how the reform was conceptualized, justified, and even enacted.

These events might as well be coincidental. But the very language that reformers used—identifying themselves as "reformers," discussing the "vectors of development," and describing ways of how they went about enacting change—all drawn from Barber's works—suggested that there might be more to it. In 2009, Michael Barber was invited to work as a professor at a Russian university. He taught a course and gave numerous speeches across the country, often invited by the reformers. In September 2012, right before the core group started putting together the new proposal, he visited Russia again. During that visit, he gave a talk at LEU and several interviews, in which he praised the reformers' efforts but stated that good ideas were not enough—they had to be realized in practice. A consistent message appeared across his public engagements, "It is not enough to simply reform an educational system; decisive innovations that will radically transform the system are necessary."[8] This position heavily resonated across the reformers' work and provided support for their reform efforts.

Despite close contacts with him, reformers did not acknowledge Barber's influence in public interviews about teacher education reforms or in presentations of the Concept. This distancing was reasonable given the contestations over international influences in Russian education (more on that in chapter 6). If the language of the Concept was used in such a way that it would mask international influences in it (chapter 2), then it is understandable why international experiences were presented to the public as something that informed the choices proposed in the policy but did not necessarily serve as a script.

All of these factors point to the possibility that in the political theater of Russian teacher education reform, Michael Barber was a playwright. His reports became the scripts for reform, both in the production of the Concept and in its actual implementation. The language he used—one of the key tools playwrights utilize—became the rallying cry of reform: if "the quality of the educational system cannot exceed the quality of its teachers," then teacher education has to be "radically transformed." He himself, however, disappeared from the stage—his influence on the reformers' ideas appeared in the bibliographies of their articles and in their interviews with me, but not in any other public engagements they gave or documents they produced. Similar to a playwright of a theatrical play, Michael Barber constructed "an imaginary world" (Barranger 2006, 82) in his reports and stepped back as the reformers transformed his work into their own performance.

Michael Barber's influence on how teacher education modernization became conceptualized and implemented reveals that reformers' personal connections with global policy entrepreneurs affected their choice of scripts. As I explained in chapter 1, many reformers knew him personally and some described him as a warm and charismatic personality. The OECD's reports on the teaching profession were also published in Russian in the same journal as Barber's reports, yet they did not have the same profound effect his work did. His ideas created traction because they aligned with reformers' aspirations and theoretical orientations. That is the point that I will explore next.

Overlaps in Scripts

There are several dimensions of alignment between the transnational scripts provided by Michael Barber and the ideologies to which reformers subscribed. This alignment is important because it helped create traction between the globally circulated scripts and nationally defined agendas (Tsing 2005). Here I will briefly describe three areas of overlap in scripts: the pursuit of leadership positions, the relationship between education and economic development, and the focus on activity-based learning.

First, Michael Barber and national policy actors pursued revolutionary change, arguing that it will allow Russia to restore leadership positions. When Michael Barber gave a speech on innovations in education in Russia in 2012, he emphasized the need for a revolution in education for a country to become a global leader. Laying out the historical trajectory of industrial and postindustrial shifts throughout the nineteenth and twentieth centuries, he called for radical transformations that could allow a leap forward toward a position of global leadership. Similar ideas were promoted by Shchedrovitsky's son—Pytor Shchedrovitsky—who fused his father's activity systems theory with the theories of neoclassical economics.[9] His main argument was that in order for Russia not to fall behind in the economic competition, it needed a revolution in production and it had to create a new division of labor. The historical trajectories that he drew on echoed Barber's arguments, as did his calls to introduce radical transformations—in economic activities as well as in education—to allow Russia "to leap forward toward a leadership position" (Field Notes, June 2014). This agenda was actively pursued by reformers who, as I showed in an earlier section, argued for the need to introduce reforms to reach leadership positions that Russia lost in the last twenty years.

Globally circulated neoliberal approaches to social engineering (Anderson 2005) aligned with Shchedrovitsky's writing on the role of education in society. Barber's reports, along with Hanushek's articles and OECD publications, published in a Russian educational journal, promoted the application of human capital theory in Russian policymaking. According to these publications, schools had to develop certain competencies in students for the country to be competitive in the global economy. The focus on developing students' "soft skills" and preparing them for economic competition resonated with Shchedrovitsky's engineering designs for using pedagogy to mold younger generations into the appropriate economic and social positions (chapter 4). A common description of learners in Barber's writing and in the reformers' explanations of the need for change was that students needed to be trained to be highly "adaptable for the challenges of the modern world." This focus on adaptability and flexibility of human beings to the environment around them yet again found resonance in Shchedrovitsky's systems theory and his writing on the role of pedagogy in blueprinting societies.

Finally, activity-based learning as the instructional approach that could improve the quality of education was common both in the global and national scripts. It emerged in Barber's second report (Mourshed, Chijioke, and Barber 2010), where the authors praised India's state of Madhya Pradesh for improving education by introducing "activity-based learning." The report also stated that the United Kingdom raised the quality of teaching when local agencies provided teachers with support to carry out "classroom activities." Oddly, the McKinsey report promoted activity-based learning that emerged out of "a highly standardized teaching model" (47) and "prescriptive teaching materials" (29). The Russian reformers similarly promoted activity-based learning as the approach that would improve educational quality and raise Russia's PISA scores. Of particular importance to them was the fact that Vygotsky's theories of active learning received worldwide recognition and therefore constituted Russia's "competitive advantage" (FS 2013). Reformers pushed for activities that were project-driven, research-related, meta-disciplinary, and heavily individualized (Alekseyeva et al. 2010). The new school standards in Russia echoed globally circulated constructivist teaching approaches developed by Vygotsky but were also linked to more recent works in Russian educational psychology. Elkonin and Davydov, whose works are referenced in explanations of new school standards, focused on activity in "developmental education," whereas Shchedrovitsky developed a "systems-activity approach." His work on the relationship between activity, thinking, and systems of knowledge came down to one main tenet that "activity should not be regarded as an attribute of the individual but rather as an all-embracing system that 'captures' people and 'forces' them to behave a certain way" (Grigorenko 2004, 201). When applied to school standards for compulsory schooling and coupled with teachers' professional standards that prioritized development and regulation, this conceptualization of activity reveals a reform course toward greater social control and authoritarian social engineering.

In sum, the overlaps between global and national scripts (adhered to mostly by the reformers themselves) created traction for the reform. In the ensuing drama, reformers got to act on their concerns as engineers of the national soul and designers of the national future. But for their performance to "create real benefit," it was important that those affected by the reforms would be willing to engage with the scripts offered to them. This, however, remained an area of struggles and conflicts, as I show next.

Universal versus National:
The Drama of Preserving the Difference

In June 2014, when the Concept transformed into an experiment, LEU organized professional development sessions for the participants of the reform project. On the last day, Oleg Victorovich explained how teacher preparation was organized in the United States. When he finished, an elderly gentleman asked him, "But how about the Russian mentality? Would any of this fit the Russian mentality?" Oleg Victorovich answered without a pause, "I don't believe there is such a thing as mentality. That's just a word that lazy people use when they don't want to do something. What works there, works here. What does not work there, won't work here" (Field Notes, June 2014).

This was one of the rare moments when someone from the team publicly stated that universal solutions worked regardless of cultural contexts. The audience did not appreciate this response. Heads started turning; whispering began. The elderly gentleman shrugged his shoulders and looked away.

Oleg Victorovich's response echoed the claim in the first McKinsey report that "the same broad policies are effective in different school systems irrespective of the cultural context where they are applied" (Barber and Mourshed 2007, 16). Other reformers also adhered to this position. Dmitriy Grigoryevich posted on his blog later that year that he regretted saying that he believed that Russia could have its own unique path of development. Principles and strategies for development were universal and Russia should just follow those. This sentiment was articulated in the study of international experiences that Anton Mikhailovich supervised and the article in an educational newspaper that followed (described in an earlier section).

Not all actors involved in teacher education reform agreed with the notion that international scripts were universal and applicable to the Russian context. Soon after the professional development sessions, a petition appeared on change.org with an appeal to stop the destruction of Russian teacher education in general and Lyutvino Pedagogical University No. 1, where Fedor Aleksandrovich had been appointed rector, in particular. The petition argued that the country had strong national traditions of pedagogical education. According to its author, a retired professor of that university, the introduction of the liberal arts models and practice-oriented teaching degrees would destroy national education and the nation's future. The proposals for reform that were associated with the Concept were portrayed as an attempt to Westernize Russia and turn it into a colony. The international origin of the ideas was not the only area of contention—the rector's nepotism and allegations of rampant corruption were also included in the text. The petition received almost ten thousand signatures and several hundred comments, mostly of support. It was forwarded to the president's administration. United Russia Party representatives announced that they would investigate the matter but it was soon forgotten.

Similar concerns about the search for universal solutions and their poor fit for national contexts emerged during my interview with the president of OSPU. In the years before, he held a prominent position in society and in the educational world. He pioneered some of the earlier reforms in pedagogical education, such as the introduction of bachelor's and master's degrees as well as the tenets of the Bologna Process. Despite his own active involvement in introducing some international practices into the Russian context, he was skeptical about reformers' agendas: "At the end of the eighties, beginning of the nineties, I had a chance to learn more or less deeply about how teachers are prepared in higher education in the United States, Great Britain, France, Sweden, and the Netherlands. And I reached a conclusion, that each country has its own national system of education, a universal system does not exist. And when they say, 'global educational system,' 'European education,' those are just notions because educational systems that emerged naturally [are national ones]. One of our problems nowadays is associated with a certain degree of uncertainty because the system is not being built up naturally, through gradual transformations and approximations of society's needs, but through borrowing of external forms. But, unfortunately, this borrowing of external forms is not creating a productive result. Because, and I repeat myself, there is no such a thing as a universal system. Each country has its own. And external forms create contradictions. . . . So, everything seems to be going in this struggle of reformers and conservatives. But maybe another way of looking at it would be to say that the problem is that there is no clarity about what type of system is desirable" (Interview 8, November 2013).

Other interviewees from pedagogical universities or the educational sector made a similar point with slightly different language—they responded to global scripts as problematic because "they did not evolve organically" and therefore did not match the national context. Gradual evolution that is responsive to the social needs and cultural contexts seemed more preferable to revolutions based on borrowed designs. Reflecting on the contradictions between the borrowed models and mentality, the dean of the psychology department in Dobrolyubov spoke about the problems that Western forms created. She mentioned how Russian students' lack of independence negatively affected their achievement when new curriculum plans decreased the number of contact hours and increased the time set aside for independent learning. She spoke of cultural differences in thinking. "Russian children like to contemplate. That's important! But what happens when you ask a person with such nonstandard thinking to take a test? They will fail it. But it has nothing to do with their abilities. It is their thinking that is different" (Interview 62, April 2014).

Concerns about the contradictions between global scripts, borrowed models, or Western forms of education were shared widely by participants in different educational institutions. Rarely did they display a belief that universal models or global scripts were effective regardless of the context or that they would "create real benefit." On the contrary, teacher educators felt that the context determined what happened in the classroom and struggled to preserve their approaches amid growing standardization and control of their work (Aydarova 2015a). Similar to reformers, they worried about the future of the nation, but not from the perspective of the global race. Rather it was a concern about preserving national distinctness or locally meaningful knowledge.

Describing the emergence of large-scale international assessments in the twentieth century, Nordin and Sundberg (2014) suggested that "the drive for rigour and standardisation in the education sector . . . arose in response to a world in which local knowledge, and the uncertainty accompanied with it, had become increasingly unsatisfactory" (12). Scott's (1998) analysis of government's efforts to improve human conditions that resulted in failure counteracts this position. He shows that governments' attempts to standardize local practices show that the eradication of local communities' knowledge—*mētis*, or "a wide array of practical skills and acquired intelligence in responding to a constantly changing natural and human environment" (Scott 1998, 313)—can lead to disastrous consequences. He contends: "What has proved to be truly dangerous to us and to our environment, I think, is the combination of the universalist pretensions of epistemic knowledge and authoritarian social engineering. . . . When schemes like these come close to achieving their impossible dreams of ignoring or suppressing *mētis* and local variation, they all but guarantee their own practical failure" (Scott 1998, 340). While it is too early to judge the long-term effects of the reformers' efforts, it is worth contemplating whether these reforms will bring more harm than good.

Concluding Thoughts

In this chapter, I analyzed how reformers deployed international influences to accomplish their agendas. From using PISA as a prop for constructing a crisis narrative to utilizing McKinsey reports authored by Michael Barber as policy scripts, reformers continually engaged with the Other. This engagement, however, was not always visible to the public. In constructing a crisis around PISA results or Russia's failure in the global education race, reformers organized and participated in events that drew large crowds. But when it came to the script for the policy, they were less forthcoming, using the study of international experience as a guise for the actual source of ideas. If not outright rejection, then clear ambivalence toward foreign ideas common among educators and society at large was a potential reason for their circumspect references to the influences on their work.

Russian reformers, yet again, are not unique in how they engage with global discourses. In England, Secretary of Education Michael Gove in his speech for the Education World Forum in 2011 focused on Michael Barber and Andreas Schleicher of the OECD as two of the most influential people in global education policymaking. He went on to say, "No nation that is serious about ensuring its children enjoy an education that equips them to compete fairly with students from other countries can afford to ignore the PISA and McKinsey studies. Doing so would be as foolish as dismissing what control trials tell us in medicine. It means flying in the face of the best evidence we have of what works" (Gove 2011). Focusing on English students' poor performance on PISA and evoking the language of the "global education race" (Morris 2016), he went on to argue for "the instigation of transformative reforms" (Adamson et al. 2017, 4) based on the policies of high-performing education systems. What ensued was "policymaking as pantomime" where English policymakers "already knew what the magical solutions were" (13) and imposed their beliefs on the international practices they observed.

Seeing PISA and McKinsey in the same sphere of influence reveals the complexities of the emergent global governance of education. Multiple actors' performances interact to produce new constellations of influence and power. These constellations are not just the effect of international organizations influencing decisions with abstract or theoretical arguments. Rather, they are the effect of "simple narratives of educational good and evil . . . drawn from scientific and global data (such as PISA) [that] provide a powerful and flexible resource from which simple policy stories can be constructed and complexity and conditionality marginalized" (Adamson et al. 2017, 14). One such simple policy story is a claim that better PISA results will improve a country's economic performance, circulated worldwide despite its flawed and ahistoric analysis (Berliner 2015). Another one is that universal solutions work regardless of cultural contexts. The simplicity of these policy stories comes at a price, often paid by populations that they affect rather than policymakers themselves.

In her analysis of PISA's push for standardization and for a reductionist technocratic view of education, Gorur (2016) raised concerns about the threat for diversity that PISA poses. She contends that "in the new, standardised school systems of PISA calculations, it is possible to (mis)understand teaching and school administration as standardisable and routinisable practices which can be codified in universally applicable terms—as matters of management rather than pedagogic expertise" (608). Extending these observations, Münch (2014) argued that this would lead to the "McDonaldization of education." In other words, if PISA proceeds with the imposition of universal reforms that prioritize accountability, measurability, and economization of education, it will eliminate the existing diversity of educational approaches and threaten our collective futures. Takayama (2018) critiqued the assumption that PISA's constructions of literacy are universally applicable, calling superficial the OECD's "attempt for cultural diversity and inclusivity without questioning how uneven power is exercised" (233). Similar concerns can be raised about the McKinsey reports because universal solutions they advocate eliminate possibilities for exercising local knowledge and undermine cultural variation in how teaching and learning are constructed. Moreover, the OECD and McKinsey reconstructed neocolonial structures of domination as the implementation of recommended reforms often requires assistance from global consultancies and edubusinesses (Aydarova 2017a; Meyer 2014; Morris 2016). These observations reflect the concerns raised by Russian educators that global scripts can be dangerous for educational systems. The question remains how Russian teacher educators engaged with the reform once it started.

6

Money Matters

In November 2015, less than two years after the Concept was first displayed on the ministry's website for public discussion, LSEU and LEU organized a conference to report the results of the first stage of the teacher education modernization reform. Among the conference presenters and attendees were teacher educators and administrators from pedagogical universities, many of whom in 2014 were either highly skeptical of the reform or actively engaged in the struggle to block it. Now, as they took turns making their presentations, they praised the project and emphasized the radical transformation it brought to their institutions. For example, Pavel Bogdanovich, who headed OSPU's efforts to create an alternative reform proposal in the fall of 2013 (chapter 3), now praised the project during his speech: "What has been done is a revolution! There has never been anything like this in terms of its effects. I am confident that despite the fact that Anton Mikhailovich or Maksim Davydovich said that they did not know what would happen when the project ended, whether the participants would die out like mammoths, the process has started . . . Dear colleagues, I think that the result of this project is enormous. There will be a continuation of this project because the changes have already started taking place. The process of change is not only the most difficult, the most labor-intensive, the most painful, but also the most interesting thing" (Field Notes, November 2015).

I could not believe what I was hearing. Pavel Bogdanovich was not alone. Many among those who criticized the Lyutvino group two years ago for failing to understand the challenges teacher preparation was facing or for imposing a Western model on them, were now enthusiastically using such terms as "modular structure of the program," "practice-based approach," "activity-based learning," "results-oriented design," and "feedback loop." All those words and phrases were the language of reform ideology that never surfaced in teacher educators' speech during earlier stages of my fieldwork. How in the world did all of this come about?

Recent scholarship in educational policy has examined how philanthropic organizations and conservative think tanks use competitive grant funding to disseminate their reform ideologies (Reckhow 2012; Scott and Jabbar 2014; Tompkins-Stange 2016). When reform measures they promote become tied with federal funding, such as Race to the Top or Innovation 3 grants, educational institutions find themselves under pressure to take on these ideologies in pursuit of much-needed resources (Owens 2015). While philanthropic organizations and think tanks were not the main actors of this Russian modernization drama, reformers found their techniques useful for the project. They used competitive grant funding to recruit and train acolytes to perform reform ideology that otherwise seemed unpalatable to reform participants. Together, these elements allowed reformers to push their agenda across the expanses of the Russian Federation and accomplish a great deal more than anyone anticipated.

Battle Over the Concept

In March of 2014, the mood at LEU was gloomy. The reformers repeated a refrain that as soon as the president signed the directive approving the Concept, it would take effect. Yet that signature was slow in coming. Every discussion of the Concept turned into a confrontation. As Joseph Abramovich noted, when the President's Council discussed the Concept, the former minister of education asked if the reformers were planning to train nurse practitioners instead of doctors, implying that it deprofessionalized teaching and significantly lowered teacher education standards. Oleg Victorovich lamented during our interview that once the Concept was published, a number of bloggers responded with very negative reviews and the Ministry of Education backed down on its promises of support. To counter these reviews, Maksim Davydovich organized a group interview with several people from the core group. The article that came out did not receive as much attention as all of the oppositional writing.

The Committee on Education in the State Duma had a heated debate about the Concept. According to published reports of that discussion, members of parliament raised many critical questions about the policy proposal (UG, February 25, 2014). The most open criticism of the Concept came from a former rector of a pedagogical college who expressed concerns over "the wash-out effect of applied bachelor's degrees on the whole system of higher education," arguing that these degrees would decrease the status of the teaching profession even further. His position was that the Concept did not solve the real problem that pedagogical education faced—a lack of state funding. Another criticism came from the first assistant to the head of the committee, Oleg Smolin. He was perplexed how "a liberal artist who got a little preparation for teaching would be better than someone initially prepared for teaching." In other words, using a poor translation for a person with a liberal arts degree, Smolin questioned how a decrease in professional preparation could produce better teachers. Finally, a pedagogical university graduate and a first assistant to the head of the Committee on Science, Education, Culture, and Informational Politics noted that because "the purposes for which it was created were not clearly stated," the Concept should not be brought up for any more public discussions. Not only did this debate fail to provide the approval for the Concept that the reformers were so eagerly anticipating, it also taught them "to avoid the parliament as much as possible" (Field Notes, July 2014).

The teacher education community mobilized its opposition as well. When the Concept was supposed to be discussed during the ministry's open session, teacher educators rallied behind closed doors and succeeded in removing it from the agenda. When Boris Ivanovich, an administrator at Lyutvino Pedagogical University No. 2, heard about my interest in the Concept, he responded with pride over the apparent victory of the teacher education community, "You don't need to look at some silly documents that will probably never take effect. No one needs that" (Field Notes, March 2014). According to him, because teacher educators "managed to block it at the ministry level," I should focus on something else in my research.

The reformers seemed downcast, too. Their concern was not just the barriers that the Concept was facing, but rather Russia's potential involvement in the military conflict in Ukraine. As Anton Mikhailovich shared with me during our meeting in March 2014, wars are costly and it was unlikely that at such a time the ministry would find money to carry out the project. The reformers seemed to sense a real danger that the project would die without ever taking off.

Policy Metamorphosis

When I returned to Lyutvino in June of 2014, the battle over the reform shifted grounds. Even though pedagogical universities mobilized enough opposition to block the Concept of Teacher Education Modernization from being signed into law, reformers and their supporters found a way around this barrier. The Concept itself was allegedly dropped but its proposals became a part of the new policy titled the Comprehensive Program of Improving the Qualifications of Pedagogical Workers in General Education Schools (Government of the Russian Federation, 2014) issued May 28, 2014. As a result of this strategic maneuvering, the Concept disappeared from the policy landscape, but its ideology reappeared in the program that was quickly signed into law and funded by the Ministry of Education without any debate or dialogue.

The Comprehensive Program consisted of four strands that focused on the introduction of teachers' professional standards, teacher education modernization, merit-based pay, and increasing the prestige of the teaching profession. The first three strands were connected to highly contested and unpopular policies that received a lot of opposition from teachers, teacher unions, teacher educators, and the public (fig. 9). The last strand was added earlier as a concession to those who opposed the first three reforms

Figure 9. December 1, 2013—A day of protests against educational reforms across Russian cities. Merit-based pay and the new teachers' professional standards were among other items on the agenda.

to address what most people saw as the main problem teachers faced in Russia (Aydarova 2016).

In our final interview, Maksim Davydovich underscored the vital link between the Concept and the teacher education modernization strand in the program: "Those [teacher education reform] priorities exist in the form of a text. This text exists in two versions: one as the Concept of Teacher Education Modernization and another one as a constitutive part of another more encompassing document called the Concept of Increasing the Levels of Pedagogical Workers where the Concept of Teacher Education became one of the program strands." Despite this connection, the title "Concept of Teacher Education Modernization" was dropped from the project's documentation. Instead, project managers and participants were urged to use "Comprehensive Program of Improving the Qualifications of Pedagogical Workers in General Education Schools" in all reports and project products. This move underscored that the policy continued to operate under masks (chapter 2) as the new guises obscured the connections between the unpopular Concept and the new reform initiatives.

The second strand of the Comprehensive Program titled "Modernization of Teacher Education" focused on "changing the contents of federal state educational standards in . . . 'Education and Pedagogical Sciences' and the technologies of teaching so that those correspond to the requirements of the new professional teachers' standards and . . . school standards" (Government of the Russian Federation 2014, 7). This strand sought to "implement a networked collaboration among higher education institutions," "significantly increase the amount of practical preparation," introduce "individual learning trajectories for students," develop "programs of multi-profile bachelor's degrees" that included both humanities and pedagogy components, as well as create "a model of pedagogical education for those who do not hold a degree in pedagogical education." These goals echoed the Concept's measures (appendix A and chapter 2).

Some modifications were also present in the new text. For example, the primary focus of the Concept was the creation of new models of teacher preparation, whereas the program added the changes in the federal teacher education standards to its priority areas. The push for a variety of preparation paths remained, but instead of using the contentious notions of "liberal arts" or "applied bachelor's," the strand focused on "multi-profile bachelor's degrees" or "increased practical preparation." All measures in the Concept that focused on attracting high-quality students to pedagogical education or high-achieving graduates into schools were dropped from the program.

Suggestions to introduce higher monetary compensation for better practical preparation were also omitted. Finally, there was no longer any mention of induction into the profession.

While the strand description in this program was only a page and a half long, its eventual implementation reflected a pursuit of drastic changes in teacher preparation. First, two types of bachelor's degrees could lead to the teaching profession: an applied bachelor's with a heavy focus on practice and an academic bachelor's as a liberal arts degree that allowed students more easily to opt in and out of becoming teachers. Two types of master's degrees were supposed to be developed: a master's with a strong focus on practical preparation and a master's with a focus on research. These degrees increased the number of pathways into teaching as some of them were specifically designed for those who had no prior pedagogical preparation. The driving ideology behind all of these degrees was that instead of being a subject specialist, a teacher had to know how to teach. This meant that all degrees had increased focus on practice supported by school-university partnerships. Taking heed from similar efforts in the United States and the United Kingdom (e.g., professional development schools, clinical models, and school-based teacher training), reformers wanted to see schools as equal or leading partners in teacher preparation and teachers as the main supervisors for teacher candidates. In some proposals, school-based experiences constituted a third to half of undergraduate curriculum plans.

The signature distinction of this reform was that it focused on the development of modules rather than programs. Even though the Concept mentioned modules only once in a description of potential master's programs, Maksim Davydovich called modules "a key quality improvement mechanism," constituting a "coherent whole for different types of teachers' labor functions and professional activities." Modules reflected a competency-based approach as they had to correspond to the labor functions laid out in teachers' professional standards (chapter 4) rather than to any bodies of knowledge in academic or professional fields. Modules were also supposed to create opportunities for student mobility because they could take modules anywhere they wanted, not just at the universities they were attending. In that regard, this move echoed the OECD's recommendations that Russian professional education needed "a competency-based module system [that] would permit students to move in and out of the system depending on their needs and on those of the changing labour market" (OECD 1998, 64).

When the reform started as a funded project with different institutions designing different modules, however, no one designed a whole model or a whole program of teacher education. In November 2015, when the first stage of the reform was complete, it remained unclear how modules could be put together to create models or programs of teacher education. The modular structure, however, opened possibilities for other providers to offer if not the whole then at least some parts of teacher education programs. The modular approach created variation in the paths available to students, but it was not clear how it would support program coherence and cohesion.

To create opportunities for academic mobility, institutions offering teacher preparation had to develop networked collaborations among themselves, with pedagogical colleges and with schools. Academic mobility and increased practical preparation required a rethinking of how students moved through their studies. Traditionally, Russian students were assigned to academic groups with which they stayed for the duration of their studies in their respective universities. This reform meant that this group structure had to be abandoned so that students could design their own individual educational trajectories. While the practice of students accumulating credits of their own choosing is familiar in many European and North American universities, in Russia, where most schedules for each group were still designed with paper and pencil by a department's office staff, this was a revolutionary idea that required technological infrastructure unavailable in most state universities.

Finally, programs had to be result and outcome oriented. The focus was on producing an effective teacher. The LSEU team designed an external assessment to measure students' competencies and the alignment of these competencies with teachers' professional standards, making it the centerpiece of all reform efforts. Even though the LEU team wanted to create a qualification exam that would allow candidates to bypass teacher education altogether, it did not happen. The LSEU team insisted that it should only be used for screening among those who were trained to be teachers. Together all these measures revealed a technocratic approach based on standardization, modularization, fragmentation, individualization, and outcome-based orientation of teacher education.

All of these drastic changes generated a lot of resistance. When the debates raged about the Concept, to mitigate opposition reformers argued that they were not proposing a reform but an experiment. For example, I asked Joseph Abramovich during our interview about concrete ways in which the Concept could be implemented (e.g., how to create an exit from pedagogical education when higher education institutions follow rigid frameworks of per capita funding for specific majors). In response, he shared: "This project that we are starting now, we insist that it is not a reform. It is an experiment. And through this experiment, we hope to build all these different constructions." Among themselves, reformers continued calling this project a reform. During the group interview about the Concept, for instance, Anton Mikhailovich compared this reform to a dental procedure in which a patient just needed to have his teeth removed without anesthesia. Unsurprisingly, perhaps, this description of the project never made it into the final article.

So, framing this reform as an "experiment" was strategic. It meant to disarm opposition. Most importantly, however, as reformers learned in the past, reforms fail because they do not get funded. Pitching this project as an experiment placed it in the recognizable frameworks of scientific and educational explorations that required funding. Even while the public engaged in debates about the Concept, reformers knew that the ministry had already allocated money for their project through the Federal Program of Educational Development.

Funding to Purchase Acquiescence

Sources of Funding

When I heard about the allocations for the Concept through the Federal Program of Educational Development, I wondered whether any international organizations were providing funding for Russian teacher education modernization. After all, the foreignness of the ideas embedded in the proposal seemed to suggest that this could be a distinct possibility. When I asked a Ministry of Education official closely connected to the reformers' network whether teacher education modernization was financed by the World Bank or any other international organization, he gave me a cryptic answer: "I did not participate in all the discussions. Maybe such decisions were made. Maybe those were just conversations. But I am not sure what came out of it. From my point of view, any investment into the country, if it does not destroy it, is beneficial [for its development]."

Sensing his discomfort, I tried to soften my question. "I am just trying to understand."

There was a moment of silence. Then he looked me in the eye and slowly said, "Money is very important. But it is important to remember the Persian saying, 'If you take someone else's handkerchief, you take someone else's scent'" (Interview 70, June 2014).

The saying the MOE official used indicated that borrowing money is often accompanied by borrowing values—a loan is not only about finances but also about priorities and orientations. In the Russian context where the struggle between Western-oriented and nationalist groups has deep-running historic roots (Figes 2002), this is a sensitive topic. But one could interpret this saying differently, too. There might be negative consequences for those who borrow money from external sources—the money leaves a scent that can be picked up and leads back to the lender. Why would this be a matter of concern for the MOE official?

International organizations, such as the World Bank, USAID, Open Society Foundations, and others were very active in Russia in the 1990s, but in the 2000s, they gradually started exiting stage. First, George Soros announced that he was closing the Open Society Institute in 2003. Then scandals erupted about the British Council's activities in Russia. In 2012, the Russian government demanded that USAID stop its operations because it was "meddling in the national affairs."[1] Several of my interviewees noted that among international actors in education only the World Bank kept an office with full-time staff in Russia. Other organizations only hired experts for specific projects. When I went to the World Bank office to conduct an interview with one of its representatives, I noticed that the building had no signs bearing the name of the organization and was under heavy security surveillance.

State-sponsored media created much hype around international organizations' involvement in Russia. In an article justifying the State Duma's law that required NGOs to declare themselves "foreign agents" if they received foreign aid, *Russia Today* explained: "In the past 25 years, billions of dollars have been pouring into Russia from the US State Department and its subsidiary agencies like the US Agency for International Development (USAID alone—nearly $3 billion), as well as from so-called '*private foundations*' like the National Endowment for Democracy, Freedom House, and George Soros's Open Society Institute. All of these institutions, judging by their activities and leadership's biographies, have important ties to the US State Department, the intelligence community, Cold War and the '*color revolutions*.'[2] The goal of all this money was not to express Washington's generous love of Russia, its culture or its people. In addition to building a loyal infrastructure, it aimed at 'winning hearts and minds'—and along the way oil, gas, and military capacity. It has all been about '*opening*'—'*open society*,' '*open economy*,' '*open Russia*,' '*open government*'—open for brainwashing, economic plunder, for hijacking Russia's domestic and foreign policies."[3]

This was how the involvement of international organizations was constructed for the public. They were not there to support the development of Russian education but rather to use their projects for advancing their own agendas or promoting the interests of Russia's competitors. That is why the MOE official was careful in how he framed his response.

I was not alone trying to figure out who was funding teacher education reforms. There were a few people that I met during fieldwork who were trying to trace international organizations' involvement in the reform efforts. Some faculty members in Ognensk and Dobrolyubov spoke at length about the impact of the World Bank and WTO on Russian education. In Lyutvino, a forty-year-old administrator from one of the pedagogical universities shared with me, "We all know it is the World Bank's doing. All they want is to destroy Russian education. Teacher education was the best that was left from the Soviet era. Now they got to it, too. I was in the State Duma and one of the politicians showed me the documents about the loan that the World Bank gave and how it was going to transform Russian education. Teacher education was there, too" (Field Notes, February 2014). From his perspective—a perspective shared by those who try "to follow the scents" of international organizations' involvement—the World Bank's money was used to pursue "an intentional politics of destroying pedagogical education" (Interview 61, March 2014). This sentiment was widely circulated on oppositional websites and blogs.

The representative from the World Bank, however, did not acknowledge that the bank was involved in the current wave of teacher education reform: "There have been no projects in pedagogical education. Moreover, the bank has not had any recent projects in education in principle. Meaning, projects that are projects, where there is an international loan and there is involvement from the regions, there have not been projects like this for the past eight years. The last project ended in 2007. It was 'E-Learning Support Project.' After that we have had no projects in education. There has been a project in higher education with the OECD's involvement with one university in one of the regions, but that project does not involve pedagogical education in any way."

After this, he explained to me that the bank often produces "analytical reports" and those may or may not lead to a project. I was aware of two World Bank reports that focused on teacher preparation in Russia: *Reforming Education in the Regions of Russia* (Canning, Moock, and Heleniak 1999a) and *Teaching in Transition* (Gasparishvili et al. 2006). It did not seem that there was any activity in teacher education reforms after those were published. I asked whether the Russian officials paid attention to those analytical reports. "Reforms of teacher education started; there were a lot more conversations about teacher education after that. Those were just happening without the bank's involvement. Russia has a strong enough expert community to carry out this work without the bank's assistance" (Interview 71, June 2014).

The working group members similarly stated that there was no support from international organizations for this reform. When I asked Joseph Abramovich, who used to work for the World Bank, if that organization was involved in the current reform, he explained that it was not the case. "The World Bank pays little attention to *teacher training. More specifically, there are a lot of conversations, but very few innovations in this area" (Interview 47, February 2014). According to Vadim Alekseyevich, analytical reports on teacher education that the World Bank provided remained in the background and no funding was allocated for the current stage.

Publicly available information about World Bank activities suggests that it funded several projects in Russia, but the Education Reform Project focusing on general education (Loan No.: 4605-RU for US$ 50 million) ended in 2007. A 2004 World Bank memo for that project identified teacher education reform as one of its "political priorities." At least in this respect the Lyutvino administrator was right—pedagogical universities were on the World Bank's agenda (coincidentally, at the time when Joseph Abramovich was working there). But the final report focused primarily on the introduction of per capita funding, making no mention of initial teacher education (World Bank 2007). At the time of my fieldwork, the World Bank officially had only one project in education focusing on financial literacy. According to the Russian Ministry of Foreign Affairs, in July 2014 Russia stopped receiving funding from the World Bank because of sanctions against Russia.[4] It is possible this reform received no funding from international organizations. But it is also possible that policy actors would not divulge donor involvement for fear of political and social repercussions.

Grant Competition

Regardless of the sources of funding, the Ministry of Education announced the competition for funding to oversee Concept implementation on December 28, 2013—only two months after it was presented at the LEU seminar and two weeks before it was released for public discussion on January 14, 2014. The competition's title—"Expert and Analytical Support for Implementing Projects of Pedagogical Master's, Pedagogical Bachelor's, and Variegated Paths of Teacher Education"—made no mention of the Concept but contained references to its key elements. The competition for funding remained open during the months when the Concept was hotly debated. Despite the debates and multiple conflicts, LSEU was awarded 86 million Russian rubles (approximately $2.3 million) at the beginning of March 2014—around the time when it seemed that the policy would be ultimately blocked. Even though, based on Russia's laws, competition for funding required a transparent process and multiple bidders, reformers described this process as hoops they had to jump through. Four institutions allegedly participated in the competition—three of them so obscure that even a furtive look at the list made it clear that only Lyutvino Special Education University could have won the competition because only they possessed "the technical expertise." The LEU team wrote the technical specifications for the grant in consultations with the team from LSEU, set the rules for the competition, found other groups who would bid against LSEU, and decided who would win the competition (i.e., LSEU) to make sure that the ideology of the reform remained intact. As Tatyana Borisovna casually mentioned during one of our chats, "Of course, we need to make sure that our own people work on the project" (Field Notes, February 2014).

Initial announcements for grant funding to design different aspects of the reform were also posted on December 28 but then reposted again in March and April of 2014. The National Training Foundation (Rus. NFPK), originally created to administer the World Bank loans and now overseeing the financial side of the Federal Program of Educational Development, initially projected that nineteen grants amounting to over 354 million rubles would be distributed in March of 2014. Those grants were supposed to range from about eighteen to twenty million rubles each. In March 2014, most of competitions for these grants were announced again but with smaller amounts and an additional group of awards added to it (see summary of final grant announcements in table 5). While the funding was intended for the development of modules for different types of bachelor's and master's programs envisioned by the Concept but not included in its final text, none of that was clear from grant descriptions. For example, instead of stating clearly that grant funding was supposed to be used to develop modules for an academic bachelor's, the grant competition focused on "the development of bachelor's programs . . . that can facilitate students' academic mobility." Instead of stating that the last group of grants would be used to develop an applied bachelor's, the competition referred to them as "strengthening the practical preparation in bachelor's programs through networked collaborations

Table 5. Summary of Grants Awarded to Project Participants in 2014

Number of Awards	Type of Activity	Maximum Possible Amount for Each Award (in Russian Rubles)	Date of the Award
7	Strengthening practical preparation of future teachers based on networked collaborations between higher education institutions and general education schools (i.e., applied bachelor's)	15,704,113	April 17/May 27, 2014
5	Development of modules and rules for implementing bachelor's degree programs that facilitate students' academic mobility based on networked collaborations (different subject areas in pedagogical education; i.e., academic/liberal arts bachelor's)	15,276,609	April 22, 2014
3	Development of modules and rules for implementing bachelor's degree programs that facilitate students' academic mobility based on networked collaborations (nonpedagogical education; academic/liberal arts bachelor's)	15,276,609	April 17, 2014
6	Development of modules and rules for implementing master's degree programs with in-depth practical preparation (pedagogical education)	15,029,705	April 22, 2014
2	Development of modules and rules for implementing master's degree programs with increased research and practical preparation (pedagogical education)	14,005,970	April 17, 2014
TOTAL: 23		335,302,128	

between higher education institutions and general schools." Yet again, the language was used to mask the intentions of reform but also to guarantee that only those in the know, that is, those who belonged to reformers' networks, could win the competitions.

The distribution of funds for different award categories revealed the ideology driving the reform: more than half of the awards went toward increasing practical preparation, whereas research-based master's programs often associated with stronger professionalization (similar to the Finnish model) received only two grants. How awards were advertised also reflected behind-the-scenes struggles. There was little acceptance of the applied bachelor's model as a notion, so this category of grants was added last. Both liberal arts and applied bachelor's models received a lot of negative attention, therefore grant announcements avoided those terms altogether. Once awarded, however, those grants were grouped together based on these program types in all public announcements about the reform.

Eventually, the total available grant funding ran up to over 335 million rubles (or approximately $9 million). Together with the eighty-six-million-ruble grant awarded for overseeing the project, these grants amounted to over four hundred million rubles for the first stage of the "experiment." The following year, another three hundred million rubles were supposed to be distributed among project participants again, according to Anton Mikhailovich (Field Notes, July 2014). All of this was a substantial sum of money. To put it into perspective, the Federal Program of Educational Development for 2013–2020 signed into law on April 15, 2014, projected that only about 170 million rubles per year would be used for "pedagogical education, leadership training, and professional development of educational workers" (Government of the Russian Federation, 2014). Double that amount was spent during the first year of project implementation alone. At that time, Russia was also beginning to face severe economic sanctions, which made these allocations appear even more generous and surprising.

Together these grants created a three-pronged relationship: the Ministry of Education as the client for whom the project was administered (Rus. *zakazchik*), LSEU and LEU as managers of the project (Rus. *operatory*), and project participants as implementers or executors of the project (Rus. *ispolniteli*). The irony of this role distribution was that those on whom this reform was implemented were paid to design its actual implementation, and the ministry that is often perceived as the initiator of reforms (chapter 3) acted as a client for whom reform implementation was performed. The reformers yet again served as directors staging the play but evoked the ministry as the final arbiter of all disagreements when it was expedient.

On April 7, 2014—a month after the first grant for overseeing project implementation was awarded—Lyutvino Special Education University along with Lyutvino Economics University began providing "the expert and methodological support for the project participants" (Project Website, 2014–2015). In two months between the beginning of March when LSEU received the funding to oversee the project and May 29, 2014, when the Comprehensive Program was signed into law, the reformers selected project participants and arranged to bring them to Lyutvino for professional development that served as the project kick-off (described in the next section). Thirteen institutions joined as participants-implementers, with some winning several different grants from this project. LSEU alone won three of the twenty-three grants in addition to the grant to oversee the project. Of the thirteen implementers of the reform, seven were pedagogical universities. The rest were either classical universities or institutions that specialized in other areas. One of the interesting participants in the project was an institution that specialized in heavy metallurgy. Their budding interest in teacher education was evidence of reformers' efforts to break up the monopoly of institutions traditionally involved in teacher preparation.

It is important to note that project participants were often selected through reformers' personal connections and their networks. The very first list of participants included on the project's website had only six universities: two universities that supervised the project (LSEU and LEU) along with Lyutvino Pedagogical Universities Nos. 1 and 2, Nikitinsk State Pedagogical University, and Ognensk State Pedagogical University. Apart from OSPU, rectors of these institutions expressed enthusiastic support for the reform and were often involved in co-presenting its measures with the reformers (chapter 3). Gradually, other universities were added, often from reformers' networks as well. For example, some of the participants were from universities where the LEU team had done their consulting projects (chapter 1) and others were from institutions whose rectors participated in Skolkovo's 100 Rectors program (chapter 3). One way or the other, the presence of like-minded people mattered significantly for including institutions in the list of grant awardees. OSPU was the only institution whose leadership opposed the reform.

Selecting project participants from reformers' networks did not diminish the resistance to the reform, however. For example, Dmitriy Grigoryevich—

the rector of Lyutvino Pedagogical University No. 2—was the reformers' close ally. The university won one of the grants, but the faculty members did not seem to buy into the reform ideology. When the project kicked off as professional development for teacher education faculty and administrators, the group that came from that institution was agitated and angry. Boris Ivanovich—the same administrator who told me that I should study something else because this policy would never take effect just two months before—said to the reformers, "Don't teach us how to do what we have been doing all of our lives. Give us the money and we will ourselves decide how to spend it" (Rus. *Dayte nam den'gi i my sami ikh raspilim*). Visibly frustrated by the professional development sessions, he announced in the middle of the day, "I just got a call from my boss. We have to go. Can we wrap this up in thirty minutes?" As he was leaving, he noted, "There is a meeting at the ministry tomorrow. Hopefully, we can still somehow influence this whole thing." What these conflicts underscored was that even though university rectors expressed alignment with the project ideology, the faculty and administrators who eventually had to engage in the project were less inclined to accept the vision and measures of the reform. After seeing the confrontations that happened during her presentation, one of the LEU faculty invited to speak at the professional development event noted, "I am getting the impression that they are here for the resources, nothing else" (Field Notes, June 2014).

Her comment about resources pointed to the role of finances in purchasing acquiescence that reformers actively pursued. They realized that it was not the seductive ideology or the promise of change that attracted people to the project or kept them involved in it but the funding that project participants could bring to their home institutions by implementing the reform. This understanding that external funding would play the central role in transmitting the new ideology of educational reform emerged at the very beginning of the project. As Anton Mikhailovich explained to me once higher education institutions were selected to participate in the reform: "There was a meeting at the ministry where the minister and his two assistants got all the rectors from the higher education institutions participating in the project and told them that if they don't do something for real they will be responsible for the money. They won't get the money for the next year and they will have to give account for how they have spent this money. The minister threatened them" (Field Notes, July 2014).

Similar understandings of how central funding was to spreading the project's ideology were reiterated multiple times during the cumulative event in Lyutvino in November 2015 as well as in my follow-up interviews with the reformers. Anton Mikhailovich during his speech at the opening plenary of the conference noted that he was hoping that those who participated in the project would not die out like dinosaurs when the project is over. "The university administration tolerated your work because you were bringing in some resources. Who knows what will happen if those resources are not there afterward," he quipped. Similarly, during our last interview, he described the monumental changes that had to happen in higher education because of the project's new ideology and noted: "While the project is going on, [project participants] face few obstacles because there is external funding. . . . University leadership tolerated the transformations that were introduced by the project because the changes brought in additional resources: money, as well as consulting support and glory—'I am a participant of a federal project, I am a leader.' If we stop this now, everything will go back to the way it used to be before" (Interview 80, December 2015).

Funding mattered not only in the additional resources universities received for accepting the reform's ideology but also in the threats participants faced if they disagreed with some of the changes reformers wanted to see. Even though the Concept had a clause about reducing the scale of teacher preparation (chapter 2), that part of the policy was tabled, but reformers continued to argue that the ministry should decrease the number of students pedagogical universities could admit with full funding from the federal government (Rus. *control'nye tsifry priyema*). During the November conference, different reformers noted that only those universities that could demonstrate results aligned with reform ideology would continue receiving federal support for their students. If they chose not to comply with reform measures, such as an increased number of school-based practicums or greater involvement of schoolteachers in supervising students during their field placements, they would lose "free money from the federal government." With other sources of funding being limited or completely nonexistent, this became a sore point for many administrators.

Reformers strategically used funding to purchase acquiescence of teacher education faculty and administrators. Eager to bring funding to their home institutions, teacher educators attempted to take on the ideology of the reform no matter how foreign it seemed to them before. To create convincing performances, however, project participants had to be trained in reform ideology. In the rest of this chapter, I will explore the process of training that started in June 2014 and took a year and a half to complete before it culminated in a November conference during which project participants had to perform reform compliance for ministry officials and other academic audiences.

Training the Actors

Initial Training

As I noted before, what teacher educators viewed as a victory in March became a defeat in June when the same people who scoffed at the Concept were now assembled into a room where they were undergoing "professional development" on how to implement the new principles of teacher education in their institutions. It was the reformers' turn to celebrate. When I saw Anton Mikhailovich in the middle of June, he had a huge grin on his face and savoring each word said, "I still can't believe that the project took off" (Field Notes, June 2014). The task before the reformers now was to immerse project participants into the reform ideology.

To accomplish that, reformers organized the project kickoff in the middle of June 2014 as professional development sessions that focused on different aspects of the "experiment." Project participants were split into four groups based on the strand of their work and the level of preparation: LSEU supervised and trained the teams that were designing modules for applied bachelor's and master's programs with increased practical preparation, whereas LEU worked with teams developing modules for academic bachelor's (or liberal arts) and research-based master's programs. Because of my closer ties with the LEU team, I observed the sessions they offered. The composition of groups attending their sessions changed from day to day depending on the topic discussed—one day there were about ten or twelve people in the room, the next about twenty-five. Sessions varied in their contents: some attempted to create a shared understanding and language among the participants about what this project entailed, while others described models in place at LEU or other institutions that reflected reform ideology, such as designing programs based on desired outcomes. No matter what direction the sessions took though, project participants tended to take issue with what they were told.

To develop a shared understanding and language of the reform, project participants were invited to review the criteria for evaluating their projects when those were completed. After an LEU professor's presentation about a master's program she developed, Roman Valeryevich urged the participants to apply the criteria for their projects to evaluate this program. Boris Ivanovich dominated much of the conversation that ensued. "We agree on some things but disagree on many more others," he started. When the LEU presenter acknowledged that most, if not all, LEU programs are not modular, participants responded with angry disbelief. This was the major requirement for the grants they received, but at that stage it was not clear what constituted a module and there were no clear examples of what a module looked like at a Russian higher education institution. Hearing that LEU did not have modular programs only added fuel to the fire. In the midst of this conversation, Boris Ivanovich exclaimed, "I feel like I am a character in the play *The Dowerless Girl* when Larisa asks, 'Do you also have chains?' and Vozhevatov responds, 'Shackles!' We don't just have chains, we have shackles that the client [the ministry] locked us into with those modules." Similar to many other questions and comments throughout the day, this response revealed how critical many participants were of the reform ideology. As they asked presenters questions, they challenged the overall task before them. For the rest of that day, verbal battles over the meaning of "contemporary," "measurable," and "scientifically based" unfolded before me.

During the next two days, invited speakers shared with project participants principles and models that exemplified reform ideology. Thursday sessions focused on competencies and program design based on professional activity and professional tasks. After an LEU presenter completed a part of her presentation on how competency matrices could be developed based on the Bologna Process guidelines and Tuning[5] specifications, she was confronted with questions over the need for such detailed breakdowns. One participant explained: "What scares me is that breaking things down into details leads to complete absurdity. When we reach tiny details of a competency, we actually lose it. Besides, when we tell instructors that they have to help students develop competencies, but not the whole thing, just parts of it, they don't understand, they don't know how to apply this to their own work, and they can't describe what they are doing. But the biggest problem is that when we create these clusters and develop these matrices, we are introducing a hardline system . . . And that's why I think this Westernization (Rus. *zapadnichestvo*) will only create damage" (Field Notes, June 2014). This push-back against standardization and fragmentation that she shared resonated with the group as people nodded while she was speaking.

The last day of professional development was dedicated to the liberal arts model. Tensions escalated when two morning presentations focused on US approaches to teacher education. After Oleg Victorovich described the US model of teacher preparation, one of the older professors from Bratsk challenged his presentation: "This is an absolutely socialized model that corresponds to the society where it operates. To what extent can it be engrafted onto our society? Our consciousness? Our tradition?" Someone else questioned how reasonable it was to look at the US example if Americans have average results on PISA themselves. Trying to salvage the situation, Fedor Alexandrovich stepped in with his own commentary: "We have just heard a great presentation. It has only one downside. We constantly heard the word 'American.' And then we got a question—what do we do with all of this, when it is so alien for us? Let's cross out the word American from the entire presentation and let's listen as if it was all about us" (Field Notes, June 2014).

I was asked to present next and share how the liberal arts model worked in teacher preparation in the United States. After my presentation, among other things, I was asked, "Wouldn't the absence of academic depth in teacher preparation lead to, I'll say like a doctor, the 'Psaki syndrome' with this whole scenario of the US Navy reaching Belarusian shores? [Jennifer Psaki] received a bachelor's degree. Wouldn't such a system lead to the absence of academic depth in teacher education?" Referencing the mishaps of a White House communications director during Obama's presidency who mistakenly claimed that the US Navy reached the shores of a landlocked country, the project participant implied that borrowing a US model would create an intellectual decline in Russia.

What I observed during these professional development sessions offered by LEU in June 2014 seemed like a tug-of-war between reformers and project participants. Reformers explained the main ideological principles of the reform or shared models that exemplified some of the reform aspects, and project participants challenged those principles and models. In response, reformers evoked a higher authority—the ministry—as the final arbiter on the matter and as the main client of the reform who put constraints both on them as the managers of the project and on the project participants themselves. Among themselves, however, during tea and lunch breaks, reformers scoffed that the ministry would want what they told them to want because ultimately they were the ones who were deciding what direction the reform should take. Every day there was much frustration on everyone's part. The project participants fought the imposition of what they saw as an alien ideology and the reformers were angry with the resistance they observed.

Ongoing Training

The "experiment" did not end with the June professional development sessions. Those who participated in the professional development had two months to develop modules that would match the reform ideology. To support their work on this project, participants received access to the web portal hosted by LEU so that they could use the resources provided by the reformers, ask questions about the challenges they were facing, and collaborate with colleagues from other institutions. At the end of August of 2014, project participants were expected to present those modules to the ministry. This ambitious plan appeared to be more challenging than reformers anticipated. The deadlines for submitting modules were extended as there continued to be uncertainty about what those modules entailed and how they could be created. In October 2014, a conference was held in Lyutvino to discuss midpoint results of the project. During this conference, project participants presented the modules that they were able to develop to ministry officials and to higher education faculty from other institutions.

In December of 2014, twenty-three additional institutions joined the project as co-implementers of the reform. In spring of 2015, all participating institutions tested and evaluated more than one hundred modules that project participants had designed. After students went through the modules, they took a new assessment of professional competencies that LSEU developed as a part of this project. Students' results on this assessment were used to gauge the effectiveness of the modules. This new assessment was described by Maksim Davydovich as "the radical innovation" and "the drastic difference that sets this project apart from others" because it evaluated "actual educational outcomes" (Project Website, 2014–2015). All modules were compiled into an online library and made accessible to participants through the project website. To disseminate reform ideology even further, reformers envisioned making the module library accessible to other institutions that had not yet participated in the reform efforts. In addition to disseminating reform ideology, this library of modules worked as a mechanism of standardization through sharable materials and potential building blocks for program models.

In May 2015, during a conference in Lyutvino, participants shared how they implemented their modules at other institutions. Eight more institutions joined as co-implementers of the reform, bringing the total number of participating institutions to forty-four. With the ministry's ongoing efforts to reduce the number of pedagogical universities, the growing numbers of institutions participating in the reform reflected how the landscape of teacher education was being redrawn through reform efforts. Many participating institutions were either classical universities or institutions not traditionally involved in teacher preparation at all.

Amid all of this activity, LSEU and LEU continued to provide training to project participants. A day of workshops and group work set aside specifically for project work preceded all conferences. Webinars and seminars brought participants together to discuss turning points in project implementation, such as the rollout of the competency assessment. In addition to these events, reformers put together several special issues of academic journals that highlighted the ideology of the reform and introduced the projects developed by some of the participants. Yet the most important work happened during professional development sessions for small groups that took place in Lyutvino or occasionally at the participants' institutions where reformers traveled in teams.

As Roman Valeryevich explained, and later a faculty from LSEU confirmed, many of those professional development sessions took the form of Shchedrovitsky's organizational activity games. The fact that those games were deployed in the process was not public knowledge, but those who were involved in the process shared that it was through these games that participants' thinking was aligned with the project's goals (see chapter 4 on Shchedrovitsky's work in this area). According to Roman Valeryevich, to accomplish transformations in participants' thinking, reformers worked with small teams of six to seven people from each university. He described what happened during group work this way: "This is what the system of that work was like. It was explained to them how [a program] can be organized and participants were shown different prototypes. At the same time, people presented what they were going to do. Not what they were going to say, but what they were actually going to do. Ninety percent of the time was spent on talking things through. People asked questions and transformed their products. We set a task for them, explained to them what it meant, engaged them in interpretation of that task and its problematization. We fought with them, made things up with them. They engaged in design. They had to give presentations not as theoreticians but as designers . . . They had to design starting from the results they had to accomplish" (Field Notes, November 2015).

The language used to describe these processes, particularly problematization and design, pointed to the work conducted by Shchedrovitsky and his disciples in the design of sociocultural change. As Anton Mikhailovich explained, this was a difficult project because it had "to change people's perceptions about how things ought to be [Rus. *predstavleniya o dolzhnom*]." During the November 2015 conference, some of the participants described their experiences as "getting their heads blown off" or "experienc[ing] total reboot." Borrowing language from Shchedrovitsky's followers, they described their project tasks as "reshaping notions of the future" and "designing the society of the future." Those training sessions—or "personally targeted work" as Roman Valeryevich described them—played an important role in getting participants to take on the new ideology and the vision of change.

The vision of introducing cultural change by working with small groups of change agents who could then spread the new ideology further also stemmed from Shchedrovitsky's work and, according to Roman Valeryevich, was a part of the reformers' strategy. Yet, the teams from different universities were relatively small. When seven or eight people were brought to Lyutvino for professional development, as I learned during a follow-up study in Dobrolyubov, thousands of others working for the same institution knew little about ongoing reform efforts, to say nothing of the fact that their own university was participating in the project.

Final Run-Through to Streamline the Performance

The conference reporting the results of the first stage of reform implementation took place in November 2015, about a month before final reports were due at the ministry. I was invited to attend this event as a "foreign expert." Reformers brought project participants together for a day of preconference workshops held at LEU, which were spent on debates about participants' projects and practice runs of their presentations. Members of reformers' teams told participants how to make changes in their presentations or simply edited their PowerPoints for them. In anticipation of the project participants' performance for ministry officials, reformers wanted to make sure that all presentations were ideologically aligned and that all participants would be invested in praising the project to get funding for the next stage. When I joined the group that worked on the applied bachelor's model, I learned that these run-throughs were not without their own tensions.

Most of the time during the preconference workshops, reformers tried to address participants' faulty performances. What constituted a faulty performance varied but was often connected to participants' failure to introduce new ideology into their projects to the extent desired by the reformers. For example, one of the thorny issues in the applied bachelor's group was the question of academic disciplines and modules. Traditionally, curricular documents were based on academic disciplines, but the ideology of the project required that those should be replaced with modules. At the beginning of the day, Maksim Davydovich, who was in charge of this group, stated with some irritation in his voice: "The ministry receives from us the documents that you turned in to us and sees 'academic discipline' and then they ask us as the managers of the project what we had been doing this entire time if the teams of implementers continue to use the term 'academic discipline.'"

In their defense, several participants shared that the technical specifications for the projects that they received from the ministry listed "academic disciplines." Maksim Davydovich responded that ministry officials knew reform ideology well and that when they received documents that didn't match that ideology, they feared that participants were faking their work on the project. Even though after several rounds of negotiations Maksim Davydovich conceded that participants could use "academic disciplines," he urged them to explain how their use of the term was different from its traditional meaning. Throughout the rest of the day he continued emphasizing the project's focus on a modular structure of teacher preparation as the driving ideology of the reform that participants had to clearly demonstrate in their presentations.

A similar confrontation happened when the group attempted to come to a consensus regarding the number of credits that should be allocated to preservice teachers' practical preparation—another key ideological principle of the reform. When some participants started saying that fifty to seventy credits out of 240 total credits for undergraduate degrees would be enough for practical preparation, Maksim Davydovich asked them how their proposals differed from what was traditionally done in teacher education, implying that this change was not radical enough to match reform ideology. When someone else recommended that a range of credits between seventy and ninety should be listed in standards documents, Maksim Davydovich noted that the ministry should be notified that some participating institutions refused to increase the amount of practical preparation even though this is one of the main tenets of this reform.

He continued, "You have to understand that as we are trying to modernize teacher education, we also have the processes of reorganization and creation of leading regional universities. When we introduce a qualifying exam and it becomes clear that your graduates cannot pass it, that they have not developed the practical competencies necessary to engage in this work, no one will give you per-student funding from the federal budget" (Field Notes, November 2015). Evoking reorganization and the creation of "leading regional universities" through mergers, Maksim Davydovich implicitly threatened participants that their institutions could be completely eliminated. Speaking more directly, he argued that if they did not implement the reform according to its ideology, they could lose federal funding—the main source of financial support for pedagogical universities. All of these direct and indirect threats had major implications for the presentations that project participants had to give during the conference. Unless their performance was adjusted to reflect reform ideology more closely with a much bigger increase in practical preparation, participants' presentations would put in danger the future of the project and of their own institutions.

This final run-through showed that disagreements about key points of reform remained despite reformers' ongoing efforts to change participants' thinking. Recognizing these challenges, reformers used these rehearsals to streamline participants' performances so that they would clearly demonstrate a move away from the previous approaches. Reformers conducted these final run-throughs to ensure that MOE officials attending the conference would see ideological congruity between participants' presentations and the main principles of the reform and authorize continued funding for the project. This is how Anton Mikhailovich made this point clear at the beginning of the preconference day, when he spoke to all project participants: "Our main task for today is to make sure that the results that are going to be aired for the client [the Ministry of Education] . . . eh . . . that your messages would not contradict one another. This does not mean that we want you to say exactly the same thing. Not at all. But in our speeches we need to have some commonality, some points that we all agree on. . . . Today we have a very important day. The impressions from this project will depend on how people will present their work [. . .] Tomorrow, we would need to show ourselves in such a light that we would have a chance to keep this party going" (Field Notes, November 2015).

At the end of day, Maksim Davydovich reiterated this message when he offered closing remarks for the group working on the applied bachelor's projects: "It is very important for us to adequately convey to the ministry our position, so that the ministry would support us and so that we could move on to the next stage of the project, which would entail changing [Federal] Teacher Education Standards. So, let me say it again, tomorrow and the day after tomorrow you have an opportunity to show how amazing you and your university are. Do not restrain yourself in any way when you do that [Rus. *Ni v chem sebe ne otkazyvayte*]" (Field Notes, November 2015).

These repeated references connecting conference presentations with the subsequent funding for the project revealed the tenuous relationship between the reformers and project participants. It was convincing performances of the latter that could ensure ongoing financial support from the ministry for the reformers' efforts. Even the presentations of foreign experts, such as myself and my colleague from the United Kingdom, underwent a rehearsal in the LSEU rector's office at the reformers' request to make sure that our evaluations would not put the project in danger. Without these final run-throughs, the danger of losing support for the second stage when teacher education standards would be changed ran high.

The November Conference: The Final Performance or a Premiere?

The official part of the November conference took place in LSEU's main building over three days: Wednesday, Thursday, and Friday. The large lecture hall where all sessions took place was set up as an amphitheater with the lectern and a large desk facing the audience at the bottom of the stairs. Reformers and ministry representatives that occasionally joined them sat at that desk throughout the conference. When project participants had to present, they came to the lectern from their seats in the amphitheater. This unequal status between project participants who were mostly women and reformers who were men became most visible in the interactions that followed presentations. Reformers interrupted participants when they offered comments or questions and talked down to them through most of the conference. As I looked around the room, I saw many familiar faces. Although people were greeting one another and waving hello, there was no familial closeness that I saw at the conferences organized by pedagogical universities.

The first session was delayed because the ministry representative was running late. As soon as he entered the room, the conference started with a short video highlighting the project's key accomplishments. The LSEU rector gave several opening remarks, thanking the Ministry of Education for the support extended to this project. The ministry official spoke for twenty minutes, highlighting the need for reform because of the new teachers' standards and school standards. His presentation was organized around three questions he saw as central in the reform: what to teach, how to teach, and who should teach. Promising that the ministry would use "all [available] pressure mechanisms to support the work that has been completed," he noted that forty-five universities were already participating in the project. So, the task was "to ensure that all higher education institutions of the Russian Federation that prepare teachers took part in this program so that not a single educational establishment was left out of this project." In their subsequent talks, reformers reiterated this sentiment—the project had to become an all-encompassing reform that would be implemented across the entire country. The project's ideas also had to be disseminated through reports and publications generated by participants, so that the ideology of reform would become accessible to more academic communities. Even how reformers constructed the audience for this conference—"the whole country is now watching you"—pointed to the scale of their ambition. For "an experiment" that had minimal evaluation and research (external reviewers were invited to evaluate only descriptions of modules prepared by project participants), the sights were set high to expand the project as broadly as possible.

After the ministry official, Vadim Alekseyevich, Anton Mikhailovich, and Maksim Davydovich took turns sharing their visions for the future of the project. In their talks, they urged participants to consider additional changes that the reform required. New teacher education standards had to be created based on the reform ideology. University structures also had to be transformed so that instead of faculties (or departments), universities would consist of programs. Students' ability to choose modules had to extend beyond their university, which, along with the greater involvement of schools in teacher preparation, required a change in legal and regulatory frameworks for higher education institutions. The number of students admitted with allocations from the federal budget had to be reduced. The preparation of teacher education faculty had to change drastically as well so that new faculty members would be trained in the new ideology. A ministry official who joined the conference on the last day shared during her talk that she was hoping that this experiment would become the blueprint for the reform of the entire higher education sector. For an experiment that was "not that radical" (Interview 78, December 2015), this reform within a year and a half of its implementation began to reach far beyond traditional teacher preparation.

Apart from setting sights on new horizons, during their talks reformers discussed what they saw as accomplishments of the project. Anton Mikhailovich noted in his opening speech that he was proud that the project was not just about "a stack of papers" but a "real project with real results." "We have started speaking the same language," he said to the project participants, "when one person says a word, other people know exactly what this word means and to me that is the real outcome of this reform." The use of shared language was important because it signaled to observers that the new ideology was now accepted as the blueprint of the future. With so many projects that did not lead to real results and failed because there was no shared language (chapter 1), this project finally generated a change in reformers' eyes.

And shared language participants did seem to speak. Despite disagreements that emerged the day before, during their conference presentations, teacher educators consistently used the key words from the project's core principles—"system-activity-based approach" to educational processes, "modular structure of the program," "increased practical preparation," "networked cooperation among higher education institutions and schools," and so on. Many of these words appeared in the OECD's (1998) and the World Bank's (1999, 2004) reports in the 1990s and 2000s; many others came from activity theories developed by Russian psychologists. But it was unlikely that these words would have received so much attention without all the training that the reformers provided.

An important channel for infusing these words into participants' performance were the PowerPoints they read from and the reports they eventually submitted to project managers. As the participants used the same key words, they also fairly consistently emphasized the need for further financial support. From one presentation to another, faculty and administrators described how finances were necessary to support students' internship placements, facilitate faculty mobility among different institutions, and keep the project going in general. For three days, teacher education faculty and administrators worked hard to convince reformers and MOE officials that they had bought into the ideology of the reform and were implementing it faithfully to ensure continued grant support.

This performance was not necessarily always disingenuous. In informal conversations with me, reformers highlighted the teams whose projects showed a real departure from past approaches. At the same time, during some of the presentations, they also pointed out the teams that dressed up what they always did in new terminology. In such contexts, shared language that project participants tried to adopt acquired a comical effect. During a coffee break, Joseph Abramovich smirked about the presentation of the OSPU rector, "Look at the big words they've learned! 'Reengineering'!" Acknowledging this uneven spread of project ideology in our final interview, Anton Mikhailovich shared that about half of the institutions "implemented most of the project ideas."

Despite everyone's efforts to demonstrate "commonality" and acquiescence, disagreements continued to stew. After my presentation, a couple of participants from Nikitinsk approached me during a coffee break to share their concerns about the loss of subject area preparation that reformers advocated. The rector of their university supported reformers since the Concept's early days, their team was highlighted as one of the eager adopters of reform ideology, but they still were worried about the reformers' focus on practice that aimed to move preservice teachers away from being subject specialists. Yet they did not voice those concerns publicly at any of the sessions. Only one presenter spoke directly about the decision not to rely on modules in program design because of the problems the latter created. After that presentation, Anton Mikhailovich used LEU as an example of an institution where modules were used without any problems and angry whispers filled the room.

Even reformers had a spat about the academic bachelor's program created to attract those who chose other majors into teaching. "Do we even have enough people interested in pursuing this option?" exclaimed Maksim Davydovich in frustration after Stepan Sergeyevich finished his presentation on multiple points of entry into and exit out of teacher education that were developed during the project. To smooth over these disagreements, Anton Mikhailovich urged everyone not to "air dirty laundry" during the closing session when the MOE representative with decision-making power was going to be present. Overall, however, MOE officials for whom all of these performances were set up were hardly ever present to either become convinced by participants' compliance or notice the contestations—they rarely stayed long enough to see much of what was happening. Most of them showed up to give their own talk, stayed for half an hour to an hour to answer additional questions, and left soon afterward. Only one of the officials met with a select group of participants for a half-hour chat about the project.

After the last session on Friday, reformers and project participants gathered in a small room with hors d'oeuvres and spirits to celebrate a successful event. Toasting each other over cold cuts and canapés with caviar, they said their words of gratitude and well wishes for productive future collaborations on the reform efforts. The training of the actors into which the reformers poured so much energy paid off. By mid-December, they received official word that the project would receive continued funding.

The Aftermath

Summing up more than two years of active work, reformers celebrated many victories. Having learned from global policy edupreneurs, such as Michael Barber, how to orchestrate change in an educational system, they deployed additional strategies to initiate an ideological shift in Russian teacher education. The use of competitive grants along with intensive training in reform ideology for project participants allowed reformers to bring together teacher educators and administrators into performances that signaled the latter's acquiescence to the reform. Moreover, what reformers managed to push through against much opposition as "an experiment" quickly grew into an all-encompassing reform. The second stage of the reform was supposed to create new teacher education standards that would solidify reform ideology in binding legal documents intended for quality control and university accreditation. This step would make the change irreversible and much more long-lasting than anything gained through grants and professional development sessions. Furthermore, the project's alleged success set sights high for transforming not only the entire field of teacher education but also Russian higher education at large.

The performances during the November conference played a critical role in ensuring the continuation of this project. As Anton Mikhailovich explained during our last interview, "Despite the difficult financial situation,[6] the project has received money [for the second stage]" (Interview 80, December 2015). But it was not only the continued funding that would now guarantee the ongoing reform efforts. In December 2014, the Ministry of Education created Coordinating Councils to oversee different sectors of higher education. Vadim Alekseyevich became chairman of the Coordinating Council for Education and Pedagogical Sciences. Among its seventeen members, there were Joseph Abramovich, Fedor Aleksandrovich from Lyutvino Pedagogical University No. 1, Dmitriy Grigoryevich from Lyutvino Pedagogical University No. 2, the rector of Lyutvino Special Education University, the rector of Nikitinsk Pedagogical University, and even the MOE official I had interviewed about the funding for this project. All of these actors were active in supporting the reform since its inception. Even as the composition of the Coordinating Council changed, reformers moved into other positions in Federal Curricular and Methodological Associations. Their influence now was no longer that of outside experts "whom the Ministry trusted" but rather insiders setting the trends and orchestrating many of the activities in the field.

Reformers' activities often continued with the ideas that were originally proposed in the Concept but were removed for political reasons. For example, one of the driving principles of the Concept was opening entry to the teaching profession for those without pedagogical education. The reform created a variety of teacher education degrees for those who wanted to teach. To address the goal of attracting others into teaching, reformers supported the introduction of Teach For America into the Russian context. In 2015, "Teacher for Russia"[7] started its first pilot program under their guidance.

Despite the reformers' commitment to "real projects with real results," the reform continued to be discussed through the metaphor of theater. A month after the conference in an interview with me, Anton Mikhailovich reflected on the results of the reform: "Our goal was to make sure that no one remains indifferent. We managed to split the audience in two. That's the main result. As Meyerhold used to say, 'The play has taken place.' That's the result of it." Drawing on his own experiences in directing amateur theater, he went on, "I lose interest in the play once it has premiered. I get excited about all the work leading up to the premiere. But once it has been staged, I am no longer interested in it. I look for other things I could do." Evoking the theater metaphor, Anton Mikhailovich spoke of closure and of his readiness to move to other projects. The political theater of educational reform would soon resurface in other initiatives spearheaded by the LEU team.

Epilogue

> Theater is change and not simple presentation of what exists: it is becoming and not being.
>
> —Augusto Boal, *Theater of the Oppressed*

Political theater of educational reforms does not end when a project is completed. The new Federal Program of Educational Development issued December 26, 2017, identified providing quality education as measured by PIRLS, TIMSS, and PISA, with the expectation that Russia would attain "no less than the twentieth position by 2025" in PISA rankings, as its top priority. In spring of 2018, Russian news was peppered with announcements of a new educational reform that would "dramatically change everything in education" for a modest cost of eight trillion rubles (approximately 120 billion dollars). The struggle to peek through policy masks, to decipher the origins of scripts, and to follow the money goes on. Educational modernization continues to be rolled out following directives from President Putin, the government of the Russian Federation, and the Ministry of Education but orchestrated by reformers and experts in their networks.

As more countries engage in reforming their education to increase their competitiveness on the global stage, the drama described in this book resonates in other contexts. Global policy networks that facilitate the spread of relatively standard reform packages extend far beyond Russian borders. The move away from governments toward governance is becoming more widespread, which allows a variety of stakeholders apart from traditionally assumed state actors (S. Ball and Junemann 2012) to enter the stage but operate as shadow elites whose presence is not visible to the public (Wedel 2009). Michael Barber's work continues to be referenced in policy briefs and proposals in the United States, United Kingdom, Mexico, South Africa, India, and in many other corners of the world. Global policy networks have changed not only the set of actors participating in teacher education reforms but also transformed the terms of the conversation (Paine, Aydarova, and Syahril 2017). Attempts to end university-based teacher education in the United States (Kumashiro 2010; Sleeter 2008; Weiner 2007, 2011; Zeichner 2010) and England (Beauchamp et al. 2016; Ellis and McNicholl 2015; Furlong 2013) show that more governments hold teacher education responsible for the low quality of teachers and students' underachievement on international assessments in order to disguise the involvement of private sector actors (Akiba 2013; Trippestad, Swennen, and Werler 2017).

In what follows, I provide a summary of the modernization drama, the exploration of several theoretical insights that stem from this work, as well as practical implications of this study that have relevance not only for educational policymaking in Russia but also for other contexts. Taking my cue from Edelman's argument that art and theater provide an antidote to political spectacle, I turn to Bakhtin's (1981, 1984, 1986), Brecht's (Willett 1964), and Boal's (1979) writing for insights into policymaking and global transformations in education.

Summary of the Modernization Drama

This book presents a story of a Russian teacher education reform that officially started in February of 2013 when the Ministry of Education issued a decree to initiate the work of a large working group brought together to create a plan for institutional transformations in teacher education. The group met and discussed the plans with various stakeholders until the reform received widespread approval.

The unofficial story of this reform, however, suggests that it actually started in the eighties—at the time of perestroika in the Soviet Union, the UK government's attacks on teacher education in England (Judge et al. 1994), and the rise of the New Right in the United States (Apple 2006). That time of drastic change in Russia brought together a constellation of actors who perceived themselves as change agents and embarked on multiple projects that transformed the Russian educational landscape. Their rise was predicated on several factors: Shchedrovitsky's events brought together like-minded people who formed networks of experts; as a type of a collective, reformers lent support to each other to climb up the power ladder; reformers' movement between government positions, consulting businesses, and international projects amplified the amount of resources they could garner. International organizations' involvement did not so much impose a certain direction of reform as provide frameworks that supported the network's activities and allowed reformers to broadcast their message to wider audiences. Reformers attempted several times to reform teacher education, each time unsuccessfully. Ultimately, a constellation of factors involving changes in school standards as well as the introduction of teachers' professional standards created a conducive environment for change. Prolonged contacts with Michael Barber provided reformers with the scripts for conceptualizing the policy and for performing its implementation.

In less than two years of intense activity—between October 2012 and June 2014—the reformers staged auditions for their drama to increase the legitimacy of their proposal, organized dress rehearsals for the release of the policy text, presented the policy to the public, and fought hard to defend their proposal. Throughout all of this time, they referred to the president and the Ministry of Education as initiators of reform and themselves as mere implementers. Key in reformers' performances was their ability to deploy multiple masks to disguise the new ideologies that the policy was attempting to introduce. Selective focus on the "low" performing pedagogical universities obscured a complete reorientation in the purposes of schooling and teachers' roles in society. Schools now had to provide socialization and teachers had to develop students' personalities. This reorientation runs the danger of deepening social stratification because children from privileged backgrounds will receive the best education their families can afford, whereas those from marginalized groups will be left with teachers who use tools of psychology and pedagogy to solve their problems. This move also depoliticizes education because issues of social inequality and injustice are eliminated from the agenda.

Driven by the vision of a corporate dystopia that many in the reformers' network pursue, modernization drama intends to create an undemocratic and regulated space-time intolerant of dissent that directs human activity toward knowledge production for the benefit of corporate growth. In the context of these transformations, pedagogical universities as a remnant of the Soviet past had to be if not completely eliminated then at least radically transformed. Even though the policy was never signed into law, reformers staged the implementation of reform as an experiment to create new teacher education models.

Those who became the target of reforms—pedagogical university faculty and students—provided alternative readings of the situations, contested the constructions presented, and argued for a more contextually relevant script. Yet when participation in the reform came attached to competitive grant funding, many institutions joined the project of teacher education modernization. As project participants engaged in the project, they continued to wrestle with the reform ideology but put up performances of acquiescence and faithful implementation to continue receiving funding. Reformers' deployment of dramaturgical techniques used in their performances along with the (un)intended outcome of their drama—more docile minds and bodies regulated by teachers trained in psychology and pedagogy techniques—unveil futures to fear. The production of spectators and consumers rather than knowledge creators not only presents a rupture in knowledge economy discourses (Åstrand 2016) but also suggests that future generations will be schooled to accept the status quo instead of questioning it.

This book's focus on the micro-politics of educational policymaking shows that regimes can collapse, new leaders can assume government offices, donors can come and go, but those who identify as educational reformers will continue pursuing transformations in education to bring forth conservative social change. Whether they will succeed with that ultimate goal remains to be explored in future studies.

Critical Reflexivity

Before I delve into the theoretical insights this work provides, however, I want to subject this text to some scrutiny. Research that taps into the blurry lines between reality and fiction places researchers in a position of constant uncertainty. This conversation about "borrowing handkerchiefs" and "borrowing scents"—is it an attempt to avoid an answer or provide insight into the challenges of political struggles? These constant references to Michael Barber in interviews but not in any published materials—can his presence be interpreted as an influence as reformers claim or are mentions of his name just an attempt to elevate their status? These elusive links between the reformers' networks and Shchedrovitsky's circle—are his theories the foundation for their proposals, or is it a coincidence that so many of them are associated with his foundation? I wrestled with many of these questions throughout my fieldwork, analysis, and writing. After conducting this research, I certainly feel that I have more questions than answers.

I share these observations to reveal the space of uncertainty from which this research stems. I compared several sources when it was possible; I conducted member checks sharing general observations I developed and specific policy-related facts I needed to confirm. But throughout all of these endeavors, I could not get rid of one nagging thought so beautifully captured by Debord (1994)—that in the midst of political spectacle, "truth is a moment of falsehood" (14). When so much remains hidden, when so many aspects are intentionally obscured, when so many connections are intentionally elevated or dropped, producing a text that beams with confidence becomes an impossible feat. There were times I pursued paths based on my intuition; there were texts that I had to read between the lines; there were some connections made through faith in reasoning rather than in undisputable facts. Thus, the observations I make are tentative, the descriptions I provide are partial, the conclusions I draw are tenuous, and the implications I suggest are mere invitations.

My own role in the fieldwork, particularly with the reformers, is another aspect that should be considered critically. In examining reformers' performances and the masks the policy text wore, I was reminded of my own performances and my own masks. As I noted in the introduction, Bakhtin's writing on Europe in the Dark Ages captures how in duplicitous environments, the clown, the joker, and the fool play an important role of questioning and critiquing power (Aydarova "Jokers"). Throughout interviews, chats, and observations, I often actively claimed the position of a naïve young woman who needed help understanding the convoluted processes of political decision-making. Sometimes I was placed in that position without my own active attempt to occupy it.

This role, however, was not the only position available to me. In the opening of the first chapter, I described my trip to Fevral'sk where I was asked to be a foreign expert. It was a role that I performed torn by the duplicity of my own act: researching teacher education reform and being a tool in the hands of those who are engaged in dismantling it. This was one occurrence that I described in the text, but there were other occasions when I found myself in similarly compromising positions: being asked to contribute to the reform efforts even though I could not fully and wholeheartedly support them. I moved through these situations on a case-by-case basis, getting myself out of participating in some cases, sharing the resources that I had in others. But as Holmes and Marcus (2005a, 2005b) observe, I was aware that to have access to experts' networks there would be a price to pay and wearing a mask of like-mindedness was the price tag. This mask, however, is relevant only for the proposals for reform. In terms of my interactions with the reformers, I was deeply impressed by their extraordinary thinking and was thankful for the respect I was afforded. Their passionate pursuit of change resonated with many of my own feelings, albeit our visions of the future and assumptions about desirable paths of getting there were not the same. I hope that my narrative captures my respect for them, despite our potential disagreements on teacher education reforms or the vision of futures to come.

Theoretical Insights

Actorhood

Contemporary analyses of the emergence of global governance in education often focus on the macro-level processes overlooking the agency exercised by individual policy actors, experts, or academics who participate in co-constructing and fabricating educational change (Lawn 2006; Ozga 2012). Accounts of spectacle in educational policymaking, on the other hand, focus on how policymakers manipulate their audience into accepting their reform proposals (Adamson et al. 2017; Tröhler, Meyer, Labaree, and Hutt 2014; Smith et al. 2004; Wright 2005). While my account has attempted to examine critically the tools that policy actors employ to manage their audience's perceptions of the policy, it also shows that policy actors' multiple positions and biographies serve as an important window into the proposals they create or educational realities they fabricate. In the case of Russian reformers, they were contemporaneously academics at high-profile institutions of higher education, scholars who conducted comparative studies of what works (Morris 2016), authors of international organizations reports' (e.g., World Bank), and national policy creators. The multiplicity of positions they occupied collapse multiscalarity of global policies (Verger, Novelli, and Altinyelken 2012) into one person's actorhood.

Actorhood in political theater becomes an important element that connects the circulation of global policies with national reforms and neoliberal discourses with social change. In the context of global change, dramas of modernization, standardization, modularization, and fragmentation have become recognizable across cultural contexts and national boundaries (Münch 2014; Mundy et al. 2016; Rizvi and Lingard 2010). Often these transformations are examined at the macro level of international organizations, national governments, and educational systems. This book, however, shows that it is important to attend to individual actors whose biographies incorporate connections to the hubs of policy circulation that allow for similar ideas to traverse throughout the globe. The trouble of English teacher education in the 1990s became the trouble of Russian pedagogical universities in the 2010s because several key actors visited Britain and met Michael Barber, who offered solutions for reforms. While "traveler tales" have had profound effects on educational systems for hundreds of years (Phillips 2000), what might be different about the current stage is the ability of policy entrepreneurs to establish connections, develop networks, and maintain contact with like-minded collectives when they conceptualize reforms. Personal contacts, real-time connections, and occasional visits from those who trade policy scripts serve as regulating mechanisms that streamline policy processes. Most importantly, the outsourcing of international organizations' operations to local experts, be it data collection for SABER, analysis of PISA results, or production of project memos, creates opportunities for "policy ventriloquism," in which it is no longer clear who the speaking subject is and whose agenda is actually being pursued.

Second, actors' biographies allow not only a connection with the global movement of ideas, but also reveal connections between the socialist past and the neoliberal present. As reformers sought to destroy the Soviet past to build a neoliberal future, they drew on the very techniques, discourses, and rhetorical tropes that were in circulation during Soviet times. From the construction of a New Man through education to the evoking of country leadership to justify new reforms; from the metaphorical use of the "International Anthem of Socialism" to the tricks of fiction-making with fabricated data—these are all familiar performances of Soviet-era actors. As Yurchak (2005) contends in his study of late socialism, those who came of age in the sixties and seventies learned how to use performative shifts "to render many of their activities invisible to, or misrecognized by, the state" (298). The biographic resources that policy actors brought extended their performances and developed paradoxical continuities with the Soviet past—the very past that they were actively trying to dismantle. Their performances demonstrated how socialism and neoliberalism are co-constitutive contradictions (Bockman 2011; Brandist 2014, 2016).

Finally, reformers were genuinely concerned about Russia's future and that concern became the driving force of their proposals. Similar to Shchedrovitsky, from whom many of them took their cue, they sought to reform education to make Russia great on the global stage. Their concerns reflected commitments to market-based ideology and the rule of elites. These commitments emerged in their pursuit of "open entry" into the teaching profession and their support for different schools based on students' socioeconomic status. Coupled with reformers' other initiatives that are beyond the scope of this book, these commitments revealed an overt agenda to protect social stratification and normalize inequality. Russian greatness pursued through these reforms is likely to benefit only a select few who already occupy privileged positions. Reformers' own biographies, however, illustrate how their (past) frustrations with institutions that created social mobility at the expense of their own opportunities could have shaped their policy priorities.

Visibility and Responsibility

Rational models of global policy analysis rarely differentiate between visible and disguised performances. Yet this distinction is important in order to attend to the illusions these performances create, the erasures they afford, and the involvements they obscure. The visible performances captured in letters to the ministry, institutional reports, or interviews created the illusion of democratic participation, dialogue, and straightforward role allocation. These performances suggest that MOE creates working groups to design policies that the educational community subsequently discusses, critiques, and reshapes. Those who participate in the discussions (are) believe(d) to have a voice. These visible performances obscure, however, that it remains the voice of elites—political, social, and economic—who use policies to create the world that protects their status and their social standing. Other voices added to perpetuate the illusion of dialogue matter only as a number in a total tally of participants who allegedly engaged with the policy and offered their support. This portrayal creates an illusion that the educational community accepted global designs for national polices, that legitimation of a policy took place, and that consensus over the suitability of global norms emerged.

Moreover, policy performances are orchestrated in ways that allow actors, directors, and playwrights to reshuffle roles and diffuse responsibility for the change. When role reshuffling assigns the role of the director to the representative of an institute of power—the president or the minister of education—it erases the faces of policy authors and obscures the identities of directors who are actually orchestrating the reform. This erasure legitimizes the policy because it now comes fused with the power of the institution that the representative stands for. It also eliminates the falsifiability of assumptions built into the text. The policy proposal is no longer a text prepared by someone whose position can be called into question because of his association with international organizations, such as Joseph Abramovich; or someone whose ideas can be repealed because of other failed or controversial reforms he already pioneered, such as Vadim Alekseyevich; or someone the quality of whose research is critiqued by scholars in his community, such as Anton Mikhailovich. The script is no longer a product made by an individual whose work was discredited by scholars in his home country, such as Michael Barber, but rather a summary of "best international experiences." The absence of an individual's face or name that goes along with a policy proposal, similar to the framing generally afforded international reports (Grek 2009; Sellar and Lingard 2013, 2014), increases the legitimacy of the policy's claims as a stake in objective truth rather than a subjective opinion with little grounding in empirical or conceptual foundations.

Selective focus accomplishes a similar purpose of obscuring who is involved in the staging of modernization dramas. State institutions stand in the limelight, while the corporate actors remain protected by the shadows (Gunter, Hall, and Apple 2017; Tompkins-Stange 2016). Researchers, scholars, teacher educators, and preservice teachers continue to look to the state as the answer to their troubles and the manager of their fate. Individuals and their networks, corporations and their spokespeople, remain mostly invisible amid the trouble of educational reforms. This invisibility protects their continual involvement from being called into question and creates a shroud for their growing spheres of influence, making them unknowable, and unanswerable for the reforms (Au and Ferrare 2015). The trouble is that when so much remains hidden from the public eye, searching for facts and asking questions verges on conspiratorial thinking.

Ethics in Political Theater

Bakhtin's writing on ethical responsibilities is helpful for considering visibility and role reshuffling through the lens of ethics. The translator who worked with Bakhtin's text *Toward a Philosophy of the Act* made a distinct choice: instead of using the word "responsibility," he chose "answerability" to "foreground the root sense of the term—answering; the point is to bring out that 'responsibility' involves the performance of an existential dialogue" (Bakhtin 1993, note 80 by Liapunov). In describing the center of answerability, Bakhtin (1993, 12) states, "the ought becomes possible for the first time where there is an acknowledgment of the fact of a unique person's being from within that person; where this fact becomes a center of answerability—where I assume answerability for my own uniqueness, for my own being." This center of answerability is the core of ethical acting.

The opposite, such as "prov[ing] my alibi in Being" or "pretend[ing] to be someone [else]," creates a rift in the ethics of the act. According to Bakhtin, in every act, in every product of a creative activity, we are answerable both for the contents of it and for its moral overtones. Bakhtin combines a variety of elements in his conception of ethics: the author's or the actor's acknowledgment of their unique contribution to the act, the veracity of the message conveyed, as well as the melding of the cultural and situational elements to reflect the context-sensitivity of the act.

In the political theater of education reforms, in contrast, authors who create global policies traverse international borders and rarely acknowledge authorship of the ideas that become translated into national reforms. Reformers who use those ideas to draw up policy proposals hide behind the anonymity of the policymaking process to eschew the position of answerability, creating for themselves an "alibi in Being." The position of anonymity precludes a possibility of substantive dialogue and deliberation because no one occupies a position from which to answer the utterances traversing societies and nations in regard to policy texts, direction of educational reforms, or the futures they seek to create. Anonymity only further intensifies the "illusion of democratic participation" (Smith et al. 2004) and creates conditions for more authoritarian measures of control and imposition of social change by protecting policy authors from any form of accountability or retribution.

What goes without saying in an ethical analysis of an act is its ability to prove the veracity of its facts. As Bakhtin (1993, 4) observes, "veridicality or being-true is the ought of thinking." Fictionalized data, masks of evidence, or claims based on missing statistics greatly undermine the ethical dimension of the performances onstage. Perhaps it is here that the anonymity and a lack of answerability become most salient because "the ought gains its validity within the unity of my once-occurrent answerable life" (5). If the policy actors choose to occupy unanswerable positions, they step away from the responsibility for the data they use or the evidence they rely on to substantiate their claims.

Finally, Bakhtin finds suspect formal ethics that postulates that there are abstract universal norms applicable in all contexts. Instead, he returns to the individual act, which never occurs in the theoretical abstract, but in specific situations circumscribed by cultural and historical contexts. It is here—at the intersection of a specific situation with the culture and historicity of the moment—that an answerable act can occur. This observation is worth extending to the claims regarding the universality of policy proposals. When reformers claim that abstract theoretical ideas are universally applicable or can work anywhere regardless of the context, they make problematic assumptions that render their proposals "an empty demand for legality" (26). Those who respond to their claims bring in the concreteness of cultural contexts or the contingencies of historical development to debunk myths of universality. In this case, those targeted by reforms are most cognizant of the ethical dimension of policymaking that needs to correspond to "a living act performed in the real world" (27). Perhaps, it is these voices that need to be amplified in global policy research to disrupt the reigning ideology of universalism or cultural neutrality on which much of the global governance infrastructure rests (for examples, see Aydarova 2015a; Gorur 2016; Münch 2014; Takayama 2018).

Aesthetics in Political Theater

If politics is the art of governing, then policy as a text needs to be considered as a work of art constructed by an artist: from the perspective of relationships between the author, the characters of the text, and its final audience. Bakhtin (1990) emphasizes ways in which powerful art emerges out of an artist's relationship with the characters characterized by freedom and respect. When an artist does not attempt to control his characters, giving them rather freedom to grow, experiment, and undergo an open-ended process of becoming, he enters a dialogic relationship with them that transforms him and his creation. Art in which characters are controlled and manipulated is dead art, not generative and aesthetically pleasing. Holquist (2002) explains that artists' excessive authority over their characters leads to texts in which a woman kissing a tractor is no different than a woman kissing a man. This reading of a policy as a tool that represents the art of governing raises questions about those who populate the Concept's text as characters: students of pedagogical universities, those who switch careers to become teachers, regional administrations, and faculty members at pedagogical universities. Even though reformers claimed that the Concept introduced an experiment, the policy set out to control, shape, and regulate activities in ways that foreclose creativity and imagination. Rigid criteria for evaluating participants' projects foreclosed any possibility of freedom and play. Little freedom was afforded real and imagined participants to exercise their agency and pursue change that they find meaningful in their contexts. The "singular vision" (Wu 2016, 224) for improving teacher education erased the complexity in "orientations, anxieties, and strategies" (224) pursued by different participants in Russian teacher education.

The relationship between an artist and the characters he creates is also predicated on the artist's "excesses of seeing." The artist who chooses to typify his characters and to reduce them to one or two defining features that position them as villains or as failures produces a "work . . . contrived rather than created" (Bakhtin 1990, 18). The antidote to this is seeing "all of [the character] in the fullness of the present and admir[ing] him as such" (19). Policy construction as a form of art would greatly benefit from expanding ways policymakers and reformers see the populations they seek to govern. Approaching these participants as whole, rather than reducing them to their weaknesses, may contribute to the generation of policies that are more sensitive to the historical emergence of various organizational forms, the meanings that different participants imbue them with, as well as the contradictions and conflicts that their existence may be wrought with. Seeing the whole of policy characters would entail considering their full humanity, together with the value of the local knowledge they possess. Approached this way, policies could become aesthetically sound products, not grotesque exaggerations of contrived forms that threaten to eliminate diversity and local ways of knowing (Gorur 2016).

The appearance of the Concept in tandem with teachers' professional standards and school standards raises troubling questions about the authoritarian control over the characters and subsequently over participants in the reform process. Those texts set out to authoritatively foreclose possibilities of becoming and set the parameters of human development not just of teacher educators who belong to a small segment of the educational sector but rather all of the country's school-age children. In their links to Shchedrovitsky's (1993) theory of pedagogy as well as the overall "radical constructivism and antihumanist thinking"[1] of his works, those texts seek to blueprint members of the future society. An interesting contrast between Shchedrovitsky's writing on molding students into their positions in a society is Bakhtin's (1981, 1984, 1986) writing on becoming. Shchedrovitsky sets out to design a formula for a desired human being and argues that pedagogy should develop as a technology that provides tools for shaping students to fit into that formula. Bakhtin (1981, 1984), on the other hand, emphasizes that becoming is an open-ended and unfinalizable process that emerges through revisiting historical experiences and imbuing them with new meanings, engaging in carnivalesque play, and participating in a dialogue with alterity—the Other that can enrich one's understandings, make visible one's position in the world, and reveal that which lies beyond one's horizon. Shchedrovitsky's teaching has been used by anthropotechnicians to change the thinking of corporations' workers, whereas Bakhtin's theories became the foundation of dialogic and emancipatory pedagogies (A. Ball and Freedman 2004; Stetsenko 2012).

There are two fundamental differences in how these philosophers conceptualize subjects' agency. One is the likelihood of their subjects' rebellion. Bakhtin's subjects subvert authority, defy established norms, and create new worlds, whereas Shchedrovitsky's subjects undergo ideological treatment to accept the control of higher authority over their lives. Shchedrovitsky's subject is a surprising match for the neoliberal subject, the construction of which is now actively pursued in educational systems around the world. By focusing on the minutiae of measurable knowledge, character qualities, and "soft skills" (Meyer and Benavot 2013; Spring 2015a, 2015b), global policies, circulated through the OECD's PISA apparatus and consulting businesses such as McKinsey, echo Shchedrovitsky's approach. Instead of subjects who take an agentive stance in the world—to shape it, to mold it, and to change it—these policies seek to create spectators, workers, and consumers (Åstrand 2016; Labaree 2014; Ozga 2012). Ironically, Bakhtin's construction of becoming that captures human beings as actively constructing and changing worlds around them corresponds more closely to the New Man envisioned by the Soviet educational system.

Another difference lies in authority imbued with the right to determine the direction for the change in subjects. Bakhtin (1981) wrote about subjects wrestling with authoritative and internally persuasive discourses in pursuit of liberation from the hold of another's word over their lives. Shchedrovitsky, on the other hand, believed that a higher authority in society should determine what functions students would have to carry out in the future; his followers debate whether it is even necessary to have an actor who ensures that certain boundaries in this human programming are not overstepped. Leaving no room for the subjects to determine their own path, those who follow this ideology also try to eliminate actors who can restrict the power of higher authorities over human development. These transformations, even though specific to Russia, raise important questions about the processes of subjectivation fostered by neoliberal education policies worldwide. In the context where corporate control of education is increasing, it is important to consider who could call these developments into question and limit their reach into students' and teachers' souls (Spring 2015a, 2015b).

Political Theater as a Tool of Coercion

To shed light on how political theater of educational reform works as a tool of coercion, I turn to Brecht's (Willett 1964) writing on drama that coopts the audience into accepting the status quo. When applied to educational policy, it shows that reformers stage performances to convince the audience of the need for reform and of the steps they propose as the only way to address the problem. Despite claims that the policymaking process is democratic and participatory, it ends up being monologic, authoritarian, and manipulative. Props onstage are set to depict a changing world in which competition is the only form of possible relationships and economic advancement is the only viable goal for education. Then the staging of rehearsals for the release of the policy proceeds in ways that minimize opportunities for critical engagement or transformative interventions into the production of the policy text. Throughout the whole staged performance, reformers afford their audience members limited roles for participation—either to support the measures or remain silent—the very roles that are afforded for theater spectators. In the case of teacher education modernization, the role of new rectors is particularly important because the audience that comprises pedagogical university faculty is expected to identify with them as representatives of its own establishment and empathize with their enthusiastic support for reform.

Matters do not improve when the reform becomes implemented as an experiment. For underfunded institutions that rely heavily on federal subsidies for their students, participation in grant competitions is important for bringing in much-needed funding. In the context where the Ministry of Education evaluates institutions on their ability to win grants, choosing not to participate can be doubly costly as the danger of being labeled ineffective and becoming nominated for closure is very real. So, no matter how much resistance and opposition the project's ideology unleashed, connecting it to grant awards left little room for teacher educators to pursue alternative paths. With strictly specified criteria and participants' ongoing training in reform ideology, only the reformers' vision for the future of teacher education and specific steps for reaching it come to matter.

The tragedy here is twofold. First, the measures are proposed as the only truth there can be. The audience or actors in training are not given room to critique the proposals, but only accept them as givens. Substantive engagement with such proclamations is futile because reformers are the ones who possess the truth. Second, the measures construct the world as changing on its own and not as a world that can be changed through participants' actions. This places the audience in the passive position of accepting change and molding its members to adapt to the changing world. Coercion emerges in spaces where educators are not afforded opportunities to reflect on the world, on the social conditions around them, on the sociopolitical contexts of their lives, and on the contradictory and conflicting purposes of education, so that they could strive for social transformation. Through these tools of coercion, the political theater of educational reforms precludes possibilities of dialogue and preserves social stratification, injustice, and inequality (Boal 1979; Willett 1964).

Practical Implications

Political Theater as a Tool of Liberation

Political theater does not have to be only a tool of coercion. Theater is not only a space for recreating fictions but also for mobilizing populations, for raising political consciousness, and for engaging in dialogue to create alternatives (Goldbard 2001; Reinelt 1998). Both political theater and the tools that reformers employ in their performances can be reclaimed and reappropriated in the struggle against authoritarian reforms. The masks of the policy text can serve as a guise. Masks can also be used in the process of critical reflection or the healing process when participants imagine other worlds and channel their inner struggles onto external means.

Boal's (1979) work on emancipatory theater along with Bakhtin's (1984) writing on carnival identify ways in which reformers' performances can be challenged. Several aspects are important here. Boal emphasizes that the audience cannot remain apathetic; they cannot continue to assume the role of spectators. Liberation occurs when those who were assigned the role of the audience walk out on stage to challenge the script presented to them. This might require creating alternative stages or using other spaces to challenge policymakers' constructions of problems and solutions. But ultimately this requires an active position or what Bakhtin referred to as "think[ing] participatively" (Bakhtin 1993, 19). Just as reformers should not act as if they had "an alibi in Being," so the audience should not seek alibis for themselves in a passive reception of the performances staged for them. Along with other scholars (Owens 2015, Ravitch 2013), I urge educators and researchers to take an active position of contesting corporate-driven reforms in their contexts. In what follows I share observations on what can be done in response to such reforms.

Dialogic Engagement

One way to create conditions for emancipatory theater is through dialogic engagement with the proposals. In my attempts to learn about faculty's perspectives on the Concept, I often faced a challenge: very few people that I interviewed were aware, either as a matter of time or challenging circumstances of their work, that there was a reform under way. After all, searching for information on different reform initiatives is an all-consuming endeavor. Sometimes, it was a problem of a lack of information. But quite often it was also a conscious choice—many among the people that I interacted with believed that what was happening "above" had little bearing on their lives. This is a common response in times of crisis—to disengage, to pretend that nothing is happening, or to choose not to know that change is under way. The example of teacher education reform in England (Ellis and McNicholl 2015; Furlong 2013; Judge et al. 1994), however, shows that nonengagement is rarely a viable option. Emancipatory theater is about taking on the active role of demanding to know what the reformers seek to accomplish and engaging with those proposals in public spaces. It is also about creating a dialogue and finding ways to move reformers back into "answerable" positions, so that they are required to give accounts for the data they use, the claims they make, and the evidence they manipulate.

The problem, however, is that not everyone has equal access to information about global policies. During my fieldwork, I met the leader of Russia's independent teachers' union actively involved in contesting educational reforms. He immediately asked if I could explain what is happening in education in other countries. "We keep being told about what the West is doing, but we have no information and no language skills to figure out whether that is true or not on our own," he explained (Field Notes, December 2013). Making knowledge about global education policies more publicly accessible, for example based on the model of the National Education Policy Center in the United States, would go a long way in helping different communities around the world gain deeper understandings of the changes under way in order to be better equipped for the struggle. An added benefit would be to provide access to policy briefs in different languages.

Collectivity

The next part of active engagement concerns the notion of collectivity. Bakhtin's (1984) writing on carnival makes it clear that social transformations occur when groups manage to overcome the individualizing processes that separate them. It happens in moments when participants recognize the power that can be unleashed by a collective struggle. Teacher educators and administrators who engaged in critiquing the Concept often struck out on their own. The performances that occurred in pedagogical universities in response to the Concept were often elements of individual struggles.

To present an active response to the reformers' performances, individual efforts will not suffice. After all, theater is not an individualizing experience—it is rarely a one-man show. Basic principles of building collectives and developing networks around shared goals in policy can be an important step toward emancipation. Working together with schools, communities, and other higher education institutions could be an important dimension of fostering collectives that amplify different voices silenced by the drumbeat of reforms (Aydarova and Berliner 2018; Paine, Blömeke, and Aydarova 2016).

Collaboration Across Borders

Another important element for potential emancipation is collaboration and dialogue with the Other. While policymakers, policy actors, and policy entrepreneurs enjoy free movement across national borders, educators often remain constrained by their belief that what they do is contextually determined. While I support the general premise of this belief and, as I have argued before, I see this as a more ethical framing than policymakers' assertions, I also believe that it is dangerous to use this belief to justify nonaction. There are significant ways in which educators can both learn from each other and draw on each other's strengths to contest narrowing purposes of schooling, market-based solutions for improving education, or growing corporate involvement in education that are traversing the globe.

This learning is not about transplanting the models that are used elsewhere. That is what reformers are already trying to do, disregarding the local contextual and adaptable knowledge that this may eradicate. Instead, this learning can be directed at debunking the myths and constructions that support reformers' performances (e.g., Berliner and Biddle 1995; Berliner and Glass 2014; Cochran-Smith 2006). For example, collaborative cross-national studies that examine relationships between educational achievement and economic development might address the myth that increases in PISA scores lead to increases in national GDP (cf. Hanushek and Woessmann 2010). Or, cross-national collaborations could explore the claims in the McKinsey reports about successful reforms and identify alternatives that do not lead to deprofessionalization of teaching or increased inequality of educational outcomes for students.

Another possible area of exploration can be multi-sited cross-national work that examines what is gained and what is lost when teacher education is reoriented toward practice at the expense of deep theoretical learning. What happens to the profession at large when shared knowledge that has been historically accumulated by the profession becomes individualized and deintellectualized (Judge et al. 1994)? Carnoy (2006) noted that comparative work is helpful for seeing the changing relationships between the state and the education sector. Attacks on teachers' unions, according to him, have to be considered from the perspective of teachers being a powerful political force. What happens to this political force when the preparation of its members is moved to classrooms in schools where teachers are increasingly called to teach from scripts and standardized teaching materials? Collaborative work could also be directed toward tracing the impact of global actors, such as Michael Barber, or global corporations on educational approaches and practices worldwide. Across borders, it would be possible to examine the reach of McKinsey or Pearson into classrooms, schools, communities, societies, and the very souls of those who embark on educational journeys. Collaborative knowledge generation could reveal this reach and identify ways to develop alternatives.

Historicity

A turn to history provides additional possibilities for emancipation. There are ways in which we need to learn from history not only as it pertains to political theater as an instrument in social struggle but also to learn from history as it reveals the significance of teachers and schools on the national and global stage. This is important as an antidote against creating old practices anew and against uncertainty. As I showed, "base schools" were once established with little success; creating them again without having learned from that experience is unlikely to support students' professional growth. A similar trend is occurring in the United States: without having analyzed the experience of professional development schools (which was not always smooth), the turn to "clinical practice" is hailed as the solution that will revolutionize teacher preparation (National Council for Accreditation of Teacher Education 2010). Such historical amnesia is damaging for education because it treats existing practices as inconsequential, which inevitably leads to repeating the same mistakes and squandering already limited resources on recreating practices that have been (unsuccessfully) tried before.

Faced with attacks on their identity, authority, or professional knowledge when international assessment results are released or new reform plans are announced, many in education respond with ambivalence. Wishing away the reform or pursuing grant funding to create the visibility of accepting reform ideology were responses of some Russian teacher educators. Accepting the market as a regulating force or engaging with educational philanthropies, such as the Bill and Melinda Gates Foundation and the Eli and Edythe Broad Foundation, were some reactions to change among the teacher education community in the United States. These responses are rooted in uncertainty and precarity (Ellis and McNicholl 2015; Furlong 2013; Null 2008). But it is important to remember that access to schooling, educators' professional rights and protections, and university scholars' social status are not historical givens. They are an outcome of collective struggles and ongoing negotiations. It is necessary to draw on the lessons of history across different nations to develop insights into what is possible and what might be dangerous in the current designs of global policies.

In all of these processes, I want to emphasize the richness of resources that theater holds for social science at large in those tumultuous times. Brecht (Willett 1964) reminds us that theater can serve not only to entertain but to alert, inform, and educate. Educate not in a moralistic and paternalistic sense of top-down instruction but rather educate politically—to raise awareness of injustice and unfairness as well as to mobilize marginalized groups for struggle. Here the historic precedents of Brecht's (Willett 1964), Boal's (1979), and Conquergood and Johnson's (2013) work with oppressed groups point to the need to reimagine how we think of theater. Perhaps we should consider learning from history about ways in which theater was instrumental in kindling revolutions and raising masses toward unrest. There might be a worthwhile lesson to gain from those experiences—to know how to reach across social divides in response to reformers on national, regional, or global stages in order to build a different future more kind and just for all.

Appendix A

Summary of the Policy

The Concept of Support for the Development of Teacher Education, also known as the Concept of Teacher Education Modernization, was a nine-page Word document displayed on the websites of the Ministry of Education and several pedagogical universities for most of 2014. The heading included the word "Project," indicating this proposal was not signed into law.

The first part of the text was an introduction that laid out the justification for the reform. The first paragraph stated that new school standards and new teachers' standards required a change in "the organization, contents, technology,[1] and scale [Rus. *masshtab*] of teacher preparation." The second paragraph described what was "inherited" by the Russian Federation: a system of teacher preparation built for a regulated market in which students were assigned to postgraduation teaching placements—or *raspredelenie*. The government used to "strictly regulate the number of students" and "limit students' mobility." Then the text moved into describing the system as one that "has not changed for many years" but in which "the number of pedagogical universities is declining." The number of universities offering teacher preparation decreased (from 196 in 2008 with seventy pedagogical universities, to 167 with forty-eight pedagogical universities in 2012).

The money from the federal budget was used to support fifty-seven thousand students who study disciplines under the umbrella of "Education and Pedagogy" and 133,100 people graduated with specialist degrees (see part 1) in that area of specialization in 2012. Next, the text stated that a large proportion of pedagogical universities were found to have indicators of ineffectiveness based on the Ministry of Education's monitoring of higher education institutions: thirty out of forty pedagogical universities (71.43%)

and twenty-nine out of thirty-seven of their branches (78.38%).

At the bottom of the first page, the text laid out the key claim: "data based on the enrollment numbers and academic achievement results, and also data on students' employment . . . show the existence of a 'double negative selection' when 'not the best' students enter pedagogical universities and 'not the best' graduates go to work in schools." A chart from a sociological study of pedagogical education students was provided to show that "a significant portion of students do not go to work in schools or in the social sphere over all." The legend for the chart contained the reference to the sociological study that it came from.

The text acknowledged that "a number of contradictions" affected the situation, such as "the low prestige of teachers' work" and "the absence of a career ladder in the teaching profession." It immediately moved on to state that the Concept addressed these problems in three ways. First, the Concept would solve the problems associated with the "entry into the profession," which included "low scores on the Unified State Exam of students entering pedagogical education programs," "the absence of an opportunity to select applicants motivated to become teachers," and low percentage of graduates obtaining employment in the educational system. Second, the Concept would address "the problems of preparation," which included such elements as "unsatisfactory quality of graduates' preparation," "outdated methods and technologies," "the absence of a sufficient number of hours dedicated to practicums and on-the-job training," "the absence of an activity-based approach in preparing students," and so on. Third, the Concept could solve the problems of "maintaining teachers in the profession," such as the "absence" of statistics on teaching vacancies in the regions, "absence of regional governments' responsibility" for enrollment numbers and graduates' job placement, "low effectiveness of the mechanisms of attracting the most talented graduates into teaching," and several others.

The list of problems culminated in the main goal of the program: "increasing the quality of preparation of the teaching force, aligning the system of pedagogical education with the teachers' professional standards and federal standards of general education, and overcoming the 'double negative selection.'" To achieve this goal four "tasks" had to be resolved. The "improvement of pedagogical education students' quality" was supposed to happen through "rejecting a linear trajectory of education" and through creating "free entry" into teacher education programs, including such means as a "universal bachelor's degree." The change in the "contents and technologies of education" should be accomplished by "establishing connections between all disciplines and teachers' professional standards," creating a system of practical and on-the-job training, and "preparing students for specific contexts and tasks through a network of university-school partnerships." The effectiveness of pedagogical universities and colleges should be improved by increasing graduates' "practical preparation" in the form of "applied bachelor's" degrees and by developing master's programs for those who want to get a job in the system of education. The last task dealt with the development of the "system of independent professional certification of teachers" and the creation of "a system of quality evaluation of pedagogical education programs."

Next, the text stated that when the Concept was implemented, "a new system of teacher education should be created," which would have ten key elements in it:

1. Development of practical competencies, including through school partners
2. "Applied bachelor's as the main model of teacher preparation"
3. Programs of pedagogical education for the third and fourth years of nonpedagogical education program students
4. "Universal bachelor's degree (similar to *Liberal Arts) in pedagogical universities with higher entry requirements for those who enter pedagogical education programs"
5. Master's programs for methodologists and administrators
6. "Practical modular master's programs with an opportunity for a quick entry into the profession of those who do not have pedagogical education"
7. Introduction of qualification exam based on the new teachers' professional standards that will "simplify entry into the profession" and "allow evaluations of the quality of teacher preparation"
8. "Accompanying beginning teachers"[2]
9. Financing of students' practicums in schools
10. Students' independent practical work in schools should be stored in electronic portfolios and shown to potential employers

The implementation of the Concept was expected to happen in two stages. In 2014–2015 "pilot programs in seventeen to twenty-five universities will be rolled out" in order to create "new models and programs" and prepare "the carriers of new ideology and technology." Also, during this stage, proposals for a new mechanism of determining target admission numbers should be proposed. In 2016–2017, this new mechanism was supposed to be implemented, new models and technologies should be supplemented with "methodological support," and "the new models should be spread throughout the entire system of teacher education in the Russian Federation." The last part of the document presented a road map of implementing the Concept, with ten steps to be undertaken in 2014–2015 and fifteen in 2016–2017. Most of these steps replicated what had already been described.

Appendix B
Theoretical Foundations

Social theorists have long drawn on theater as a framework that can elucidate social and political processes. Even though I did not embark on my research with that framework in mind, the preliminary analysis of activities I observed and interactions I witnessed pointed me to the need to explore how theater can be used productively to make sense of the data I gathered. It was both how some of the participants described their experiences and how I came to make sense of the processes in which I participated. I found theater particularly helpful in exploring the blurring of boundaries between "real" and "fictional," "performed" and "lived."

In the fields of comparative and international education, educational policy, and teacher education, it is not customary to use theatricality to understand the processes at hand. Even though some notable exceptions exist (see Adamson et al. 2017; Smith et al. 2004; Wu 2016), more rational and positivist frames predominate. To address this gap, I explore different theories of performance and theater to demonstrate how they informed this study.

Performance

Goffman's (1959) analysis of everyday behaviors through the lens of theater helps us attend to the performances that actors present to convince the audience of their definition of the situation, which represents their "claim to what reality is" (53). Performers may sincerely believe in the performance they are presenting; or, they may cynically employ it to accomplish their own goals. Through this analysis, a new perspective on public behaviors emerges, which presents participants of social interactions—couples, parents, mechanics, lawyers—as actors engaged in dramatizing their roles to validate their worth or to manage their impression on the audience. This dramaturgical arrangement of a performance focuses both on that which is revealed and that which is concealed. For example, performers might occasionally conceal the dirty work that went into putting the service forward, or they might downplay the sacrifice that is necessary to keep the performance going.

Several important observations are important for my analysis. Goffman refers to those who engage in a shared performance of defining a situation a particular way as a team. Those who belong to a team belong to a secret society, not by virtue of their own choosing but rather by the roles that are being carried out in a particular situation. Members of the same team will display a degree of solidarity in protecting each other's faces and promoting the same definition of the situation. They might also collude in convincing the audience of particular messages. The performance put up for the audience onstage (the front region) is likely to be different from that which happens backstage (back region). Members of the same team have access to the backstage, whereas the audience can view only the front stage. In the back region, an individual performer or a team might relax or let his guard down. It is in the back region that teammates might share perspectives among themselves that don't match the definition of the situation that they gave while onstage. To preserve their reputation, however, that mismatch would be a carefully protected secret. Certain people might occupy discrepant roles—acting as spies for another team or shopping for this team's success to use it elsewhere. Goffman's explanations are helpful for understanding that reformers are not alone in engaging in performances they put up.

Goffman (1974, 83) also examines fabrications, or performances that are put up in order to "manage activity so that a party of one or more others will be induced to have a false belief about what it is that is going on." Fabrications can include both benevolent play and "experimental hoaxing." What brings different fabrications together is the unsuspecting audience who becomes the target of deceit. The key to their undoing can be either a willing unmasking of the actors who designed the fabrication or a discrediting that emerges out of a disruption of the fabrication. Once a disruption reveals that a fabrication was involved, it has both a backward and a forward impact: actors' prior and subsequent performances are subject to more suspicion and distrust.

Goffman's writing is helpful in beginning to consider ethnographic work in educational institutions and in the world of educational policymaking.

The metaphor of theater helps with identifying ways in which participants forge performances that match the team's party line, police their words not to overstep the boundaries, and regularly engage in impression management. Yet an opportunity to peek behind the stage curtain and observe the backstage interactions can reveal fabrications that were put up on stage. This holds some promise for ethnography of policy that an analysis that identifies discrepancies and disruptions has a chance to discredit some of those fabrications.

While Goffman's perspective sheds light on ways one could make sense of mundane or routine interactions, three possible areas of his theory remain largely unattended. Goffman's construct of performance is largely depoliticized: issues of power, justice, inequality, or oppression receive scant attention in his theory. Teams might put up performances that will help them receive financial gain from an interaction, they might operate in ways that might allow them to control the situation, but what the consequences of those performances might be either for the audience or for other types of participants in it (such as the effects some interactions have on people from a lower social class) is left largely unexplored or is not problematized.

The second area is the question of impact. Certain teams might have limited audiences that are bound by local contexts where people might come into constant contact with each other on a regular basis (see, for example, Anderson-Levitt's (2012) explanation of "local"), whereas other teams' performances might reach national audiences and have an impact on broader swathes of society. Goffman's analysis does not seem to attend to the differentials in the power different teams can exert on other participants. A policymakers' team that puts together a proposal that then is performed for a nation has a more profound impact than the performances of those whose work this proposal targets. Differentials in social positioning, power differences, scale, and reach among various teams' performances, however, is an important area of consideration for the world of educational policymaking.

Finally, Goffman's analysis represents interactions of a relatively static society: teams in it follow the scripts that they have created, attempt to protect their performances from disruptions, and continue with their performances on a regular basis. What remains unattended then is the process of social change and the struggles over definitions of situations with an eye toward the future. To consider what role performance plays in social change, I draw on Turner's (1974) construct of social drama. To address struggles over definitions, I turn to Edelman's (1988) and Debord's (1994) theories of spectacle. Political theater conceptualized by Brecht (Willett 1964) and

Boal (1979) offers insights into how alternative futures can be constructed. Before moving on to those, however, I briefly consider Scott's (1990) analysis of different forms of disguise employed by groups in their communication.

Performance of Disguise

Goffman's writing on fabrications runs short of highlighting basic mechanisms that different individuals and groups employ to disguise their "real" intentions or "true" feelings. James Scott's work on hidden transcripts sheds light on some of the mechanisms that might be employed in those contexts. Scott writes that subordinate groups cannot risk openly challenging those in power. Thus, in public, they perform according to agreed norms. But offstage, they draw on what Scott calls "hidden transcripts"—or a form of dissent that is shared only with the members of one's own group—to critique, challenge, and subvert dominant groups. Occasionally, ruptures occur and that which was contained by the hidden transcript becomes public, often resulting in social unrest and potential social change.

Scott's work has been cogently critiqued for bringing together disparate pieces of evidence, simplistically dividing societies into dominant and subordinate groups, and ascribing certain behaviors to one group but not the other (Gal 1995). Yet it has also provided insights into forms of disguise employed by groups to hide their message in plain sight. Scott describes three such approaches: anonymity, euphemization, and grumbling, but I will only focus on the first two as they bear significance for the present study.

Anonymity is used to make a hidden transcript public "while disguising the identity of persons declaring it" (Scott 1990, 140). Scott lists such activities as spirit possession, gossip, or anonymous letters as means of deploying anonymity in revealing the hidden transcript. In the world of policymaking, particularly in Russia, anonymity that is evoked in policy proposals and policy implementation serves a similar purpose, albeit in the situation where power is distributed unevenly and those who engage in anonymity do not necessarily belong to a subordinate group (chapter 2). Anonymity allows the authors to disguise their identities, so that their reputations do not suffer and they maintain their freedom to continue with their activities, despite the discrepancies between their expressed views and the norms of public communication.

Another technique is euphemization, which constitutes "disguis[ing] the message just enough to skirt retaliation" or "the veiling of the message [that] represents the application of varnish" (152). In Scott's analysis, euphemization occurs when subordinate groups disguise curses directed at their masters under the cover of blessings or in contexts where folk tales are used to communicate messages about subordinate groups' "true" desires and aspirations, even those that might be sanctioned by the dominant groups. Euphemization is helpful for considering ways in which policy texts wear masks that disguise the "true" intentions of their makers (explored in chapter 2). If in Scott's work it is the subordinate groups who deploy these techniques to protect the hidden transcript that might eventually lead to social change, then in this study it is the powerful groups who draw on these techniques to extend their domination into new contexts and to decrease potential retaliation to their methods of governing.

Social Drama

Turner's contribution in extending observations about performance lies in his application of theatrical metaphor to the situations where conflict results in social change. Turner (1974) calls such situations "social dramas," or "units of aharmonic or disharmonic processes, arising in conflict situations" (37). Social dramas consist of several phases. The first phase—"breach"—occurs when an individual or a group violates a social norm. As a result, if a breach widens and community experiences rising tensions about the broken norms, "crisis" occurs. Turner treats the phase of crisis as a turning point "when it is least easy to don masks or pretend that there is nothing rotten in the village" (39). The third stage is "redressive action" during which "mechanisms" are introduced to address the crisis that emerged. Turner argues that what happens at this stage reveals most the propensities and the potentialities for social change. He asks scholars to attend to the processes occurring at this stage to observe what mechanisms are deployed to secure the pre-crisis status quo, who is involved, and how precisely they go about addressing the crisis state. If social change is to occur, it most likely occurs as a result of resolving tensions among different groups at this phase. The final stage in Turner's social drama lies either in "reintegration of the disturbed social group" or "the social recognition and legitimization of irreparable schism between the contesting parties" (41). Thus, the final stage represents a "temporary climax, solution, or outcome" that is opportune for "taking stock" (42), as it can reveal how relationships in the "political field" were reconfigured through the several stages of the social drama.

Turner's focus on social drama as the site of social conflict that can generate change is instrumental for conceptualizing this study. The focus on conflict and the reordering of political and professional roles that emerge out of this conflict is captured in part 2 of this study. The emphasis of Turner's work on conflict bearing potentialities for change is also helpful for considering possible outcomes of the struggles recorded here with one caveat. Crises do not only occur when individuals or social groups break established norms; crises can be manufactured, constructed, and artificially created, particularly in the realm of modern-day politics. To understand these processes, I turn to Edelman's work on political spectacle.

Political Spectacle

Edelman (1988) draws on the metaphor of theater to examine how political events are constructed as political spectacle. He notes:

> Accounts of political issues, problems, crises, threats, and leaders now become devices for creating disparate assumptions and beliefs about the social and political world rather than factual statements. The very concept of "'fact'" becomes irrelevant because every meaningful political object and person is an interpretation that reflects and perpetuates an ideology. Taken together, they comprise a spectacle which varies with the social situation of the spectator and serves as a meaning machine: a generator of points of view and therefore of perceptions, anxieties, aspirations, and strategies. (Edelman 1988, 10)

In his analysis, Edelman focuses on several constructions employed in the deployment of political spectacle—constructions of social problems, political leadership, enemies, and political news. The first two carry most relevance for the analysis of teacher education reforms in this text.

In writing about social problems, Edelman emphasizes that among the damaging conditions that negatively affect human lives, many remain unnoticed and unaddressed. In the production of social problem narratives, different groups struggle over their own definition of the situation and their proposed solutions. In Edelman's analysis, "a problem is a signifier" (16), which "focuses on a name for an undesirable condition or a threat to well-being" (17). Government's responses to that problem are likely to be "inconsistent" because it deals with a variety of social groups and attempts to accommodate multiple definitions of the problem. The "bricolage of claims" that emerges out of this struggle can make the situation better or it can make it worse, "but some consequences of the policies pursued are always inversions of the value formally proclaimed as the goal of the activity" (16). Naming reasons for problems in general reflects the dominant ideology, and solutions often come before the constructions of problems.

What becomes identified as a problem and what does not largely depend on public support for a particular construction of a problem. Identifications of problems come bundled together as "a radiation of signifiers" (36)—a construction of one problem justifies a construction of another and rationalizes a whole set of policies. Attention to history or to social structure is often excluded. The audience of the spectacle gets evoked as agents of change in solutions to some problems or gets excluded in the definitions of others. For those who attempt to analyze these processes, it is important "to recognize the range of meanings and of strategies *implicit* in each item that emerges from the radiation of signifiers" (Edelman 1988, 36, emphasis added). These considerations have informed much of the analysis presented in chapter 4.

With regard to construction of political leadership, Edelman observes that leaders are perceived as if they are independent actors able to set a new course of action, even though the social forces operating on them and discourses that speak through them make this an unlikely occurrence. Yet he also acknowledges that it would not be reasonable to state that leaders make no difference at all in how political events are shaped. Ultimately, "the term 'leadership' . . . catalyzes an intricate language game that draws its appeal from a complex of psychological needs including an incentive to blame or praise identifiable people for changes in well-being and an effort to understand why changes take place" (Edelman 1988, 64). This is an important point to which I turn in chapter 3 as I examine how participants in decision-making levels of educational hierarchy hide behind the masks of those above them to justify their own actions and decisions. Yet I also extend this analysis by showing how those who conceptualize policies use leaders as faces of change to eschew responsibility for the reforms they are proposing.

Spectacle in the Postmodern Society

The reach of political spectacle and the power of its deception need to be considered in light of society's postmodern condition. Debord's (1994) exploration of a new form of social relationships in which the spectacle works as an organizing force presents a provocative stance on contemporary social conditions. While many approach his analysis as focusing exclusively on media, I propose to consider his tenets on a wider scale, in which spectacle has reached into restructuring meanings and relationships. In stating that "the spectacle is the opposite of dialogue" (17), Debord emphasizes the fragmentation of meanings that emerges in modern societies and that is exacerbated by atomization of individuals alienated from the world of their work and from a meaningful life outside of work. This fragmentation is important in considering ways in which temporal and spatial isolation of some performances precludes a possibility of shared meaning-making: "spectators are linked only by a one-way relationship to the very center that maintains their isolation from each other. The spectacle thus unites what is separate, but it unites it only in its separateness" (Debord 1994, 22). The pervasiveness of fragmentation that precludes the audience from accessing all the aspects of political performances became reflected in the structure of this text. I created a text in which individual chapters capture an element of the story and depend on each other to present the full plotline.

Debord's observation regarding the relationship between truth and falsehood sheds further light on existing fragmentations: "In a world that *really* has turned on its head, truth is a moment of falsehood" (Debord 1994, 14). Images and representations, illusions and masks that saturate social life only further break down social relationships of trust and diminish a sense of shared responsibility for society's future. Permeations and mutations in what the spectacle promises for the future with its emphasis on the pursuit of development and the elusiveness of reaching those promises fosters cynicism and further cements the evolving fragmentations. Debord continues:

> The spectacular character of modern industrial society has nothing fortuitous or superficial about it; on the contrary, this society is based on the spectacle in the most fundamental way. For the spectacle, as the perfect image of the ruling economic order, ends are nothing and development is all—although the only thing into which the spectacle plans to develop is itself. (Debord 1994, 15–16)

Debord's (1994, 1998) critiques of development—as a spectacle that "plans to develop [into] itself"—applies equally well to the project of modernization. The drama of modernization, even though framed as an attempt at social change, ultimately seeks to recreate an unequal society and cement the stratification that already exists.

Political Theater

Observing the blurry lines between fiction and reality, truth and falsehood can easily turn into cynicism that only reproduces the existing structures (Rancière 2011, 2016). Political theater as a tool of liberation can be a useful antidote for this condition. Drawing on Marxist theories, Brecht (Willett 1964) differentiates between two types of theater: dramatic and epic. Dramatic theater hypnotizes the audience, lulls them into empathy for the characters on stage, pushes them to reach catharsis at the end, and forces them to accept the status quo in society at large. Brecht criticizes this theater as performance based on feeling that "wears down [a spectator's] capacity for action" (37). Epic theater, on the other hand, appeals to "spectator's reason" and gets him or her to "come to grips with things" (23). Drawing on the principle of alienation, it encourages the audience to dissociate themselves from actors on stage and take on the position of critical observer. Alienation engages the audience intellectually, so that they would consider how the performance onstage can propel them to action to transform the world around them. Brecht's epic theater is what has become widely known as political theater.

Boal (1979) extends Brecht's work by arguing that it is not enough for spectators to simply analyze what the performance reveals. They have to step onto the stage and take over the performance, so that new solutions to the depicted problems can be found. Boal invites his spectator "to practice theatrical forms in which . . . he ceases to be an object and becomes a subject, is changed from witness to protagonist" (126).

Brecht's and Boal's writing inform how I frame the role of education and how I approach the power of political theater. Conservative neoliberal policies in education, like dramatic theater, seek to adapt subjects to the world. Emancipatory education can serve as an alternative to those policies and, akin to epic theater, invites subjects to transform the world in pursuit of justice and equality. These theories also inform how I envision the reader's engagement with this text. Instead of empathizing with the main characters of this text, I hope readers can take on the role of observers who can use what they learn in order to intervene in realities around them. Political theater has enormous power because, as Kushner observes:

the secrets of theater—that a life lived at play is preferable to a life lived in drudgery; that things are not always what they seem to be; that the unpredictability and vibrancy of actual human presence contains an inimitable power and a subversive potential; that there is an impurity, a fluidity at the core of existence—these secrets speak to the liberationist, revolutionary agenda of our day. (Kushner 1997, 34)

Appendix C

Methodology and Data Analysis

In this appendix, I build on the explanation of the methodology that I provided in the introduction and throughout the text. To avoid repetition, I only add elements that might not have been treated in sufficient detail before.

Critical Ethnography

As I explained in the introduction, this study is a critical ethnographic study of teacher education reforms in Russia. As a critical ethnography, it draws primarily on Bakhtin's philosophy of dialogism (Holquist 2002): it emphasizes multivoicedness and acknowledges participants' unequal positions in hierarchies of power and access to resources (Quantz and O'Connor 1988). Rooted in Bakhtin's philosophy, this study privileges the speaking subject and the word (Bakhtin 1981) both in data collection and in the analysis. In my field notes I captured chats, conversations, and brief exchanges more than bodily comportment or elements of physical attributes. In the final text, I attend to what is said and unsaid, but not necessarily to how bodies, spaces, or nonhuman objects contribute to the story. While I recognize that this limited my analysis, I also believe that this allowed me to focus on what I saw was crucial and better attend to the details of verbal exchanges. The focus on the spoken word also allowed me to focus on the performative and constitutive roles of language and discourse (Austin 1975).

My approach to interviewing was deeply influenced by Bakhtin's writing as well. Drawing on Spradley's (1979) suggestions for conducting ethnographic interviews, I designed standard interview protocols with a set of open-ended questions that addressed different elements of reforms. When I began piloting the interviews, I realized that my participants' ability to comment on the reform varied depending on their position, academic rank, geographic location, and a host of other factors. Bakhtin's work prompted me to reconsider my interview protocols. Recognizing that different actors occupy distinct social positions, I started tailoring some or most of the questions for each participant based on what I had learned about him or her prior to our conversation. When conducting interviews, I followed open-ended conversations with my participants and allowed them to share what was within the purview of their horizons and their social worlds (Holquist 2000). One could argue that such an approach would limit trustworthiness of obtained data because participants could choose to turn conversations to irrelevant subjects or use interviews to mislead me. But framed within Bakhtin's writing on language and its social life, this was invaluable data for me even when that happened. In such cases, body language and changes in speaking allowed me to register that what is shared is intended as a performance. Being a native speaker of Russian and a person of Russian origin helped me navigate some of these circumstances. At the same time, my openness and flexibility allowed me to "get out of the way" (Bernard 2011, 160) to let participants speak about their perspectives, experiences, and expectations for the reforms.

Bakhtin's writing was also influential in how I conceptualized dialogue and brought in knots of contestations across different sites in my analysis. Bakhtin's construct of an utterance that includes any verbal act allowed me to position on the same plane elements that belong in different social worlds, recreating in the text dialogues and contestations that would be separated by time and space in life. An example of such a knot is "teacher as facilitator" in chapter 4, where I juxtapose reformers' conflicts over this phrase with the interactions around it in a pedagogical university. While these actors occupy positions in different social worlds, their utterances focus on a common kernel and reflect a conflict over problem construction in teacher education reforms.

Multi-Sited Ethnography of Policy

Both multi-sited ethnography and anthropology of policy respond to the challenges posed by globalization and neoliberal governance to the traditional notions of ethnography. Following the movement of ideas requires a rethinking of one's attachment to a site; tracing how different groups participate in policy formation, contestation, and appropriation calls for what Feldman (2011) identifies as "nonlocal ethnography." The ethnographer's movement attempts to follow the mobility of ideas, actions, and discourses. This leads to varying degrees of engagement in different spaces and events, which invariably causes descriptions to be both thick and thin (Marcus 1998, 2011). This, however, is of less significance because multi-sited ethnography focuses on time, change, and movement. In my work, multi-sitedness was reflected in two aspects: identifying varying interpretive policy communities (Yanow 2000), such as the policymaking hub in Lyutvino and pedagogical universities in Dobrolyubov and Ognensk, as well as following reformers' networks to trace the flow of policy ideas.

The variability of sources in multi-sited ethnographies in general precludes a possibility of an even account and thus requires an inventive approach to constructing ethnographic texts (Marcus 2011). The ethnography is no longer a coherent story of typical events and behaviors but rather a story of contingencies, connections, and ambivalences. My study is no exception and, partly in response to this challenge, I constructed a fragmented ethnographic text in which chapters complement each other but capture different elements of reformers' endeavors.

Fieldwork

My experiences of gaining access to the sites varied across locations. In Dobrolyubov, I was initially able to establish contact with the department in 2011 through a family member who asked the department head for permission for me to come and conduct a research study. While I maintained that relationship throughout all three trips (fieldwork: May–June 2011; June 2012; March–June 2014), by the end of my fieldwork, the dean started expressing dissatisfaction with the informal association between me and the university. On the new monitoring exercise that I describe in chapter 4, this relationship "does not count for anything" and she found that to be quite disappointing. I taught classes, conducted seminars for faculty, and assisted in organizing events for the students (where my association with an American university constituted valuable symbolic capital for the department and for the organizers). Faculty and students appreciated my efforts, but the administrators for the most part did not. Without an official contract, my contributions did not count as "international activity" on the ministry's monitoring of effectiveness. This shift, unfortunately, eventually led to an uncomfortable end of my relationship with the department, even though I still keep up with many of the faculty and students.

I made my first visit to Ognensk in 2012. I was fortunate to receive permission to conduct my research by the dean of the department, whom I contacted by email with a request to come (May 2012). However, when I returned in 2013 (September–December 2013), the new dean required that I go through the "official channels." This required that I sign a contract with the international office and pay for access to the university at a cost of $500 a month. This became a protracted engagement with the university's bureaucratic machine that was at times painful, at times dehumanizing (Aydarova 2017c). As a part of the official arrangement, I was assigned a supervisor. In my research at the Foreign Languages Department, I was able to arrange my own observations and interviews. My supervisor, on the other hand, provided assistance in scheduling interviews with some of the university administrators and several key figures involved in the educational sector in the city. Because my supervisor was involved in the university's efforts to counter the proposal prepared by LEU, I learned a lot about the struggle that was unfolding through conversations with her. My ability to access various resources, however, was very uneven. Despite my "official" and "formal" association with the university, I had to rely on participants' goodwill when I asked for syllabi, curriculum plans, or other documents. In some situations, I received rejections, but in others, people went out of their way trying to help me in my research. In one instance, one faculty member snuck into the faculty office to download curriculum documents onto a flash drive for me and, à la James Bond, gave it to me only on the stairs so that no one could see us. As she handed it to me, she whispered, "You go and tell them 'above' that we just can't go on like this." She knew that the dean had refused to let me have access to curricular plans because those were now the university's "intellectual property and know-how." She was risking her job because she was hoping that through my research those in power would hear the stories I collected about the problems created by educational reforms.

Finally, my fieldwork in Lyutvino took place due to a series of fortunate events. I secured permission to conduct research at LEU during a conference in the United States. In the fall of 2013, I established contact with the secretary of the working group and arrived in LEU in January 2014 (fieldwork: January–March 2014; June–July 2014; November–December 2015). Throughout my time at LEU, I was very well taken care of. There was a university van that picked me up at the airport and took me to the student dormitory when I first arrived. I ended up getting housing on my own (which was significantly more expensive and terribly inconvenient because it added a two-hour commute), but the option to stay at the dormitory was open to me. I was given a pass to enter the building and even received assistance for registering with the immigration authorities. All of that happened without me signing the contract and paying monthly fees for an "official" association with the university. I was stunned by how different my experience at LEU was compared to other universities. I was treated as a guest and I was thankful.

At the same time, my relationships at the site developed quite differently from the other sites. As I explained in the introduction, LEU's organizational culture was much more business-oriented than the culture of other institutions. I got to observe some classes in the master's programs and participated in some of the meetings, but for the most part my life was confined to working in an office, conducting interviews, and analyzing documents connected to the reform. This created a bit of tension because I did not have a clearly identifiable role to fulfill and my presence was occasionally viewed with suspicion. To develop a better understanding of reformers' activities, I read the books they mentioned, saw plays they recommended, and watched online lectures they discussed.

I shared an office with the second working group secretary (and two other LEU employees) and spent a significant amount of time talking to her and learning about what was happening. She helped me arrange my first interviews and shared with me the list of those who belonged to the large working group. But I also tried to navigate the spaces on my own, contacting people on the list of the working group and reaching out to those who were not directly associated with the LEU. After each interview, I asked for suggestions about who else I could interview. Those who knew about the reform gave me a standard list of names—those who belonged to the core working group. Sometimes the names of the new rectors were also added to the list of suggestions. Prior to conducting interviews, I found interviewees' publicly available bios and read their publications. This, as I mentioned before, allowed me to tailor my interviews to each specific person, keeping only some questions in common across all interviewees. Most interviews lasted about an hour. They were audiotaped and transcribed. I treated what I was learning in a cumulative manner and by the end of my time at LEU, I was not only conducting interviews to learn from new people but also to check what I was beginning to understand from previous interviews and additional document analysis.

In addition to site research, I participated in other events related to my topic or discussed by my participants in the cities where I conducted research: an anti–educational reform protest in Ognensk, a Pedagogical Olympiad in Lyutvino, or May Day mock parades in Dobrolyubov. During these events, I met new people and scheduled additional interviews. Quite fortuitously, for example, during the Pedagogical Olympiad in Lyutvino, I came across a professor from the reformers' network who gave a lecture on pedagogical education reform and corporate vision for education, which I quote extensively in chapter 4.

Analysis

I started preliminary analysis when I was still in the field, writing memos about key themes that were emerging, and checking my observations with participants whenever it was possible. To conduct member checking, I created charts and matrices (Miles and Huberman 1994) to capture different relationships as well as sequence of events and participants in the policy process. Upon my return, I transcribed and analyzed interviews, uploaded the documents I collected into NVivo, and coded them there. I inductively developed a set of broad themes (Ryan and Bernard 2003) associated with key elements in the study and traced those across the different texts I had at my disposal. Themes included such items as pedagogical education, international assessments, actors, problems, educational reforms, desired outcomes, values, and others. Themes were then broken down into smaller codes that captured more discrete elements within each theme. For example, the theme associated with the Concept had the following elements: sources of ideas (foreign experience/practical experience), consensus, drawbacks of the Concept, discussion of the Concept, proposals for the Concept, problems in pedagogical education, reactions, implementation of the Concept. During coding, I listened to the recordings several times and reread transcripts continuously. The list of themes was revisited several times to revise them, combine them, and reduce their numbers.

Apart from a thematic analysis, I also annotated texts and hyperlinked segments of different texts across the database as knots of contestations or consensus. In the segments of data that captured key elements of the themes or represented important ruptures, I analyzed the language use in tandem with analysis of the statements. I relied on the techniques of critical discourse analysis (Fairclough 1995, 2001, 2003) to trace intertextual connections and attend to discrepancies that shed light on the competing ideologies and discursive tools employed to disguise them. Importantly, Fairclough (1995) observes how moments of ruptures in texts can be instantaneous and non-repetitive but that in no way reduces the import they carry.

Despite my efforts to engage in systematic data analysis, I realized that repetition in assertions in the data did not increase the veracity of the statements and checks across participants, particularly among the reformers, did not lead to attainting greater degrees of truthfulness in the stories. Members of the same team, as Goffman (1959) explains, have to uphold the same fictional account, so cross-checking with different participants would only verify the plot of the fiction rather than facts about the policy. As Edelman's (1988) writing indicates, political language operates on mystifications and guises, so techniques of attaining trustworthiness become more elusive. That is why instead of drawing on the construct of triangulation, I approach ensuring the quality of the study through the notion of "crystallization" offered by Richardson (2000, 934), who argues that it "provides us with a deepened, complex, thoroughly partial, understanding of the topic. Paradoxically, we know more and doubt what we know."

I traced multiple sources of information and examined how events, accounts, and explanations refracted across different sources. Tracing these refractions helped me identify areas of discrepancies and ruptures. Taking Goffman's perspective on this, participants in a performance have to be "prepared to see that the impression of reality can be shattered by very minor mishaps" (36). Mishaps and cracks in the definitions of situations reveal struggles that performers may attempt to conceal and provide insight into the events unfolding backstage. Ultimately, I recognize the challenges that my study represents, but I also see its strength not in having attained a truer portrayal of Russian policymaking but rather in disrupting assumptions of how it is made to be seen.

Text

The challenges of conducting research in areas where the lines between truth and fiction are blurred drew me toward a more narrative approach in presenting my account. I chose it because it gave me the freedom to face the uncertainties of the project. A narrative approach allowed me to capture the complexity, the fluidity, and the fragmentation of the policyscape (Carney 2009) that I was trying to navigate. My goal was to write the kind of ethnography that

> reaffirms the common threads of our humanity, which, in turn, deepens your sensitivities to the human condition. Considered in this light, ethnography can sometimes be a bridge that connects two worlds, binding two universes of meaning. It can be a path that entwines the distant lives of others to our more familiar being, a gift to the world. (Stoller 2007, 181)

I pursued a narrative flow, rather than a more traditional structure, to challenge the technocratic rationality and assumed objectivity in policy studies. I make no claims of being a detached observer. My body and soul are very much a part of this story.

Insider/Outsider

After identifying as Russian all of my life, it was through my fieldwork that I became an American. Scholars writing on "native research" or "insider research" often note that either members of the scholarly community or researchers themselves make assumptions that an insider status would afford an easier access to the community, provide a significant amount of shared knowledge, and create trust with the communities where research is conducted. My experiences, similar to others engaged in such research (see Ghaffar-Kucher 2015) challenged these assumptions: sites where I expected to be welcome because of much shared professional ground were not welcoming; sites where I expected to face multiple barriers were the easiest to navigate. In each context, different aspects of my identity mattered in different ways. Narayan (1993) emphasized this point in her call to move away from the binary of insider/outsider status and consider how researcher's multiplex identities "with many crosscutting identifications" (676) might influence one's experience in the field.

When I was moving into the field, I relied on the assumptions of benefits that my insider positions would bring: that as a Russian with native-language proficiency, I would be able to navigate the spaces of everyday life with relative ease. Yet, for getting assistance at the hospital or a deposit back from an internet company in Russia, Russian proficiency alone became insufficient—one also needed a Russian passport. My Ukrainian citizenship positioned me as an immediate outsider who had no right to receive benefits afforded citizens or permanent residents, such as getting health care or a bank account where the refund for the deposit could be transferred. This made me vulnerable to the illicit practices common in that context.

But there was also a moment in which it became clear that this vulnerability provided access to understanding the challenges of everyday life with which my participants had to cope daily. During one of the conversations with foreign-language students at the university, several of them noted, "You never had to go to the hospital to get help, or fight to get internet installed, or argue about the services that cell phones companies provide. If you don't know how frustrating it is, it might not make sense why some people would dream of leaving this country." By that time I did indeed struggle with those issues. My prior assumptions about the familiarity with those struggles would not have done justice to their experiences and their perceptions.

My connections with the United States were imbued with new meanings depending on the situation and the prevalent mood of the day. A particularly challenging moment was the time when the 2014 conflict in the east of Ukraine started. In conversations with Russian participants, my American connections were evoked to place blame for the conflict on me as the most immediate American proxy. In my defense, I drew on my Ukrainian connections to reclaim the status of a person negatively affected by the conflict. In other situations, I was asked to provide "expert" linguistic opinion on the use of English or life in the United States because I was "from America." Furthermore, as I mentioned before, I was invited to carry out functions at official events that were dutifully photographed and placed online (without my knowledge) with the Americanized version of my name (Helen) and the name of my American university displayed under the picture. Throughout my research, I came to see my identity as pieces of a puzzle that my participants and I arranged in different constellations to pursue different goals.

Insider/outsider categories matter most for accessing the insider knowledge of the community. This, ultimately, was a similar struggle. In the reformers' network, I was no insider, regardless of my language proficiency, which as Shore (2011) notes, is common among those who do research with policymakers. With students and faculty I had more in common. But the changes were so abrupt and dramatic that even faculty returning to the same department after maternity leave could not make sense of what was happening around them. Insider knowledge, in the end, became as elusive as a clear identification of who I was in this study.

Notes

Introduction

1. Most geographic and personal names in this text are pseudonyms to protect participants' confidentiality and anonymity.

2. All translations from Russian into English are mine. To protect my participants' anonymity, I use neither full citations of texts that could reveal their identities nor the exact links for the news stories connected to reforms.

3. In Russia, teacher education is commonly described as pedagogical education. While I translated the titles of policies using "teacher education" as the term commonly used in English, the reader should be aware that the original titles are "The Concept of Pedagogical Education Modernization" and "The Concept of Support for the Development of Pedagogical Education." I use "teacher education" and "pedagogical education" interchangeably throughout the text.

4. Teaching and Learning International Survey administered by the OECD, http://www.oecd.org/education/talis/.

5. Systems Approach for Better Education Results administered by the World Bank, http://saber.worldbank.org/index.cfm.

6. More on the challenges of conducting ethnographic research in Russia and particular identities that were constructed for me can be found in Aydarova (2017c).

Part I. Historical Context: Sowing the Seeds of Discontent

1. GARF is the State Archive of the Russian Federation in Moscow that contains a significant portion of Soviet-era documents. Numbers provided are *fond*, *opis'*, and *delo*.

2. It is important to remember that K–12 standards in the United States often require that students are taught allegiance to capitalism as the only acceptable form of social and economic organization. Despite the rhetoric of democratic deliberation and freedom of ideas, US students are subjected to similar forms of indoctrination rarely recognized as such (Popkewitz 1982).

3. Humanitarization sought to increase the proportion of humanities-oriented subjects in school programs to counteract a heavy polytechnic emphasis introduced in the sixties and seventies.

Part II. Directing Social Change: Russian Policy Dramas

1. Actors

1. Because the text in this part is a narrative ethnography, I do not use block quotations.

2. In Russian, institutions in social spheres would include schools, libraries, kindergartens, social services, and so on. Because the English phrase "social institutions" incorporates a much wider range of establishments, I use the translation of the Russian phrase "institutions in social spheres" throughout the text.

3. Those who were targeted by those scandals claim that corruption investigations were "politically motivated" (Clover 2013).

4. Http://www.yras.ru/news/202-future-school.html.

5. Http://izvestia.ru/news/536971.

6. In developing these sketches, I used characterization techniques used in ethnodrama (Saldaña 2003). To create these, I relied on reformers' publicly available bios, interview data of how they described themselves or their "life objectives" (Saldaña 2003, 221) and of how other participants described them, my observations and interactions with them during fieldwork, as well as their interviews for the media.

7. Fevral'sk State University is a classical university and not a pedagogical university. This is important for understanding some reformers' disdain for pedagogical universities.

8. In constructing this chart, I relied on interview data, field notes, and participants' publicly available bios. There were many more people and organizations that could be included, but for the sake of clarity I chose to focus on the aspects that were relevant for this text. Individuals' names are for the most part pseudonyms that appear in rectangular boxes. Organizations' names appear in oval boxes and are pseudonyms when they refer to specific higher education institutions in Russia. The short names of policies appear in triangles. Straight lines denote current connections through employment, official association, or personal contacts; lines in dashes denote past connections through former employment, place of study, or past personal contacts.

9. I use the asterisk to show which English words or phrases appeared in Russian interviews or documents. Reformers' and experts' code-switching and use of English words is in general atypical for older generations of those involved in education.

10. I did not have personal contact with Michael Barber (real name) during my research, but I participated in a conference in Russia where Barber gave a plenary

speech. This sketch is based on Jenny Ozga's (2014) interview with Michael Barber, an article about him published in the *Guardian* (Wilby 2011), several Russian resources, and my field notes of the conference event.

    11. I draw on Shchedrovitsky's autobiography, articles about his work, as well as field notes of the conference organized in his honor.

    12. Http://www.fondgp.ru/gp/archive/texts.

    13. I tried to ask a number of different people about this aura of secrecy but was never able to get a full response. Some people shared that Shchedrovitsky manipulated human consciousness; others were annoyed by Shchedrovitsky's followers' devout and almost religious admiration for him. Still others divulged that scandals associated with some of his followers in positions of power put a certain stigma on the group as a whole.

2. Masks and Guises

    1. In framing this argument, I use "front-stage" to capture Goffman's notion of "front region" as the "place where the performance is given" (1959, 107) as opposed to backstage "where suppressed facts make an appearance" (112).

    2. My treatment of the text's masks rests on three analytical approaches: critical discourse analysis (Fairclough 1995, 2001, 2003); comparative analysis between Lyutvino Economics University's version of the policy and the final version provided by the Ministry of Education; and dialogic juxtaposition between the text of the policy and reformers' explanation of its various points.

    3. The metaphor of violence conveys the charged atmosphere that reformers' attempts to transform the system of teacher preparation created, but it was shared as a humorous account of the caution that had to be exerted in presenting these proposals for change.

    4. While I personally find such comparisons problematic, reformers used them in their presentations of the policy.

    5. This saying is an adaptation of the Soviet-era aphorism commonly used in the field of education—"to sow the seeds of intelligence, kindness, and eternity." The journalist drops "eternity" as a sarcastic commentary on the collapse of the Soviet Union—it was supposed to be eternal but is no more.

    6. In 2014, the *New York Times* ran an insightful story about the connections between this publishing house and President Putin that can be found at https://www.nytimes.com/2014/11/02/world/europe/putins-friend-profits-in-purge-of-schoolbooks.html.

    7. The abrupt ending of this conversation was indicative of my other attempts to understand corporate involvement in educational reforms, which will be discussed in chapter 4.

    8. The use of this term matches the translation of the sources of these ideas into Russian. Barber and Mourshed's (2007) report described internships that could increase the quality of teaching. In that text, internship was translated as *stazhirovka*.

9. This word was indeed used in the Russian translations of Barber and Mourshed (2007) and Schleicher (2011).

10. Russian parliament.

3. Dress Rehearsals and Missing Directors

1. This is a term commonly used in Russian sociology and political science. While it may represent an outdated understanding of power as unequally distributed among different levels of the political and social structure, I believe it aptly captures how power is perceived and experienced in the Russian context—as a top-down, hierarchical, and often authoritarian mode of control.

2. In conceptualizing my work on policy formation, I draw on the sociocultural approaches to policy analysis (Levinson, Sutton, and Winstead 2009; Sutton and Levinson 2001), anthropology of policy (Shore, Wright and Però 2011), as well as interpretive policy analysis (Yanow 2000). As Sutton and Levinson (2001, 2) note, "one approach to official policy formation involves 'researching the powerful' (Walford, 1995) and examining the specific social arenas where the interests and languages comprising a governing policy charter get negotiated into some viable form."

3. Many of the reformers and experts in their network used foresight technology as a means of "collectively constructing the future" (http://asi.ru/molprof/foresight/).

4. The description of this event provides further support for my earlier claim that the script was selected before the official timeline began. Articles about it appeared on LEU's and MOE's websites. According to the two texts, the problems that plague pedagogical education were so numerous that it was imperative that reforms be implemented soon. The group supposedly identified problems in teacher education, such as the introduction of new general education standards, the absence of a qualifying exam for entry into the profession, and the double negative selection, and agreed on the principles of the reform.

5. Larisa Nikolayevna did not elaborate on how the business game was organized or what the problem-posing seminar was like. What struck me in that moment was that both of these formats are usually used in Shchedrovitsky's Moscow Methodological Circle; games and seminars are also used by the LEU team during their consulting work.

6. Reformers' use of medicalized metaphors in describing their work on this Concept deserves to be noted. Some of this language will emerge in chapter 4. What is particularly interesting about it is that it reflects transnational trends of how reformers construct their work on changing educational systems.

7. Http://www.kremlin.ru/events/president/news/16764.

8. Http://kremlin.ru/events/president/news/12515.

9. Http://kremlin.ru/events/president/news/12733.

10. Http://kremlin.ru/events/councils/14677.

11. Http://kremlin.ru/events/president/news/. I am not providing the exact news article to protect the anonymity of my participants.

12. Http://kremlin.ru/events/president/transcripts/5979.

13. Http://nasha-novaya-shkola.ru/?q=node/4.

4. Light and Shadows

1. *Doctor House* is the Russian name for *House, MD* featuring Hugh Laurie.

2. *Interns* is a Russian version of *Scrubs*.

3. Their observations about students' weaknesses were based on students' high school graduation grades because the Unified State Exam was introduced in the entire country only in 2009.

4. The Russian word *effectivnost*, which is used to describe this monitoring, can be translated into English as both "effectiveness" and "efficiency," which creates difficulties both in policy interpretations in Russia and in the telling of this story. I chose to translate this term as "effectiveness" because it resembles the Russian wording, but the reader should be aware that this semantic ambiguity exists and causes significant problems of interpretation among the different policy communities.

5. The quote the speaker uses represents surprising parallels between this framing of the teacher education problem in Russia and in the United States. As Wilson (2014) notes, entrepreneurs who target American teacher education with reforms follow a similar logic. Speaking of the use of alternative routes to increase competition in teacher preparation, Wilson (2014) argues that "this new wave of alternative approaches contain within them some high visibility programs that may have intentions to—in Schumpeter's (2008) words—'destruct,' so that new and better teacher preparation can arise from the rubble" (185).

6. I take this story as a piece of institutional folklore, where what is important about the story is not its veracity but people's construction of their lifeworld and their perceptions of transformations.

7. Http://base.garant.ru/55170694/.

8. It is important to point out that the term "socialization" is a relatively new term in Russian education. Throughout most of the twentieth century, the role of schools was conceptualized as "teaching" (Rus. *obuchenie*) and "upbringing" (Rus. *vospitanie*). The term "upbringing" overlaps with "socialization" in its focus on value transmission, but it retains the freedom of individuals to become that which they have the potential to become. "Socialization" carries stronger connotations of individuals being molded into particular social roles—the focus of my exploration here.

9. Http://strategy2020.rian.ru/news/20111122/366204765.html.

10. Http://www.aif.ru/dossier/1399.

11. Because Shchedrovitsky's followers used very technical and jargon-laden language, I am paraphrasing here. To check my own understanding of the exchange,

I asked Marina Nikolevna during our interview whether I appropriately reconstructed the meaning of that exchange.

5. Props, Scripts, and Playwrights

1. Trends in International Mathematics and Science Study (TIMSS) is an international comparative assessment carried out by the International Association for the Evaluation of Educational Achievement since 1995. More information about this assessment can be found at http://timssandpirls.bc.edu/.

2. Progress in International Reading Literacy Study (PIRLS) is an international comparative assessment carried out by the International Association for the Evaluation of Educational Achievement since 2001. More information about this assessment can be found at http://timssandpirls.bc.edu/.

3. Programme for International Student Assessment (PISA) is an international comparative study that focuses on math and reading literacy skills carried out by the Organisation for Economic Co-operation and Development (OECD). Most recently, Pearson joined OECD to provide support in carrying out and disseminating findings of these studies. More information about PISA can be found at http://www.oecd.org/pisa/.

4. Teacher Education and Development Study in Mathematics (TEDS-M) is an international comparative study of primary and secondary mathematics teacher education carried out by the International Association for the Evaluation of Educational Achievement. More information about this study can be found at http://www.iea.nl/teds-m.html.

5. Http://fip.kpmo.ru/fip/info/13430.html.

6. Http://www.i-russia.ru/all/articles/14508/.

7. Http://ria.ru/edu_news/20120910/747200309.html.

8. Http://www.i-russia.ru/all/articles/14508/.

9. My point here is not to suggest that the two men have influenced each other but rather to demonstrate an overlap in scripts circulated by global and national actors.

6. Money Matters

1. Http://www.bbc.co.uk/russian/russia/2012/10/121001_lavrov_usaid_british_council.

2. The term "color revolutions" refers to the large-scale protests in Ukraine ("Orange Revolution," also known as "Maidan" in Russia; see chapter 4), Georgia ("Rose Revolution"), and other post-Soviet states that toppled the government. In Russia, as this quote illustrates, a common perception is that these revolutions were conducted with support from the West.

3. Http://rt.com/politics/russia-ngo-usa-funding-101/.

4. Http://www.mid.ru/rossia-v-gruppe-20-rossia-i-specializirovannye-mezduna rodnye-ekonomiceskie-organizacii-mvf-vto-oesr-fseg-opek-i-dr-/-/asset_publisher/ uFvfWVmCb4Rl/content/id/2149294.

5. Project Tuning is a part of the Bologna Process and provides a framework of competencies to assist institutions undergoing harmonization to become a part of shared European educational space.

6. When these interviews were conducted, Russia had already gone through at least eighteen months of sanctions, with the ruble having lost half of its value against the dollar.

7. Http://choosetoteach.ru/.

Epilogue

1. Radical constructivism in this context refers to the assumption that anyone and anything can be changed, molded, and transformed based on predetermined designs (Il'ia Kukulin, personal communication, December 2015).

Appendix A. Summary of the Policy

1. In the last several years, it has become more common to use the word "technology" in education, not to refer to information technologies as is customary in other countries but rather as a synonym for methods and educational approaches that focus on structural organization of educational processes. It is likely that in this text "technology" is intended to convey this meaning, but it is open to individual interpretation.

2. This phrase is as confusing in Russian as it is in English. It stands for mentoring. Chapter 2 explores the reasons why this phrase might have been chosen.

References

Adamson, Bob, Katherine Forestier, Paul Morris, and Christine Han. 2017. "PISA, Policymaking and Political Pantomime: Education Policy Referencing Between England and Hong Kong." *Comparative Education* 53(2): 192–208.
Agar, Michael H. 1996. *The Professional Stranger: An Informal Introduction to Ethnography.* San Diego: Academic Press.
Akiba, Motoko. 2013. *Teacher Reforms around the World: Implementations and Outcomes.* Bingley: Emerald.
Alekseyeva, L. N., M. V. Dargan, Y. L. Zaytseva, O. B. Kalinina, and I. A. Petrunina. 2010. *Razrabotka novogo soderzhaniya obrazovaniya: Podhody i otsenka kachestva* [The development of new contents of education: Approaches and assessment of quality]. Moskva: Tsentr "Shkol'naya Kniga."
Alexander, Robin J. 2000. *Culture and Pedagogy: International Comparisons in Primary Education.* Oxford: Wiley-Blackwell.
———. 2009. "Towards a Comparative Pedagogy." In *International Handbook of Comparative Education*, edited by Robert Cowen and Andreas M. Kazamias, 923–39. Dordrecht: Springer.
Amann, Ron. 2003. "A Sovietological View of Modern Britain." *Political Quarterly* 74(4): 468–80. doi:10.1111/1467-923X.00558.
Amrein-Beardsley, Audrey. 2014. *Rethinking Value-Added Models in Education: Critical Perspectives on Tests and Assessment-Based Accountability.* New York: Routledge.
Anderson, Gary L. 2005. "Performing School Reform in the Age of the Political Spectacle." In *Performance Theories in Education: Power, Pedagogy, and the Politics of Identity*, edited by B. K. Alexander, G. L. Anderson, and B. P. Gallegos, 199–220. Mahwah: Lawrence Erlbaum Associates.
Anderson-Levitt, Kathryn M. 2003. *Local Meanings, Global Schooling: Anthropology and World Culture Theory.* New York: Palgrave Macmillan.
———. 2012. "Complicating the Concept of Culture." *Comparative Education* 48(4): 441–54.
Apple, Michael W. 2006. *Educating the "Right" Way: Markets, Standards, God, and Inequality.* New York: Routledge.

———. 2013. *Can Education Change Society?* New York: Routledge.
Åstrand, Björn. 2016. "From Citizens into Consumers: The Transformation of Democratic Ideals into School Markets in Sweden." In *Global Education Reform: How Privatization and Public Investment Influence Education Outcomes*, edited by Frank Adamson, Björn Åstrand, and Linda Darling-Hammond, 73–109. New York: Routledge.
Au, Wayne, and Joseph J. Ferrare, eds. 2015. *Mapping Corporate Education Reform: Power and Policy Networks in the Neoliberal State*. New York: Routledge.
Austin, John Langshaw. 1975. *How to Do Things with Words*. Cambridge: Harvard University Press.
Aydarova, Elena. 2016. "Teachers' Plight and Trainees' Flight: The Perceived, Lived, and Conceived Spaces of Schools." *Voprosy Obrazovaniya* 2: 183–207.
———. 2017a. "Discursive Contestations and Pluriversal Futures: A Decolonial Analysis of Educational Policies in the United Arab Emirates." *Education Policy Analysis Archives* 25(111).
———. 2017b. "'I Want a Beautiful Life': Divergent Chronotopes in English Language Teacher Education." *Critical Inquiry in Language Studies* 14(4): 263–93.
———. 2017c. "Pedagogical Peep Show: The Challenges of Ethnographic Research in a Post-socialist Context." In *Reimagining Utopias: Theory and Method for Educational Research in Post-Socialist Contexts*, edited by I. Silova, N. W. Sobe, A. Korzh, and S. Kovalchuk, 65–81. Rotterdam: Sense Publishers.
———. n.d. "Fiction-Making in Audit Cultures: Disrupting Designs for Modernization and Conservative Social Change." Working paper. Department of Educational Foundations, Leadership, and Technology, Auburn University.
———. n.d. "Jokers and Fools in the Public Square: Ethnography in the Age of Spectacle." Working paper. Department of Educational Foundations, Leadership, and Technology, Auburn University.
Aydarova, Elena, and David C. Berliner. 2018. "Navigating the Contested Terrain of Teacher Education Policy and Practice: Introduction to the Special Issue." *Education Policy Analysis Archives* 26(25).
Aydarova, Elena, Zsuzsa Millei, Nelli Piattoeva, and Iveta Silova. 2016. "Revisiting Pasts, Reimagining Futures: Memories of (Post)socialist Childhoods and Schooling." *European Education* 48(3): 1–11.
Aydarova, Olena. 2013. "Package, Seal, and Sell: Global Flows and Transformations in Teacher Education." *Global Studies Journal* 5(2): 171–82.
———. 2014. "Universal Principles Transform National Priorities: Bologna Process and Teacher Education." *Teaching and Teacher Education* 37(1): 64–75.
———. 2015a. "Global Discourses and Local Responses: A Dialogic Perspective on Educational Reforms in the Russian Federation." *European Education* 47(4): 331–45.
———. 2015b. "Glories of the Soviet Past or Dim Visions of the Future: Russian Teacher Education as the Site of Historical Becoming." *Anthropology and Education Quarterly* 46(2): 147–66.

Baker, David, and Gerald K. LeTendre. 2005. *National Differences, Global Similarities: World Culture and the Future of Schooling*. Stanford: Stanford University Press.
Bakhtin, Mikhail. 1981. *The Dialogic Imagination*. Austin: University of Texas Press.
———. 1984. *Problems of Dostoevsky's Poetics*. Minneapolis: University of Minnesota Press.
———. 1986. *Speech Genres and Other Late Essays*. Austin: University of Texas Press.
———. 1990. *Art and Answerability: Early Philosophical Essays*. Austin: University of Texas Press.
———. 1993. *Toward a Philosophy of the Act*. Austin: University of Texas Press.
Ball, Arnetha F., and Sarah Warshauer Freedman, eds. 2004. *Bakhtinian Perspectives on Language, Literacy, and Learning*. Cambridge: Cambridge University Press.
Ball, Stephen. 2003. "The Teacher's Soul and the Terrors of Performativity." *Journal of Education Policy* 18(2): 215–28.
———. 2007. *Education, Plc: Understanding Private Sector Participation in Public Sector Education*. London: Routledge.
———. 2012. *Global Education, Inc.: New Policy Networks and the Neoliberal Imaginary*. Oxon: Routledge.
———. 2016. "Following Policy: Networks, Network Ethnography and Education Policy Mobilities." *Journal of Education Policy* 31(5): 549–66.
Ball, Stephen J., and Carolina Junemann. 2012. *Networks, New Governance and Education*. New York: Routledge.
Barber, Michael, and Mona Mourshed. 2007. *How the World's Best-Performing School Systems Come Out on Top*. London: McKinsey & Company.
Barranger, Milly S. 2006. *Theater: A Way of Seeing*. Belmont: Thomson Wadsworth.
Baudrillard, Jean. 1997. *Fragments: Cool Memories III*. London: Verso.
Bauman, Zygmunt. 1995. *Life in Fragments: Essays in Postmodern Morality*. Oxford: Blackwell.
Beauchamp, Gary, Linda Clarke, Moira Hulme, Martin Jephcote, Aileen Kennedy, Geraldine Magennis, Ian Menter, Jean Murray, Trevor Mutton, Teresa O'Doherty, and Gillian Peiser. 2016. *Teacher Education in Times of Change*. Bristol: Policy Press.
Berliner, David C. 2006. "Our Impoverished View of Educational Research." *Teachers College Record* 108 (6): 949–995.
———. 2015. "The Many Facets of PISA." *Teachers College Record* 117(1): 1–20.
Berliner, David C., and Bruce J. Biddle. 1995. *The Manufactured Crisis: Myths, Fraud, and the Attack on America's Public Schools*. Reading: Addison-Wesley.
Berliner, David C., Gene V. Glass, and Associates. 2014. *50 Myths and Lies That Threaten America's Public Schools: The Real Crisis in Education*. New York: Teachers College Press.
Bernard, H. Russell. 2011. *Research Methods in Anthropology: Qualitative and Quantitative Approaches*. 5th ed. Lanham: Altamira Press.
Bieber, Tonia. 2010. "Playing the Multilevel Game in Education—the PISA Study and the Bologna Process Triggering Swiss Harmonization." In *Transformation*

of Education Policy, edited by Kerstin Martens, Alexander-Kenneth Nagel, Michael Windzio, and Ansgar Weymann, 105–31. Basingstoke: Palgrave.

Boal, Augusto. 1979. *Theater of the Oppressed*. New York: Urizen Books.

Bochenkov, S. A., and I. A. Val'dman. 2013. "Interpretatsiya i Predstavlenie Rezul'tatov YeGE: Problemy i Vozmozhnye Resheniya" [Interpretation and Presentation of the Unified Exam Results: Problems and Possible Solutions]. *Voprosy Obrazovania* (3): 5–24.

Bockman, Johanna. 2011. *Markets in the Name of Socialism: The Left-Wing Origins of Neoliberalism*. Stanford: Stanford University Press.

Bogdanov, Ivan Mikhaylovich. 1964. *Gramotnost' i Obrazovanie v Dorevolyutsionnoy Rossii i v SSSR: Istoriko-Statisticheskie Ocherki* [Literacy and education in pre-revolutionary Russia and in the USSR: historical-statistical essay]. Moscow: Statistika.

Boli, John. 2005. "Contemporary Developments in World Culture." *International Journal of Comparative Sociology* 46(5–6): 383–404.

Boli, John, Francisco O. Ramirez, and John W. Meyer. 1985. "Explaining the Origins and Expansion of Mass Education." *Comparative Education Review* 29(2): 145–70.

Bondarenko, S. M. 1974. *Urok—Tvorchestvo Uchitelya* [Lesson—teacher's art]. Moscow: Pedagogika.

Brandist, Craig. 2014, May 29. "A Very Stalinist Management Model." *Times Higher Education*. Retrieved from https://www.timeshighereducation.com/comment/opinion/a-very-stalinist-management-model/2013616.article.

———. 2016, May 5. "The Risks of Soviet-Style Managerialism in UK Universities." *Times Higher Education*. Retrieved from https://www.timeshighereducation.com/comment/the-risks-of-soviet-style-managerialism-in-united-kingdom-universities.

Brown, Amy. 2015. *A Good Investment? Philanthropy and the Marketing of Race in an Urban Public School*. Minneapolis: University of Minnesota Press.

Busemeyer, Marius R., and Janis Vossiek. 2016. "Global Convergence or Path Dependency? Skill Formation Regimes in the Globalized Economy." In *The Handbook of Global Education Policy*, edited by Karen Mundy, Andy Green, Bob Lingard, and Antoni Verger, 145–61. Malden: Wiley.

Canning, Mary, et al. 2004. *Modernizatsiya Rossiyskogo Obrazovaniya: Dostizheniya i Uroki* [Modernization of Russian education: accomplishments and lessons]. Washington, DC: World Bank.

Canning, Mary, Peter Moock, and Timothy Heleniak. 1999a. *Reforming Education in the Regions of Russia*. World Bank Technical Paper No. 457. Herndon: World Bank.

———. 1999b. *Russia Regional Education Study*. Report No. 18666-RU. Washington, DC: World Bank.

Carney, Stephen. 2009. "Negotiating Policy in an Age of Globalization: Exploring Educational 'Policyscapes' in Denmark, Nepal, and China." *Comparative Education Review* 53(1): 63–88.

Carney, Stephen, Jeremy Rappleye, and Iveta Silova. 2012. "Between Faith and Science: World Culture Theory and Comparative Education." *Comparative Education Review* 56(3): 366–93.

Carnoy, Martin. 2006. "Rethinking the Comparative—and the International." *Comparative Education Review* 50 (4): 551–70.

Caruso, M. 2008. "World Systems, World Society, World Polity: Theoretical Insights for a Global History of Education." *History of Education* 37(6): 825–40.

Cave, Tamasin, and Andy Rowell. 2015. *A Quiet Word: Lobbying, Crony Capitalism and Broken Politics in Britain.* London: Vintage Books.

Chatterjee, Choi. 2015. "Imperial Incarcerations: Ekaterina Breshko-Breshkovskaia, Vinayak Savarkar, and the Original Sins of Modernity." *Slavic Review* 74(4): 850–72.

Chudgar, Amita. 2013. "Teacher Labor Force and Teacher Education in India: An Analysis of a Recent Policy Change and Its Potential Implications." In *Teacher Reforms around the World: Implementations and Outcomes*, edited by Motoko Akiba, 55–76. Bingley: Emerald.

Clover, Charles. 2013. "Political Backlash Blamed for Woes at Russia's 'Silicon Valley.'" *Financial Times*, May 21, 6.

Cochran-Smith, Marilyn. 2005. "The New Teacher Education: For Better or for Worse?" *Educational Researcher* 34(7): 3–17.

———. 2006. "Teacher Education and the Need for Public Intellectuals." *The New Educator* 2(3): 181–206.

Coffield, Frank. 2012. "Why the McKinsey Reports Will Not Improve School Systems." *Journal of Education Policy* 2 (1): 131–49.

Conquergood, Dwight, and E. Patrick Johnson, eds. 2013. *Cultural Struggles: Performance, Ethnography, Praxis.* Ann Arbor: University of Michigan Press.

Counts, George S. 1961. "A Word about the Soviet Teacher." *Comparative Education Review* 5(1): 13–16.

Danticat, Edwidge. 2011. *Create Dangerously: The Immigrant Artist at Work.* New York: Vintage Books.

Darling-Hammond, Linda. 2010. *The Flat World and Education.* New York: Teachers College Press.

Darling-Hammond, Linda, and Ann Lieberman, eds. 2012. *Teacher Education around the World: Changing Policies and Practices.* London: Routledge.

Darling-Hammond, Linda, and John Bransford, eds. 2005. *Preparing Teachers for a Changing World: What Teachers Should Learn and Be Able to Do.* San Francisco: Jossey-Bass.

Davidov, Veronica. 2012. "Forest Masters, Forest Borders, and the Escalation of Logging and Mining in Karelia: The Transformation of Vepsian Forests as Social and Metaphysical Spaces." Paper presented at the American Anthropological Association 2012 annual meeting, San Fransisco, California, November 13–18.

Davies, Bronwyn, and Peter Bansel. 2007. "Neoliberalism and Education." *International Journal of Qualitative Studies in Education* 20(3): 247–59.

Davydova, G. A. 2005. *G. P. Shchedrovitsky: Biografiya* [G. P. Shchedrvotisky: biography]. Institut Razvitiya imeni G.P.Shchedrovitskogo. Retrieved from http://www.fondgp.ru/gp/bio.

Debord, Guy. 1994. *The Society of the Spectacle*. New York: Zone Books.

———. 1998. *Comments on the Society of the Spectacle*. London: Verso.

DeStefano, Joseph. 2013. "Teacher Training and Deployment in Malawi." In *Teacher Reforms around the World: Implementations and Outcomes*, edited by Motoko Akiba, 77–97. Bingley: Emerald.

Dimov, Vadim M. 1981. *Narodnoe obrazovanie v sotsial'noi politike razvitogo sotsialisticheskogo obshchestva* [People's education in the social policies of a developed socialist society]. Moscow: Moscow University Press.

Dmitriev, Igor'. 2012. "Nee'ffektivnyi 'monitoring e'ffektivnosti' " [Ineffective monitoring of effectiveness]. *Rossii'skie vesti*, November, 19.

Dneprov, Eduard. 2006. *Obrazovanie i politika: Noveyshaya politicheskaya istoriya Rossiyskogo obrazovaniya* [Education and politics: The newest political history of Russian education]. Moscow: Geo-Tech.

Donnelly, Katelyn, Michael Barber, and Saad Rizvi. 2012. *Oceans of Innovation: The Atlantic, the Pacific, Global Leadership and the Future of Education*. London: Institute for Public Policy Research. Retrieved from https://www.ippr.org/files/images/media/files/publication/2012/08/oceans-of-innovation_Aug2012_9543.pdf?noredirect=1.

Duncan, Arne. 2016, October 4. "An Open Letter to America's College Presidents and Education School Deans." The Brookings Institute. Retrieved from https://www.brookings.edu/blog/brown-center-chalkboard/2016/10/04/arne-duncan-letter-education-school-deans/.

Earley, Penelope M., David G. Imig, and Nicholas M. Michelli. 2011. *Teacher Education Policy in the United States: Issues and Tensions in an Era of Evolving Expectations*. New York: Routledge.

Edelman, Murray. 1988. *Constructing the Political Spectacle*. Chicago: University of Chicago Press.

Edwards, D. Brent, Taeko Okitsu, Romina da Costa, and Yuto Kitamura. 2017. "Regaining Legitimacy in the Context of Global Governance? UNESCO, Education for All Coordination and the Global Monitoring Report." *International Review of Education* 63(3): 403–16.

Ellis, Viv, and Jane McNicholl. 2015. *Transforming Teacher Education: Reconfiguring the Academic Work*. London: Bloomsbury.

Ertl, Hubert. 2006. "Educational Standards and the Changing Discourse on Education: The Reception and Consequences of the PISA Study in Germany." *Oxford Review of Education* 32(5): 619–34.

Ewing, E. Thomas. 2004. "A Stalinist Celebrity Teacher: Gender, Professional, and Political Identities in Soviet Culture of the 1930s." *Journal of Women's History* 16(4): 92–118.

Fairclough, Norman. 1995. *Critical Discourse Analysis: The Critical Study of Language*. London: Longman.
———. 2001. *Language and Power*. 2nd ed. London: Longman.
———. 2003. *Analysing Discourse: Textual Analysis for Social Research*. London: Routledge.
Farquharson, Karen. 2005. "A Different Kind of Snowball: Identifying Key Policymakers." *International Journal of Social Research Methodology* 8(4): 345–53. doi: 10.1080/1364557042000203116.
Feldman, Gregory. 2011. "Illuminating the Apparatus: Steps Toward a Nonlocal Ethnography of Global Governance." In *Policy Worlds: Anthropology and the Analysis of Contemporary Power*, edited by Cris Shore, Susan Wright, and Davide Però, 32–49. New York: Berghahn Books.
Ferguson, James, and Akhil Gupta. 2002. "Spatializing States: Toward an Ethnography of Neoliberal Governmentality." *American Ethnologist* 29(4): 981–1002.
Figes, Orlando. 2002. *Natasha's Dance: A Cultural History of Russia*. New York: Metropolitan Books.
Freire, Paulo. 1970. *Pedagogy of the Oppressed*. New York: Continuum.
Fuller, Edward J. 2013. "Shaky Methods, Shaky Motives: A Critique of the National Council of Teacher Quality's Review of Teacher Preparation Programs." *Journal of Teacher Education* 65(1): 63–77.
Furlong, John. 2009. *Education—An Anatomy of the Discipline: Rescuing the University Project?* London: Routledge.
Furlong, John, Marilyn Cochran-Smith, and Marie Brennan, eds. 2013. *Policy and Politics in Teacher Education: International Perspectives*. London: Routledge.
Furlong, John, Geoff Whitty, Caroline Whiting, Sheila Miles, and Len Barton. 2000. *Teacher Education in Transition: Re-forming Professionalism?* Buckingham: Open University Press.
Fursenko, A. A., ed. 2006. *Prezidium TsK KPSS 1954–1964: Chernovye Protokol'nye Zapisi Zasedanii, Stenogrammy, Postanovleniia* [The Presidium of the Central Committee of the Communist Party of the Soviet Union 1954–1964: drafts of meeting protocol records, transcripts, directives]. Vol. 2. Moscow: ROSSPEN.
Gal, Susan. 1995. "Language and the 'Arts of Resistance.'" *Cultural Anthropology* 10(3): 407–24.
Gasparishvili, A. T., A. A. Ionov, A. Y. Ryazantsev, and Anna Smolentseva. 2006. *Uchitel' V Epohu Peremen* [Teacher at the time of change]. Moscow: Logos.
Gee, James Paul. 2004. "New Times and New Literacies: Themes for a Changing World." In *Bakhtinian Perspectives on Language, Literacy, and Learning*, edited by Arnetha F. Ball and Sarah Warshauer Freedman, 279–306. Cambridge: Cambridge University Press.
Ghaffar-Kucher, Ameena. 2015. "Writing Culture; Inscribing Lives: A Reflective Treatise on the Burden of Representation in Native Research." *International Journal of Qualitative Studies in Education* 28(10): 1186–1202.

Gillette, J. Michael. 1997. *Theatrical Design and Production: An Introduction to Scene Design and Construction, Lighting, Sound, Costume, and Makeup.* 3rd ed. Mountain View: Mayfield.

Gladwell, Malcolm. 2009. "Most Likely to Succeed: How Do We Hire When We Can't Tell Who's Right for the Job?" In *What the Dog Saw and Other Adventures*, 314–35. New York: Little, Brown and Company.

Goffman, Erving. 1959. *The Presentation of Self in Everyday Life.* New York: Anchor Books.

———. 1974. *Frame Analysis: An Essay on the Organization of Experience.* Boston: Northeastern University Press.

Goldbard, Arlene. 2001. "Memory, Money, and Persistence: Theater of Social Change in Context." *Theater* 31(3): 127–37.

Gonzalez, Gerardo M., and Charles L. Carney. 2014. "Challenging the Spectacle: A Case Study on Education Policy Advocacy." *International Journal of Leadership and Change* 2(1): 19–27.

Gorur, Radhika. 2016. "Seeing Like PISA: A Cautionary Tale About the Performativity of International Assessments." *European Educational Research Journal* 15(5): 598–616.

Gounko, Tatiana. 2008. *Translating from Soviet to Neoliberal: Policy Transitions in Russian Higher Education and the Role of the World Bank, the OECD, and the IMF.* Saarbrucken: VDM Verlag.

Gounko, Tatiana, and William Smale. 2007. "Russian Higher Education Reforms: Shifting Policy Perspectives." *European Education* 39(2): 60–82.

Gove, Michael. 2011. "2011 Speech to the Education World Forum." Retrieved from http://www.ukpol.co.uk/michael-gove-2011-speech-to-the-education-world-forum/.

Government of the Russian Federation. 2010. *Nasha novaya shkola* [Our new school]. Retrieved from http://nasha-novaya-shkola.ru/?q=node/4.

Granger, David A. 2008. "No Child Left Behind and the Spectacle of Failing Schools: The Mythology of Contemporary School Reform." *Educational Studies* 43(3): 206–28.

Gramsci, Antonio. 1971. "On Education." In *Selections from the Prison Notebooks by Antonio Gramsci*, edited by Q. Hoarse and G. N. Smith, 24–43. New York: International.

Grek, Sotiria. 2009. "Governing by Numbers: The PISA 'Effect' in Europe." *Journal of Education Policy* 24(1): 23–37.

———. 2013. "Expert Moves: International Comparative Testing and the Rise of Expertocracy." *Journal of Education Policy* 28(5): 695–709.

Griffiths, Tom G., and Robert F. Arnove. 2015. "World Culture in the Capitalist World-System in Transition." *Globalisation, Societies and Education* 13(1): 88–108.

Grigorenko, Elena L. 2004. "Is It Possible to Study Intelligence Without Using the Concept of Intelligence? An Example from Soviet/Russian Psychology."

In *International Handbook of Intelligence*, edited by R. J. Sternberg, 170–211. West Nyack: Cambridge University Press.

Grigor'yev, V. V. 1900. *Istoricheskiy Ocherk Russkoy Shkoly* [Historical essay on the Russian school]. Moscow: Tovarishchestov Tipografii A.I. Mamontova.

Gritsevskiy, I. M., and S. E. Gritsevskaya. 1990. *Ot Uchebnika—k Tvorcheskomy Zamyslu Uroka* [From the textbook to the creative design of a lesson]. Moscow: Pedagogika.

Gunter, Helen M., David Hall, and Michael W. Apple. 2017. *Corporate Elites and the Reform of Public Education*. Bristol: Policy Press.

Hakuta, Kenji. 2011. "Educating Language Minority Students and Affirming Their Equal Rights: Research and Practical Perspectives." *Educational Researcher* 40(4): 163–74.

Hamann, Edmund T., and Lisa Rosen. 2011. "What Makes the Anthropology of Educational Policy Implementation 'Anthropological'?" In *A Companion to the Anthropology of Education*, edited by Bradley A. U. Levinson and Mica Pollock, 461–77. Malden: Blackwell.

Hanushek, Eric A., and Steven G. Rivkin. 2004. "How to Improve the Supply of High-Quality Teachers." In *Brookings Papers on Education Policy 2004*, edited by Diane Ravitch, 7–25. Washington, DC: Brookings Institution Press.

Hanushek, Eric A., and Steven G. Rivkin. 2010. "Generalizations About Using Value-Added Measures of Teacher Quality." *American Economic Review* 100(2): 267–71.

Hanushek, Eric A., and Ludger Woessmann. 2010. *The High Cost of Low Educational Performance: The Long-Run Economic Impact of Improving PISA Outcomes*. Paris: Organisation for Economic Co-operation and Development.

Hemment, Julie. 2009. "Soviet-Style Neoliberalism?" *Problems of Post-Communism* 56(6): 36–50.

Hess, Frederick M. 2002. "Break the Link." In *Handbook of Research on Teacher Education: Enduring Questions in Changing Contexts*, edited by M. Cochran-Smith, S. Feiman-Nemser, D. J. McIntyre, and K. E. Demers, 974–80. New York: Routledge.

Heyneman, Stephen P., et al. 1995. *Russia: Education in the Transition*. Report No. 13638-RU. Washington, DC: World Bank.

Hilton, Gillian L. 2012. "Changing Policies Changing Times: Initiatives in Teacher Education in England." Paper presented at the Bulgarian Comparative Education Society. Kyustendil, Bulgaria, June 12–15.

Hogan, Anna, Sam Sellar, and Bob Lingard. 2015. "Network Restructuring of Global Edu-Business." In *Mapping Corporate Education Reform: Power and Policy Networks in the Neoliberal State*, edited by W. Au and J. J. Ferrare, 43–64. New York: Routledge.

Holmes, Douglas R., and George E. Marcus. 2005a. "Cultures of Expertise and the Management of Globalization: Toward the Re-Functioning of Ethnography." In *Global Assemblages: Technology, Politics, and Ethics as Anthro-*

pological Problems, edited by A. Ong and S. J. Collier, 235–52. Malden: Blackwell.

———. 2005b. "Refunctioning Ethnography: The Challenge of an Anthropology of the Contemporary." In *The Sage Handbook of Qualitative Research*, edited by N. K. Denzin and Y. S. Lincoln, 1099–1113. Thousand Oaks: Sage.

Holmes Group. 1986. *Tomorrow's Teachers: A Report of the Holmes Group*. East Lansing: Holmes Group.

———. 1990. *Tomorrow's Schools: Principles for the Design of Professional Development Schools—A Report of the Holmes Group*. East Lansing: Holmes Group.

———. 1995. *Tomorrow's Schools of Education: A Report of the Holmes Group*. East Lansing: Holmes Group.

Holquist, Michael. 2002. *Dialogism: Bakhtin and His World*. 2nd ed. London: Routledge.

Hursh, David W. 2016. *The End of Public Schools: The Corporate Reform Agenda to Privatize Education*. New York: Routledge.

Il'ina, T. A., and V. I. Mishin. 1971. "Teacher Training in the USSR." *International Review of Education* 17(3): 332–37.

Indikatory Obrazovaniia 2017: Statisticheskiy Sbornik [Educational indicators: statistical report]. 2017. Moscow: Higher School of Economics.

Johnson, David, ed. 2010. *Politics, Modernization, and Educational Reform in Russia: From Past to Present*. Oxford: Symposium Books.

Johnson, Mark S. 1997. "Visionary Hopes and Technocratic Fallacies in Russian Education." *Comparative Education Review* 41(2): 219–25.

Judge, Harry, Michel Lemosse, Lynn Paine, and Michael Sedlak. 1994. *The University and the Teachers: France, the United States, England*. Wallingford: Triangle Books.

Kanstoroom, Marci, and Chester E. Finn. 1999. *Better Teachers, Better Schools*. Washington DC: Thomas B. Fordham Foundation.

Karpova, L. I., and V. A. Severtseva, eds. 1957. *Vysshaia Shkola: Osnovnye Postanovlenniia, Prikazy i instruktsiyi* [Higher school: main directives, orders and instructions]. Moscow: Sovetskaia Nauka.

Khanzhiev, N. A. 1994. *Preobrazovanie Instituta v Universitet: Opyt i Pedagogicheskie Problemy Podgotovki Spetsialistov* [Transformation of institute into university: experience and pedagogical problems of preparing specialists]. Moscow: Moskovskiy Gosudarstvenny Pedagogicheskiy Otkryty Institut.

Kingdon, John W. 2011. *Agendas, Alternatives, and Public Policies*. Boston: Longman.

Kiseleva, Tatyana G. 2002. *Narodnoe Obrazovanie i Prosveshchenie v Rossii: Real'nost' i Mify* [National education and enlightenment in Russia: reality and Myths]. Moscow: MGUKI.

Klees, Steven J., Joel Samoff, and Nelly P. Stromquist. 2012. *The World Bank and Education: Critiques and Alternatives*. Rotterdam: Sense.

Kobakhidze, Nutsa M. 2013. "Teacher Certification Examinations in Georgia: Outcomes and Policy Implications." In *Teacher Reforms around the World: Implementations and Outcomes*, edited by Motoko Akiba, 25–51. Bingley: Emerald.

Komatsu, Hikaru, and Jeremy Rappleye. 2017. "A New Global Policy Regime Founded on Invalid Statistics? Hanushek, Woessmann, PISA, and Economic Growth." *Comparative Education* 53(2): 166–91.
Kotomkina, Evdokiya Alekseevna. 2002. *Iz Istorii Narodnogo Obrazovaniya v Rossii v 1917–1932 godakh* [From the history of national education in Russia in 1917–1932]. Tver': Izdatel'stvo "Liliya Print."
Kovacs, Philip E. 2011. *The Gates Foundation and the Future of US "Public" Schools*. New York: Routledge.
Kovaleva, G. S., L. O. Denishcheva, and N. V. Sheveleva. 2011. "Pedvuzy Dayut Vysokoe Kachestvo Pedagogicheskogo Obrazovaniya, No Ih Vypuskniki Ne Speshat v Shkolu" [Pedagogical universities give a high-quality pedagogical education, but their graduates do not hurry to go to school]. *Voprosy Obrazovania* (4): 124–47.
Koyama, Jill. 2010. *Making Failure Pay: For-Profit Tutoring, High-Stakes Testing, and Public Schools*. Chicago: University of Chicago Press.
———. 2013. "Global Scare Tactics and the Call for US Schools to Be Held Accountable." *American Journal of Education* 120(1): 77–99.
Koyama, Jill, and Candace Cofield. 2013. "The Theatre of Competing Globally: Disguising Racial Achievement Patterns with Test-Driven Accountabilities." *The Urban Review* 45(3): 273–89.
Koyama, Jill, and Lesley Bartlett. 2011. "Bilingual Education Policy as Political Spectacle: Educating Latino Immigrant Youth in New York City." *International Journal of Bilingual Education and Bilingualism* 14(2): 171–85.
Kukulin, Il'ia. 2011. "Alternative Social Blueprinting in Soviet Society of the 1960s and the 1970s, or Why Left-Wing Political Practices Have Not Caught On in Contemporary Russia." *Russian Studies in History* 49(4): 51–92.
Kumashiro, Kevin K. 2010. "Seeing the Bigger Picture: Troubling Movements to End Teacher Education." *Journal of Teacher Education* 61(1–2): 56–65.
Kushner, Tony. 1997. "Notes about Political Theater." *Kenyon Review* 19(3/4): 19–34.
Labaree, David F. 2014. "Let's Measure What No One Teaches: PISA, NCLB, and the Shrinking Aims of Education." *Teachers College Record* 116(9): 1–14.
Lauder, Hugh, Michael Young, Harry Daniels, Maria Balarin, and John Lowe, eds. 2012. *Educating for the Knowledge Economy? Critical Perspectives*. New York: Routledge.
Lawn, Martin. 2006. "Soft Governance and the Learning Spaces of Europe." *Comparative European Politics* 4(2–3): 272–88.
Ledeneva, Alena V. 2013. *Can Russia Modernise? Sistema, Power Networks and Informal Governance*. Cambridge: Cambridge University Press.
Lemon, Alaina. 1998. "'Your Eyes Are Green Like Dollars': Counterfeit Cash, National Substance, and Currency Apartheid in 1990s Russia." *Cultural Anthropology* 13(1): 22–55.
———. 2004. "Dealing Emotional Blows: Realism and Verbal Terror at the Russian State Theatrical Academy." *Language and Communication* 24(4): 313–37.

———. 2009. "The Emotional Lives of Moscow Things." *Russian History* 36(2): 201–18.
Lemutkina, Marina. 2012. "Konets Sveta v Otdel'no Vziatykh Vuzakh" [The end of the world in some higher education institutions]. *Segodnya*, December 22.
Lenin, Vladimir Il'ich. 1957. *Lenin o Narodnom Obrazovanii: Stat'yi i Rechi* [Lenin about national education: articles and speeches]. Moscow: Izdatel'stvo Akademii Pedagogicheskih Nauk RSFSR.
Levine, Arthur. 2006. *Educating School Teachers*. Washington, DC: Education Schools Project.
Levinson, Bradley A., Margaret Sutton, and Teresa Winstead. 2009. "Education Policy as a Practice of Power: Theoretical Tools, Ethnographic Methods, Democratic Options." *Educational Policy* 23(6): 767–95.
Long, Delbert H., and Roberta Long. 1999. *Education of Teachers in Russia*. Westport: Greenwood Press.
MacBeath, John. 2012. "Teacher Training, Education or Learning by Doing in the UK." In *Teacher Education around the World: Changing Policies and Practices*, edited by L. Darling-Hammond and A. Lieberman, 66–80. Oxon: Routledge.
Madison, D. Soyini. 2009. "Dangerous Ethnography." In *Qualitative Inquiry and Social Justice: Towards a Politics of Hope*, edited by N. K. Denzin and M. D. Giardina. Walnut Creek: Left Coast Press.
Maguire, Meg. 2002. "Globalisation, Education Policy and the Teacher." *International Studies in Sociology of Education* 12(3): 261–76.
———. 2010. "Towards a Sociology of the Global Teacher." In *The Routledge International Handbook of the Sociology of Education*, edited by Michael W. Apple, Stephen J. Ball, and Luis Armando Gandin, 58–68. London: Routledge.
———. 2014. "Reforming Teacher Education in England: 'An Economy of Discourses of Truth.'" *Journal of Education Policy* 29(6): 774–84.
Marcus, George E. 1995. "Ethnography in/of the World System: The Emergence of Multi-Sited Ethnography." *Annual Review of Anthropology* 24: 95–117.
———. 1998. *Ethnography Through Thick and Thin*. Princeton: Princeton University Press.
———. 2011. "Multi-Sited Ethnography: Five or Six Things I Know About It Now." In *Multi-Sited Ethnography: Problems and Possibilities in the Translocation of Research Methods*, edited by S. Coleman and P. V. Hellerman, 16–32. New York: Routledge.
Martens, Kerstin, Alexander-Kenneth Nagel, Michael Windzio, and Ansgar Weymann, eds. 2010. *Transformation of Education Policy*. Basingstoke: Palgrave.
Mathis, William J., and Tina M. Trujillo. 2016. *Lessons from NCLB for the Every Student Succeeds Act*. Boulder: National Education Policy Center.
Matza, Tomas Antero. 2010. "Subjects of Freedom: Psychologists, Power and Politics in Postsocialist Russia." Unpublished doctoral dissertation, Stanford University, Stanford, California.

Mchitarjan, Irina. 2000. "John Dewey and the Development of Education in Russia before 1930: Report on a Forgotten Reception." In *Dewey and European Education: General Problems and Case Studies*, edited by H. Rhyn and J. Oelkers, 109–31. Dordrecht: Kluwer.

Menashy, Francine. 2016. "Understanding the Roles of Non-State Actors in Global Governance: Evidence from the Global Partnership for Education." *Journal of Education Policy* 31(1): 98–118.

Meyer, Heinz-Dieter. 2014. "The OECD as Pivot of the Emerging Global Educational Accountability Regime: How Accountable Are the Accountants?" *Teachers College Record* 116(9): 1–20.

Meyer, Heinz-Dieter, and Aaron Benavot, eds. 2013. *PISA, Power, and Policy: The Emergence of Global Educational Governance*. Oxford: Symposium Books.

Miasnikov, Vladimir Afanas'yevich, and Nikolay Aleksandrovich Khromenkov. 1981. *Ot S'yezda k S'yezdu. Narodnoe Obrazovanie: Itogi i Perspektivy* [From assembly to assemby. National education: results and future prospects]. Moscow: Pedagogika.

Miles, Matthew B., and A. Michael Huberman. 1994. *Qualitative Data Analysis: An Expanded Sourcebook*. 2nd ed. Thousand Oaks: Sage.

Ministry of Education and Science of the Russian Federation. 2012. *Federal Standards for General Education*. Moscow: Ministry of Education and Science.

Morgan, Clara, and Riyad A. Shahjahan. 2014. "The Legitimation of OECD's Global Educational Governance: Examining PISA and AHELO Test Production." *Comparative Education* 50(2): 192–205.

Morris, Paul. 2016. *Education Policy, Cross-National Tests of Pupil Achievement, and the Pursuit of World-Class Schooling*. London: UCL Institute of Education Press.

Mourshed, Mona, Chinezi Chijioke, and Michael Barber. 2010. *How the World's Most Improved School Systems Keep Getting Better*. London: McKinsey & Company.

Münch, Richard. 2014. "Education under the Regime of PISA & Co.: Global Standards and Local Traditions in Conflict—the Case of Germany." *Teachers College Record* 116(9): 1–16.

Mundy, Karen, Andy Green, Bob Lingard, and Antoni Verger. 2016. *The Handbook of Global Education Policy*. Malden: Wiley.

Mundy, Karen, and Antoni Verger. 2015. "The World Bank and the Global Governance of Education in a Changing World Order." *International Journal of Educational Development* 40: 9–18.

Nader, Laura. 1972. "Up the Anthropologist: Perspectives Gained from Studying Up." In *Reinventing Anthropology*, edited by Dell Hymes, 284–311. New York: Pantheon Books.

Narayan, Kirin. 1993. "How Native Is a 'Native' Anthropologist?" *American Anthropologist* 95(3): 671–86.

———. 2012. *Alive in the Writing: Crafting Ethnography in the Company of Chekhov*. Chicago: University of Chicago Press.

National Council for Accreditation of Teacher Education. 2010. *Transforming Teacher Education Through Clinical Practice: A National Strategy to Prepare Effective Teachers.* Washington, DC: National Council for Accreditation of Teacher Education.

National Council on Teacher Quality. 2013. *Teacher Prep Review.* Washington, DC: National Council on Teacher Quality.

Nguyen, Phuong-Mai, Julian G. Elliott, Cees Terlouw, and Albert Pilot. 2009. "Neocolonialism in Education: Cooperative Learning in an Asian context." *Comparative Education* 45(1): 109–30.

Niemann, Dennis, Kerstin Martens, and Janna Teltemann. 2017. "PISA and Its Consequences: Shaping Education Policies through International Comparisons." *European Journal of Education* 52(2): 175–83.

Nikolaev, Denis, and Dmitry Chugunov. 2012. *The Education System in the Russian Federation: Education Brief 2012.* Washington, DC: World Bank.

Niyozov, Sarfaroz. 2008. "Understanding Pedagogy: Cross-Cultural and Comparative Insights from Central Asia." In *Comparative and International Education: Issues for Teachers*, edited by Karen Mundy, Kathy Bickmore, Ruth Hayhoe, Meggan Madden, and Katherine Madjidi, 133–59. New York: Teachers College Press.

Nordin, Andreas, and Daniel Sundberg, eds. 2014. *Transnational Policy Flows in European Education: The Making and Governing of Knowledge in the Education Policy Field.* Oxford: Symposium Books.

Null, J. Wesley. 2008. "Is There a Future for Teacher Ed Curriculum? An Answer from History and Moral Philosophy." *American Educational History Journal* 35(1/2): 3–18.

Ong, Aihwa. 2006. *Neoliberalism as Exception: Mutations in Citizenship and Sovereignty.* Durham: Duke University Press.

Organisation for Economic Co-operation and Development. 1998. *Reviews of National Policies for Education: Russian Federation.* Paris: OECD.

———. 2001. *The Well-Being of Nations: The Role of Human and Social Capital.* Paris: OECD.

———. 2016. "Russian Federation." In *Education at a Glance 2016: OECD Indicators.* Paris: OECD.

Owens, Deborah Duncan. 2015. *The Origins of the Common Core: How the Free Market Became Public Education Policy.* New York: Palgrave.

Ozga, Jenny. 2012. "Assessing PISA." *European Educational Research Journal* 11(2): 166–71.

———. 2014. "Data Work: Michael Barber in Conversation with Jenny Ozga." In *World Yearbook of Education 2014. Governing Knowledge: Comparison, Knowledge-Based Technologies and Expertise in the Regulation of Education*, edited by T. Fenwick, E. Mangez, and J. Ozga, 75–85. London: Routledge.

Ozhegov, Sergey Ivanovich. 2014. *Tolkovy Slovar' Russkogo Yazyka* [Dictionary of the Russian language]. 14th ed. Moscow: AST Mir i Obrazovanie.

Paine, Lynne, Elena Aydarova, and Iwan Syahril. 2017. "Globalization and Teacher Education." In *The SAGE Handbook of Teacher Education Research*, edited by D. Jean Clandinin and Jukka Husu, 1133–48. Thousand Oaks: Sage.
Paine, Lynne, Sigrid Blömeke, and Olena Aydarova. 2016. "Teachers and Teaching in the Context of Globalization." In *The Handbook of Research on Teaching*, 5th ed., edited by Drew Gitomer and Courtney Bell, 717–86. Washington, DC: American Educational Research Association.
Panachin, Fedor Grigor'evich. 1975. *Pedagogicheskoe Obrazovanie v SSSR: Vazhneyshie Etapy Istorii i Sovremennoe Sostoyaniye* [Pedagogical education in the USSR: the most important stages of history and modern condition]. Moscow: Pedagogika.
———. 1979. *Pedagogicheskoe Obrazovanie v Rossii: Istoricheskie-Pedagogicheskie Ocherki* [Pedagogical education in Russia: historical and pedagogical essays]. Moscow: Pedagogika.
Parsons, Michelle A. 2014. *Dying Unneeded: The Cultural Context of the Russian Mortality Crisis.* Nashville: Vanderbilt University Press.
Perry, Nancy, and Kadriye Ercikan. 2015. "Moving Beyond Country Rankings in International Assessments: The Case of PISA." *Teachers College Record* 117(1): 1–10.
Pesmen, Dale. 2000. *Russia and Soul: An Exploration.* Ithaca: Cornell University Press.
Phillips, David. 2000. "Beyond Travellers' Tales: Some Nineteenth-Century British Commentators on Education in Germany." *Oxford Review of Education* 26(1): 49.
Pisano, Jessica. 2014. "*Pokazukha* and Cardiologist Khrenov: Soviet Legacies, Legacy Theater, and a Usable Past." In *Historical Legacies of Communism in Russia and Eastern Europe*, edited by Mark Beissinger and Stephen Kotkin, 222–42. New York: Cambridge University Press.
Popkewitz, Thomas S. 1982. "The Social/Moral Basis of Occupational Life: Teacher Education in the Soviet Union." *Journal of Teacher Education* 33(3): 38–44.
Privalov, Alexandr. 2014. "Ob Ocherednoy Vnezapnoy Reforme" [About another sudden reform]. *Ekspert*, January 20.
Prokof'yev, M. A., P. V. Zimin, M. N. Kolmakova, M. I. Kondakov, and N. P. Kuzin, eds. 1967. *Narodnoe Obrazovanie v SSSR, 1917–1967* [National education in the USSR, 1917–1967]. Moscow: Prosveshchenie.
Quantz, Richard A., and Terence W. O'Connor. 1988. "Writing Critical Ethnography: Dialogue, Multivoicedness, and Carnival in Cultural Texts." *Educational Theory* 38(1): 95–109.
Ramirez, Francisco O. 2012. "The World Society Perspective: Concepts, Assumptions, and Strategies." *Comparative Education* 48(4): 423–39.
Ramirez, Francisco O., Xiaowei Luo, Evan Schofer, and John W. Meyer. 2006. "Student Achievement and National Economic Growth." *American Journal of Education* 113(1): 1–29.
Rancière, Jacques. 2011. *The Emancipated Spectator.* New York: Verso.

———. 2016. *The Politics of Aesthetics*. London: Bloomsbury.
Rappleye, Jeremy. 2012. *Educational Policy Transfer in an Era of Globalization: Theory—History—Comparison*. Frankfurt am Main: Peter Lang.
———. 2015. "Revisiting the Metaphor of the Island: Challenging 'World Culture' from an Island Misunderstood." *Globalisation, Societies and Education* 13(1): 58–87.
Rappleye, Jeremy, and Leang Un. 2018. "What Drives Failed Policy at the World Bank? An Inside Account of New Aid Modalities to Higher Education: Context, Blame, and Infallibility." *Comparative Education* 54(2): 250–74.
Ravitch, Diane. 2011. *The Death and Life of the Great American School System: How Testing and Choice Are Undermining Education*. New York: Basic Books.
———. 2013. *Reign of Error: The Hoax of the Privatization Movement and the Danger to America's Public Schools*. New York: Vintage Books.
Read, Robyn. 2019. "Knowledge Counts: Influential Actors in the Education for All Global Monitoring Report Knowledge Network." *International Journal of Educational Development* 64: 96–105.
Reckhow, Sarah. 2012. *Follow the Money: How Foundation Dollars Change Public School Politics*. Oxford: Oxford University Press.
Reinelt, Janelle. 1998. "Notes for a Radical Democratic Theater: Productive Crises and the Challenge of Indeterminacy." In *Staging Resistance: Essays on Political Theater*, edited by J. M. Colleran and J. S. Spencer, 283–300. Ann Arbor: University of Michigan Press.
Remington, Thomas F. 2008. *Politics in Russia*. 5th ed. New York: Pearson.
Richardson, Laurel. 2000. "Writing: A Method of Inquiry." In *Handbook of Qualitative Research*, edited by N. K. Denzin and Y. S. Lincoln, 923–48. Thousand Oaks: Sage.
Ries, Nancy. 2002. "'Honest Bandits' and 'Warped People': Russian Narratives about Money, Corruption, and Moral Decay." In *Ethnography in Unstable Places: Everyday Lives in Contexts of Dramatic Political Change*, edited by C. J. Greenhouse, E. Mertz, and K. B. Warren, 276–315. Durham: Duke University Press.
Rizvi, Fazal, and Bob Lingard. 2010. *Globalizing Education Policy*. London: Routledge.
Robertson, Susan L. 2012. "Placing Teachers in Global Governance Agendas." *Comparative Education Review* 56(4): 584–607.
———. 2013. "Teachers' Work, Denationalisation, and Transformations in the Field of Symbolic Control: A Comparative Account." In *World Yearbook of Education 2013: Educators, Professionalism and Politics*, edited by Terri Seddon and John S. Levin, 77–96. Oxon: Routledge.
———. 2016. "The Global Governance of Teachers' Work." In *Handbook of Global Education Policy*, edited by Karen Mundy, Andy Green, Bob Lingard, and Antoni Verger, 275–90. Malden: Wiley.

Robertson, Susan L., Xavier Bonal, and Roger Dale. 2002. "GATS and the Education Service Industry: The Politics of Scale and Global Reterritorialization." *Comparative Education Review* 46(4): 472–96.

Ryan, Gery W., and H. Russell Bernard. 2003. "Techniques to Identify Themes." *Field Methods* 15(1): 85–109.

Saldaña, Johnny. 2003. "Dramatizing Data: A Primer." *Qualitative Inquiry* 9(2): 218–36.

Sälzer, Christine, and Manfred Prenzel. 2018. "Policy Implications of PISA in Germany: The Case of Teacher Education." In *The PISA Effect on Global Educational Governance*, edited by Louis Volante, 109–25. New York: Routledge.

Schleicher, Andreas. 2011. *Building a High-Quality Teaching Profession: Lessons from around the World*. Paris: OECD.

Schriewer, Jürgen, and Carlos Martinez. 2004. "Constructions of Internationality in Education." In *The Global Politics of Educational Borrowing and Lending*, edited by G. Steiner-Khamsi, 29–53. New York: Teachers College Press.

Scott, James C. 1990. *Domination and the Arts of Resistance: Hidden Transcripts*. New Haven: Yale University Press.

———. 1998. *Seeing Like a State: How Certain Schemes to Improve the Human Condition Have Failed*. New Haven: Yale University Press.

Scott, Janelle, and Huriya Jabbar. 2014. "The Hub and the Spokes: Foundations, Intermediary Organizations, Incentivist Reforms, and the Politics of Research Evidence." *Educational Policy* 28(2): 233–57.

Sellar, Sam, and Bob Lingard. 2013. "The OECD and Global Governance in Education." *Journal of Education Policy* 28(5): 710–25.

———. 2014. "The OECD and the Expansion of PISA: New Global Modes of Governance in Education." *British Educational Research Journal* 40(6): 917–36.

Shahjahan, Riyad A. 2016. "International Organizations (IOs), Epistemic Tools of Influence, and the Colonial Geopolitics of Knowledge Production in Higher Education Policy." *Journal of Education Policy* 31(6): 694–710.

Shchedrovitsky, Georgiy P. 1961. "Tekhnologiya Myshleniya" [Technology of thinking]. *Izvesitya*. Available from http://www.fondgp.ru/gp/biblio/rus/7.

———. 1993. *Logica i Pedagogika* [Logic and pedagogy]. Moscow: Kastal'.

Shore, Cris. 2011. "Espionage, Policy and the Art of Government: The British Secret Services and the War on Iraq." In *Policy Worlds: Anthropology and the Analysis of Contemporary Power*, edited by Cris Shore, Susan Wright, and Davide Però, 169–86. New York: Berghahn Books.

Shore, Cris, and Susan Wright, eds. 1997. *Anthropology of Policy: Critical Perspectives on Governance and Power*. Oxon: Routledge.

———. 1999. "Audit Culture and Anthropology: Neoliberalism in British Higher Education." *Journal of the Royal Anthropological Institute* 5: 557–75.

Shore, Cris, Susan Wright, and Davide Però, eds. 2011. *Policy Worlds: Anthropology and the Analysis of Contemporary Power*. New York: Berghahn Books.

Sidhu, Ravinder. 2007. "GATS and the New Developmentalism: Governing Transnational Education." *Comparative Education Review* 51(2): 203–27.

Silova, Iveta, and William C Brehm. 2015. "From Myths to Models: The (Re) Production of World Culture in Comparative Education." *Globalisation, Societies and Education* 13(1): 8–33.

Sleeter, Christine. 2008. "Equity, Democracy, and Neoliberal Assaults on Teacher Education." *Teaching and Teacher Education* 24(8): 1947–57.

Smith, Mary Lee, Linda Miller-Kahn, Walter Heinecke, and Patricia F. Jarvis. 2004. *Political Spectacle and the Fate of American Schools*. New York: Routledge.

Smolin, Oleg. 2012. *O rezul'tatah Monitoringa Effektivnosti Deyatel'nosti Vuzov 2012* [About the results of the monitoring of higher education institutions' effectiveness]. Retrieved from http://www.smolin.ru/duma/inquiries/2012-12-12.

Smyth, John. 2006. "The Politics of Reform of Teachers' Work and the Consequences for Schools: Some Implications for Teacher Education." *Asia-Pacific Journal of Teacher Education* 34(3): 301–19.

Sobkin, V. S., and O. V. Tkachenko. 2007. *Student Pedagogicheskogo VUZa: Zhiznennye i Professional'nye Perspektivy* [A student of a pedagogical university: Life and professional prospects]. Moscow: Rossiyskaya Akademiya Obrazovaniya.

Spradley, James P. 1979. *The Ethnographic Interview*. Belmont: Wadsworth, Cengage Learning.

Spring, Joel. 2015a. *Economization of Education: Human Capital, Global Corporations, Skills-Based Schooling*. New York: Routledge.

———. 2015b. *Globalization and Education: An Introduction*. New York: Routledge.

Steiner-Khamsi, Gita, ed. 2004. *The Global Politics of Educational Borrowing and Lending*. New York: Teachers College Press.

———. 2010. "The Politics and Economics of Comparison." *Comparative Education Review* 54(3): 323–42.

———. 2018. "Businesses Seeing Like a State, Governments Calculating Like a Business." *International Journal of Qualitative Studies in Education* 31(5): 382–92.

Steiner-Khamsi, Gita, and Ines Stolpe. 2006. *Educational Import: Local Encounters with Global Forces in Mongolia*. New York: Palgrave.

Stetsenko, Anna. 2012. "Personhood: An Activist Project of Historical Becoming through Collaborative Pursuits of Social Transformation." *New Ideas in Psychology* 30(1): 144–53.

Stoller, Paul. 2007. "Ethnography/Memoir/Imagination/Story." *Anthropology and Humanism* 32(2): 178–91.

Strathern, Marilyn, ed. 2000. *Audit Cultures: Anthropological Studies in Accountability, Ethics, and the Academy*. London: Routledge.

Sutherland, Jeanne. 1999. *Schooling in the New Russia: Innovation and Change, 1984–95*. New York: Palgrave Macmillan.

Sutton, Margaret, and Bradley A. Levinson, eds. 2001. *Policy as Practice: Toward a Comparative Sociocultural Analysis of Educational Policy*. Westport: Ablex.

Szolowicz, Michael A. 2017. "Opt Out! Understanding Resistance to the Common Core's Testing Regime through Political Spectacle." Unpublished doctoral dissertation. University of Arizona, Tuscon.

Takayama, Keita. 2008. "The Politics of International League Tables: PISA in Japan's Achievement Crisis Debate." *Comparative Education* 44(4): 387–407.

———. 2010. "Politics of Externalization in Reflexive Times: Reinventing Japanese Education Reform Discourses through 'Finnish PISA Success.'" *Comparative Education Review* 54(1): 51–75.

———. 2015. "Provincialising the World Culture Theory Debate: Critical Insights from a Margin." *Globalisation, Societies and Education* 13(1): 34–57.

———. 2018. "How to Mess with PISA: Learning from Japanese Kokugo Curriculum Experts." *Curriculum Inquiry* 48(2): 220–37.

Takayama, Keita, Arathi Sriprakash, and Raewyn Connell. 2015. "Rethinking Knowledge Production and Circulation in Comparative and International Education: Southern Theory, Postcolonial Perspectives, and Alternative Epistemologies." *Comparative Education Review* 59(s): v–viii.

Timoshenko, Konstantin. 2011. "The Winds of Change in Russian Higher Education: Is the East Moving West?" *European Journal of Education* 46 (3): 397–414.

Tompkins-Stange, Megan E. 2016. *Policy Patrons: Philanthropy, Education Reform, and the Politics of Influence*. Cambridge: Harvard Education Press.

Trippestad, Tom Are, Anja Swennen, and Tobias Werler. 2017. *The Struggle for Teacher Education: International Perspectives on Governance and Reforms*. London: Bloomsbury.

Tröhler, Daniel, Heinz-Dieter Meyer, David F. Labaree, and Ethan L Hutt. 2014. "Accountability: Antecedents, Power, and Processes." *Teachers College Record* 116(9): 1–12.

Tsing, Anna Lowenhaupt. 2005. *Friction: An Ethnography of Global Connection*. Princeton: Princeton University Press.

TsK KPSS i Sovet Ministrov SSSR. 1973. *O Merakh po Uluchsheniyu Usloviy Raboty Sel'skoy Obshcheobrazovatel'noy Shkoly* [About the measures of improving the work of rural schools]. Retrieved from http://pedagogic.ru/books/item/f00/s00/z0000008/st050.shtml.

Tullar, William L. 1992. "Organizational Change in the USSR: The Activity-Inciting Game." *Leadership and Organization Development Journal* 13(1): 17–20.

Turner, Victor. 1974. *Dramas, Fields, and Metaphors: Symbolic Action in Human Society*. Ithaca: Cornell University Press.

Uchebnye Plany Pedagogicheskih Institutov [Curriculum plans of pedagogical institutes]. 1970. Moscow: Ministerstvo Prosveshcheniya SSSR.

Uchitel'skaya Gazeta. 2006, October 17. *Pedagogy of Cooperation*. Retrieved from http://www.ug.ru/archive/15485.

Urciuoli, Bonnie. 2010. "Neoliberal Education: Preparing the Student for the New Workplace." In *Ethnographies of Neoliberalism*, edited by C. J. Greenhouse, 162–76. Philadelphia: University of Pennsylvania Press.

Vazhdaeva, Nina. 2012. "Zato My Delaem Diplomy" [At least we make diplomas]. *Itogi*, December 17, 10.

Verger, Antoni. 2009. "The Merchants of Education: Global Politics and the Uneven Education Liberalization Process within the WTO." *Comparative Education Review* 53(3): 379–401.

Verger, Antoni, Mario Novelli, and Hulya Kosar Altinyelken. 2012. *Global Education Policy and International Development: New Agendas, Issues and Policies.* London: Bloomsbury.

Wacquant, Loïc. 2012. "Three Steps to a Historical Anthropology of Actually Existing Neoliberalism." *Social Anthropology* 20(1): 66–79.

Waldow, Florian. 2009. "Undeclared Imports: Silent Borrowing in Educational Policy-Making and Research in Sweden." *Comparative Education* 45(4): 477–94.

Ward, Steven C. 2012. *Neoliberalism and the Global Restructuring of Knowledge and Education.* New York: Routledge.

Webster, Colin, Iveta Silova, Amy Moyer, and Suzanne McAllister. 2011. "Leading in the Age of Post-Socialist Education Transformations: Examining Sustainability of Teacher Education Reform in Latvia." *Journal of Educational Change* 12(3): 347–70.

Wedel, Janine R. 2009. *Shadow Elite: How the World's New Power Brokers Undermine Democracy, Government, and the Free Market.* New York: Basic Books.

———. 2011. "Shadow Governing: What the Neocon Core Reveals about Power and Influence in America." In *Policy Worlds: Anthropology and the Analysis of Contemporary Power*, edited by Cris Shore, Susan Wright, and Davide Però, 151–68. New York: Berghahn Books.

Wedel, Janine R., Cris Shore, Gregory Feldman, and Stacy Lathrop. 2005. "Toward an Anthropology of Public Policy." *Annals of the American Academy of Political and Social Science* 600(1): 30–51.

Weiner, Lois. 2007. "A Lethal Threat to US Teacher Education." *Journal of Teacher Education* 58(4): 274–86.

———. 2011. "Neoliberalism's Global Reconstruction of Schooling, Teachers' Work, and Teacher Education." In *Handbook of Research in the Social Foundations of Education*, edited by Steven Tozer, Bernardo P. Gallegos, and Annette Henry, 308–18. New York: Routledge.

Wertsch, James V. 1998. *Mind as Action*. Oxford: Oxford University Press.

Wilby, Peter. 2011. "Mad Professor Goes Global." *Guardian*, June 14.

Willett, John. 1964. *Brecht on Theatre*. New York: Hill and Wang.

Wilson, Suzanne M. 2014. "Innovation and the Evolving System of US Teacher Preparation." *Theory Into Practice* 53(3): 183–95.

Wilson, Suzanne M., and Eran Tamir. 2008. "The Evolving Field of Teacher Education." In *Handbook of Research on Teacher Education: Enduring Questions in Changing Contexts*, edited by M. Cochran-Smith, S. Feiman-Nemser, D. J. McIntyre, and K. E. Demers, 908–36. New York: Routledge.

World Bank. 2002. *Constructing Knowledge Societies: New Challenges for Tertiary Education*. Washington, DC: The International Bank for Recontruction and Development/The World Bank.

———. 2007. Implementation Completion and Results Report (IBRD-46050) on a Loan No.: 4605-RU in the Amount of US $50 Million to the Russian Federation for an Education Reform Project. Washington, DC: World Bank.

Wright, Wayne E. 2005. "The Political Spectacle of Arizona's Proposition 203." *Educational Policy* 19(5): 662–700.

Wu, Jinting. 2016. *Fabricating an Educational Miracle: Compulsory Schooling Meets Ethnic Rural Development in Southwest China*. Albany: State University of New York Press.

Yanow, Dvora. 2000. *Conducting Interpretive Policy Analysis*. Thousand Oaks: Sage.

Yurchak, Alexei. 2005. *Everything Was Forever, Until It Was No More: The Last Soviet Generation*. Princeton: Princeton University Press.

Zapp, Mike. 2017. "The World Bank and Education: Governing (through) Knowledge." *International Journal of Educational Development* 53: 1–11.

Zajda, Joseph. 2003. "Educational Reform and Transformation in Russia: Why Education Reforms Fail." *European Education* 35(1): 58–88.

———. 2006. *Schooling the New Russians: Transforming Soviet Workers to Capitalist Entrepreneurs*. Albert Park: James Nicholas.

Zeichner, Kenneth M. 2009. *Teacher Education and the Struggle for Social Justice*. New York: Routledge.

———. 2010. "Competition, Economic Rationalization, Increased Surveillance, and Attacks on Diversity: Neoliberalism and the Transformation of Teacher Education in the US." *Teaching and Teacher Education* 26: 1544–52.

———. 2017. *The Struggle for the Soul of Teacher Education*. New York: Routledge.

Zeichner, Kenneth M., and Hilary G. Conklin. 2016. "Beyond Knowledge Ventriloquism and Echo Chambers: Raising the Quality of the Debate in Teacher Education." *Teachers College Record* 118(12): 1–38.

Zeichner, Kenneth M., and César Peña-Sandoval. 2015. "Venture Philanthropy and Teacher Education Policy in the US: The Role of the New Schools Venture Fund." *Teachers College Record* 117(6): 1–44.

Zinchenko, A., N. Andreychenko, A. Volkov, and S. Kraychinskaya. 2003. "Set' Igrovoy Pedagogiki: Distsiplina Uma" [The network of game pedagogy: the discipline of the mind]. *Kentavr*. Retrieved from http://circleplus.ru/archive/n/30/8.

Index

Note: Page numbers in italics indicate figures; those with a *t* indicate tables.

activity theories, 56–58, 175–76, 210
activity-based learning, 7, 28, 45, 159–60, 174–76, 210, 236
Adamson, Bob, xxiii
admission exams, 23–25, 32–33; scores on, 66, 122–26
admission numbers, 67, 238; selectivity and, 24, 67–68, 96, 169–70, 171t
admission standards, 23–25, 122–26
All-Russian Congress on Teacher Preparation, 9
alternative routes, xxxi, xxxv, 152, 167, 263n5. *See also* multiple routes into teaching
Anderson-Levitt, Kathryn M., 241
anonymity, 91–92, 224, 242
anthropology of policy, xxv–xxxii, 250–54, 262n2
anthropotechnician, 145–46, 150, 227
audit culture, xxi
Austin, John Langshaw, 249

bachelor's degree, 194–96, 195t; "applied," 70, 72–73, 79t, 172t, 185, 194–96, 195t, 207, 237; "broad," 77, 79t; liberal arts, 76–77, 96, 172t, 177, 185–88, 195t, 196, 201–02, 211, 236–37; "universal," 77, 79t, 172t, 196, 211, 236–37
Bakhtin, Mikhail, xx, 216, 223–27; on authorship, xxiv; on carnival, xxv, 219, 229, 231; on dialogism, xxxvi, 225, 227, 230, 249–50; on ethics, xxxvi, 223–24
Barber, Michael, xxxvi, 46–47, 102–3, 115, 211, 215–16; critics of, 223; on global education competitiveness, 163–64, 180; McKinsey reports of, 114, 156, 168–74, 171–72t; as policy actor, 55–56, 232; reformers' network of, *48*, 173–74, 218, 221
Barranger, Milly S., 46, 89
"base schools," 20–21, 50, 77, 232
Berliner, David C., 151, 152
Bernard, H. Russell, 250
Biddle, Bruce J., 151, 152
Boal, Augusto, xxiv, 215, 216, 229, 233, 242, 247
Bochenkov, S. A., 123
Boland, Eavan, xxxii
Bologna Process, xxvii, 31–32; Project Tuning of, 32, 201, 265n5
Brecht, Bertolt, xxiv, 216, 228–29, 233, 241–42, 247

Brodsky, Joseph, 40
"budget students," 32, 66–67, 199, 206, 209, 228, 235–36
Bush, George W., 113

certification exam, 102, 172t. *See also* license exam and qualification exam
Chijioke, Chinezi, 114
civil rights movement (US), 143
"color revolutions," 191, 264n2
Comenius, Jan Amos, 40
competency-based instruction, xv, xvii, 43, 158, 159, 172t, 175, 188, 201
competitiveness, economic, xvi, 175. *See also* global education competitiveness
Comprehensive Program of Improving the Qualifications of Pedagogical Workers in General Education Schools, 119, 186–89, 197
Concept of Support for the Development of Teacher Education (Concept of Teacher Education Modernization), 31–33, 63, 155–56, 185, 235–38; chronology of, 113–20; funding of, 118–19, 190–99, 207, 211; goals of, 65, 68–70; implementation of, 70–76, 189–90, 193–200, 207, 225, 238; international comparisons with, 166–68, 178–79; McKinsey reports versus, 170–74, 171–72t; names of, 63–64, 187, 193–94; official timeline for, 90–100; opposition to, 117, 184–90, *186*; on pedagogical universities, 131; policy actors of, 46–58; public presentation of, 55; Shchedrovitsky's influence on, 144; state resources for, 66–68; unofficial timeline for, 100–106
Conquergood, Dwight, 233

corruption scandals, 32–33, 260n3, 261n6; of Skokovo institution, 45
crisis narratives, xxxvi, 84, 164, 179–80
critical discourse analysis, 261n2
critical ethnography, 249–50
critical reflexivity, 7, 42, 145, 163, 218–20
cultural continuity, xvi, 133, 177–79

Darling-Hammond, Linda, 71
Davydov, Vasily, 45, 56, 176
Debord, Guy, 143, 219, 241, 245–47
defunding, 54, 67, 206, 228
democratic participation, 87, 99–100, 112, 152, 157, 222, 224
deprofessionalization of teaching, 75, 86, 96, 167, 184, 232
deschooling theory, 53
development, economic, 7, 99, 173–76, 177; and PISA, 157, 231–32. *See also* modernization
Dewey, John, xx
dialogic engagement, xxxvi, 225, 227, 230, 249–50, 261n2
diversity, 167, 181, 226
Dneprov, Eduard, 28–29, 47
"double negative selection," 68–69, 95, 109, 122–26, *123*, 124t, 236, 262
Duma, 81, 118, 151, 184, 262n10

E-Learning Support Project, 192
economic competition, 175
economic development 7, 99, 173–76, 177; PISA and, 157, 231–32. *See also* modernization
Edelman, Murray, xxii, 216, 241, 244–45, 255
educational community, 26, 91, 99–100, 112, 222
"edupreneurs." *See* policy entrepreneurs

effectiveness, monitoring of, 126–32, *127*, 263n4
Elkonin, Daniil, 56, 145, 176
English only policies, xxii–xxiii
ethnodrama, 260n6
euphemization technique, 242–43
Every Student Succeeds Act (US), 152

Fairclough, Norman, 255, 261n2
Federal Program of Educational Development (Russia), 109, 157, 190, 194–96, 215
Federal Standards for General Education, 90–91, *135*, 135–36
Federal Teacher Education Standards, 207
Feldman, Gregory, 251
Finland, 109, 196; educational reforms in, 165, 167–68
flex nets, 58–60
Fordham Foundation, 85–86
fragmentation, 38, 189, 201, 220, 246, 256
Freedom House, 191
Fursenko, Andrey, 113

Gaidar, Yegor, 44
GARF, 7–10, 12, 17, 20, 259n1
Gates Foundation, 233
gender inequality, xxxi–xxxii, 59, 208
Gillette, J. Michael, 121
global education competitiveness, 162–64, 222–23; Barber on, 175; Gove on, 180; international reforms for, 164–68; international standards for, 156–62, 178–81, 232
globalization, 29, 86; ethnography and, 250–51; expertocracy and, 59; teacher education reforms and, xvi–xix. *See also* neoliberalism
Goffman, Erving, 239–42, 255, 261n1

Gorur, Radhika, 181
Gove, Michael, 180
grant funding, xxiii, 184, 194–97, 217–18, 233
Grigor'yev, V. V., 4–5
gymnasiums, 3–4

Hanushek, Eric A., 157, 175
historicity, 224–25, 232–33
Holmes, Douglas R., 219
Holmes Group, 71
Holquist, Michael, 225
human capital, 133, 143, 175
humanitarization, 28, 260n3

India, 175–76, 216
individualization, 45, 176, 189, 231–32
innovation economy, 132–37, 151, 157, 164
Innovation 3 grants, 184
"insider research," 60, 212, 256–57
"institute of power" (*institut vlasti*), 89
Institutes of People's Education, 9, *13*, 15
Institutional Transformations in Teacher Education, 61, 63, 91, 116, 216
International Association for the Evaluation of Educational Achievement, 264nn1–2
internships, xxxi, 39, 71, 77, 79t, 172t, 261n8

Japanese education reforms, 165, 168
Johnson, Patrick, 233

kaizen (continuous quality improvement), 150
Khrushchev, Nikita, 27
Kingdon, John W., 112

knowledge economy, 133–36, 151–53, 218
Kollontai, Alexandra, 11
Kukulin, Il'ia, 144, 265n1
Kushner, Tony, 247–48

"lab schools," 50, 79t
labor schools, 7–8, 11
Lenin, Vladimir, 6, 11
Leontyev, Alexei, 45
Levine, Arthur, 152
Levinson, Bradley A., 262n2
liberal arts degrees, 76–80, 96, 172t, 177, 185–88, 195t, 196, 202, 211, 236–37
license exam, 79t, 172t. *See also* qualification exam, certification exam
life-long learning, 135
literacy rates, 4
Livanov, Dmitriy, 115, 142
local knowledge (*mētis*), 179, 181, 226
Luxemburg, Rosa, 11
lyceums, 3–4

Maidan (Orange Revolution), 143, 264n2
Mamardashvili, Merab, 56
Marcus, George E., 219
Marginson, Simon, 163
mask(s), 63–70, 85–87, 229, 242–43; of evidence, 82–85, *83*; of intentions, 68–70, 219; of origins, 76–80, 79t; of uncertainty, 80–82
master's degrees, 171, 194, 196, 200, 237
McKinsey & Company, *48*, 55, 145, 227, 232
McKinsey reports, 56–57, 102, 114, 156, 168–74; Concept versus, 170–74, 171–72t; Gove on, 180;

on internships, 261n8; "Western" influences in, 177
Measures for the Renewal of Teacher Education, 101–2, 113, 114
medical education, 14, 21, 184; Unified State Exam scores for, 122–26, *123*, 124t
Medvedev, Dmitriy, 45, 74, 109–11, 114
mentoring, 78, 79t, 237, 265n2
merit-based pay, 117–19, 138, 186
methodology: research, xxv–xxxii, 249–54, 260n6, 261n2, 262n2; teaching, 4, 14, 142
Mexican education reforms, 165, 216
Meyerhold, Vsevolod Yemilyevich, 213
Microsoft's School of the Future contest, 45
Ministry of Education (MOE), 89–91, 112, 222; Concept implementation by, 193–99, 195t, 207; Coordinating Councils of, 212; on modular instruction, 201; monitoring by, 126–32, *127*, 263n4; reformers' network at, *49*, 59; School of the Future contest of, 45; teaching standards of, 137–43, 139–41t
Ministry of Enlightenment, 16–17, 20–21, 23
modernization, 31–34, 98, 107, 171–72t; agendas for, 46; Barber's influence on, 174; economic, 133, 147; institutional, 44–45, 228; professional standards and, 158; sociocultural, 133; teacher education, 60–65, 92–94, 101–3, 113–19
modernization dramas, xxiii–xxiv, 42–43, 216–20, 246–47; globalization and, 156, 164; nongovernment organizations and, 184; staging of, 223

modular programs, 188, 201
module, 188–89, 200–201, 203, 211
MOE. *See* Ministry of Education
monitoring of effectiveness, 126–32, *127*, 263n4
Mourshed, Mona, 102, 114, 168. *See also* McKinsey reports
multiple routes (or paths) into teaching, xv, 53, 73–75, 85–86, 96, 161, 167, 193–94, 211. *See also* alternative routes
Münch, Richard, 181

Narayan, Kirin, 256
National Council for Accreditation of Teacher Education, 77
National Council on Teacher Quality (US), 152, 167
National Education Policy Center (US), 230
National Endowment for Democracy, 191
National Training Foundation, 58, 194
neoliberalism, xvi–xix, 29–30, 60, 247; Bologna Process and, 32; environmental crises and, 147; "ideological alignment" with, 145–46; socialism versus, 221, 259n2; socialization for, 134–53, 175, 263n8. *See also* globalization
New Leaders of Higher Education program, 45, 94, 100, 104–6, 162–63, 197
"New Man," 8, 57, 145, 221, 227
No Child Left Behind policy (US), xxiii, 113, 152
Nordin, Andreas, 179

Obama, Barack, 113, 202
100 Rectors program. *See* New Leaders of Higher Education program

Open Society Institute, *48*, 58–59, 191
Orange Revolution, 143, 264n2
Organisation for Economic Co-operation and Development (OECD), xviii–xix, 210, 227, 259n4; Barber's influence and, 174; on competency-based instruction, 158; on future global workers, 153; reform recommendations of, 161–62; on Russian education, xxi, 31, 156–62. *See also* Programme for International Student Assessment (PISA)
Organizational Activity Games, 47, 52, 57, 204
Our New School policy, xiv, 42–43, 74–75, 101–3, 107, 111–12; on curriculum, 125; Medvedev on, 114; Strategy 2020 and, 102–3, 113
outcome-oriented school standards, 158
Ozga, Jenny, 261n20

Panachin, Fedor Grigor'evich, 5
partnerships with schools, 77, 79t
PDS. *See* Professional Development Schools
Pearson, *48*, 56, 232, 264n3
pedagogical colleges, 6, *13*, 72
pedagogical institutes, 9, *13*, 15, 28; base schools of, 20–21; critiques of, 18, 24–25; curriculum at, 26–27; overcrowding of, 21–22; universities versus, 14–19, 34, 64
Pedagogical Olympiad, xxix, 144, 149, 151, 254
"pedagogical specialization" (*profil'*), 80
pedagogical technical schools, *13*
pedagogical universities, *13*, 19, 39–40, 237; decreased authority of,

pedagogical universities *(continued)* 75–76; effectiveness of, 126–28, *127*; funding of, 54, 67; graduation plans after, 82–85, *83*; Medvedev on, 114, 115; monitoring by Ministry of Education of, 126–32, *127*; as second-rate institutions, 72, 85; Strategy 2020 proposals for, 43; Unified State Exam scores for, 122–26, *123*, 124t; World Bank on, 30

pedagogy, 4, 10, 17–18, 26, 28, 34, 40, 71, 75, 142–43, 175–76, 217–18, 226–27; Shchedrovitsky on, 56–57, 143–46

Pelevin, Victor, 121

PIRLS. *See* Progress in International Reading Literacy Study

PISA. *See* Programme for International Student Assessment

policy actors, 46–58, 175–76, 216–18, 220–22, 224

policy entrepreneurs, 174, 211, 221, 231, 263n5

political spectacle, xxii–xxiv, 121, 216, 219, 244–47

political theater, xxii–xxv, 247–48; aesthetics in, 225–27; ethics in, 223–25; as tool of coercion, 227–29; as tool of liberation, xxiv, 215, 229–30, 233

Pomerantsev, Peter, xxi

practical preparation, 18, 20, 63, 70–73, 77, 79t, 172t, 177, 237

President's Council for Economic Modernization and Innovative Development of the Country, 164

Privalov, Alexandr, 117

production sequence, 89–90

Professional Development Schools (PDS), 79t, 188, 232–33

Program for Educational Development, 31–32

Program of Pedagogical Education Modernization, 50, 61, 101, 109, 113

Programme for International Student Assessment (PISA), xix, 44, 156–62, 215, 264n3; activity-based learning and, 176; diversity concerns with, 181; global competitiveness and, 164, 232; Gorur on, 181; Gove on, 180; reforms and, 173, 221; Shchedrovitsky's theories and, 227; teacher preparation for, 159. *See also* Organisation for Economic Co-operation and Development

Progress in International Reading Literacy Study (PIRLS), 156–57, 159, 161, 215, 264n2

Project of Teacher Education Modernization, 64, 218

Project Tuning, 32, 201, 265n5

Psaki, Jennifer, 202

Putin, Vladimir, 44, 89, 107–10, 115; on educational modernization, 215; on teaching standards, 137; on textbook publishers, 261n6

qualification categories, 78
qualification exams, 78, 79t, 93, 172t
quality improvement (*kaizen*), 150

Race to the Top program, 113, 184
Rancière, Jacques, 247
reformers' networks, *48–49*, 58–60
Richardson, Laurel, 255
role-reshuffling, 90–91, 100, 108, 111–12, 222
rural schools, 22–24, 25, 27, 30
Russia: Duma of, 81, 118, 151, 184, 262n10; imperial, 3–7;

revolutionary, 7–13, *13*; teacher education after 2000 in, 31–33, *33*; teacher education during 1990s in, 29–31; US sanctions against, 265n6
Russian Academy of Education, *48*, 50, 158
Russian Academy of Pedagogical Sciences, 29
Russian Academy of Sciences, 15

Samsung Corporation, 150
scandals. *See* corruption scandals
Schleicher, Andreas, 161, 180
Schmidt, Otto, 10–11, 14
scholarships, 32, 66–67
School of the Future contest, 45
Schumpeter, Joseph A., 263n5
Scott, James C., 11, 179, 242–43
scripts, 155–56, 179–81, 242–43
selectivity, 16, 24, 66–68, 72, 80, 96, 98, 109, 114, 169, 172t, 236–37
seminaries, teacher training at, 4–5
Shchedrovitsky, Georgiy Petrovich, 56–59, 175, 216, 261n13; Bakhtin and, 226–27; on pedagogical specialization, 80; on pedagogy's social role, 143–48; reformers' network of, 60, 145, 150, 218; techniques of, 204–5, 262n5
Shchedrovitsky, Pyotr, 58, 175
Shchedrovitsky Foundation, *49*, 57
Shore, Cris, 257
Singapore, 109, 165, 167–68
Skolkovo Foundation, *49*, 52, 60; Moscow School of Management of, 45, 162; 100 Rectors program of, 45, 94, 100, 104–6, 162–63, 197; scandals at, 45
Smith, Mary Lee, 86
Smolin, Oleg, 185
Sobkin, V. S., 82, *83*, 125

social cohesion, 133
social drama, 243–44
social mobility, 24, 41, 125, 152, 222
"soft skills," 136, 152–53, 161, 175, 227
Soros Foundation, *48*, 58–59, 191
spectacle, 86–87, 220; Debord on, 143, 219, 241, 245–47; political, 121, 216, 219, 244–47
Spradley, James P., 249–50
standardization, 14, 179, 181, 189, 201, 203, 220
standardized assessments, 14, 32–33; international, 156–62, 178–81, 232; of teaching, 137–43, 139–41t, 207–13, 217. *See also* Unified State Exam
Stoller, Paul, 256
Strategy 2020 proposals, 42–43, 133, 157; developers of, 50; final version of, 115; Our New School policy and, 102–3, 113
Strugatsky, Boris, 52
subject knowledge, 26, 78, 138, 142, 159, 160
Sundberg, Daniel, 179
Sutton, Margaret, 262n2
Systems Approach for Better Education Results (SABER), xix, 221, 259n5
systems thinking, 57, 146, 171t, 175–76, 227

Takayama, Keita, 181
Teach For America, xxxi, 167, 213
Teacher Education and Development Study in Mathematics (TEDS-M), 156–57, 159–61, 264n4
Teacher for Russia, 213
teacher quality, 25–26, 30–31, 70–76; international assessments of, 158–62, 178–81; McKinsey report on,

teacher quality *(continued)*
  168–74, 171–72t; public policy and, xvii, 66
teachers: as facilitators, 138–42, 250; merit-based pay for, 117–19, 138, 186; professionalization of, 52, 71–72, 184, *186*; qualifications of, 63, 72, 76, 171–72t; shortage of, 21–24, 84–85, 160–61, 171t; standards for, 117, 137–43, 139–41t, 207–13, 217
teachers institutes, 6, *13*, 15, 17, 21–22, 72
teachers' labor functions, 139–41t
Teaching and Learning International Survey (TALIS), xix, 259n4
TEDS-M (Teacher Education and Development Study in Mathematics), 156–57, 159–61, 264n4
Tkachenko, O. V., 82, *83*, 125
Tolyatti Academy of Management, 58
Trends in International Mathematics and Science Study (TIMSS), 156–57, 159, 161, 215, 264n1
TRIZ, 150
tuition subsidies, 32, 66–67
Tuning project, 32, 201, 265n5
Turner, Victor, 241, 243–44

Ukraine, xxxi, 58, 143, 187, 257–58, 264n2
Unified Labor Schools, 7–8, 11
Unified Qualification Manual for Administrators, Specialists, and Workers, 137
Unified State Exam, 32–33, 236, 263n3; scores on, 122–26, *123*, 124t. *See also* standardized assessments
Union of Soviet Socialist Republics (USSR): collapse of, 12, 18, 29, 34, 261n5; perestroika in, 216; teacher education during 1920s in, 7–13; teacher education during 1930s in, 14–19; teacher education after World War II in, 19–21; teacher education during 1980s in, 28–29
United Kingdom, 112, 216; activity-based learning in, 176; educational reforms in, 167, 168; teacher education in, 85, 86
United Russia Party, 177
United States, 216; educational reforms in, 152, 166–68, 230; liberal arts curriculum in, 202; National Council on Teacher Quality of, 152, 167; National Education Policy Center of, 230; No Child Left Behind policy of, xxiii, 113, 152; Russian sanctions of, 265n6; teacher education in, 85–86; teacher preparation in, 177
United States Agency for International Development (USAID), 29, 191
universities, classical, *13*, 14–19, 34, 64, 114
Unz, Ron, xxii

Val'dman, I. A., 123
VNIK Shkola, 28–29
voucher programs, xx
Vygotsky, Lev, xx, 45, 176

Wacquant, Loïc, xvi
Weber, Max, 12
Wedel, Janine R., 58–60
"Westernization" (*zapadnichestvo*), 7, 44, 155, 177–81, 201–2
Wilson, Suzanne M., 263n5
Woessmann, Ludger, 157
Working Group on Institutional Transformations in Pedagogical Education, 91–100

World Bank, 191, 192, 210; education reform projects of, xix–xxi, 29–30, 75, 193, 221, 259n5; loans by, 192, 193; outcome-oriented school standards of, 158; reformers' network of, *48*, 58, 59
world society theory, xvii–xviii
World Trade Organization (WTO), xix, 192

Wright, Wayne E., xxii–xxiii

Yandex internet company, 148
Year of the Teacher (2010), 33
Yurchak, Alexei, 221

Zadornov, Mikhail, 64
Zeichner, Ken, *48*, 71, 143
Zinovyev, Alexandr, 56

www.ingramcontent.com/pod-product-compliance
Lightning Source LLC
Chambersburg PA
CBHW030009240426
43672CB00007B/881